INSIGHT GUIDE

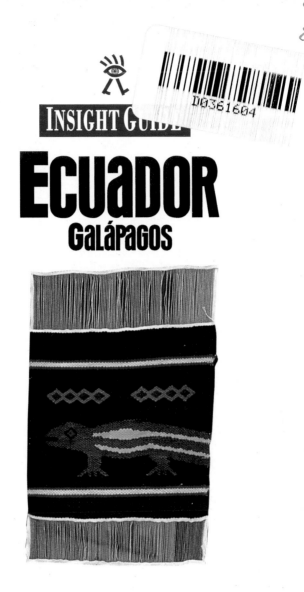

ECUADOR
GalÁPagos

KOREMATSU CAMPUS

Discovery
CHANNEL

APA PUBLICATIONS
Part of the Langenscheidt Publishing Group

ABOUT THIS BOOK

Editorial
Project Editor
Pam Barrett
Editorial Director
Brian Bell

Distribution
UK & Ireland
GeoCenter International Ltd
The Viables Centre
Harrow Way
Basingstoke
Hants, RG22 4BJ
Fax: (44) 1256-817988

United States
Langenscheidt Publishers, Inc.
46–35 54th Road
Maspeth, NY 11378
Fax: (718) 784-0640

Worldwide
Höfer Communications Pte Ltd
38 Joo Koon Road
Singapore 628990
Tel: (65) 865-1600
Fax: (65) 861-6438

Printing
Höfer Press (Pte) Ltd
38 Joo Koon Road
Singapore 628990
Tel: (65) 865-1600
Fax: (65) 861-6438

© 1999 Apa Publications (HK) Ltd
All Rights Reserved
First Edition 1991
Third Edition 1998
Third Edition (Reprinted) 1999

This guidebook combines the interests and enthusiasms of two of the world's best known information providers: Insight Guides, whose titles have set the standard for visual travel guides since 1970, and Discovery Channel, the world's premier source of nonfiction television programming.

The editors of Insight Guides provide both practical advice and general understanding about a destination's history, culture, institutions and people. Discovery Channel and its Web site, www.discovery.com, help millions of viewers explore their world from the comfort of their own home and also encourage them to explore it firsthand.

How to use this book
The book is carefully structured to convey an understanding of Ecuardor and its culture and to guide readers through its sights and activities:

◆ To understand modern Ecuador, you need to know about its past. The **Features** section covers the country's history and culture in authoritative and lively essays written by specialists.

◆ The main

EXPLORE YOUR WORLD

The contributors

This new edition was edited by **Pam Barrett** and builds on earlier editions edited by **Tony Perrottet** and updated by **Andrew Eames**.

The chief contributor was US-born writer **Lynn Meisch**, who has lived for many years in the Andes. She has contributed essays on the customs, arts, and crafts of Ecuador, and written chapters for the Places section.

Sally Burch, one of the few full-time foreign correspondents in Quito, wrote about the Ecuadorian people; **Mary Dempsey** was your guide to the two biggest cities, Quito and Guayaquil; **Sean Doyle** contributed the chapters on history and the North Coast; **Rob Rachowiecki**, who is author of two other books on the country, and leads tours into the Amazon and the Galápagos, has contributed chapters on the Oriente and the Western Lowlands; and **Betsy Wagenhauser**, the former head of the South American Explorers' Club, wrote about adventure travel. Much valuable updating work has been done by **Jane Letham** and **Mark Thurber**, both based in Quito. Jane works for the South American Explorers' Club, on which she has written a short essay; and Mark, a geologist and guide, also contributed the new chapter on Ecuador's economy and ecology.

The chief photographer for the book was Argentine-born **Eduardo Gil**, director of the prestigious Buenos Aires Cultural Center. Many of the portraits of indigenous life were taken by **Eric Lawrie** and **Stephen Trimball**. **André Bartschi** did much of the stunning wildlife photography for the Oriente chapters; and Galápagos resident **Tui de Roy** photographed some of the islands' extraordinary creatures.

Places section provides full details of all the areas worth seeing. The chief places of interest are coordinated by number with full-color maps.

◆ The **Travel Tips** listings section offers information on travel, hotels, restaurants, and adventure travel organizations. Information may be located quickly by using the index printed on the back cover flap – and the flaps are designed to serve as bookmarks.

◆ **Photographs** are chosen not only to illustrate the geography of the country and the beauty of its cities, but also to convey the everyday activities of its people.

Map Legend

— ·· —	International Boundary
— —	Disputed Boundary
----	Province/ State Boundary
⊖	Border Crossing
—·—	National Park/ Nature Reserve
----	Ferry Route
✈	Airport
🚌	Bus Station
❶	Tourist Information
✉	Post Office
♁ ♂	Church/Ruins
∴	Archaeological Site
⋂	Cave
★	Place of Interest

The main places of interest in the Places section are coordinated by number with a full-color map (e.g. ❶) and a symbol at the top of every right-hand page tells you where to find the map.

CONTENTS

Taking the
baby to
Pujilí
market

Insight on....

Information panels

Places

LATITUDE 0° 00'

Straddling the equator, Ecuador is becoming one of the most popular holiday destinations in Latin America

The Republic of Ecuador took its name in the early 1800s from the equatorial line that runs through its heart. As far as the rest of the world was concerned, these geographical peculiarity would long remain Ecuador's major claim to fame. When outsiders did consider Ecuador, it was as a kind of giant natural laboratory. In 1736 Charles-Marie de la Condamine and Pierre Bouguer headed a pioneering expedition mounted by the French Academy of Scientists; almost 70 years later, the German explorer Alexander von Humboldt made discoveries here that were vital for the development of physical geography; and in 1835 Charles Darwin studied wildlife in the Galápagos Islands.

All these men, as well as the eminent English traveler, Edward Whymper, who came here in 1879, published adventure-spiced volumes about their experiences, recounting a land of fantastic animals, ice-capped volcanoes and impenetrable Amazonian jungles, but few of their compatriots followed in their footsteps. Had they done so, they would have found a harsh but beautiful country, in which the Catholic Church held considerable sway over people's lives, and where political assassination and periods of military rule were common.

Ecuador still does not come into the world's eye very often today – a fact that many Ecuadorians may feel thankful for, considering that it has been the chaos of war, revolution, and staggering debt that has made many of the country's neighbors internationally known. During the latter part of the 20th century the Ecuadorians have lived in relative tranquility. It was the flamboyant nature of President Bucaram and the confusion surrounding his removal from office in early 1997 which made many people in the West aware of the country's existence. But despite this minor upheaval, Ecuador is now one of the most politically stable countries in Latin America. It is also among the safest in which to travel, even though nuisances such as pickpocketing are on the increase in some tourist areas.

Ecuador is not, and has never been, a prosperous country, but it has largely avoided the most bitter extremes of poverty that afflict other Andean countries, such as Bolivia and Peru. The Ecuadorians remain an approachable and easy-going people. They are a culturally diverse population, who include descendants of the Spanish *conquistadores* and of the original pre-Columbian inhabitants, many of whom still speak Quichua and maintain traditions from Inca times and earlier. Divided into 10 distinctly different communities, the latter prefer to be called *indígenas* (natives or indigenous people) rather than the Spanish *indio* (or "Indian" in English). Given the history of repression that has marked their country's evolution they are remarkably open and friendly to foreigners

Ecuador's cultural diversity is matched by its great geographical differences. Although only half the size of France – or somewhat larger than Britain – it contains the snow-capped Andes, a string of volcanoes, both extinct and active, the wide, deserted beaches of the Pacific Coast, and expanses of steamy Amazon jungle. Until recently Ecuador was almost entirely a rural country, but the past few decades have been marked by rapid urbanization, although about half of the population still lives in rural areas. Its two main cities – Quito, the capital, and Guayaquil, the industrial heart – are trying hard to cope with the problems that such expansion inevitably brings, and are all too obviously characterized by extremes of wealth and poverty. But they are vibrant, exciting places to explore, and visitors are generally welcomed.

Given all this, together with the relatively low cost of living, which makes traveling inexpensive, you begin to see why Ecuador is rapidly earning a reputation as one of the most popular new destinations in South America.

PRECEDING PAGES: clouds over the Western Cordillera; minding sheep in the windswept Sierra; patchwork fields in the Chimborazo province; cruising past Kicker Rock in the Galápagos Islands.
LEFT: young girl in typical Otavaleño dress.

COAST, SIERRA AND JUNGLE

Sandy beaches, snowy volcanoes, Amazon rainforests, the Galápagos Islands…

Ecuador's vivid diversity is one of its greatest attractions

Straddled across the Andes on the most westerly point of South America, Ecuador is about half the size of France (271,000 sq. km/103,000 sq. miles) making it the smallest of the Andean countries.

The Andean mountain chain divides the country into three distinct regions: the coastal plain known as the Costa, the Andean mountains, or Sierra, and the Amazon jungle, or Oriente. The fourth region is the Galápagos Islands, a group of volcanic islands situated in the Pacific Ocean some 1,000km (620 miles) due west of the mainland. The striking geographical and cultural contrasts between these regions in one small country are what make Ecuador such a fascinating place to visit.

Contrasting ecosystems

The gently rolling hills of the Costa lie between sea and mountains, varying in width from 20 to 180km (12 to 112 miles). The low-lying areas and marshlands frequently become flooded, making access difficult in the rainy season. Much of this area was virgin coastal rainforest at the turn of the century but now is devoted primarily to agriculture.

The shore-line offers long stretches of relatively unspoilt sandy beaches, lined with coconut palms, and the sea is warm all year round. The river estuaries harbor mangrove swamps, important breeding grounds for land and marine wildlife, though many of these are being converted to expansive pools for commercial shrimp ranching, which has become an important industry. Further inland, particularly on the fertile lowlands irrigated by the Guayas and Daule rivers, there extend plantations of bananas, sugar-cane, cacao and rice. A low mountain range called the Mache-Chindul, near the coast, rises to a height of 800 meters (2,550 ft) and is one of the few spots that still supports virgin coastal rainforest and scattered indigenous communities, known as *chachis*.

The Andes consist of an eastern and western range, joined at intervals by transverse foothills. Nestling between the ranges are the valleys of the Sierra, with highly productive volcanic soils that have been populated and farmed for several thousand years. From the valley floors, a patchwork quilt of small fields extends far up the mountain sides, illustrating the intensive use that has been made of every available inch of land. The Quichua indigenous communities who own this land hoe their own small-holdings by hand, producing a variety of crops such as potatoes, corn, beans, wheat, barley and carrots.

VOLCANIC AVENUE

The term "Avenue of the Volcanoes" was coined by the German explorer Alexander von Humboldt.

The northern end of the Ecuadorian Andes is dominated by 10 glaciated volcanoes that tower to over 5,000 meters (16,000 ft). The Pan-American Highway follows the central valley, the Avenue of the Volcanoes, with excellent views over these snowy giants. Chimborazo, in the western chain, is the highest peak in Ecuador (6,310 meters/20,700 ft). A little further north, in the eastern range, is Cotopaxi, at 5,900 meters (19,350 ft) the highest active volcano in the world. The upper slopes of these peaks are covered by active glaciers that beckon mountaineers from all over the world.

Equally enchanting for trekkers are the surrounding sub-alpine grasslands known locally as *páramo,* which host a diversity of wildlife, including the Andean condor, Andean fox, and spectacle bear, as well as hundreds of wildflowers. Lower down on the eastern Andean slope there is a dense cloudforest that remains largely unexplored because of cliffs, thick vegetation and dismally heavy rains all year round.

The Amazon rainforest of the Oriente begins in the foothills of the eastern Andean slope. River systems flowing from this rainy wilderness become tributaries of the Amazon, the longest being the Río Napo (855km/530 miles). The shores of these wide and slow-moving rivers traditionally have been the location of set-

LEFT: the awesome Mount Chimborazo.

tlements and the principal means of transport through a hilly and densely vegetated terrain. However, this lifestyle is rapidly being transformed by an expanding road network initiated by the oil industry in the early 1970s. Settlers, agricultural interests and expanding indigenous communities are now converting once virgin rainforest into pastures and croplands. For the moment, most of the original forest survives and offers both magnificent scenery and ideal terrain for adventure.

The Galápagos Islands, home to the famous giant tortoises, blue-footed boobies and marine iguanas, consist of 13 islands and 40 to 50 islets, some of which are no more than large rocks. The biggest island, Isabela, measures more than 4,000 sq. km (1,520 sq. miles).

The Galápagos are the product of a hot spot volcanic center which actively erupts basalt lava on several of the islands. Since this archipelago never had direct connection to the mainland, the wildlife that exists here evolved in isolation and many species are endemic. Because the area is biologically unique, virtually all of the islands are protected within the Galápagos National Park and by the United Nations as a World Heritage Site.

Land of sun and rain

Being right on the equator, Ecuador lacks the four seasons of the temperate zones. Every location in the country generally has a wet (winter) and dry (summer) season, but it is difficult to predict the weather on a day to day basis, especially during an *El Niño* year, when the whole country gets dumped on by heavy rains.

The rainy season for the Costa is between January and June. It rains most of the time in the Oriente, though December to February are usually drier. Both these regions are hot (above 25C/80F) all year round. The Galápagos Islands have a hot and arid climate.

Weather patterns in the Sierra are complex and each region has its own micro climate. Generally, the central valleys are rainy between February and May, while the rest of the year is drier, with a short wet season in October and November. The climate overall is mild, and Quiteños brag about their perpetual spring where gardens bloom all year round.

The distinct ecological zones of this diverse

LEFT: sea lion in the Galápagos Islands.

country account for the broad variety of wildlife. For example, of the 2,600 species of birds existing in this part of the world, no fewer than 1,500 can be found in Ecuador.

A dynamic landscape

The forces of tectonic plates, volcanoes and water have sculpted an exquisite array of landscapes, but have also caused devastating natural disasters throughout Ecuador's history. In April 1996 an earthquake shook the province of Cotopaxi, causing 30 deaths and destroying many rural adobe houses, leaving thousands homeless. Several days later, a massive block of ice, loosened by the same earthquake, broke off in the hot afternoon sun and avalanched down the slope, burying the climbers' hut and taking the lives of nine visitors.

Another earthquake in 1987 in the Oriente destroyed parts of the transcontinental oil pipeline, the country's primary source of income, which crippled the economy for six months. Tragically, several thousand people drowned as the floods of ice and mud were unleashed from the glaciated peaks in the eastern Andean range.

In 1660, a century after the colonial city of Quito was founded, the nearby volcano of Guagua Pichincha erupted catastrophically, dumping several feet of ash onto the city. The volcano is expected to erupt again, and the houses in the poor marginal *barrios* of the much expanded city, often located on steep, unstable slopes, rarely meet earthquake codes, a fact which has many politicans and planners understandably worried.

Demographics

The population of Ecuador is around 13 million, about half of whom live in the cities. Population growth is fairly rapid at around 2.7 percent annually.

The country is divided into 21 provinces, many of them named after mountains (Chimborazo, Cotopaxi, Pichincha) or rivers (Guayas, Napo, Esmeraldas). The capital city is Quito, situated in the northern Sierra, at an altitude of 2,800 meters (9,300 ft). It has about 1.5 million inhabitants. Guayaquil is the largest city, with a population nearing 2 million, and its seaport is the economic nerve-center of the country.

LEFT: rainforest in the Amazon basin.

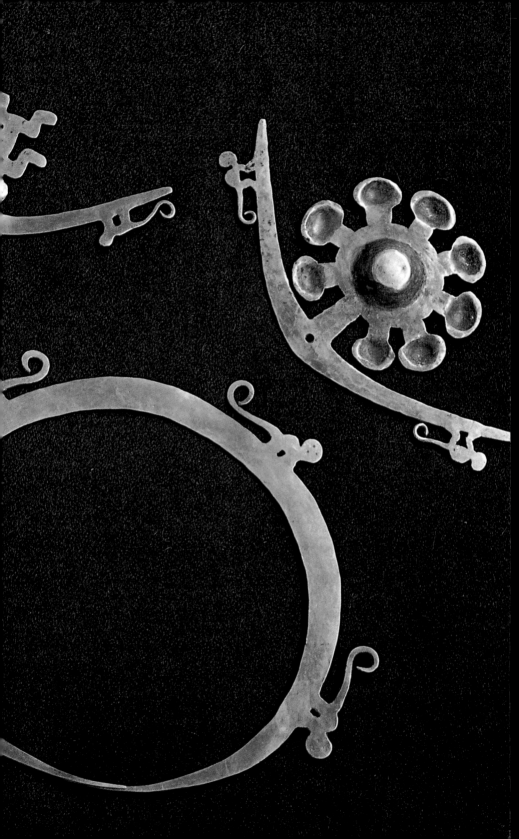

Decisive Dates

Pre-historical 30,000–3000BC
Hunter-gatherer societies inhabited the Andes.
6000BC: manioc cultivated in the Amazon basin.

Valdivian period 3500–500BC
The first evidence of permanent settlements and communities. Surviving pottery testifies to sophistication of the society.
3500BC: earliest Valdivian site, Loma Alta, was established.
1500BC: ceremonial temples built in Real Alto.

300BC–AD700 La Tolita period
A society of gold- and metal-workers.

AD500–1500 Manta period
Crafted objects of gold, silver and pottery, plus cotton textiles.

Sierra cultures 10th-16th century
10th century: the Cara people, ruled by the Shyri dynasty, established in the land of the Quitus.
The Cañaris emerged as the most powerful and well-organized culture.
The Puruhás were ruled by the Duchicela dynasty.
14th century: Shyri and Duchicela familes intermarried, creating the greater kingdom of Quitu.

1460: Inca invasion. Tupac-Yupanqui subdues the Cañaris.
Late 15th–early 16th century: the Incas consolidate their victories; the city of Tomebamba is built, with a Temple of the Sun; the Inca Huanya-Capac builds Ingapirca (Inca Stone Wall); indigenous people are forcibly transferred from Ecuador to Peru and vice versa; the Incas introduce coca, sweet potatoes and peanuts, plus the habit of chewing coca leaves; the Imperial Highway is extended from Cuzco to Quito.
1492: the city of Quitu taken by the Incas.
1527: Huascar, son of Huanya-Capac, ascends the Cuzco throne, and civil war breaks out between him and his half-brother Atahualpa, heir to the Kingdom of Quito.
1532: war ends with Huascar's defeat.

Spanish conquest
1526: first *conquistadores*, under Bartolomé Ruiz, land near Esmeraldas and discover people decked with gold.
1530: Francisco Pizarro lands near Manabí.
1530–32: constant battles and massacres of indigenous people in the Spanish quest for gold.
1532: Atahualpa captured and killed.
1534: Pedro de Alvarado lands in Manta.
1534: an army led by Simón de Benalcázar defeats the Incas when thousand of Indians in the Inca army stage a mutiny. Benalcázar founds the Villa de San Francisco de Quito on the ruins of the city the Incas had destroyed.
1535: the city of Guayaquil is founded.
1549: the Spanish conquest is completed but the *conquistadores* fight each other for gold until subdued by the Spanish crown in 1554.

Colonial period c.1550–1832
The land is divided up among the Spaniards and worked under the *encomendero* system, a form of serdom on huge estates. The Church becomes a major landowner.
1550s: *obrajes* (textiles workshops) using forced labor were established in Otavalo.
1563: Quito becomes the seat of a royal *audencia* (colonial assembly).
17th century: seminaries and universities established in Quito, which becomes an intellectual center.
1720: *encomiendas* abolished, but Indians become serfs on large haciendas under the *wasipungo*, or debt peonage, system.
1736: expedition by the French Academy of Sci-

ences, led by Charles de la Condamine and Pierre Bouguer, measures a degree of the meridian near the equator and determines the circumference of the earth; also conducts the first scientific exploration of the Amazon.

18th century: Enlightenment ideals reach Ecuador. Eugenio Espejo (1747–95) campaigns against imperialism and dies in prison.

1768: Mount Cotopaxi ends 20 years of devastating eruptions.

1802: Alexander von Humboldt arrives in Ecuador. He climbs Mount Chimborazo and makes numerous important geographical and meteorological discoveries. He is the first to identify altitude sickness.

1835: Charles Darwin spends five weeks on the Galápagos Islands where he makes many of the observations underpinning his theories of evolution.

1809: members of the criollo oligarchy seize power in Quito but are harshly subdued.

1820: Guayaquil establishes a revolutionary junta.

1822: Battle of Pichincha: the forces of Antonio José de Sucre defeat the royalist army and liberate Quito.

1822: Simón de Bolívar arrives in Quito.

1823: Bolívar's ideal, Gran Colombia, incorporating Ecuador, Venezuala and Colombia, is formed, but lasts only seven years.

1830: General Juan José Flores announces the creation of the Republic of Ecuador. Sucre is assassinated, and Bolívar later dies in exile.

1843–58: years of political disorder

1858–75: Gabriel García Moreno imposes a harsh dictatorship and is finally assassinated. Improves the country's infrastructure, enhances agriculture, and develops Guayaquil's port facilities.

1912: Eloy Alfraro, liberal president, is killed by a pro-clerical mob.

1922: crippling blight strikes banana industry, in which Ecuador is the world's largest exporter.

1930s: first oil explorations in the Oriente.

1934–61: José María Velasco Ibarra, a populist leader, enjoys five presidential terms.

1941: Peru annexes almost half of Ecuador's territory, taking much of El Oro, which is rich in gold and coffee.

1942: Río de Janeiro Protocol ratifies the new borders. Ecuador will later renege on the deal.

1950s: crisis in the hacienda system.

PRECEDING PAGES: gold earrings and bracelets from the Carchi culture, 1400–500BC. **ABOVE LEFT:** Francisco Pizarro, the Spanish conqueror who landed in 1530. **ABOVE RIGHT:** member of the palace guard.

1960s: beginning of foreign tourism.

1964: Land Reform Act outlaws debt peonage system and gives Indians title to their plots of land.

Early 1970s: oil starts to flow through new trans-Ecuadorian pipeline, the beginning of a period in which great damage will be done to the Oriente and the indigenous people.

1972: oil becomes the major export.

1978: constitution grants the vote to 750,000 illiterate adults. The center-left government of Jame Roldós launches literacy and housing programs, increases wages and encourages unions.

1981: Roldós killed in a plane cash. Osvaldo Hurtado takes over and continues reforms.

1982: devasting *El Niño* floods ruin crops and destroy roads and railways.

1984: Conservative León Febres Cordero wins elections and forms a government.

1987: earthquake sweeps away oil pipeline, causing massive ecological and economic damage.

1988–92: Social Democrat Rodrigo Borja Cevallos heads a fair and progressive government.

1992–96: years of unpopular right-wing government under Sixto Durán Bellén.

1995: border dispute with Peru.

1996: Abdala Bucaram, nicknamed El Loco, wins elections. Campaigns as champion of the poor but his initial popularity soon fades, amid allegations of corruption.

1997: Bucaram ousted. Fabian Alarcon sworn in.

LOST WORLDS

*Ancient civilizations bequeathed a rich variety of cultural remains
which continue to intrigue both archaeologists and visitors*

The archaeology of the Americas shines, in the public mind, with just a few specially bright stars: the Incas of Peru, the Aztecs of central Mexico and the Maya of southern Mexico and Guatemala. The many pre-Colombian cultures beyond those centers are still relatively little known, in spite of some astonishing recent discoveries.

Ecuador comprises one of those *tierras incognitas*, even though it has a fabulously rich archaeological heritage. Because of the close proximity between coast, Sierra and Amazonia, experts are able to study the movements that shaped civilization on the entire continent. It is becoming clear that many key developments defining pre-Colombian South America took place in Ecuador.

The oldest pottery in all of the Americas has been found here. Cultures have been discovered that worked in platinum, a metal unknown in Europe until the mid-1800s. Ancient trade links have been established between Ecuador, Mexico and Amazonia. And it seems likely that pre-Colombian Ecuadorians sailed to and explored the Galápagos Islands.

The remote past

The first human beings who came to Ecuador were hunters and gatherers. The approximate period of their arrival is still debated, but it is certain that human beings have been in the Andes for 15,000 years, probably 30,000 years, and perhaps even for as long as 50,000 years. But the crucial question in Ecuador itself surrounds the gradual, all-important transformation from the hunting and gathering way of life to what archaeologists call the "formative lifestyle."

While hunters and gatherers lead a nomadic existence, formative cultures feature permanent settlements and communities. Most archaeologists believe that this transformation in the Americas occurred over a 2,000- or 3,000-year

period, starting around 3000BC in the most advanced areas. To the great surprise of many archaeologists, the earliest pottery and other evidence of formative cultures in the whole of South America has been found on the coast of Ecuador, from a culture known as Valdivia.

The Valdivian culture stretched along the

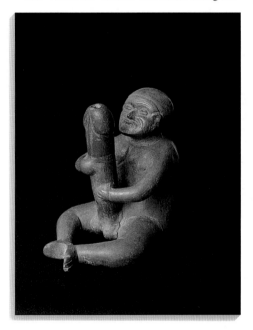

Ecuadorian coast of the modern-day province of Manabi, with its extensive, ecologically rich mangrove swamps, reaching inland to the drier hilly country. The earliest Valdivian site, dating back perhaps to 3500BC, is called Loma Alta. A range of extraordinary pottery has been found at this site, decorated with different carved motifs and a variety of colored clays. The Valdivian potters also formed multi-colored female figurines that turn up in late strata in the archaeological sites.

In Real Alto, a large Valdivian town continuously inhabited for over 2,000 years, archaeologists have found the remains of over 100 household structures, each of which may have

---

LEFT: Jama Coaque. figurine, 500BC.
RIGHT: priapic pottery from the Carchi culture.

housed 20 or more people. By 1500BC, the Real Alto people had built ceremonial temples on the tops of hills in the center of their town, where complex rituals obviously took place. A large number of female figurines have been found here, displaying sculpted hair, and long, slender legs.

The problem for the archaeologists and historians of pre-Colombian South America was not that the earliest and most advanced formative culture was found in Ecuador, although that certainly surprised them. The real problem was that the Valdivian culture, with highly developed pottery, agricultural cultivation, and social organization firmly under its belt, could not have appeared out of nowhere. There must have been a long series of precursors, of trial-and-error development, which led up to these cultural achievements.

The evidence to show that these developments occurred on the coast of Ecuador, ultimately giving birth to Valdivia, is not completely convincing. Investigations have uncovered earlier pottery on the coast, yet supporting data linking these oldest clay chips to Valdivia is lacking.

The daring and well-publicized voyages of Thor Heyerdahl encouraged such archaeologists as Emilio Estrada (see panel below), even though Heyerdahl's rafts sailed from Peru to Polynesia, not from Japan to Ecuador. The acceptance of the Jomon-Valdivia connection was wholehearted in some quarters. Indeed, visitors to the Museum of the Banco Central, Quito's most important archaeological museum, may still encounter this theory as an almost proven fact, presented as the most up-to-date

hypothesis by many of the museum's guides.

But, in fact, the Jomon theory has been largely discarded. No single phase in the development of Valdivian pottery corresponds to a particular phase in the Jomon cultural development. In fact, the decorative motifs common to both Jomon and Valdivia are found all over the world because the techniques that produced them are precisely those which potters choose almost automatically when they experiment with the results of applying a finger, a bone tool, a leaf or a stone to the wet clay.

On a deeper level, the views of Estrada and his colleagues strike an important chord for all archaeological studies in the Americas. There seems to be an irresistible tendency to assume that technological and artistic advances originated in the "discovery" of these lands by Asians or Europeans. The most vulgar expression of this tendency is to be found in the still-popular theory of the writer Eric van Daniken, which connects advanced pre-Colombian civilizations with extra-terrestrials.

Origins in the Amazon

In the Oriente region of Ecuador, as elsewhere in Amazonia, the persistent presence of hunting and gathering peoples has led many observers to regard Amazonia as an historical backwater, incapable of supporting large populations and advanced civilizations. The first hint that this could not be the case came from agricultural scientists investigating the domestication of manioc, which they concluded had taken place in the Amazon basin at least 8,000 years ago.

Archaeologists believe that large cities of more than 10,000 people, supported by manioc cultivation, grew up on the Amazon's fertile flood-plain as well as in the jungles on the eastern slope of the Ecuadorian and Peruvian Andes. These new historical concepts view modern tribes as being descended from the inhabitants of these undiscovered cities, the survivors of the plagues, wars and forced dislocations caused by the Spanish Conquest.

The cultures of the Amazonian cities, which archaeologists are now starting to find in Ecuador and Peru, gave pottery and manioc to South America. Manioc, along with corn (which came to Ecuador from Central America by way of trade), formed the agricultural foundation for a series of advanced coastal cultures, starting with Valdivia, according to current thinking.

THE JAPANESE IN ECUADOR?

The well-known Ecuadorian archaeologist, Emilio Estrada, at first working alone, and later with the collaboration of Smithsonian Institute archaeologists Betty Meggers and Clifford Evans, postulated that Valdivia's origins were to be found on the Japanese island of Kyushu. The Jomon culture, which existed on Kyushu around 3000BC, produced pottery strikingly similar to that found in the Valdivian sites, with predominantly curved and zig-zag lines and wedge shapes, and with combinations of ridges, lines, dots and grooves. However, this theory never caught on and now it has been virtually abandoned.

The Andes, or Sierra, at first acted as a thoroughfare between the Amazon and the coast.

An important site near Cuenca, called Cerro Narrio, is situated at the crossroads of a natural, easy route, following the drainages of the Pastaza and Paute rivers. From around 2000BC, Cerro Narrio may have been a key trading center, where exchanges of technologies, products, and ideas from the coast, Amazonia, and the Sierra took place. Ceramics bearing unmistakably similar designs to those of coastal cultures have been found at Cerro Narrio, but archaeologists are unable to determine whether these pots were imported from the coast or were made

whole area. Meanwhile, Amazonian societies were renowned for their ritual vessels, made for more than 3,000 years, and for their hallucinogenic concoctions.

Flowering of coastal activity

Following the establishment of formative cultures and of wide-ranging trade and exchange networks, stretching from Mexico to Peru and from the Amazon to the coast, archaeologists describe a period of "regional development" (500 BC–AD 500) followed by a period of "integration" (AD 500–1500). The final period culminated in the conquest of all of present-day

at Cerro Narrio by potters who had come from the coast to live in the Sierra.

Archaeologists now believe that a number of important items were traded between coast, Sierra and jungle. Coastal societies collected spondylus shells, which were processed into beads in the Sierra and traded in Amazonia, where the shell design appears on much of the pottery that has been discovered. The Sierran societies domesticated the potato which was used for trade, as well as coca – crucially important in rituals and ceremonies throughout the

ABOVE: pre-Colombian copper pieces which have been found in the Sierra.

Ecuador by the Inca Empire, which undertook an extensive program of city building and artistic creativity, before being itself destroyed by the Spaniards. A grand flowering of cultural activity preceded the Inca conquest of Ecuador, and the abundance of distinctive phases, especially on the coast, is overwhelming. The extraordinary achievement of these coastal cultures is embodied in the goldwork and sculpture of the La Tolita and Manta civilizations.

La Tolita civilization

The La Tolita culture reached its zenith around 300BC and its star shone for perhaps 700 years on the coast of northern Ecuador and south-western Colombia. The key site is a small, swampy lowland island in the mouth of the Santiago River in the coastal province of Esmeraldas. Now inhabited by Afro-Ecuadorian fisherfolk, La Tolita came to the attention of Westerners in the 1920s, when several European explorers announced the discovery of unprecedented numbers of finely crafted gold objects .

The merciless pillage of these priceless objects went on for years, and was even industrialized by a prospector named Yanuzelli, who mechanized the milling of thousands of tons of sand from which gold artifacts were extracted and then melted down into ingots. Despite this,

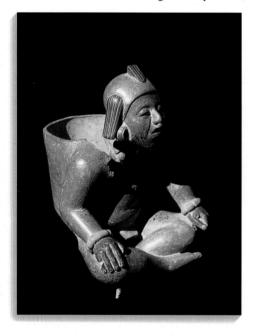

many gold objects are still found on La Tolita.

The magnificent mask of the Sun God, with its ornately detailed fan of sun rays, which is the symbol of Ecuador's Banco Central, was found on La Tolita. So much gold has been uncovered there that archaeologists believe that the island was a sacred place, a pre-Columbian Mecca or Jerusalem, a city of goldsmiths, devoted to the production of holy images. It may have been the destination of pilgrims from the coast, the Sierra and possibly Amazonia, who went there to obtain the sacred symbols of an ancient cult that influenced most of what is now Ecuador.

The quality and beauty of La Tolita goldwork is matched by the sculpture found on the island.

The freestanding, detailed figures in active poses make La Tolita sculpture unique in pre-Colombian art. The sculptures depict both deities and mortals, the latter displaying deformities and diseases, or experiencing emotions of joy, sadness or surprise.

La Tolita artisans also excelled in a metalcraft unknown even in Europe until the 1850s. Metalsmiths on the island worked in platinum, creating intricate masks, pendants, pectorals, and nose-rings in a metal with a very high melting point. Archaeologists have long puzzled over how La Tolita metalsmiths were able to do this, with only rudimentary tools and technology. One theory is that by combining pure platinum with bits of gold, which melts at a much lower temperature, the smiths created an alloy with which they could work.

The Manta culture

The Manta culture, in the modern province of Manabi, flowered during the period of integration, and also produced objects of surpassing beauty in gold, silver, cotton textiles, pottery and stone. The great city of Manta housed more than 20,000 people, and by including the population of outlying villages, archaeologists have arrived at very high numbers of people who lived during the Manta culture. This culture produced the greatest mariners of pre-Colombian Ecuador, and there is evidence that the Manta people settled extensive coastal areas, and traded with the coastal peoples of western Mexico and central Peru.

There is an intriguing theory held by some archaeologists that Manteña mariners, along with pre-Colombian Peruvian sailors, discovered the Galápagos Islands. A quantity of ceramic shards, almost certainly of pre-Columbian vintage, have been found on three of the islands; the presence of cotton plants, domesticated on the continent, also indicates some sort of contact between the islands and the mainland. Whether the contacts were only occasional, or just accidental, as some believe, whether the islands were used as a seasonal fishing outpost, as Thor Heyerdahl and others favor, or whether they were settled by groups of Manteñas, as a few archaeologists assert, has yet to be established.

LEFT: Jama Coaque drinking cup. RIGHT: figurine from the Bahía culture, 500BC–AD500.

ON THE SIDELINES OF HISTORY

Although never a major player on the world stage,
Ecuador was fought over and dominated by the Incas and the conquistadores

The forces of historical change have frequently been imposed on Ecuador from beyond its borders. Successive invaders – the Incas, the Spaniards and, more recently, bellicose neighbors – have swept across the country in great waves of destruction, each seeking to remake it in their own image. Their success is reflected in the varied ethnicity of the Ecuadorian people – 40 percent Indian, 40 percent *mestizos* (mixed European–Indian blood), and the remainder an assortment of full-blooded Europeans (*criollos*) and the descendants of black Caribs and Africans (*morenos*). Their legacy of brutal exploitation constitutes an ongoing struggle for modern Ecuadorians.

Sierra cultures

The land that is now Ecuador was first brought under one rule when the Incas of Peru invaded in the middle of the 15th century. By this time, the dazzling cultures of Manta and La Tolita on the Ecuadorian coast had flowered and faded, while an increasingly powerful series of agricultural societies had divided the region's highlands among them.

The greatest of these cultures was the Cañaris, who inhabited the present-day sites of Cuenca, Chordaleg, Gualaceo and Cañar. Theirs was a rigidly hierarchical society. Only the Cañari elites were allowed to wear the fine, elaborate gold and silver produced by their metalsmiths. Among the Cañari artifacts, figures of jaguars, caymans and other jungle animals predominate – showing their strong links with Amazonian groups.

Another advanced group were the Caras, forefathers of the modern Otavaleños, and ruled by the Shyri dynasty. Arriving in Ecuador "by way of the sea," the Caras ascended the Río Esmeraldas during the 10th century and established themselves in the land of the Quitus. They worshipped the sun and believed the

moon was inhabited by humans. They built an observatory to chart the solstices, and identified the equator as "the path of the sun." Their economy was based on spinning and weaving wool, and there was a traveling class of merchants who traded with tribes in the Oriente.

The Puruhás, ferocious warriors based around

Ambato, were ruled by the Duchicela family, which intermarried with the Shyri in the 14th century and created the greater kingdom of Quitu. While little social or economic influence was exerted over the kingdom's lesser tribes, they nevertheless expanded the numbers of men who could be deployed in battle.

The Inca invasion

On to this landscape of tribal identity marched the Incas – literally, "Children of the Sun" – who were to be the short-lived precursors of the Spaniards. Although established in the Peruvian Andes from the 11th century, it was not until about 1460 that they attacked the Cañaris, with

LEFT: Alexander von Humboldt and his fellow traveler Aimé Bonpland. **RIGHT:** a fanciful European depiction of the Inca Atahualpa.

the ultimate objective of subjugating the kingdom of Quitu. From this moment in history,
Ecuador became brutally embroiled in imperial
ambitions as armies dispatched
from distant capitals turned the
country into a battlefield.

The Cañaris fought valiantly
against superior odds for several
years before being subdued by
the Inca Tupac-Yupanqui. His revenge severely
depleted the indigenous male population: when
the Spanish chronicler Cieza de León visited
Cañari territory in 1547, he found 15 women to
every man. Inca occupation was focused on the

BATTLE DRUMS

The stomachs of enemies
were turned into drums to be
beaten at the next battle.

served as temple, storehouse and observatory.

Inca conquest along the spine of the Andes
continued inexorably. Quitu, which had fallen
by 1492, became a garrison
town on the empire's northern
frontier and, like Tomebamba,
the focus of ostentatious construction. Battles continued to
rage: for 17 years the Caras
resisted the Inca onslaught before Huayna-
Cápac, Tupac's son, captured the Caras' capital,
Caranqui, and massacred thousands.

The Incas at war were a fearsome sight.
Dressed in quilted armor and cane or woollen

construction of a major city called Tomebamba
on the site of present-day Cuenca. It was
intended to rival the Inca capital of Cuzco, from
whence stonemasons were summoned to build a
massive Temple of the Sun and splendid palaces
with walls of sculpted gold.

But by the time Cieza de León arrived, Tomebamba was already a ghost town. He found
enormous warehouses stocked with grain, barracks for the imperial troops and houses formerly occupied by "more than two hundred
virgins, who were very beautiful, dedicated to
the service of the sun." At nearby Ingapirca,
the best preserved pre-Hispanic site in Ecuador,
the Incas built an imposing fortress that also

helmets, and armed with spears, *champis* (head-
splitters), slingshots and shields, they attacked
with blood-curdling cries. Prisoners taken in
battle were led to a sun temple and slaughtered.
The heads of enemy chieftains became ceremonial drinking cups, and their bodies were stuffed
and paraded through the streets.

Imposing the new order

Inca colonization brought large numbers of
loyal Quechua subjects from southern Peru to
Ecuador, and many Cañaris and Caras were in
turn shipped to Peru. The Incas introduced their
impressive irrigation methods and some new
crops – sweet potatoes, coca and peanuts – as

well as the llama, a sturdy beast of burden and an excellent source of wool. The chewing of coca, previously unknown in highland Ecuador, soon became a popular habit. The Imperial Highway was extended to Quito, which – although 1,980km (1,230 miles) from Cuzco – could be reached by a team of runners in just eight days. Loyalty to the Inca, with his mandate from the sun, was exacted through the system of *mita* – imperial work or service – rather than taxation. As large areas came under centralized control for the first time, a nascent sense of unity stirred; but it was an alien and oppressive regime, attracting little genuine loyalty.

Huayna-Cápac, seeking to unite his domain through marriage, achieved just the opposite.

Huanya-Cápac had been born and raised in Tomebamba; his favorite son, Atahualpa, was the offspring of the Duchicela marriage and heir to the kingdom of Quito. Atahualpa's half-brother, Huascar, was descended from Inca lineage on both sides, and thus the legitimate heir. In 1527, Huascar ascended the Cuzco throne, dividing the empire for the first time. Civil war soon broke out, and continued for five years before Atahualpa defeated and imprisoned Huascar after a major battle near Ambato.

Atahualpa, an able and intelligent leader,

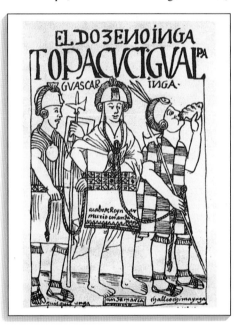

The Ecuadorian Indians who suffered Inca domination were proud, handsome peoples. Cieza de León spoke of the Cañaris as "good-looking and well grown," and the native Quiteños as "more gentle and better disposed, and with fewer vices than all Indians of Peru." Tupac-Yupanqui married a Cañari princess, and Huayna-Cápac, in turn, the daughter of the Duchicela king of Quito. This was to play a crucial part in the collapse of the empire, for

established the new capital of Cajamarca in northern Peru. But the war had severely weakened both the infrastructure and the will of the Incas, and by a remarkable historical coincidence, it was only a matter of months before their death-knell sounded.

The bearded white strangers

Rarely have the pages of history been stalked by such a greedy, treacherous, bloodthirsty band of villains as the Spanish *conquistadores*. With their homeland ravaged by 700 years of war with the Moors, the Spanish believed they had paid a heavy price for saving Christian Europe from Moslem domination. When news reached

LEFT: famous Inca masonry at Ingapirca ruins. **ABOVE LEFT:** Inca society boasted a well-ordered system of public works. **ABOVE RIGHT:** the capture of Huascar during the Incas' bitter civil war.

Into the Amazon

O nce Quito had been settled, the *conquistadores* began to seek new lands and new adventures. Tales of El Dorado and Canelos (a Land of Cinnamon, supposedly to the east), filled the air. Francisco Pizarro appointed his brother, Gonzalo – "the best beloved of any man in Peru" – to lead an expedition to find these magical destinations. On Christmas Day, 1539, Gonzalo left Quito with 340 soldiers, 4,000 Indians, 150 horses, a flock of llamas, 4,000 swine, 900 dogs, and plentiful supplies of food and water.

Surviving an earthquake and an attack by hostile Indians, the expedition descended the Cordillera. At Sumaco on the Río Coca, they were joined by Francisco de Orellana, who had been called from his governorship of Guayaquil to be Gonzalo's lieutenant.

Hacking their way through dense, swampy undergrowth, and hampered by incessant heavy rain, they were reduced to eating roots, berries, herbs, frogs and snakes. The first group of Indians they met denied all knowledge of El Dorado, so Gonzalo had them burned alive and torn to pieces by dogs.They met another group who spoke of an inhabited city, supposedly rich in provisions and gold, just 10 days' march away at the junction of the Coca and Napo rivers. A large raft was constructed, and 50 soldiers under de Orellana's command were dispatched to find the city and return with food: already 2,000 Indians and scores of Spaniards had starved to death.

Hearing nothing of the advance party after two months, Gonzalo trekked to the junction, but there was no city. The pragmatic Indians had very sensibly lied to save their skins. In early June, 1542, the 80 surviving Spaniards from Pizarro's group staggered into Quito, "naked and barefooted."

By then, Francisco de Orellana was far away. The brigantine's provisions were exhausted by the time the party reached the river junction: sailing back upstream against the current was impossible, and the difficulties of blazing a jungle trail would have killed the weary men. Hearing the call of destiny and whispers of El Dorado across the wilderness, de Orellana sailed on.

For nine months the expedition drifted on the current, never knowing what lay round the next bend. Crude wooden crosses were erected as they progressed, purporting to claim the lands in the name of the Spanish king. They encountered many Indian tribes: some gave them food – turkeys, turtles, parrots and fruits – and ornaments of gold and silver; others attacked with spears and poisoned arrows, claiming many Spanish lives.

On one occasion 10,000 natives are said to have attacked them from the river banks and from canoes, but the Spaniards' arquebusses soon repelled them.

They heard frequent reports of a tribe of fearsome women known as "Amazons," who lived in gold-plated houses. Near Obidos, the "Amazons" attacked. These fearsome women were "very tall, robust, fair, with long hair twisted over their heads, skins round their loins, and bows and arrows in their hands." From this report, the great South American river and jungle area took its name.

Finally, in a lowland area with many inhabited islands, de Orellana noticed signs of the ebb of the tide and, in August 1541, sailed into the open sea. For the first time, Europeans had traversed South America.

Today, if you want to emulate this experience, but in rather more style and comfort, book a trip on the riverboat *Flotel Orellana* – rather like a Mississippi riverboat – which takes visitors up and down the Amazon (see the *Travel Tips* section at the end of this guide for details).

ABOVE LEFT: *conquistadores* abuse one of their pressganged porters.

Spain of the glittering Aztec treasury, snatched by Cortéz in 1521, it fired the imaginations of desperate owners of ruined lands – and the Church – and spawned dreams of other such empires in the New World.

The first *conquistadores* to set foot on Ecuadorian soil landed near Esmeraldas in September, 1526. They had been dispatched from Colombia by Francisco Pizarro to explore lands to the south. The party, led by Bartolomé Ruíz, discovered several villages of friendly natives wearing splendid objects of gold and silver, news of which prompted Pizarro himself, with just 13 men, to follow a year or so later. Near

passes. Arriving exhausted in Cajamarca in November, 1532, they formulated a plan to trap the Inca Atahualpa. At a pre-arranged meeting, the Inca and several thousand followers – many of them unarmed – entered the great square of Cajamarca. A Spanish priest outlined the tenets of Christianity to Atahualpa, calling upon him to embrace the faith and accept the sovereignty of the Spanish king, Charles V. Predictably, Atahualpa refused, flinging the priest's Bible to the ground; Pizarro and his men rushed out from the surrounding buildings and set upon the astonished Incas. Of the Spaniards, only Pizarro himself was wounded when he seized

Tumbes, he found an Indian settlement whose inhabitants were similarly adorned, and so planned a full-scale invasion. Late in 1530, having traveled to Spain to secure the patronage of King Charles V and the title of Governor and Captain-General of Peru, Pizarro – this time with 180 men and 27 horses – landed in the Bay of San Mateo near Manabí.

For two years the *conquistadores* battled against the Indians and against the treacherous terrain of mosquito-infested swamps and jungles, and frozen, cloud-buffeted mountain

Atahualpa, while the Incas were cut down in their hundreds.

Atahualpa was imprisoned and a ransom demanded: a roomful of gold and silver weighing 24 tons was amassed, but the Inca was not freed. He was held for nine months, during which time he learnt Spanish and mastered the arts of writing, chess and cards. His authority was never questioned: female attendants dressed him in robes of vampire bat fur, fed him, and ceremoniously burnt everything he used. The Spaniards melted down the finely wrought treasures, and accused Atahualpa of treason. Curiously, Pizarro baptized him "Fransisco," and then garotted him with an iron collar.

ABOVE: 16th-century depiction of the Spanish advance during the Conquest.

Two worlds collide

To the Incas, the Spanish conquest was an apocalyptic reversal of the natural order. In the eyes of a 16th-century native chronicler, Waman Puma, these strangers were "all enshrouded from head to foot, with their faces completely covered in wool…men who never sleep." The Incas had no monetary system and no concept of private wealth: they believed the only possible explanation for the Spaniards' craving for gold was that they either ate precious metals, or suffered from a disease that could be cured only by gold. Their horses were "beasts who wear sandals of silver."

Conversely, the Spaniards perceived the natives as semi-naked barbarians who worshipped false gods, and were good for nothing; Cieza de León's positive remarks only illustrate his unusual fair-mindedness.

While Pizarro continued southward towards Cuzco, his lieutenant, Sebastian de Benalcázar, was dispatched to Piura to ship the Inca booty to Panama. But rumors of these treasures had traveled north, and Pedro de Alvarado, another Spaniard in search of riches, set out from Guatemala to conquer Quito. With 500 men and 120 horses, he landed at Manta in early 1534, and during an epic trek slaughtered all the coastal Indians who crossed his path.

Hearing of this, Benalcázar quickly mounted his own expedition to capture Quito. Approaching Riobamba in May, he encountered a massive Quiteño army under the Inca general Quisquis. Fifty thousand Indians, the largest Inca force ever assembled, were deployed, hopelessly outnumbering the Spaniards. But the Indians, owing no loyalty to the Incas, mutinied and dispersed, and the best opportunity to defeat the Spanish was lost. Alvarado was paid a handsome sum by Pizarro to abandon his Ecuadorian excursion and return quietly to Guatemala.

Benalcázar marched northward with thousands of Cañaris and Puruhás in his ranks, for both tribes sought revenge on the brutal Incas. Arriving in Quito in December, 1534, he found the city in ruins; Rumiñahui, the Inca general, had destroyed and evacuated it rather than lose it intact. Atop Cara and Inca rubble, with a mere 206 inhabitants, the Villa de San Francisco de Quito was founded on December 6, and Guayaquil the following year. Rumiñahui launched a counter-attack a month later, but was captured, tortured and executed.

By 1549, the conquest was complete: a mere 2,000 Spaniards had subjugated an estimated 500,000 Indians. The number of casualties is impossible to ascertain, but tens of thousands died in this 15-year period, through starvation, disease and suicide as well as in battle.

The Spanish yoke

With the restless natives quietened, the *conquistadores* fought each other for the prizes: not until 1554 did the Spanish Crown finally subdue them. In 1539, Pizarro appointed his brother Gonzalo governor of Quito, but when the first Viceroy to Peru passed through shortly thereafter, he found the colonists in revolt. Gonzalo fought off the Viceroy's forces in 1546, only to be deposed and executed by another official army two years later. During Gonzalo's governorship, an expedition was mounted to explore the lands east of Quito. The undertaking was a disaster (see *Into the Amazon,* page 36) but under the renegade leadership of Francisco de Orellana, the first transcontinental journey by Europeans was made in 1541.

When Cortéz cried, "I don't want land – give me gold!," he spoke for all *conquistadores.* But the immediately available treasures were soon exhausted. The land and its inhabitants were

and slaves brought from Africa to man the coastal cacao plantations. Ecuador escaped the grim excesses of mining that befell Peru and Bolivia, as the Spanish, to their disappointment, found few precious metals here.

As well as horses, pigs and cattle were introduced, and Ecuador nurtured the first crops of bananas and wheat in South America. The Spaniards also imported diseases such as smallpox, influenza, measles and cholera. But with much of the highlands and all of the Oriente so inaccessible, Spanish settlement was relatively light, so geography saved the Indians from extermination, if not from subjugation.

divided among the *conquistadores,* and the first settlers soon followed. Of the Quito region, in contrast to the damp, ghostly barrenness of Lima, Cieza de León wrote: "The country is very pleasant, and particularly resembles Spain in its pastures and climate."

The Avenue of the Volcanoes, the strip of land 40 to 60km (25 to 40 miles) wide running the length of Ecuador between two towering rows of volcanoes, was ideal farmland. In addition, workshops were established to produce textiles,

OPPOSITE: Francisco Pizarro, the great conqueror.
ABOVE LEFT: colonial depiction of weaving.
ABOVE RIGHT: a *criollo* noble.

Colonial administration was based on the twin pillars of the *encomienda* system and the Church. The former effected the transition from conquest to occupation. The *encomenderos,* or landowners, were given tracts of land and the right to unpaid Indian labor, and in return were responsible for the religious conversion of their laborers. The Indians were obliged to bring tribute, in the form of animals, vegetables and blankets, to their new masters, as they had to the Incas. It was a brutally efficient form of feudalism whereby the Spanish Crown not only pacified the *conquistadores* with a life of luxury, but also gained an empire at no risk or expense.

For centuries, the main landowner was the

Church, as dying *encomenderos* donated their estates, in the hope of gaining salvation. Pragmatically, *indígenas* accepted the new faith, embellishing it with their own beliefs and rituals. Days after Benalcázar founded Quito, the cornerstone of the first major place of Christian worship, the church of San Francisco, was laid. Franciscans were followed by Jesuits and Dominicans, each group of missionaries enriching themselves at the Indians' expense while claiming a monopoly on salvation.

Methods of conversion could be brutal: children were separated from their families to receive the catechism; lapsing converts were

protesting against increased taxes on food and fabrics. The authorities put an end to the agitation by executing 24 conspirators and displaying their heads in iron cages.

During the 18th century, the ideas of the European Enlightenment crept slowly towards Quito University. The works of Voltaire, Leibnitz, Descartes and Rousseau, and the revolutions in the United States and France gave intellectual succor to colonial libertarians. The physician-journalist Eugenio Espejo, born in 1747 of an Indian father and mulatto mother, emerged as the anti-imperialists' leader.

Espejo was a pioneering, fearless humanist.

imprisoned, flogged, and their heads shaved. Some priests took Indian women as mistresses, and their children contributed to the numbers of *mestizos*, people of mixed Spanish-Indian blood. Quito – seat of a viceregal court or *audencia* from 1563 – grew into a religious and intellectual center during the 17th century as seminaries and universities were established.

Push for independence

In reaction to the Spaniards' oppressive socioeconomic actions there sprouted violent popular uprisings and nascent cries of "Liberty!" As early as 1592, the lower clergy supported merchants and workers in the Alcabalas Revolution,

He published satirical, bitterly combative books on the subject of Spanish colonialism; and as founding editor of the liberal newspaper *Primicias de la Cultura de Quito*, was probably the first American journalist. He was repeatedly jailed, exiled to Bogotá for four years, and finally died, aged 48, in a Quito dungeon. From his cell, he wrote to the President of the *Audencia*: "I have produced writings for the happiness of the country, as yet a barbarian one." His name now graces the National Library and countless streets in Ecuador.

ABOVE: a contemporary depiction of the quay at Guayaquil.

Von Humboldt: the first travel writer

Simón Bolívar described Humboldt as "the true discoverer of America because his work has produced more benefit to our people than all the *conquistadores*." Praise indeed from the liberator of the Americas. But how did this wealthy Prussian minerologist come to play such a vital role in the history of the continent?

Alexander von Humboldt was born in Berlin in 1769. As a young man he studied botany, chemistry, astronomy and mineralogy, and traveled with Georg Forster, who had accompanied Cook on his second world voyage. At the age of 27 he received a legacy large enough to finance a scientific exploration, and made such an impression on Carlos IV of Spain that he received permission to travel to South America – the first time a non-Spanish scientist had been granted this privilege since Charles de la Condamine in 1735. With his companion Aimé Bonpland, Humboldt set off for Caracas in November 1799. During their five-year expedition the two men covered some 9,600km (6,000 miles) on foot, horseback and by canoe. They suffered from malaria, and were reduced to a diet of ground cacao beans and river water when damp and insects destroyed their supplies.

Following the course of the Orinoco and Casiquiare rivers, they established that the Casiquiare channel linked the Orinoco and the Amazon. In 1802 they reached Quito, where Humboldt climbed Chimborazo, failing to attain the summit but setting a world record (unbroken for 30 years) by reaching almost 6,000 meters (19,500ft). He coined the name "Avenue of the Volcanoes" and, after suffering from altitude sickness, was the first to connect it with a lack of oxygen. Between ascents he did a vast amount of work on the role of eruptive forces in the development of the earth's crust, establishing that Latin America was not, as had been believed, a geologically young country.

It was while in Ecuador that Humboldt began assembing notes for his *Essays on the Geography of Plants*, pioneering investigations into the relationship between a region's geography and its flora and fauna. He claimed another first by listing many of the indigenous, pre-conquest species: vanilla and avocado, yucca, maize and manioc, among others; and he was responsible for the birth of the guano industry, after he sent samples of the substance back to Europe for analysis.

Humboldt's contributions seem endless: off the west coast he studied the oceanic current, which was named after him; his work on isotherms and isobars laid the foundation for the science of climatology; he invented the term "magnetic storms" and as a result of his interest the Royal Society in London promoted the establishment of observatories, which led to the correlation of such storms with sun-spot activity.

Humboldt viewed the natural world through the

eyes of a 19th-century Romantic. He was also deeply interested in social and economic issues. Despite good relations with the Spanish crown, he called himself "a Republican at heart"and was adamantly opposed to slavery which he considered "the greatest evil that afflicts human nature." His admirers were many: Goethe, a close friend, found him "exceedingly interesting and stimulating," a man who "overwhelms one with intellectual treasure;" while Charles Darwin had been inspired by the Prussian scientist's earlier journey to Tenerife, in the Canary Islands, and his description of the volcanic Pico de Teide and the dragon tree. Darwin knew whole passages of Humboldt's *Relation historique* off by heart, and described him as "the parent of a grand progeny of scientific travellers."

RIGHT: the young Humboldt, who received a legacy at the age of 27, enabling him to finance his research.

INDEPENDENCE AND AFTER

*From the battle for independence to recent oil exploitation
in the Amazon, the history of modern Ecuador has been turbulent*

As the Crown's grip on its colonies began to loosen, the ghost of the *conquistadores* stirred from its slumber. From the beginning of the Spanish era, money and muscle had meant power; laws, constitutions and governments were subject to the greed of reckless individuals. Cortéz and de Orellana disobeyed orders and attained greatness, and Pizarro answered to no one. The ethos they bequeathed to those who came after them was devoid of ideas and morality. Through the age of *caudillos* in the 19th century, and of military dictators in the 20th, Ecuador was viewed as a treasure, like Inca gold, conveniently there for the taking.

The road to freedom

Ecuador's first step towards independence was also its first coup. In response to the fall of Spain to Napoleon in 1808, a new wave of repressive measures was enforced in the colonies, prompting members of the *criollo* oligarchy to seize power in Quito in August, 1809, and imprison the president of the *Audencia*. Within a month, loyalist troops from Bogotá and Lima had displaced the usurpers, but the subsequent reprisals were so harsh that they prompted a second rebellion two years later. This time, a constitution for an independent state was formulated, but the uprising remained confined to Quito, and so was easily suppressed.

But the whole continent was moving inexorably towards liberation. With English support, Simon Bolívar – *El Libertador* – had taken on the Spanish loyalists in his native Venezuela, where he become dictator, then in Colombia. In October, 1820, Guayaquil ousted local authorities and established a revolutionary junta; and following the Battle of Pichincha in May, 1822, when forces led by Antonio José de Sucre resoundingly defeated the royalist army, Quito was liberated.

A few weeks later, Bolívar arrived in Quito.

PRECEDING PAGES: political mural in Latacunga.
LEFT: a worker overlooking the Quito of the 1890s.
ABOVE RIGHT: Simón Bolívar, *El Libertador*.

He was the archetypal *criollo* – ambitious, paternalistic, impatient, never doubting his methods or goals. His brilliance sprang from the singular intensity of his vision, which brought liberation to a continent, but he failed to appreciate the dynamics of the new nations. His Argentinean counterpart, José de San Martín,

was stoic, taciturn and self-effacing – Bolívar's ideal complement. But at their only meeting, in Guayaquil in July, 1822, to plot the future of a proposed Gran Colombia – they had a fundamental disagreement: Bolívar wanted a republic, while San Martín envisaged a monarchy. What exactly passed between the two men at that meeting is not known, but Bolívar triumphed, and San Martín went into self-imposed exile in Europe.

Gran Colombia was formed in 1823, incorporating Ecuador, Colombia and Venezuela. But the new, united nation lasted just seven years: in September, 1830, the military commander of Quito, General Juan José Flores – a Venezuelan who had married into the Quiteño aristocracy – announced the creation of the Republic of Ecuador. The new republic's population stood at approximately 700,000 and its ill-defined borders were based on those of the colonial *Audencia*.

That same year, Marshal Sucre – Bolívar's chosen successor – was assassinated en route from Bogotá to his home in Quito, prompting Bolívar to grieve, "They have slain Abel." On the northern shores of the continent that he had transformed, *El Libertador* died a broken man: overcome with frustration, he said of his life's work, "We have ploughed the sea."

Rocafuerte was bribed into exile, and Flores held power for two more years before being toppled by the Liberals.

In the subsequent period of chronic political disorder, the next 15 years saw 11 governments and three constitutions come and go, while the economy stagnated. Border disputes sprang up with both Peru and Colombia, with the mayor of Guayaquil actually ceding his city and southern Ecuador to Peru. This morass was tidied up by one of the strong men of Ecuadorian history, Gabriel García Moreno, who had risen from humble origins to the rectorship of the University of Quito.

False freedom

The inequalities of the colonial social structure were preserved with ruthless duplicity by the new Ecuadorian elite. While cries of "Patria" and "Freedom" echoed across the country, the poor remained enslaved in workshops, on *haciendas* and plantations. National power was up for grabs, and the struggle between the Conservatives of Quito and the Liberals of Guayaquil, which has characterized Ecuadorian politics, began immediately. Flores made a deal with the opposition Liberal leader, Vicente Rocafuerte, to alternate the presidency, with Flores retaining military control, but in 1843 he refused to step down from his second term.

During his decade in power, the nation became a theocracy where only practicing Catholics were allowed to vote. He renamed the best regiments "Guardians of the Virgin" and "Soldiers of the Infant Jesus" and frequently indulged in acts of self-humiliation: sepia photographs capture him, clad in black, carrying a heavy wooden cross on his shoulders through the streets, followed by his entire cabinet.

Freedom of speech and the press were nonexistent, and political opponents were imprisoned or exiled. But while the country's mind was being repressed, its body matured: hospitals, roads and railways were constructed; schools were opened to Indians and women for the first time; Guayaquil's port facilities were improved; and new crops enhanced agricultural productivity. From this era there emerged a spirit of national identity.

García Moreno's critics were many, but they trod a dangerous path, all too aware of the fate that awaited enemies of the regime. Quiteño journalist and leading intellectual Juan Montalvo railed against the president's tyrannical clericalism. From his enforced exile in Colombia, he rejoiced on hearing of the president's assassination in 1875, declaring: "My pen has killed him."

As the century turned, the liberal President barriers, and on one occasion cried, "Give me a balcony and I will be president again!"

War in the Amazon

Ecuador was originally more than double its present size, but Brazil, Colombia and Peru have each taken generously from its portion of Amazonia. In 1941, Peru snatched almost half of Ecuador's territory in an invasion that was largely uncontested, as President Arroyo, fearing a coup, kept most of his troops in Quito. Much of El Oro, a region rich in gold, oil and coffee, was lost, though Ecuador has subsequently reneged on the Rio de Janeiro Protocol

Eloy Alfaro managed to improve the Indians' lot, modernize the legal code, and separate Church and state before an incensed pro-clerical mob tore him to pieces.

Political assassination has not been a feature of more recent years, but nepotism and mindless populism have characterized the political landscape. José María Velasco Ibarra, who enjoyed five presidential terms between 1934 and 1961, was known as "The National Personification" for his ability to transcend regional

LEFT : the victorious Marshal Sucre signing the Act of Independence in 1822. RIGHT: workers on a banana plantation in the 1880s.

VIEWS FROM ABROAD

In *Four Years Among Spanish-Americans*, Friedrich Hassaurek, US Minister-Resident in Quito from 1861– 66, paints a vivid portrait of life in Ecuador. He found "convents instead of printing presses, military barracks instead of schoolhouses", and Indians doing "more work than all the other races together" but flocking to church "to break the monotony of daily life". The English mountaineer Edward Whymper, who visited Ecuador in 1879–80, spoke of Indians living in abject misery and exhibiting "hospitable instincts and an extreme timidity, heightened by an all-pervading mistrust".

of 1942 which ratified the new boundary. Several skirmishes have broken out since then, the most recent one, in 1995, developing into a more serious conflict that lasted three months, cost both sides several hundred casualties and had a damaging effect on the Ecuadorian economy. A ceasefire finally took place, with Ecuador reluctantly accepting the Rio Protocol. Further hostilities remain a possibility but a resolution of the dispute is believed to be on the horizon. In August 1997 interim president Alarcon met in Bolivia with Peru's President Fujimori for continuing peace strategies, about which the government appears to be optimistic.

The economy has expanded from its original bases of cacao and textiles to include coffee, Panama hats, shrimp farming, fresh flowers, tourism and, particularly, bananas. Under the iron fist of the Boston-based United Fruit Company, Ecuador became, and remains, the world's leading exporter of bananas. The accompanying ethos of rampant capitalism produced a crisis in the archaic *hacienda* system in the 1950s as, for the first time, money spread beyond the few hundred dominant *criollo* families. The long-overdue land reforms of 1964 further eroded traditional socio-economic ties, and the discovery of massive oil deposits in the Oriente has – in addition to changing the face of that neglected region – permanently shifted Ecuador's economic emphasis away from agriculture. Oil is now the major industry, controlled by the state-run Petroecuador and several multinationals; in 1994 the value of oil exports amounted to more than a third of the nation's exports, bringing in over $1,000 million.

Democratic leaders

Ecuador was the first Latin American country to attain democracy. In 1978, the army drew up a constitution which extended the vote to the country's 750,000 illiterate adults. The center-left government of Jaime Roldós, elected the following year, launched massive literacy and housing programs. Emphasizing issues instead of personalities, the government increased workers' wages and encouraged the emergence of a politically articulate middle class, and of mass-based organizations such as peasant co-operatives and labor unions. But an economic crisis loomed as oil prices dropped and payments on foreign debt fell due, and for a while rumors of a military coup were rife.

In 1981, Roldós died in a plane crash, sending the nation into mourning. Vice-President Osvaldo Hurtado fulfilled his pledges to serve his full term, to continue Roldós' reforms, and to maintain civil liberties – despite the added difficulty of the great *El Niño* floods of late 1982, which ruined banana and rice crops and destroyed roads and railways.

León Febres Cordero, a Conservative, won the 1984 elections. Febres oversaw sustained economic growth, but was brought down over charges of misuse of public funds which he allegedly paid to an Israeli counter-insurgency adviser for helping to dismantle a troublesome guerrilla movement.

Elections in 1988 brought to power President Rodrigo Borja Cevallos, a Social Democrat from Quito. He set an honest, competent political course: civil disturbances such as transport workers' strikes and student riots over price rises were handled leniently. Inflation fell, the foreign debt was serviced regularly and foreign investors continued to be attracted, both under Borja and under his successor, Sixto Durán Bellén of the Christian Social Party, who was elected in 1992. Sixto was not a very popular president, although the border dispute with Peru did produce a temporary surge in support. One of his more unpopular policies was the introduction of a privatisation program for telecommunictions, electricity and parts of Petroecuador, but Congress stalled the program.

Jaime Nebot, a right-wing Christian Socialist, looked set to lead Ecuador through the late 1990s, until Abdala Bucaram, a fiery populist, led the Ecuadorian Roldosista Party (PRE) in a surprise victory and formed a coalition government in 1996. Bucaram, a former mayor of Guayaquil nicknamed "El Loco" (a name he originally coined himself), gained much support from the country's poor and disenfranchised.

After singing and dancing his way into office, newly elected President Bucaram continued his extravagant behavior by recording a CD which many government employees were "encouraged" to buy. But the country soon became tired of the show.

Bucaram introduced steep increases in the prices of all utilities; natural gas more than trebled in price. Those already living in poverty – the people he had promised to help – were the worst affected. There was also much controversy over his plans to introduce a new unit of currency and peg it to the US dollar. Most serious though was the blatant corruption in administering state funds. A scandal over a Christmas telethon appeal for gifts for underprivileged children highlighted the extent of government corruption. Donations disappeared under mysterious circumstances and Bucaram and company were blamed.

On February 5, 4 million citizens dresssed in black took to the streets in a peaceful protest. A two-day general strike brought the country to a standstill with road blocks preventing any interprovincial traffic. The military maintained order but, exercising considerable restraint, refused to take sides. By the end of the second day Congress had found a clause in the constitution that enabled them, by the vote of a simple majority, to get rid of Bucaram on the grounds that he was mentally incapacitated .

During this confusing time there were three people who claimed the presidency for themselves : Abdala Bucaram, Rosalia Arteaga (the vice president) and Fabian Alarcon, the president of Congress. Thousands of people congregated around the presidential palace shouting for Abdala to leave. He fled to Panama (as he

had once before) leaving behind rumors that he had left the palace carrying black plastic sacks filled with sucres.

On February 11 Congress officially voted in Alarcon as interim president until August 1998, when democratic elections would be held.

Alarcon called a referendum in May 1997, asking 14 questions regarding the constitution. Some of these were complex issues, more suitable for lawyers than for the general public, but basically "yes" answers legitimized Alarcon's presidency. In April 1997 Congress formed a committee to investigate corruption within the government. It found that funds had leaked out

of Bucaram's office to a private one, where false invoices were written and bribes to various deputies made.

With this evidence Congress threw out 13 (and later another four) of its own deputies who were guilty of embezzlement. The high court (with documentation received from Congress) began legal action and issued arrest warrants against the 17. Two deputies gave themselves up; the rest went into hiding or fled the country.

With this refreshingly firm attitude towards corruption, and with the conflict over the border with Peru close to resolution, Ecuador has been able to plan for the 21st century in a mood of healthy, if cautious, optimism.

LEFT: political graffiti in Otavalo. **ABOVE RIGHT:** Abdala Bucaram, president, 1996–97.

ECONOMY AND ENVIRONMENT

*Ecuador has a difficult balancing act to perform if it is to
conserve the environment while boosting the economy*

The most significant event for the economy and ecology of the Oriente was the discovery by Texaco in 1968 of large petroleum reserves in pristine Amazon rainforest. The development of these oil fields spurred an economic boom in the 1970s but also resulted in profound damage to the rivers, rainforest and the indigenous people. Today oil accounts for 45 percent of Ecuador's exports and it will remain an important source of foreign income into the next century.

The government of the day negotiated a profitable deal with the petroleum companies in 1972 when oil first started flowing through the transcontinental pipeline. At the same time, world oil prices rose dramatically. The government quadrupled its budget in three years and public spending on social services was proportionally higher than any other country in Latin America. Investments were made in education, health and infrastructure that improved the lives of most Ecuadorians.

The history of the Oriente took a different course, however. Settlers, large corporations and Indians competed for land and resources. Little thought was given to the potential impacts on the environment as drilling wastes and oil spills flowed directly into rivers and lakes. The indigenous people had no concept of ownership and allowed oil companies to build roads and drill in exchange for gifts.

Settlers were awarded plots of land if they were willing to "improve" it, which meant clearing most of the native vegetation for agriculture or pasture. As their land was usurped by settlers, the indigenous people in the Lago Agrio area were forced to enter the new Ecuadorian society, often at the bottom social rung as laborers, domestic workers and prostitutes. Or they fled deeper into the rainforest, coming into conflict with other tribes.

With the support of the environmental lobby in the 1980s, however, tribes such as the Quichua, Siona-Secoya, Cofan, Achuar, Shuar

and Huaorani began to raise awareness in Ecuador and abroad through protests, putting pressure on the government to recognize their land rights and for the oil companies to clean up their act. In the early 1990s a division within the Ministry of Energy and Mines was created to regulate the oil industry: today environmental impact studies are required before each phase within a oil concession.

Attempts at protection

One of the most controversial areas for oil production is in the petroleum concession of Block 16 which partly lies within the Yasuni National Park. The park was severely reduced in size after Conoco revealed plans to construct a pipeline. Intense pressure to abandon the project was exerted by indigenous Huaorani, and international environmental organizations such as the Rainforest Action Network.

The block was sold to Maxus, which is a less visible Texas-based company and so less vulnerable to press criticism. Honest efforts were made to minimize impacts by using the latest technologies such as drilling 10 wells from a single platform, similar to offshore drilling methods. Most of the water extracted from the wells was re-injected, avoiding the practice of polluting the rivers with high levels of toxic heavy metals and hydrocarbons. However, YPF, an Argentinean company, purchased Maxus in 1996 and expenditures for environmental studies have been drastically reduced.

The biggest impact is the construction of a 120km (75-mile) long all-weather access road. Guard stations have kept settlers from the Sierra out but Quechua and Huaorani now use the road as the primary means of reaching the Napo River and are beginning to clear areas alongside for agriculture. In addition heavy rains in this hilly terrain have resulted in large and frequent landslides which have silted up many small streams and threaten to break the pipeline.

Three multinationals, ARCO, Triton and CGC, are now attempting to work in the Pastaza province but are up against well organized and

---

LEFT: oilman on a dusty road through the Oriente.

funded indigenous organizations. In order to allay fears about colonists moving into the area there will be no roads in a plan for a new pipeline. If implemented, this would be a revolutionary step in oil development.

Oil will continue to be a vital source of income for Ecuador but it remains to be seen if the battling groups will be able to come up with effective protection for the rainforest.

Burning the forests

The strong link between the need for economic development and environmental protection in Ecuador was made clear during the summer of

1997 when poor *campesinos* burned forests and fields in the "green-belt" that surrounds Quito to clear areas so grass would grow to graze their livestock. Once rain falls the topsoil is washed from the steep slopes leaving an impermeable surface of compacted volcanic pumice.

This practice of burning is common throughout the country and has been partially responsible for one of the highest rates of deforestation in Latin America (280,00 hectares/6.9 million acres). As a result almost 30 percent of the productive soils of the intra-Andean valleys have been lost to erosion.

But it is hard to blame the *campesinos* for the destruction since their average wage is about

US$6 a day, and creating more pasture land with fire is an act of survival.

Natural gas

A successful example of a government policy designed to alleviate poverty and protect the environment is the subsidy on natural gas. In July 1997 the retail cost of a 10-gallon tank was approximately US$1.20 which is within the budget of even the poorest *campesino*. The subsidy is designed to improve public health by providing a cheap source of fuel for cooking and boiling water. Since gas is less expensive than wood and charcoal, it saves the forests from being cut. Air pollution is also reduced in urban areas. Former president Abdala Bucaram's bid to remove the subsidy for natural gas in 1997 was among the austerity measures which helped oust him.

Pesticides

The agricultural industry, accounting for 40 percent of foreign earnings, is just behind petroleum in importance. In order to maximize production pesticides are used extensively to keep a thriving population of insects from devouring the crops. Officially the laws regulating pesticide use and residues on vegetables are strict but they are rarely enforced. Most farmers have no training on what to use, or how much; nor do they use protective equipment.

Climate change

The rainfall record since the beginning of the last century shows a pronounced decrease. Glaciers along the Avenue of the Volcanoes have retreated on average 300 meters (950 ft). The reduction in rain is most pronounced in the southern part of the country. During 1995 and 1996 Ecuador rationed electricity because the Paute hydroelectric plant which provides 65 percent of the country's electricity was dry.

Due to rationing, almost $4 billion in production was lost. The lack of rain in the Paute river basin was the first problem. Deforestation was also a culprit, since the soils are losing the ability to absorb water. Also, silt from eroding fields is filling the reservoir. When rationing means you can't even turn on your lights, the vital connection between conservation of scarce resources and the health of the economy really hits home.

ABOVE LEFT: knocking a highway through the jungle.

INEFAN: The National Parks Service

The Ecuadorian National Parks Service, INEFAN, was created in 1992 in an attempt to protect Ecuador's extraordinary variety of largely intact ecosystems. This agency has the daunting task of managing and protecting 24 national parks, ecological reserves and recreation areas that cover 4,619,021 hectares (11,413,850 acres), or 17 percent of the total area of the country.

The entrance fees from the two most popular parks, the Galápagos and the Cotopaxi National Parks, help subsidize some of the less visited and threatened reserves. For instance, coastal mangrove swamps, which are vital breeding grounds for marine fish species, have been destroyed in the past 15 years by the construction of expansive pools for "shrimp ranching".

The Cayapas-Mataje and the Manglares-Churute Reserves were created to protect a small portion of the rapidly disappearing mangroves, but many locals are unaware that these reserves exist. INEFAN's biggest task is community education on sustainable use of fish resources within these reserves.

Cloud forests were being cleared from the Andean central valley long before the Spanish conquered Ecuador in the first half of the 16th century, but the Andean eastern slope has never been cut because it is so wet, rugged and inaccessible.But as more roads are punched into the Oriente and colonists begin to fell the old growth mahoganies and alders, protected areas such as Cayambe-Coca Ecological Reserve, Llanganates and Sangay National Parks become important refuges for rare species such as the Andean spectacle bear, woolly mountain tapir and Andean condor.

Yasuni National Park in the Oriente is considered the most biologically diverse place in the world, where over 900 different species of trees have been identified in a single 2-hectare (5-acre) plot. Even with UNESCO World Heritage status, however, the howler monkeys and jaguars of Yasuni still have to share their habitat with an oil company and aggressively colonizing indigenous groups. Conservationists are extremely wary of this experiment since the nearby Cuyabeno Reserve recently had

ABOVE RIGHT: a jaguar – one of the creatures in need of protection.

its western half lopped off because the area is now filled with colonists and oil wells.

Mediating land use conflicts perhaps presents the greatest challenge to INEFAN. Multiple and often environmentally damaging activities such as homesteading, timber production, grazing, water projects, mining and oil production are permitted by other federal agencies in protected areas.

INEFAN has benefited to a very substantial extent from the financial assistance given by several international aid agencies. Perhaps the most significant help came in 1995 in the form of a five-year so-called "debt-for-nature" grant of US$ 9 million from the Global Environment Fund – which is a

branch of the now "greening" World Bank.

This grant supports high-tech research projects, such as a satellite image study to map out potential new parks in Ecuador's southern provinces, as well as providing much-needed funding for basic management in the field.

Cynics have been known to refer to Ecuadorian protected areas as "paper parks" since essential environmental policing is still lacking, but it is nevertheless remarkable that a country with only limited resources has had the foresight to sketch out the natural areas that are worth saving in the future.

If you are interested in learning more about INEFAN's work and would like to contact the organization, their offices can be found at Amazonas y Eloy Alfaro, 8th Floor, Quito, tel: 548924.

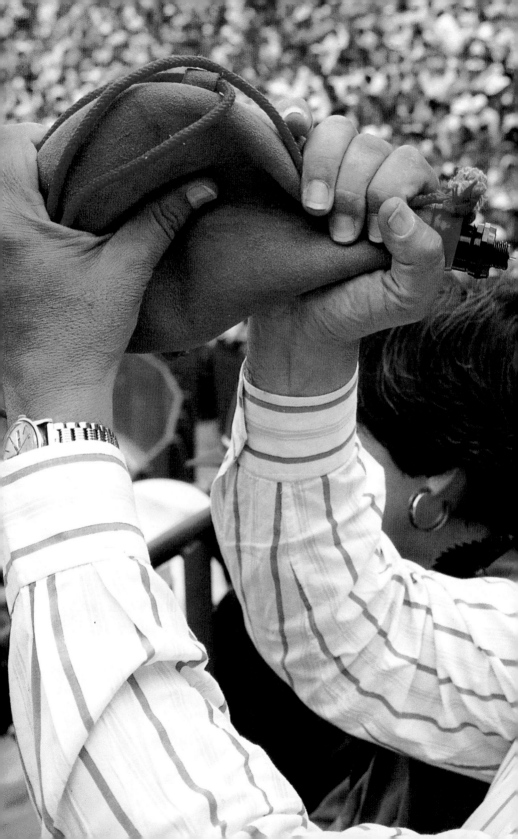

THE ECUADORIANS

The people of Ecuador inhabit a relatively small land, but they are as diverse and colorful as the landscape

Like other Andean countries, Ecuadorian society reflects divisions that can be traced back to the Spanish Conquest of the early 16th century. But the people have been shaped as much by Ecuador's wild geography as its history: the racial makeup, temperament and outlook of Ecuadorians is radically different on the coast, in the Sierra and in the jungle.

Until the discovery of oil in the early 1970s prompted an urban explosion, Ecuador was an almost completely rural society. To a large extent it still is, although roughly half the population live in towns or cities: how they behave and think is closely linked to their relationship with the land, and modern urban life conserves elements of traditional rural customs. To understand the differences between Ecuador's three regions, one should first look to village life.

Images from the countryside

The typical *campesino* (peasant) of the Sierra works hard to obtain a meagre living from rocky, volcanic soil. Andean families live in a harsh environment, where bare mountains descend into shelving ravines and gentle valleys. The land is rarely flat, except on the valley bottom, which generally belongs to the rich landowners. So the *campesino* must use ingenuity to terrace and cultivate the steep mountain sides on slopes with up to 60-degree angles, where the topsoil is easily washed away by rain.

In harmony with this environment the typical *serrano* tends to be tough, patient, frugal and resigned to the difficulties of life. Yet *serranos* can be elated and vivacious when their imaginations are fired. Andean music, with its plaintive tones, melodic pipes and sorrowful lyrics, admirably expresses the *serrano* temperament.

The peasants of the Costa live in contact with the abundant nature of the green lowlands,

PRECEDING PAGES: impromptu concert at Otavalo market; light refreshment at Quito bullfight; steaming afternoon on the Amazon frontier.
LEFT: marcher in the Mamá Negra parade, Latacunga.
RIGHT: laundry in the Napo River.

where the warm climate and fertile soil make daily living easier. But life is also more uncertain because of the dangers of disease, floods and other hazards. Like their environment, the *costeños* tend to be easygoing and exuberant but also quick-tempered and careless about what tomorrow may bring.

The Oriente is a case apart, as it has begun to be colonized only in recent years, and represents scarcely 2 percent of the population. The Indians there have lived for centuries in relative isolation and their way of being is very different from that of the people of the Sierra who have suffered long years of discrimination. Light-hearted and self-confident, they are accustomed to a generous natural environment and a free lifestyle. This situation has begun to change with the presence of timber and oil companies that are endangering their environment, as well as encroaching colonization which has brought about an accelerated process of assimilation.

Natural differences between the regions have

been accentuated by slow, hazardous transport and difficult communications. But within each region, society is characterized by diverse racial and ethnic groups.

Traditional Andean society

The rigid social order that reigned in the Sierra from colonial times until the land reform of 1964 is the basis on which modern society was built. Cut off by the difficult mountain passes from the rest of the world and under the strong influence of the Catholic Church, Andean society engendered a world of traditional values centered around the family.

The traditional social order of the Sierra began to disintegrate in the 1960s with the introduction of agrarian reform. In the face of rapid population growth and increasing unrest among the peasants, who were pressing for more land, the authorities passed legislation to break up the larger estates and *haciendas* and hand over uncultivated land to the peasants.

Frontier settlements

While the Sierra has mainly produced food for local consumption, the Costa, with the advantage of its navigable rivers, sea-ports and extensive fertile plains, has been developed over the

The nucleus of rural life was the *hacienda*, or estate. These large properties were the main pole of production. Their owners were descendants of the Spanish *conquistadores* who controlled the country's economy and politics. They would allow Indian families a small plot of land for their own subsistence in exchange for their labor. This form of dependence, akin to European feudalism, still exists in a few areas, though it was officially abolished in 1971.

The *mestizos* were employed on the *haciendas* as managers, stewards or clerks, in charge of running the estates. The power they wielded over those under their authority, fueled racial animosity between Indians and *mestizos*.

CONFLICTING VALUES

The typical Spanish settler in the Sierra considered work degrading, whereas in comparison the Indian valued it and disapproved of laziness. This was a further element which exacerbated racial tension, since the Spaniard expected the Indian to work for him, but then despised him for doing so.

These perceptions – Spanish intolerance and Indian incomprehension – survive in diluted forms today, particularly within the realm of public service, contributing to the fundamental social disunity which so markedly characterizes the country.

past 100 years for export crops. Cocoa, bananas and, more recently, cultivated shrimps have each had their boom period.

Landless peasants from the Sierra traveled to the coast in search of work on the plantations or a piece of undeveloped land to till. Thus, in the space of a century, the inhabitants of the Costa changed from being a small fraction to slightly more than half the total population.

The owners of the *haciendas* on the Costa, tended to be more business-minded and enterprising than their Sierra counterparts and generally did not mind dirtying their hands alongside their wage-earning farmhands. This

export oil, which meant more jobs and the promise of new opportunities in the cities. At the same time, those peasants who had been unable to obtain land under the agrarian reform of 1964 had to leave the *haciendas,* and many of them sought work in the towns.

In just two decades, one quarter of Ecuador's population moved from the countryside to the towns, causing an urban explosion which the country was unable to support. Housing, and water and electricity supplies, could not keep up with the huge increase in demand. Today Ecuador is short of an estimated one million homes; half the existing houses lack running

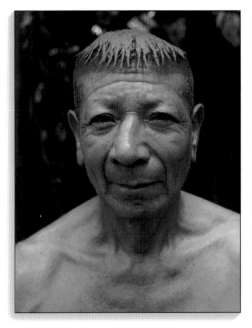

helped to create a more liberal and egalitarian society, which was accelerated by greater contact with the outside world via the sea-ports.

Today the Ecuadorian Costa has a Caribbean flavour, which has led to Guayaquil being called "the last port of the Caribbean."

The urban explosion
In the 1970s, following the discovery of petroleum deposits in the Oriente, Ecuador began to

LEFT: a Sierra *indígena* from Cañar; an Afro-Ecuadorian woman from the coastal region.
ABOVE: healer from Santo Domingo de los Colorados.
ABOVE RIGHT: schoolgirl from Quito.

water and sewage facilities, and a third have no electricity.

With the foreign debt crisis of the 1980s, unemployment increased dramatically. The new urban population had nowhere to turn, except to the streets to scrape together a living by their wits. Vendors of trinkets, sweets, clothes or electrical goods of doubtful origin throng the city centers, competing for the attention of passers-by. The more enterprising ones announce their wares on the buses. And on street corners, five-year-olds sell newspapers, shine shoes or urge you to buy chewing-gum in the hope of earning their daily meal.

Today, barely half the workforce has a steady

full-time job; 38 percent are in the informal sector of street-vendors and self-employed craftsmen and 12 percent are unemployed. Unofficial sources put these figures even higher.

Meanwhile, the well-to-do can find all the comforts of modern life in high-rise apartment blocks, protected by armed guards. Miami-style shopping precincts display a broad variety of consumer goods, and chauffeur-driven limos wait at the doors of luxury restaurants.

These contrasts are an expression of the erratic modernization of Ecuador which has radically changed living and working conditions in scarcely two decades, without being able to

answer the basic needs of its population. The most flagrant social contradictions are to be found in Guayaquil, center of the nation's wealth, which is surrounded by vast slum areas built on marshland, the scene of abject poverty and rampant delinquency.

Chronic poverty

It is ironic that in Ecuador, a country rich in natural resources with its fertile valleys, abundant marine life, extensive forests and reserves of oil and gold, most people face a daily struggle to scrape together the bare necessities. UNICEF estimates that about two-thirds of Ecuadorian families live below the critical poverty line. Even

so, compared to the level of poverty in neighboring Peru and Colombia, Ecuador does not come off so badly. The cost of living is relatively low and as Ecuador produces most of its own food, few families are unable to get a square meal each day and most do have a roof of some kind over their heads.

Hardship is not reserved to the towns. In rural areas, life is increasingly difficult for the peasants. Those who became small landowners cannot keep up with production costs, which rise faster than the price they receive for their crops, and they can rarely get cheap credit or adequate technical help. And once the paternalistic relations of the *hacienda* disappeared, the lack of social services became acute.

Successive governments have implemented social welfare programs in health care, aid to small farmers, food distribution, cheap housing, child care, employment and other needs, but there are never enough resources.

All the same, in spite of hardship, the Ecuadorian people are patient, peaceable and honest. The violence that has become typical in Colombia and Peru is practically unheard of here, and though the crisis has brought about a rise in delinquency and crime, the level of violent crime (with the possible exception of Guayaquil) is lower than in many of the industrialized world's big cities.

Indigenous groups

The visitor to Ecuador is readily seduced by the colorful costumes and skilful handicraft of the Indians: the women's embroidered blouses, the ponchos, the woven belts. But these are just the outward embodiment of a whole culture, an identity and a long history of resistance to assimilation by colonial society.

There are 10 different ethnic groups in Ecuador, each of which considers itself a distinct nationality, with its own language and culture. Together, they make up between a quarter and a third of the population. The most numerous are the Quichua Indians who live mainly in the Sierra and are related to the Quechuas of Peru and Bolivia.

In Ecuador, the terms *indígena* and *blanco* (Indian and white) are social and cultural, rather than racial definitions. The term *mestizo* (mixed blood) is not used frequently, although it is probably the most accurate description of the genetic heritage of most Ecuadorians. About half the population are self-identified as indigenous: people are considered *indígenas* if they live in an indigenous community, speak Quichua (or another indigenous language) and dress in a particular way.

Ethnicity in Ecuador is, to some degree, fluid and malleable. To some extent, over a generation or two, people can change their ethnic identity. An indigenous family can move to Quito, send their children to school dressed in modern, clothes and the children will generally be considered white. But these same children can return to their parents' community, and identify themselves as *indígenas* should they so choose.

ing aside their traditional dress, language and identity are often those who show the most virulently racist attitudes. "Stupid Indian" or "dirty Indian" are typical epithets used about people who for years were excluded from public education, while their cultural heritage and language were treated with disdain.

Many *indígenas* have defied attempts to integrate them into *mestizo* society, manifesting a tacit resistance to the ill-treatment and discrimination practiced against them.The survival of Indian culture and identity, their festivals, their languages and their dress, despite the odds, is witness to their endurance.

Some Ecuadorian indigenous groups have been residents of the land for centuries, while others are descendants of groups of people (called *mitmakuna)* who were moved around the Andes by the Incas: there were loyal Inca Quichua-speakers who were sent to recently conquered areas to serve as a teaching and garrison population; and people who were moved far from their homelands as a punishment for resistance to Inca rule.

Racism is deeply engrained in Ecuadorian society. Indians who become "white" by leav-

The Quichuas and the native Amazonian Indians in the Oriente have retained their own identities more than most. They lived for centuries in almost complete isolation from the rest of the world, apart from a few missions that were established there. But when oil companies began to dig pipelines and build roads into the region, settlers soon followed, and the Indians with whom they came into contact were rapidly assimilated into modern society.

Recently, with international campaigning for protection of the Amazonian forest, Indian groups who are still seeking to preserve their environment and lifestyle have found a worldwide audience for their claims, which gives

LEFT: children have to earn a living.
ABOVE: woman selling roots for tea-making.

them greater leverage on governments. In July 1990, CONAIE (the Confederation of Indian Nations of Ecuador) held a meeting in Quito with representatives of indigenous groups from throughout South, Central and North America. Their slogan is "500 Years of Resistance and Survival" and they are pushing for land rights, economic reform and recognition as separate nations within their larger nation states.

Afro-Ecuadorians

Many coastal people have curly hair and darkish skin, revealing their descent from the African slaves brought over in previous centuries. But in two areas, the warm Chota Valley in the mountainous province of Imabura, and the north-western province of Esmeraldas, there is a predominantly black population. In both areas there is a strong African cultural heritage, which has mixed with Indian culture. The people of the Chota Valley, for example, play the plaintive Indian music of the Sierra on African-type instruments, while the Awa Indians north of Esmeraldas have adopted the *marimba*.

Immigrant groups

There has been little immigration to Ecuador, apart from an influx of Colombians in the north,

LEGACY OF SLAVERY

Historians believe that a Spanish frigate loaded with slaves was shipwrecked off the northern coast of Ecuador around the middle of the 17th century, and that the Africans who survived the wreck spread gradually across the province of Esmeraldas, living practically in isolation there for many years.

The black population of the Chota Valley, on the other hand, are the descendants of people who were brought to Ecuador to work on the sugar-cane plantations at the height of the slave trade, and given their freedom when slavery was abolished.

and a substantial number of Chinese who settled in Guayaquil. The only other sizeable foreign ethnic group is the Lebanese, popularly known as "Turks," who came to Ecuador at the beginning of this century and have accumulated considerable economic and political power.

Religious fervor

Since the arrival of the early missionaries, Ecuador has been under the strong influence of the Catholic Church. The word of the local priest or bishop still has great weight, especially in the rural Sierra. However, since the end of the last century, when the anti-clerical liberal movement of the Costa took power, state and church have been separated. In state schools, the curriculum does not include religion.

In recent years the Catholic Church in Latin America has reaffirmed its intention to work on behalf of the poor. Some Catholic groups have taken this attitude further and are promoting political organization among the rural and urban slum populations as a means of seeking solutions to their grave problems.

Meanwhile, Protestant groups are engaged in active evangelization, particularly among Indians. Their success is due partly to the funding they provide for development projects and infrastructure, but also to the Protestant work

laws. Another facet of the community spirit is the *minga* – a collective work effort inherited from Inca times via the *hacienda* system which has been adopted by the population in general.

Ecuadorians are generally glad to share whatever they have with family and friends, whether there is abundance or scarcity. The kind of individualism typical in northern countries, such as wanting to live alone, is considered a strange and anti-social aberration.

But this sense of community operates only within the immediate group of family and acquaintances. Outside, in the cement jungle of the cities, the rule is everyone for himself.

ethic, which has been favorably received in many communities, as it has much in common with the Indian belief in the dignity of labor. For several Protestant sects, however, the priority is to counteract the work of progressive sectors of the Catholic Church.

Community life

Indian culture greatly values the community. For example, *indígenas* advocate communal ownership of land – a concept which often comes into conflict with Ecuadorian tenancy

The family unit

Middle-class families in Ecuador are typical of Latin countries: they value strong family ties and close supervision of the womenfolk, while men tend to take their sexual freedom for granted, priding themselves on their gallantry and their *machismo*.

Among the poorer urban classes, especially those in the Costa, family relations are often far more informal, and it is not unusual for a man to have several families with different women, with whom he lives in turn, rarely contributing much to their upkeep. Young Indian couples often live together in a "trial marriage" before taking the wedding vows.

LEFT: an *indígena* couple admire an amusement park in Riobamba. **ABOVE:** Holy Week Passion Play, Otavalo.

The status of women

Although Ecuador was the first country in South America to grant women the right to vote, it has been one of the slowest to embrace the principle of equality of the sexes in the workplace and at home. However, attitudes are beginning to shift. In 1989 a law prohibiting all forms of discrimination against women was introduced and in 1995 an inter-American law against violence to women was written, signaling increased recognition of women's rights. People may be unaware of these specific laws but many organizations, particularly CEPAM (Center for the Promotion and Action of Ecuadorian Women)

are working towards making the laws effective in practice. One breakthrough has been free legal assistance to women when proceeding with charges of violence against them.

In the past few years women's organizations have grown and there are 36 national centers which deal with women's issues. Notably there has been active participation of indigenous women in promoting such issues in the Sierra. The migration of more men than women from the Sierra to urban areas has led to indigenous women taking on new responsibilities in their communities. Organizations are focusing on providing education and health care for women. Approximately 40 percent of women are now economically active. Many started work due to financial pressure, but as family size has decreased to an average of two or three children in urban areas, women are freer to pursue careers. They have entered most fields, although you will not see a female bus driver or welder. In 1990 women made up 5 percent of the police force. At high school, many girls take a pre-military training course but very few pursue it as a career. The number of women and men studying at university level is now more or less equal.

Despite ingrained attitudes about traditional gender roles in Ecuadorian society, women are making inroads into the "old boys' network" of national politics. The first female vice president of Ecuador, Rosalia Arteaga, was elected in 1996 on a ticket with the now deposed President Abdala Bucaram. Political analysts believe that he specifically chose her as a running mate to woo female voters, a constituency largely ignored by other candidates. She proved politically savvy, avoiding the corruption of the Bucuram administration and surviving his impeachment in February 1997.

Urban youth

Lifestyles in urban Ecuador are rapidly modernizing and changing the face of Ecuadorian culture. A middle-class teenager from Quito or Guayaquil probably identifies more with peers from the United States or Europe than with those in an isolated mountain village. These young people have access to cable TV, videos, Internet, and CDs. Western rock and pop are often more popular than traditional Latin music.

Shopping malls have become popular meeting places for teenagers, before a night out at one of the modern multi-screen cinemas or meeting friends at a Burger King or Pizza Hut. On weekends *discotecas* playing salsa and rock music are bursting at the seams until 3 or 4am.

The best jobs for young professionals are often with foreign companies. As a result, night schools are as full as the *discotecas*, with students studying English and computer programming. As Ecuadorian yuppies enjoy their symbols of success – cellular phones, credit cards, espresso coffees and copies of *Newsweek* – they are worlds away from the rural *campesino* who still earns about $5 a week.

LEFT: growing up in the city. **RIGHT:** allegorical figure in the Mamá Negra parade, Latacunga.

THE BRIGHT COLORS OF EVERYDAY WEAR

The distinctive clothes of Ecuador's indigenous people are not just worn on high days and holidays, but can be seen in any market or village street

The diversity of Indian dress in Ecuador is witness to the strong sense of identity which the various groups have retained throughout the centuries. Some of the clothes that the *indígenas* wear so proudly today are in fact adaptations of the 16th-century Spanish-style costumes which were once a kind of uniform, indicating which *hacienda* they belonged to.

INCA INSPIRATION

Some items go back further: it is said that the indigo and black clothing of the Saraguro people is worn as a sign of perpetual mourning for the Inca Atahualpa, killed in 1533 at the beginning of the Spanish conquest. Hats, too, date back to the colonial period. Even the Panama is an adaptation of the headgear worn by the Manabí people at the time of the conquest. Fragments of *ikat* tie-dyed textiles from the pre-Hispanic period have also been found.

Traveling around the many markets in Ecuador, you are bound to notice the wide variety of colors and styles of shawls, ponchos and *macanas*, the ubiquitous carrying cloths which are used to carry various items from kindling to babies.

◁ **CHAPS WITH CHAPS**
Shepherds of Cañar province, north of Cuenca, wear sheepskin chaps, along with deep red ponchos. Broad brimmed white felt hats are worn by all Canãri men.

▷ **WOMEN OF THE CLOTH**
Carrying traditional cloth, these Otavaleñas are dressed in their habitual finery: intricately embroidered cotton blouses, hand-spun skirts and shoulder wraps. Their luxuriant black hair is bound with brightly coloured ribbons called *cintas*. Teeth are often capped with gold.

△ **MEN'S BRAIDED HAIR**
The men of Cañar, Otavalo and Saraguro province wear their hair in a thick braid, bound with cloth.

▷ **SILVER TRINKETS**
Large, intricate silver filigree earrings and stunning indigo-blue ponchos are worn by the women of Pujilí in Cotapaxi Province.

COLORS TO DYE FOR

The rich colors of the Indian ponchos, shawls and scarves are the most striking thing about the dress of Ecuadorian Indians.

Many of the shades come from natural dyes: the deep indigo blue worn by the Saraguro Indians comes from the Indigofera, a tropical bean-producing plant, and the rich red of the scarves and wraps worn by *indígenas* of Salasaca is produced from cochineal, which is extracted from the crushed bodies of female insects (*Dactylopius coccus*) which live on the Opuntia cactus. *Ikat* textiles – ponchos, shawls and belts – are also richly colored. They are made by a process of tying and dyeing (see far left picture) before the garment is woven.

The indigo-dyed cotton shawls called *paños*, which are made around Gualaceo, are the best-known of the *ikat* products. These shawls have macramé fringes which are an art form in themselves, as they can take many months to make.

△ **SEED-BEAD STATUS**
The color and number of rows of the Saraguro seed-bead necklaces indicate the community to which a woman belongs.

▷ **SHIGRAS**
Shigras are brightly-colored bags of agave fiber, which are hand-made in the central Sierra and found nowhere else in the Andes.

LIFE AND LORE IN THE SIERRA

*Ancient values, traditional healers and Christian festivals
are all part of life in the Sierra*

Every nook and valley of the Ecuadorian highlands is populated by distinct indigenous groups, some descendants of original Ecuadorian tribes, others descendants of the Incas or of people imported by the Incas from other areas of the country. It's difficult to travel in Ecuador without wondering what kinds of lives indigenous people lead and what kinds of tales they tell. Any guide book that assures you "the people lead lives unchanged since Inca times" should be tossed right out of the window because indigenous Ecuadorians don't live in a static universe any more than we do.

Europeans and Ecuadorian *indígenas* have been in contact for nearly 500 years, and Europeans have influenced the lives of *indígenas* in profound ways. Language, clothing, food, housing and religion all have a European imprint. The influence has also worked the other way round: for example, more than half the food crops consumed in the world today were domesticated in the Americas before the arrival of Europeans. Most significant are corn (maize) and potatoes, which were the economic foundation of the Inca empire.

Distinctive subcultures

One of Ecuador's attractions for visitors is that indigenous people still retain a number of customs of pre-Hispanic origin. Although the various groups have distinctive subcultures they share a number of traits. Some might argue that a poor, evangelical Protestant family in Chimborazo which ekes out a living on half an acre of bad land has nothing in common with a wealthy, Catholic weaving family in Otavalo which has just finished the construction of a four-story apartment building in town. Yet both families consider themselves *indígenas*, both wear a distinctive dress that identifies them as members of a particular ethnic group, and both families speak Quichua in their homes.

To paraphrase Sir Winston Churchill, the

PRECEDING PAGES: market day, Zumbagua.
LEFT: market stalls. **RIGHT:** Easter procession in Cacha.

indígenas of Ecuador are separated by the barrier of a common language: Quichua or Runa Shimi (The People's Tongue). Quichua is part of the Quechua language family. There are five different Quechua languages spoken today in Peru, and two or three different Quichua languages spoken in Ecuador. This means that *indí-genas* from different regions of Ecuador do not necessarily understand each other.

The origins of Quechua are unknown, but we do know that it was spoken around the time of Christ by the Chinchay, a trading group on the coast of Peru. The Incas adopted Quechua from the Chinchay and spread it throughout the Andes as they expanded their empire in the 14th and 15th centuries. Then the Spanish employed Quichua as a *lingua franca* to help them Christianize the *indígenas*. The Quechua language family is growing; more people speak it now than in Inca times, including several million people in Ecuador. Today most *indígenas* are bilingual in Quichua and Spanish, but some older people, especially in remote communities, speak Quichua only.

Quechua and Quichua were not written languages when the Spanish arrived. Various alphabets have been devised over the centuries and this accounts for inconsistencies in spelling. The Quichua word for baby, for example, can be spelled *wawa*, *guagua* or *huahua*.

Co-operative values

If there is a core value in indigenous society it is reciprocity, and naturally there are Quichua words which express this. One such word is *minga*, a collective work effort, which operates

in various ways. In community *minga* the leaders organize an effort to repair the roads, or clean the irrigation canals, and every family must furnish several workers. If they fail to show up some communities levy a fine.

Then there is a private *minga*. If a family needs to roof a house, for example, they invite the neighbors to a roofing *minga,* supplying copious quantities of food and *chicha* (a local beer made from *yucca)* for the workers, and people come because they know they'll need help themselves one day. In the same way, *compadres* (two couples who are ritual kin because they are godparents to each others' children) also know they can call upon each other for help

– anything from a loan of money to working in the kitchen at a fiesta.

Before the Spanish conquest money did not exist in indigenous societies. Items were bartered or labor was traded. Under the Incas, people paid their taxes in the form of labor (*mita*) or goods, and were taken care of in return with food from central storehouses in times of famine. In many places, reciprocity still means the exchange of goods or services rather than money. It is useful, as a tourist, to bear this in mind: for example, if you have a Polaroid camera, giving people photographs is much better than paying them to let you take their picture. However, this is not always applicable in public places such as markets, where you're likely to draw a huge crowd. In the same way, sharing food or gifts of food is culturally appropriate in most situations.

Sacred mountains

Indígenas throughout the Andes have worshipped mountains for millennia. In Ecuador mountains are seen as male or female individuals, inhabited by powerful spirits. Mountains are also believed to control the rain and therefore the fertility and well-being of the entire region. The highest peak in any area was considered to be a *waka* (*huaca*) or sacred spot by the Incas. The Spanish constructed Catholic shrines over Inca sacred places, which is why you will see so many isolated chapels on hilltops.*

Chimborazo, in the western *cordillera* of central Ecuador, is the highest mountain in the country, an enormous snowcap that looms over the province like a giant ice cube. It is known as Taita (Father) Chimborazo, while slightly to the north and in the eastern *cordillera* is Mama Tungurahua. Lesser peaks in the region are also seen as male and female pairs. Offerings such as guinea pigs, *trago* (a fierce sugar-cane liquor) or plants are sometimes made to the mountains to propitiate them.

In Imbabura Province, Mama Cotacachi reigns to the west of Otavalo while Taita Imbabura dominates the east. When Cotacachi's peak is snowcapped the *indígenas* say it is because Taita Imbabura visited her during the night. Needless to say, this encounter resulted in a baby, Urcu (Mountain) Mojanda, which lies just to the south of Otavalo. The connection of mountains with fertility is obvious here, and many *indígenas* carry it even further. When, for example, people who live on the flanks of Imbabura plant crops they first ask Taita Imbabura to give them an abundant harvest. And when it rains in the region people say that Taita Imbabura is peeing on the valley.

If the mountains send the rain, Mother Earth (Allpa Mama or Pacha Mama) feeds the people by producing crops. Like the mountains, Mother Earth should be thanked so it is customary to throw the last few drops of an alcoholic drink on the ground as an offering to her. The concept of reciprocity not only holds

SACRED PEAKS
The highest peak in any area was considered by the Incas to be a *waka* (*huaca*) or sacred spot.

(witches), or *hechiceros* (sorcerers, witches). In Quichua traditional healers are called *yachaj mamas* or *yachaj taitas* (knowledgable mothers or fathers). There are also midwives, who are known as *parteras*.

The details of healing vary among the different ethnic groups, but in the Sierra people might go to a local healer for a number of reasons: it might be because they have intestinal parasites, or because they believe an envious neighbor has cast a spell on them (*envidia*) or because they are looking for suc-

among humans, but carries over to relations between the human and natural world. If Mother Earth feeds us, she should also be fed, and she likes alcohol.

Shamanism and healing

Virtually every Ecuadorian community has a man or woman who knows the healing properties of various plants, or who can diagnose and cure by correcting spiritual imbalances or undoing spells. Healers are known by various Spanish names: *curanderos* (curers), *brujos*

LEFT: a smile in the Sierra. ABOVE: family sifting grain in Guamote.

cess in love or business. In addition, many people in the highlands have combined the Quichua belief in an inner and outer body, which must be kept in balance, with the medieval European belief in humoral medicine. This ancient tradition held that the body was composed of four humors: yellow bile, black bile, phlegm and blood, whose relationships determined a person's disposition and health.

Today people believe that such illnesses as infant diarrhoea occur because the baby has had a fright (*susto* or *espanto*) which caused the inner and outer bodies to become unbalanced. If the inner body actually flees, then death can result, so the healer performs a ceremony known as "calling the soul" to bring back the baby's inner body. Bodies can also become diseased because of bad air *(wayrashka* in Quichua), known as *mal aire* in Spanish. *Mal aire* gave us our word malaria, because people initially believed that the disease came from swamp vapors rather than from the bites of mosquitoes that lived in the swamps.

Calling the soul involves a cleansing, in which the patient's body is rubbed with a raw egg. The egg is shaken and the sounds it makes indicate that the bad air is being absorbed. After the cleansing a child is sent to hide the eggs in the fields nearby. Calling the soul also includes prayers in Quichua to God the Father, Son and Holy Spirit, the Virgin Mary and the saints. The healer tells the patient's heart to rise up (that is, to come back), passes alcohol to all present and smokes cigarettes, blowing the smoke on the patient. Tobacco has long been used by indigenous Americans in healing. There are many early Spanish accounts of its use among the Maya, and it is still used in healing and religious rituals throughout the Americas.

While most communities have their own healers, several areas are famous for their *curanderos.* People in the Sierra believe that the Shuar people have special healing powers, as

NATURAL REMEDIES

How effective are these spiritual healers? It depends on your belief system and on what kind of results you expect. A positive attitude is tremendously important in healing of any kind. Western doctors say that 80 percent of all illnesses are self-healing – it's the other 20 percent that need medical intervention. If local healers have an 80 percent success rate, that looks impressive. We should also bear in mind that many Western drugs, such as cocaine, curare and quinine, come from plants which local healers know well and have used in their remedies for centuries.

do the Taschila *indígenas* of Santo Domingo de los Colorados on the western slopes of the Andes. The healers of Iluman, outside Otavalo, are also famous and people come from all over the highlands to be treated by them.

A calendar full of fiestas

What's life without an occasional party to break the monotony of daily routine? In pre-Hispanic times community fiestas were organized around the agricultural and solar cycle. After the Spanish conquest, the church cleverly turned many traditional indigenous religious celebrations into Catholic feast days, on the grounds that people were going to celebrate anyway so they might as well observe a Christian occasion.

While a number of civic festivals are observed throughout the year in Ecuador, the most interesting fiestas by far are the traditional celebrations in the countryside. These mainly occur in the spring and summer, especially after the harvest and during the dry season. Every community has its own ritual calendar, so you might at any time of the year wander into a town in the middle of a fiesta in honor of their patron saint. However, here are a few of the major Sierra fiestas that are well worth catching:

Carnival (February or March) during the week before Lent begins on Ash Wednesday.

from Quito by bus, so it's well worth a day trip.

Holy Week (*Semana Santa*, the week before Easter) begins with Palm Sunday (*Domingo de Ramos*). Throughout Ecuador people buy palm fronds in the market, weave them into different shapes and take them to church on Palm Sunday. On Maundy Thursday, families visit the cemetery and bring food and drink for the dead in an observance similar to that of the Day of the Dead *(see page 82)*.

In Quito on Good Friday there is an enormous, spectacular procession through the streets of the city, complete with flagellants, men dragging huge wooden crosses, and penitents

Carnaval is a transplant from Europe, and represents a last fling before the austerity of Lent. Carnival in Ecuador is not like carnival in Rio. In fact, in the Sierra the main activity is throwing water, and it is definitely not fun to be hit in the back with a water balloon or to have a bucket of water dumped on your head in a chilly mountain village.

Ambato, however, has outlawed water throwing and has a fiesta of fruit and flowers that includes street dances and folkloric events. Hotels fill up early, but Ambato is only an hour

LEFT: Semana Santa procession, Quito. ABOVE: Corpus Christi dancers.

dressed in what look rather like purple Ku Klux Klan outfits.

There are also impressive Good Friday processions with costumed penitents in such Chimborazo towns as Yaruquies, Tixán, Chambo and Chunchi.

Corpus Christi, in honor of the Eucharist, is a moveable feast, held on the Thursday after Trinity Sunday, usually in the first half of June. Corpus Christi is a major fiesta in the central Sierra, especially in Cotopaxi and Tungurahua Provinces, but it is celebrated in many places including some communities in Chimborazo Province and in Saraguro, Loja Province.

Dancers with ornate headdresses and spectacularly embroidered costumes are now found only in such communities as Pujili, Cotopaxi and San Antonio de Pillaro, Tungurahua. In Salasaca Corpus is celebrated with music and dance. The *indígenas* wear plaster masks, bright ribbons and feathers on their hats and dance from Salasaca to the nearby town of Pelileo.

The winter solstice, Inti Raymi, on June 21, was once a major Inca festival. In the Cuzco area, far south of the equator, the winter solstice was the shortest day and longest night of the year. Closer to the equator, the differences in the length of the day and night are less dramatic, but astute indigenous astronomers still recognized

them. Today, **Saint John the Baptist** (*San Juan Bautista*, June 24) is the major fiesta in the Otavalo valley and probably replaced an ancient, pre-Inca solstice festival.

Among the Otavaleños, San Juan is a male fiesta lasting the better part of a week. On the night of the 23rd, the male vespers (*la víspera*) dress up in costumes. The dancing begins after dark both in Otavalo and in the outlying towns. The variety and ingenuity of the costumes is a sight to see – Batman, Káliman, North American plains Indians with feathered headdresses, Mexicans with giant sombreros, women, soldiers. Some *indígenas* even parody *gringos* by

RITUAL BATTLES

Also connected with the festival of San Juan is a ritual battle with rock throwing, which takes place at the chapel of San Juan, located on the west side of the Pan-American Highway from the town proper. Until the 1960s people were sometimes killed during these fights, and there are still some nasty injuries sustained. The point of spilling blood seems to be a payment or sacrifice to Mother Earth (Pacha Mamá), in gratitude for the corn harvest. Similar ritual battles (called *tinku*), fought with rocks and fists, still occur in the highlands of Peru and Bolivia, with similar casualties.

wearing blond wigs, down jackets, jeans and running shoes, and carrying backpacks.

The dancing goes on each night for a week, with groups of musicians and dancers moving from house to house and dancing (actually stomping) in a circle, with sudden reversals of direction which may represent the movement of the sun.

Saints Peter and Paul (*San Pedro y San Pablo*, June 29) is another major fiesta in Imbabura Province, and in many places the San Juan and San Pedro y Pablo festivities run together. On the night of June 28 bonfires are lit in the streets throughout the province. This seems to be a combination of indigenous and

Spanish customs. Young women who want to have a child are supposed to leap over the fires.

San Pedro is especially important in Cotacachi, where there are also ritual fights, and in Cayambe. While San Juan is important to the Otavaleños, San Pedro is the big event for the other main ethnic group in Imbabura, the people who live on the east side of the mountain in such communities as Zuleta, Rinconada, La Esperanza and Angochagua.

Because San Pedro is the patron saint of the canton of Cayambe, hundreds of *indígenas* come into town and parade under the banners of their communities. The groups dance down

ous sponsor (called the *prioste*) of local fiestas.

The feast of the **Virgin of Carmen** (July 16) is a notably larger celebration in the southern provinces than in the north. There is a fair (*feria*) in front of the church of that name in downtown Cuenca. In Chimborazo this fiesta is celebrated in Pumallacta and in Chambo.

Chambo, located just outside Riobamba, is the site of a miraculous shrine and fountain, one of those instances where a Catholic church was built on a mountain over what was undoubtedly a pre-conquest holy site. The shrine is dedicated to the Virgen de la Fuente del Carmelo de Cate-quilla (the Virgin of the Fountain of Carmelo of

the streets, around the main plaza and past a reviewing stand, where local officials award prizes to the best groups.

Among the dancers are men and women carrying roosters in wooden cages or tied to poles. These are for a ceremony called the *entrega de gallos* (delivery of roosters). In the days of *wasipungo* (serfdom) the indigenous people on the *haciendas* had to show their loyalty to the landowner by making a ceremonial gift of roosters once a year at this time. Nowadays the ceremony is most often performed for the indigen-

LEFT: fiesta of San Pedro celebrated in Cayambe.
ABOVE: All Saints' Day at a graveyard near Zumbahua.

Catequilla). *Indígenas* from throughout Chimborazo, in their finest traditional dress, visit the shrine and chapel on July 16. There is also a small fair at the base of the springs where food, drink, candles and holy items are sold.

Saint James (*Santiago*, July 25) is the patron saint of Spain, and his image (on horseback with a raised sword, killing Moors) was carried into battle by the Spanish during their conquest of the Americas. The Spanish had firearms, which were unknown to *indígenas*, who associated Santiago with their powerful god of Thunder and Lightning (called Illapa by the Incas). Today Santiago is the patron of many communities and there are many fiestas in his honor.

The feast of the **Virgin of Mercy** (*La Virgen de la Merced*, September 24) is a major two-day fiesta in Latacunga (Cotopaxi Province), where a local dark-skinned statue of the virgin is known as *La Mamá Negra*, the black mother. La Merced is also celebrated in Columbe (Chimborazo Province).

All Saints' Day and Day of the Dead (*Todos Santos y Dia de Difuntos*, November 1 and 2). These two Catholic feast days are another example of the blending of Andean and European traditions. In pre-conquest burials, food and drink were placed in graves to feed the dead in the next life. Some people believe that the spirits of the dead return to earth for 24 hours and will be unhappy if they aren't remembered.

If you are in Quito in early December you'll get swept along in the fesitivities that celebrate **The Founding of Quito** (December 6). There are parades, bullfights, dancing in the street and general merriment.

Finally, there are many beautiful Christmas (**Navidad**, December 25) pageants and celebrations throughout Ecuador; it's a wonderful time of year to be traveling there. Christmas is a religious holiday, not a commercial one, and for the most part such European and North American customs as Christmas trees and the

exchange of gifts are virtually unknown.

Among the local Christmas customs is the *Pase del Niño* (Presentation of the Christ Child). Families which own statues of the baby Jesus carry them in a street procession to the church, accompanied by musicians and by children dressed as Mary, Joseph and other nativity figures. The baby Jesus statues are blessed during a special mass and then taken back to the household crèches.

The most famous *Pase del Niño* occurs in Cuenca, on the morning of December 24. It begins at the churches of San Sebastián and Corazón de Jesús and converges on the cathedral on the Plaza de Armas. Families from

SPIRITUAL FOOD

All over Ecuador, little human and animal figures are baked from bread dough and taken to the cemeteries on November 2, where they are placed on the graves along with paper wreaths and other offerings of food and drink. It sounds as if it would be a very sad occasion, but in fact it is often quite cheerful and festive. In a nice local variation on the theme of waste not, want not, poor people come to the cemeteries and offer prayers at each grave site in return for some of the food. It's a sensible idea: they need the food more than the departed – and a few extra prayers never go amiss.

around the region bring their children, some dressed as *indígenas*, and mounted on horseback, their horses decked with gifts of food, liquor, sweets and fruits. Other children are on foot, dressed as nativity figures or as gypsies, gauchos, or Moors, each group carrying its own statue of Jesus. Inside the cathedral the children are given *chicha* (local beer) and bread, then the participants wind their way through the streets to celebrate Christmas at home.

In Saraguro, Loja Province, each indigenous community owns a statue of the Christ child which is carried in a procession on Christmas Day from the main church to the home of the

Fiesta etiquette

There are appropriate and inappropriate ways to behave at fiestas, and everyone will have a better time if you know how to act. If you want to take photographs, for example, you will be less conspicuous and find it much easier at the larger and more public events. If you are the only outsider at a small village event, then circumspection is the word. Put your camera away, watch the festivities, talk to people, and then ask if you can photograph them. *Indígenas* have been pushed around by white people for nearly 500 years and they're pushing back. They resent the arrogance of some outsiders who assume

Christ child's "godparents," the *marcan taita* and *marcan mama*. The procession is led by violinists and drummers and accompanied by costumed dancers. At the *marcan taita*'s house the statue is placed on a decorated altar, and the entire community assembles for a huge meal and an afternoon of music and dancing.

Other Christmas observances include the fiesta of the Holy Innocents *(Santos Inocentes)* on December 28 (in Quito), and the feast of Epiphany or Three Kings *(Tres Reyes* or *Reyes Magos)*, on January 6.

LEFT: dancing partners at a highland fiesta.
ABOVE: a festival to inaugurate a new mayor, Salasaca.

they can photograph anything, anywhere without asking permission. Remember, you're a guest here, not Sebastián de Benalcázar.

Ritual drinking is customary at all fiestas and by late in the day many participants are hopelessly looped. It is insulting if you refuse to drink when the *trago* bottle is passed around, so join the revellers in a drink or two and throw the dregs on the ground as an offering to *Pacha Mama*. One of the best ways to enjoy a fiesta without causing or taking offense is to arrive fairly early in the morning and leave by about 2pm, before things get seriously out of hand and before you've shared so many drinks that you can't find your way back to the bus stop.

SOUNDS OF THE ANDES

Andean pipes happily co-exist with brass bands and salsa clubs.

And then there are the weekend marimba parties...

What's a party without music? Making a joyous noise unto the Lord (or Mother Earth, maybe) seems to be a universal human activity and the Ecuadorians are no exception. At fiestas in Ecuador, two kinds of music are usually played: traditional, pre-Conquest indigenous music and Spanish (or more generally European) music. Naturally, after almost 500 years there has been considerable blending of the two.

You can hear traditional music groups (*grupos* or *conjuntos*) at many indigenous fiestas and at programs in folk-music clubs (*peñas*). There are also local and national traditional music competitions, which are usually free to the public, with an amazing variety of talent (or lack thereof).

Ancient instruments

Pre-Hispanic vocal and instrumental music was based on a pentatonic (five-note) scale, which gives Andean music its haunting, melancholic sound. Pre-Hispanic instruments were of three basic varieties: wind (flutes, panpipes, conch shells), percussion (drums), and rattles and bells. Flute-like instruments used today include the *quena*, a notched bamboo with six finger holes and a thumb hole, and a smaller flute (*pingullu*), which has three or four holes. When condors were more plentiful in the Andes *quenas* were sometimes made from their leg bones. The pre-Hispanic flutes were always held vertically; flutes (*flautas*) which are held horizontally are modeled on the European instrument.

The panpipe (*rondador*) goes back at least 2,000 years. Its modern Spanish name comes from that of the night watchman in colonial Ecuador who played the instrument on his rounds. A typical *rondador* is made of varying lengths and widths of cane or bamboo tied together in one long row; the different lengths and diameters produce distinct tones. Recently,

many Ecuadorian musicians have been using *zampoñas*, the panpipes typical of Peru and Bolivia. The *zampoña* is tuned differently from the *rondador* and usually has two rows of pipes lashed together, which musicians say makes it easier to play. The large *zampoñas* have a deep, breathy sound which has been likened to the wind off Chimborazo on a gentle day. There are many kinds and sizes of *zampoñas* with different names in Quichua and Aymara, but *zampoña* seems to be the generic name given to southern Andean panpipes.

The frequent use of Peruvian and Bolivian instruments by Ecuadorian musicians is indicative of the cross-fertilization that occurs as Ecuadorians travel in Peru and Bolivia and southern Andean musicians (or their tape cassettes) come north. The musicians teach each other songs and trade instruments. One of Bolivia's premier folk music groups, Los Kjarkas, toured Ecuador some years ago, and their music has been emulated ever since. If you

---

PRECEDING PAGES: *indígena* dance performed for tourists. **LEFT:** musicians at a fiesta near Otavalo. **ABOVE RIGHT:** school of music in Riobamba.

go to Ecuadorian *peñas* you are likely to hear some of their songs.

Percussion instruments include large and small drums (*bombos*) and gourd rattles (*maracas*). Various bells (*campanas*) are still used, especially by dancers at fiestas. In Imbabura Province, for example, 10 or 12 cowbells are attached to a piece of cowhide and are worn over the shoulder by dancers at the fiestas of San Juan and San Pedro (June 24 and June 29).

Spanish influences

Stringed instruments were introduced by the Spanish and were soon incorporated into the tra-

and joined and then the joints are bound. The tone of the *coroneta* depends on the number of horns used.

The accordion (*acordeón*) and harmonica (*rondín*) were introduced in the 19th century. The most recent addition is the portable, amplified Yamaha organ. Today, a mix of instruments is used to play music both old and new.

Brass instruments are another European introduction. Ancient trumpets, trombones, clarinets, cymbals, French horns and tubas, many of them battered beyond repair or the possibility of producing a harmonious note, are hauled out of nooks and crannies. It is traditional for brass

ditional repertoire. These instruments include the guitar (*guitarra*), violin (*violín*), mandolin (*bandolín*), *charango* and Andean harp (*arpa criolla*). The *charango* originated in Bolivia and looks somewhat like a ukulele but has five pairs of strings and eight frets. Its body is sometimes made of wood, but is more often made from an armadillo shell. The Andean harp is a homemade version of the European harp, beautiful to listen to but difficult to make and transport, which is why few musicians now use them.

After the Spanish introduced cattle into Ecuador, the *indígenas* made a unique instrument from cow horns, called a *coroneta* or *bocina*. Between 16 and 20 horns are cleaned

bands to play at small town fiestas and civic events, during which musicians pass round a bottle and are soon beyond repair themselves. In the ensuing musical interlude, volume and enthusiasm surpass musicianship.

Another venerable musical tradition is the weekend concert in the park. Many towns have municipal bands which assemble in the Plaza de Armas on Sunday mornings and rouse the populace from their Saturday night torpor. It's not exactly indigenous music: you are quite likely to get a rendition of the theme tune from from latest hit television series. As art it may be

ABOVE: impromptu sidewalk concert.

debatable, but as entertainment it's unbeatable.

In traditional music groups, men usually play musical instruments and sing, while women are only vocalists. Some music, including the *wayñu* (or *wayno*) and the *yaraví*, was probably introduced by the Incas and is almost always sung in Quichua. But the most common is the *sanjuanito*, which qualifies as Ecuador's national dance music. *Sanjuanitos* can be both instrumental and vocal and are played by folk music groups and modern bands at most fiestas.

At a *peña* a typical group will be composed of young men playing the guitar, mandolin, *charango*, violin, drum, *quena, pingullu, zampoña* and *rondador,* or a combination of the these instruments, and they will alternate purely instrumental music with songs with instrumental accompaniment. Many of the songs will be in Quichua and are considered traditional folk songs. Some you will hear all over the country, others are specific to certain provinces.

Festival music

To North American and European ears much traditional fiesta music sounds like an obsession with one theme. The same refrain is repeated over and over, endlessly hypnotic and great to dance to. During San Juan, the musical groups literally dance all night (to *sanjuanitos,* naturally), moving from house to house throughout the village.

Increasingly, traditional musical groups are being replaced by ones which use amplified instruments, especially for such occasions as weddings and other large parties. Into the house come the musicians in traditional dress, but instead of guitars and *quenas* they carry an electric sound system including microphones, amplifiers, speakers, maracas, and a Yamaha organ, which will prevent any sleep in the *barrio* for days. Such bands are hired for white and *mestizo*, as well as indigenous, events.

The musicians will tune up and launch into "La Rasca Bonita," a *sanjuanito* with a catchy little tune and upbeat tempo that qualifies as Ecuador's national party melody.The band alternates *sanjuanitos* with *cúmbias*, music of Afro-Caribbean origin from the coasts of Colombia and Ecuador. Everyone from grandparents to toddlers dances at these parties. As the band launches into its fifth *sanjuanito* you can't help tapping your toes, grabbing a bottle of *trago* and wading in to join the fray.

A dance which is done less and less at parties and now seems to be performed mainly at folk music programs is the *cueca*. It's a Spanish dance derived from the *jota* and is danced by any number of couples holding handkerchiefs.

Marimba and salsa

In the Esmeraldas region marimba is still very much alive. The Afro-Ecuadorians who settled freely in the area retained many of their customs, including their dance and music. The marimba instrument itself, the *chonta*, is similar to a xylophone, and was adapted from the African marimba, using local hardwood. It is accompanied by *bombos* (drums) *cununeros* (small tamborine) and *guasos* – bamboo stalks filled with seeds.

In the villages near Borbon, north of Esmeraldas, every single house has its own marimba. At weekends and important holidays people head out to marimba parties. The local firewater (*aguardiente*) is often thrown on the instrument itself, to signify the beginning of the marimba. Each song tells a story, moralising, instructing, illustrating daily life or recognizing death. The haunting, passionate music goes on till dawn and sometimes for several days.

Salsa, merengue and cumbia, essentially dance music from Caribbean countries, is particularly big on the coast. The most popular artists from Ecuador are Los Duques, Medardo y sus Players and Los Chigualleros.

In the modern shopping malls it is easy to find good recordings of salsa on CD. Music stores have rows of salsa and merengue compilations (and bus drivers play good selections, too, as they hurtle down the Pan-American Highway).

TAKING PART

Segundo Quintero and Carmen Gonzales are two of the better-known marimba artists, but recordings of marimba are hard to find. The Centro Cultural Afro-Ecuatoriano, Tamayo 985 y Lizardo Garcia, Quito, tel: 524 429, has videos of some of these frantic dances and information about the bigger festivals. If you have time, there are plenty of schools in Quito where you can learn to dance to the tropical rhythms of salsa and merengue, in individual or group lessons. Once you've learnt the basics, head to Sesiribo in Quito (Veintimilla y 12 de Octubre) on Thursday or Friday nights and join in.

PEOPLES OF THE AMAZON

*The Amazonian people preserve many of the old ways,
but are learning how to live with contemporary changes, both good and ill*

When Westerners think of indigenous Amazonian peoples, they conjure up strings of age-old stereotypes. The popular image is of naked men and women slipping through the jungle with Stone Age tools, isolated until recently from history and the outside world. According to this school of thought, they have always hunted for their food rather than grown it, and often engaged in brutal wars, shrinking their enemies' heads and occasionally eating their flesh. Conversely, they are held to be ecological saints, protecting their delicate environment at all costs.

Not surprisingly, the image has little to do with reality – as anthropologists in the Ecuadorian Oriente are rapidly finding out.

Coping with change

Far from being unchanging, undeveloping societies – and therefore "idyllic" – all Amazonian peoples have their own histories, and very dynamic histories at that.

Because Amazonians did not possess writing systems and, even more importantly, because their rainforest home is particularly unconducive to preserving the remains of past civilizations, there is little data with which to reconstruct Amazonian history. However, archaeologists can now show that human beings have lived in the Amazon since at least 10,000 BC, and that major technological breakthroughs occurred in the Amazon basin.

Amazonians domesticated manioc around 8000BC, and probably invented clay pottery around 4000BC, before any other indigenous cultures in South America. Migrations, new languages and vast cultural and religious transformations characterize the history of the Amazon Basin. Archaeologists believe that cultural advances moved out of Amazonia into the Andes, not the reverse.

After the arrival of the Portuguese and Spanish *conquistadores*, Amazonian societies

changed tremendously, whether they had direct contact with the invaders or not. Plagues of diseases to which indigenous peoples had no resistance moved in waves from the coast, over the Andes, into the rainforest, drastically reducing the population. Migrations of peoples away from regions conquered and colonized by the

Spanish and Portuguese provoked chain reactions of indigenous peoples being forced off their original lands into unfamiliar territories.

New technologies reached the Amazon as well, again brought by intermediaries so that no direct contact occurred with Europeans. Steel tools and new foods (especially the banana, plantain and papaya, which originated in Southeast Asia) were traded from one people to the next throughout the jungle, transforming the ways of life throughout the Amazon. In this way, the pressures created by the Spanish Conquest of Ecuador and Peru transformed Amazonia and the pre-conquest jungle lifestyle will forever remain a mystery.

LEFT: Shuar woman in traditional dress.
RIGHT: at work in the Oriente.

A range of jungle groups

The Ecuadorian Amazon is small compared with the vast jungles of Brazil, but it is nevertheless an important, even crucial, part of the region. It is inhabited by six major ethnic groups (the term "tribe," with its primitive implications, has been discarded). The largest grouping is the Quichua people (60,000), followed by the Shuar (40,000), Achuar (5,000), Huaorani (3,000), Siona-Secoya (650) and the Cofan (600).

The Huaorani people remain the most nomadic of Ecuador's indigenous Amazonians, and the least interested in cultivation, but during this century they too have partially adopted horticulture. Because they customarily went about naked, and relied so much on hunting and gathering wild foods, the Huaorani were originally called "Aucas," which means savages in the Quichua language. The Huaorani have rejected this name, which they, quite understandably, consider highly derogatory.

It appears almost certain that the Huaorani, who are composed of a number of discrete groups (Guequetairi, Pijemoiri, Baihuairi, Huepeiri, etc) are an amalgamation of survivors from many different groups diminished by disease, war and migrations. For this reason, anthropologists view the sparse material culture

MYTH AND REALITY

Although the popular Western image persists of Amazonians surviving by hunting wild game and gathering fruits and nuts, the truth is that most indigenous peoples are no longer true hunter-gatherers. In the late 20th century they obtain nearly all their foodstuffs from cultivation. They are either horticulturists, which means that they establish moderate-sized, temporary gardens; or agriculturalists, who plant crops on a permanent basis and usually on a much larger scale. The only partial exception to this is the Huaorani group, the most nomadic of the Amazonian people.

of the Huaorani, not as evidence of "backwardness," but as the basic survival mechanisms of those forest cultures that endured the most intensive stresses.

The Amazonian Quichuas are closely related to the people of the same name who dominate the Andean highlands of Ecuador. Anthropologists surmise that Quichua-speakers migrated down into the rainforests after the Spanish conquered the highlands in the early 1500s. The most numerous of the indigenous Amazonians, the Quichuas are composed of two distinct ethnic groups, the Canelos and the Quijos. These peoples brought the knowledge of well-developed agricultural systems from the Andes to the jungle, although they had to learn how to grow very different crops in their new territory. Living in dispersed, permanent settlements on individually owned plots of land, the Quichua men clear land and plant crops, while the women maintain, weed, and harvest them. They use a rotation system, resting the plot for three years after approximately five years of cultivation.

In the northern Oriente

The small ethnic groups that live in the northern region of the Ecuadorian Amazon are the Cofan (who call themselves the A'I) and the Siona-Secoya, a combination of two once sepa-

allow it to rot and mulch the exposed earth.

These peoples are semi-nomadic, which is to say that they move about within defined territories, abandoning old plots for new ones located in richer hunting grounds. They most frequently locate their gardens close to their houses, but sometimes plant smaller, less complex gardens at some distance from home. Siona-Secoya and Cofan farmers are women, and the profundity of their knowledge about soils and maintaining their fertility, about weather patterns, plant behavior and diseases, and crop combinations (beans and corn, or corn and manioc, for example) is truly astounding.

rate groups with very similar customs that unified when their numbers dwindled drastically earlier this century. These peoples practice what anthropologists call "slash and burn," a technique for creating small clearings in the forest which produce food for two or three consecutive years and then must be abandoned to replenish their fertility. The Siona-Secoya usually leave big trees standing, especially those that produce fruits, and they do not always burn off the vegetation they have cut, but sometimes

LEFT: missionaries at work in the early 1900s.
ABOVE: a Huaorani spokesman accepts land title agreement in 1990.

The Shuar people of the southern region of Ecuadorian Amazonia, and their closely related cousins the Achuar, practice a horticultural system heavily dependent upon one crop plant – sweet manioc. Women harvest the tuber 12 months or more after planting it, and they simultaneously re-sow small tuber cuttings as they harvest. When manioc is mature, it can be left in the ground to continue growing without any risk of spoilage, which has obvious advantages in tropical Amazonia. The Shuar and Achuar may perhaps be described as semi-settled, rather than semi-nomadic.

In recent years, Shuar and Achuar men have started raising cattle in increasing numbers, converting jungle to pasture. This income-earning strategy is probably not sustainable considering the fragile soil and sub-soil ecology of the jungle, yet the Shuar and Achuar are finding increasingly sophisticated methods of planning their survival in the rainforest.

Movements through the forest

It is still true that hunting, gathering and fishing determine the movements and rhythms of life for indigenous peoples. Anthropologists once assumed that hunting was the most important of these activities, but the gathering of wild fruits, honey, nuts, roots, grubs and insects – a task

the planet's ecology, coupled with a romanticization of Amazonian life. In fact, it is fairly obvious that the indigenous people of the Oriente kill animals for food until those animals become scarce. Then they move on.

Yet the nomadic and semi-nomadic lifestyles of most indigenous Amazonians have prevented and continue to prevent the extermination of game animals upon which indigenous peoples depend. The horticultural groups have always placed an overwhelming social emphasis upon having small families with no more than two children. Population stability unlocks the door to ecological stability. Amazonian belief-sys-

performed exclusively by indigenous women – actually provides the largest part of the diet. The origin of the "hunting" myth was probably due to the fact that the mostly male Western anthropologists talked almost exclusively to indigenous men, who would have discussed their own activities, and not those of their womenfolk.

Another, more recent, myth held about indigenous Amazonians is that they never kill more than they need in the rainforest, that they revere the jungle's animals, and are attuned to the natural balances of their environment. There is some validity to this view, but much of it stems from the industrialized nations' recent awareness of how they themselves have abused

BENEFICIAL TABOOS

The Shuar and Achuar people believe that deer, owls and rabbits are the temporarily visible embodiments of the "true soul" of dead human beings, and therefore they do not hunt these animals. The Siona-Secoya will never eat deer for similar reasons, and they prohibit the hunting of tree-sloths, black monkeys, opossums and weasels. They also revere and fear the pink river dolphins, and never harm them. The Quichua honor the jungle puma, a very rare feline, and would never shoot one. It is thanks to these beliefs that many of these creatures still flourish.

tems also encompass a number of iron-clad taboos against killing certain animals.

Crafts of the Oriente

For all groups except for the Huaorani (who wore nothing, even though men would use string to tie their penises up by the foreskin) a major craft used to be the making of clothes. Shuar men and Achuar women spun home-grown cotton, wove it into cloth and dyed it with vegetable-based colorings. The men wore wrap-around kilts, tied in place by bark string, and the women fastened their dresses over their right shoulders, using a belt around their waists.

induce food to rot, and are not nearly so versatile. The normal carrying basket of the Amazon is a plaited, openwork cylinder, no more than a meter high, tightly woven and very sturdy. The finest baskets are woven by the Shuar, for holding personal ornaments and other finery; they are lined with smooth banana leaves, and have an attached cover.

The tourist market has almost completely transformed another craft, pottery, which has always been the domain of women. Quichua women make clay vessels for household use, as well as sacred vessels with ritual character. These vessels are meticulously executed, elab-

The Siona-Secoya and Cofan men wove ultra-lightweight knee-length cotton smocks, called *cushmas*, which they dyed blue or red. The Quichuas adapted the forms of clothing their highland cousins wore. All of these peoples now usually wear trousers, shirts and blouses, dresses, skirts and shorts that are indistinguishable from those of other Ecuadorians.

Basket-weaving, a male craft, has survived a lot better than the production of clothes. Plastics simply do not perform as well as baskets in the tropics because they are much heavier,

orate, and eggshell thin, with geometric and zoomorphic shapes and motifs. Shuar women lavish intricate geometrical adornments on the jars used to boil and serve the hallucinogenic beverage, *ayahuasca* (*see page 97*).

Tourist demand for Amazonian pottery has transformed its production into something resembling an assembly-line, where scores of duplicates are produced with patterns that have no significance. The income derived from the sale of ceramics is, relative to the overall monetary income of indigenous Amazonians, quite considerable, and has given indigenous women a degree of power over their lives in the midst of ongoing cultural transition.

LEFT: Huaorani *indígenas* at a gathering.
ABOVE: thatch-covered huts in an Amazon village.

Most fantastic of all Amazonian arts are the feather and beadwork crowns, necklaces, earrings and other ornaments, which rely upon the plumage of toucans, parrots, macaws, hummingbirds and other magnificent birds. These stunningly beautiful works of art have always possessed enormous ritual and spiritual significance for Amazonian peoples, directly linked to their use in the *ayahuasca* ceremony *(see page 97)*. Today, tourist demand for such ornaments, to take home as souvenirs, is encouraging indigenous Amazonians to kill the most colorful, and usually the most endangered, birds at an accelerated rate.

Amazonian shamans

It was in the realm of spiritual and mythical creativity that indigenous Amazonians made their greatest strides and their most momentous discoveries. Because the Amazonian storehouse of knowledge and wisdom has always been transmitted orally, a great deal of the complexity has been lost. Indigenous spirituality has been mercilessly attacked by missionaries ever since the Spanish Conquest. In recent years Protestant groups, such as the Summer Institute of Linguistics, have worked to blot out the legacy of thousands of years, preventing the transmission of traditions from the old to the young. Never-

DON'T EVEN THINK ABOUT IT

Don't buy anything made from the plumage of Amazonian birds. Because the importation of any products which cause the death of any endangered species is prohibited by the United States, Australia and all of Western Europe, tourists who are irresponsible enough to attempt to take their "trinkets" home will inevitably have to surrender them at the customs office. This makes the death of these magnificent birds, and the devaluation of the traditions of Amazonian peoples, a tragic exercise in futility. The lower the demand for such souvenirs, the fewer birds will be killed.

theless, the enduring center of that legacy, shamanism, survives among the six principal peoples, albeit by ever more slender threads.

Shamans are the individuals who preserve the oral histories, myths, legends and other belief systems of their peoples. Among the Siona-Secoya, Quichua and Cofan groups shamans are usually men, but female shamans are not unknown in the Shuar and Achuar cultures. Many shamans devote their time to curing diseases through elaborate rituals. There are shamans who bewitch others, causing disease and misfortune to their enemies, or to the enemies of those who pay them to do so. Shamans enact the ceremonies of initiation, the rites of passage of young men and women into adulthood; and they train others to take on the role, passing on the knowledge and the rituals.

The tools they use vary. Quichua shamans own magical stones, which act as their familiars. The Shuar and Achuar shamans utilize magical darts called *tsentsak*, to bring about both healing and harm. But the most important tools they all employ are hallucinogenic substances extracted from jungle plants. The vine known as *ayahuasca*, Quichua for "vine of the soul," is the hallucinogen par excellence.

Using drum rhythms and other musical patterns, vocal incantations, the light of fires, and

The power of the family unit

In indigenous Amazonian society the most important organizational unit is the extended family. The rules of kinship define the individuals' rights of inheritance, who they should marry, and where they should live.

The Huaorani, with their very loosely defined kinship rules that do not even insist on the authority of older people over younger, can be seen, again, as a society pared down to essentials in its struggle to survive. Cofan and Siona-Secoya men may only marry women allowed to them by a patrilineal system: couples live with the family of the man's father, or in a house built

the colors provided by feather ornaments and body paint, the shamans guide those who have drunk potions derived from *ayahuasca* to see visions based on the symbolism and mythology of their cultures. The jaguar, anaconda, and harpy eagle recur over and over again in such visions. This communion with their ancestral past and the supernatural is a continuous source of social and cultural cohesion for indigenous Amazonians, and has nothing in common with the often self-destructive use of drugs encountered in Western cultures.

LEFT: Cofan family in traditional dress.
ABOVE: young Cofan *indígenas*.

close to the father's home, and they inherit property and privileges from the man's father.

Shuar men initially live close to their wives' families, before moving to their own houses, but inherit through their fathers' line. Achuar men permanently reside near their wives' families, inherit through their mothers' lines, and marry women according to matrilineal relationships. The Quichua people possess a patrilineal system, but one which is broader and more complex, defining a kinship group called the *ayllu*, several of which compose a community.

Amazonian cultures have no single leader or chief. Instead, leadership has always been provided in crises by shamans and military men.

While Quichua farmers did not wage wars or carry out raids as much as they suffered from them, the lives of all the other groups were defined by feuds, raids and war. The Siona-Secoya, Cofan and Huaorani raided to capture women and to avenge raids against them, but never for territory. For the Shuar and Achuar, warfare symbolized the spiritual quest for power: by killing a designated enemy a man could gain the visionary magical soul called *arutam*, and possess the power to lead others.

The practice of severing an enemy's head, removing the skull, and shrinking the skin is a source of great notoriety for the Shuar and

Achuar. As gruesome as this practice seems, and as perverse as it became earlier this century due to Westerners' fascination with it, the rituals associated with shrinking heads were an integral part of the shaman-leader complex that defined war and peace among these peoples. Today, far from shrinking heads, the Shuar and the Achuar have organized the most successful ethnic federation in the Amazon basin, a model for groups in Ecuador and other nations.

Twentieth-century politics

The recent discovery of oil deposits in the Ecuadorian Amazon has meant that air, water and the rainforest itself are at risk. The indige-

nous Amazonians have no choice but to change and organize in order to survive.

In the Federation of Shuar Centers, shamans no longer use their powers for vengeful purposes, but are organized around health and community issues. In addition to fighting for Shuar and Achuar land rights, the federation is involved in the protection of the environment in the southern region. The Shuar Federation has also published scores of books about the Shuar and Achuar oral traditions, which will make them far more accessible to future generations.

For the Quichuas, organizational models are available from their highland cousins, who have become intensely political. The Quichua regional federations have helped to link indigenous Amazonians and the people of the highlands; as a result, an Amazonian and highlander confederation, CONFENIAE, has been formed at national level.

For the smaller groups, the specter of demographic disappearance is real and terrifying. The Siona-Secoya community in the Cuyabeno Fauna Reserve recently helped to clean up an oil-spill in several pristine lakes, demonstrating clearly how much a part of the modern world indigenous Amazonians are, and how their knowledge and commitment is essential to the survival of the rainforest.

Faced with the multinational oil companies and the subsequent influx of outsiders, a small number of the Cofan people, the tiniest of the groups, are developing their own survival mechanisms in the village of Sabelo (see *The Gringo Chief,* facing page).

Meanwhile, working through CONFENIAE, the Huaorani have struggled with the Ecuadorian government to gain title to at least part of their former lands. In the territory they have regained, about 600,000 hectares (1½ million acres), they theoretically have enough land to create a way of life that retains some elements of hunting and gathering. Unfortunately, the Ecuadorian government maintains the right to exploit deposits of oil under these lands, which almost completely undermines the Huaorani's victory.

The survival of indigenous Amazonians is still being determined moment by moment. It can only be hoped that the *indígenas* will themselves create the forms of survival that will adequately equip them for the 21st century.

LEFT: making a canoe in the Oriente.

The Gringo Chief

Randy Borman looks like many other guides catering to the boom in Amazon tourism, as he leads groups of Westerners down the Aguarico River to visit a small Indian village, Sabelo – home to a splinter group of Cofan Indians who have moved downriver, by motorized dug-out canoe, from their main community of Dureno.

But Borman is different: brought up among the Cofan people by his missionary parents, he found it difficult to settle in the United States, and returned to the Amazon where he developed his own tourism business. Now he is the elected president of Sabelo, a village he founded and whose economy is based entirely on the American tour groups he brings to observe the traditional hunting and fishing lifestyle. The village sits on a small island separated from the shore by a narrow channel where stingrays live. During flood season, the huts are up to their stilts in water. Five of the huts are inhabited by the Cofan, two by visiting tour groups. Downstream from the central clearing are five more Cofan huts and a schoolhouse.

The Cofan and their neighbors, the Siona-Secoya, are the two peoples indigenous to the Aguarico who are facing cultural extinction. Their combined populations number just over 1,000, but in the years since 1972, when Texaco's first well in the region began pumping oil, some 10,000 *mestizo* colonists have settled in the Lago Agrio area alone. A mere hour's bus ride from Dureno, Lago Agrio has mushroomed into a rough-and-tumble regional center linking the Amazonian Oriente district to the world. Unfortunately for the Cofan, their hunting land on the Lago side of the Aguarico River was cut to ribbons by a 504-km (315-mile) oil pipeline.

Borman organized local efforts for the Cofan to win legal title to their land. Pressured by a coalition that included missionaries and American academic leaders, the government finally recognized 8,000 hectares (20,000 acres) on the Dureno side of the river as a Cofan *communa*. While *communa* status offers only tenuous protection, the victory did give the Cofan the confidence to fight for their rights.

Even if no more roads are built or wells dug, Borman believes the damage has been done. While the Aguarico's oil-eating bacteria have been able to handle the dumping and the spills, there is no such handy solution to the problem of the colonists, who have used the oil company roads to gain access to the jungle, transforming it into a patchwork of small coffee farms.

"So many of the bases of culture in Dureno have been knocked away," Borman says. "The Cofan now support themselves by growing coffee for export, just like the colonists. The majority of kids there feel kind of directionless. They tend the coffee plants, play volleyball and get drunk." He regards Sabelo as a way of giving the Cofan control over the pace of change, enabling them to retain their language and their sense of themselves as a people.

"The tourism business is a wonderful way of rob-

bing the rich and giving to the poor," says Borman.

Semioticians would have a ball with Sabelo, a traditional Cofan village that supports itself by looking like a traditional Cofan village. Borman is ready to answer the unspoken charge that he is selling culture, not preserving it. "A traveler will gain a deeper appreciation of the jungle, but also of the people. The Cofan are not selling themselves, they are enhancing their integrity."

Some might see a contradiction in the fact that Sabelo's tourist economy is dependent on the motorboat, and thus on oil. "I call it realism," says Borman. "Trying to keep the Indians in a pristine showcase denies them their dignity." Of course, Sabelo is a showcase of a kind, but at least it's one co-produced by the Cofan people themselves.

ABOVE RIGHT: Randy Borman guides a group through an Amazon tributary.

ARTESANIAS

The ancient arts and crafts of the indigenous people of Ecuador
have become much sought after by Western visitors

There are no words in the indigenous languages of Ecuador for art, nor is there a distinction between fine arts and crafts. Seduced by their beauty, Westerners have included many traditional Ecuadorian *artesanías* in our own category of fine art, particularly textiles, ceramics, and jewelry. If you have the time, there's something particularly satisfying about buying things from the artisans themselves or shopping in the market, but products from throughout the country make their way into Quito and to the famous market in Otavalo.

Woven textiles

Four or five thousand years ago, some genius in the northern Andes invented the stick loom, which is still in use and generally called the backstrap loom (local names include *awana, macana* and *telar*). This loom, sophisticated in concept and simple in form, is made of sticks and poles, with one end fastened to a stationary object and the other to the weaver's back.

When the Incas made a census of their empire they counted humans first, cameloids (llamas and alpacas) second and textiles third, before precious metals, gemstones, ceramics or food. The pre-Hispanic Andeans were textile-obsessed and the Spanish were amazed by the superb handwoven cloth made of cotton, plant and wool from the cameloid that they found in Inca storehouses. Ecuador's damper climate has not been as conducive as Peru's to the preservation of organic materials, but the few pre-Hispanic textile fragments that exist suggest a tradition as venerable and as exquisite as that of Peru.

The Spanish introduced the treadle loom, spinning wheel, handcarders, wool and silk; much later came electric looms and synthetic fibers. But an amazing number of weavers still use the stick loom. Even in Otavalo, where most

weaving is done on the treadle loom, some ponchos and virtually all belts are made on the backstrap loom. In Saraguro, blankets (*cobijas*), grain sacks (*costales*) and most items of traditional dress are handspun on simple spindles of the kind you see throughout the Sierra, and handwoven on the stick loom. These pieces are

difficult to come by, but some are sold in Quito stores. In Ecuador, by the way, men are the weavers, although many women also weave.

The Cuenca region is famous for its *ikat* textiles. *Ikat* (*amarrado* or *watado*) is a dyeing rather than weaving technique, where the warp threads are tied and dyed *before* the piece is woven. Pre-Hispanic *ikat* fragments have been found in Ecuador, so we know the method is an ancient one. The best-known *ikat* textiles are *paños*, indigo-dyed cotton shawls with elaborate macramé fringes, made in and around Gualaceo. A newer style is black and red with a macraméd, embroidered fringe. It takes only hours to wrap the design, dye and weave the shawl, but up to three months to knot the fringe.

Paños were traditionally worn by *chola* women, but young women are no longer wearing them, so fine ones are becoming rare. If you want to see the older women in their finery, proud as queens, visit the Gualaceo Sunday market. The skilled dyers and weavers have switched to making *ikat* wool belts, scarves, and shawls without fringes, usually dyed black or brown over red, blue, green or purple. Some of these shawls are made into high-fashion clothing, available in Quito.

Ikat carrying-cloths called *macanas* are made around Salcedo and in Chimborazo Province.

The Salcedo *macanas* are deep indigo blue like the Cuenca *paños*, but the designs are coarser and they have a short fringe. *Macanas* are used throughout the sierra as carrying-cloths, to haul everything from a baby to a load of firewood.

Ikat ponchos are made and worn in the Sierra from Cañar to Natabuela, north of Otavalo. The poncho is a post-conquest garment, an adaptation of the Inca tunic. Various kinds of plain ponchos are woven for daily wear, while the *ikat* ones are reserved for weddings and fiestas. Especially beautiful *ikat* ponchos are made in Cañar, Chordeleg, Cacha Obraje (outside Riobamba) and Paniquindra (near Otavalo).

And while we're on the subject of *ikat*, let's not forget blankets (*cobijas*), those mundane but necessary items. Like ponchos, *ikat* blankets are made in every highland province, but these are for daily (or nightly) use. A good one of handspun wool, woven in two sections and sewn together weighs 4.5kg (10lb) and will keep you warm in a tent on top of Chimborazo.

Belts (*chumbis*) are woven on the backstrap loom throughout the Sierra. Double-faced belts with motifs ranging from Inca pots to farm animals are woven from handspun wool or commercial cotton thread in Cañar. These are among the finest belts made in Ecuador, rivaled only by those of Salasaca. Salasaca belts are still made of handspun wool and many are dyed with cochineal, a natural dye made from crushed female insects which live on the Opuntia cactus. Running a close race are a number of double- and single-faced belts with woven motifs made in Chimborazo and Bolívar provinces, followed by belts made in Otavalo and Paniquindra in Imbabura province.

Tapestries

In the late 1950s the Andean Mission embarked on one of those craft projects that usually die a slow death. But this one was a resounding success. Weavers from Salasaca and Otavalo were taught how to make tapestries (*tapices*) on the treadle loom. This technique, in which the weft threads interlock, gives tapestries a painterly quality. Today the stores around the main plaza in Salasaca and half the Otavalo market are filled with tapestries, including wall hangings, handbags (*bolsas*) and pillow covers (*cojines*).

Handknit clothing

While Ecuadorian women have been knitting since the colonial era, a Peace Corps project in the 1960s got the modern industry off the ground. Today sweaters (*chompas*), vests (*chalecos*) and hats (*gorros*) of handspun wool are made in Cuenca and in the northern towns of Ibarra, Mira, San Gabriel, San Isidro and Atuntaqui. Exporters and Quito craft-store owners work with the knitters on the production of exclusive designs, some of which are knitted in cotton. The highest quality ones are usually sold in Quito or abroad, although some fine ones do show up in the Otavalo market. Wherever you buy a sweater be sure to try it on. The knitter's concept of small, medium and large isn't necessarily the same as yours.

Embroidery

If you look carefully in the Otavalo market you will see women from an ethnic group other than the Otavaleños, wearing pleated skirts and blouses with extremely fine, intricate embroidery on the bodice and sleeves. The women come from communities on the south and eastern sides of Imbabura Mountain, such as Gonzales Suarez, Zuleta, La Esperanza, San Isidro de Cajas and Rinconada. You can buy these blouses in the Otavalo and Ibarra markets. In addition, the

> **PRECIOUS TEXTILES**
> When the Incas conducted a census they rated textiles more highly than precious metals, gemstones, ceramics or even food.

women embroider a range of more commercial items, such as dresses, napkins, towels and tablecloths.

Hats, baskets and bags

Once and for all, Panama hats aren't made in Panama; they're made in southern Ecuador, where they're called *sombreros de paja toquilla* after the palm fiber from which they're woven. They have been made here for more than a century, with the industry going through cycles of boom and bust (see *Panama Hats* feature, page 204). In the 1960s the Peace Corps introduced other items such as nativity sets and Christmas tree ornaments to help tide the *paja* weavers over hard times.

Shigra means sack in Quichua. *Shigras* are made of *cabuya* (agave) fiber in the central Sierra provinces of Cotopaxi, Tungurahua and Chimborazo. These bags, made by hand with a buttonhole stitch, are found nowhere else in the Andes. Tied over the shoulders, they serve as a carry-all for *indígena* men and women. While originally meant for local use, *shigras* found ready acceptance in the tourist and ethnic arts markets and the best of them are true collectors' items.

Baskets (*canastas*) made from various plants including cane and *totora* reeds are made throughout Ecuador and found in every market. Giant ones with lids come from Cuenca, smaller ones from around Latacunga, and fine two-color baskets from the Oriente.

Leatherwork

Cotacachi is the main center for wallets, purses, knapsacks and clothes made from leather (*cuero*). The main street of the town is lined with shops. Leather items can also be found in

---

LEFT: woodcarving in San Antonio. **ABOVE LEFT:** making shigras. **ABOVE RIGHT:** leatherworker in Cotacachi.

the Otavalo market and in many Quito shops.The leatherwork is usually good, but be sure to check the quality of zippers and clasps.

Jewelry

One look at the pre-Hispanic gold, silver and platinum objects in the Museo del Banco Central in Quito and you know the ancient Ecuadorians were master metalworkers. In indigenous communities jewelers make silver, nickel and brass shawl pins (*tupus*), with the finest coming from Saraguro. Contemporary gold and silver filigree jewelry is a specialty of Chordaleg, where jewelry stores (*joyerias*) line the road into

town and the main plaza. The workmanship is excellent and the prices are reasonable.

In pre-Hispanic times the Ecuadorian seacoast was the source of the prized, coral-colored spondylus shell, traded throughout the Andes. Beads are still an essential part of traditional women's dress. The preference for red or coral-colored beads goes back to the days when spondylus was queen.

Ceramics

The most beautiful ceramics in Ecuador – perhaps in the entire upper Amazon – are made by the Canelos Quichua *indígenas*, or Sacha Runa (jungle people), who occupy the territory between the Napo and Pastaza rivers in the Oriente. Women make the bowls and pots for household and ceremonial use, by hand coiling. The finest pieces are eggshell thin, with painted designs representing various aspects of their life and mythology. Some beautiful ceramics are now also made for the ethnic arts market.

There are several ceramic factories with showrooms in Cuenca, turning out handmade dinner sets and tiles. The Cuenca *barrio* of Corazón de Jesús, and the towns of San Miguel and Chordaleg are also traditional producers of pottery, which is sold at the Cuenca market. These potters use the imported wheel, and in San Miguel and Chordaleg you can see their wares drying in the shade outside their houses.

The Sierra around Latacunga and Saquisilí is another pottery center, where enormous Inca-style amphoras (*tinajas* or *ollas*) for making *chicha* (the local beer) are produced in the little town of Tejar. Pujilí, noted for its Corpus Christi celebration, also has potters who make and paint figurines of birds, animals and fiesta scenes.

Woodcarving

There are two main centers of woodcarving: the Canelos Quichua region and San Antonio de Ibarra north of Otavalo. The Canelos Quichua woodcarvings of tropical birds and animals are designed expressly for the ethnic arts market, and were not made until 1975. Most of the carvings are made from balsawood, painted and laquered. Some are works of art evincing an intimate knowledge of jungle fauna.

Woodcarvings in San Antonio de Ibarra run the gamut from elaborate furniture to nativity sets, boxes, wall plaques and statues of the virgin, saints and beggars. Some are kitsch, but there are some treasures, and you can watch the carvers at work in the backs of their shops, which line the main plaza in San Antonio.

Bread figures

Producing brightly-dyed dough figures of humans and animals for sale and export is a main industry in Calderon at the southern edge of Quito. They are placed on graves as offerings to the dead on the feasts of All Saints (*Todos Santos*) and Day of the Dead (*Dia de Difuntos*) on November 1 and 2.

LEFT: a typical figure-carving of an old man.
RIGHT: tapestries hanging in Otavalo market.

A NATION OF PAINTERS

Quito has a thriving artistic scene which may yet rival the accomplishments of its 16th-century precursor

Until early in the 20th century, art in Ecuador was mainly associated with the colonial School of Quito (*see pages 164–165*) but the first three decades of this century saw the rise of a school called *"indígenismo"* (indigenism). Because Ecuadorian artists have not been isolated from currents in the international art world and many of them have studied or traveled in Europe and North America, the unifying factor of the indigenist school has not been the style of painting, which ranges from realist to impressionist, cubist and surrealist, but the subject matter – Ecuador's exploited indigenous population.

EGAS THE INDIGENIST
Camilo Egas went through an early Dalíesque period before he went on to become the most indigenist of the Ecuadorian painters.

Inspired by a Sierra life

Eduardo Kingman is perhaps the prototypical indigenist. Since the 1930s he has painted murals and canvases and illustrated books, exploring social themes and the use of color. *Jugeteria* (Toy Store), an oil painted in 1985, shows the back of a young, barefoot *indígena* girl peering into the window of a brightly lit toy shop. The toys are rendered in cheerful primary colors while the girl outside in the shadows, the picture of longing, is painted in somber burgundy, black and blue.

Such paintings as *Mujeres con Santo* (Women with Saint), *El Maizal* (The Maize Grower) and *La Sed* (Thirst) are characteristic of Kingman's work: the indigenist subject matter and highly stylized, semi-abstract human figures with heavy facial features, and huge, distorted hands. These paintings convey powerful images of oppression, sorrow and suffering, but the people portrayed in them are generic Indians rather than individuals.

Camilo Egas, who died in 1961, lived in France for long periods of time and moved through a range of styles. *Desolación* (Desola-

tion), painted in 1949, is extremely Dalíesque, with a walking eyeball and distorted women supine on a brown, barren landscape.

Then, in a surprising switch, Egas produced the most beautiful of all the indigenist works with a series of realist paintings in the 1950s. In *Indios* (Indians), three long-haired men lean diagonally into the picture, using ropes to haul an unseen burden. The painting is executed in a few bright, clear colors: blue sky, black hair, brown skin, red, white and yellow clothing. Neither the bodies nor the features of the men are abstract or distorted and the impression conveyed is one of dignity and strength rather than misery. *El Indio Mariano* is a beautiful profile portrait in the same idiom.

Finally, in another stylistic switch during the last years of his life, Egas painted a series of abstract expressionist oils in blues and grays. These cannot be classified as specifically Ecuadorian art, since abstract expressionism is not so much about any particular subject matter or theme as it is about painting itself, about color, form and the artist's attitude to the medium.

Manuel Rendón was a prolific painter who produced a remarkably diverse body of work. Artistic talent evidently ran in his family, for the paintings of his paternal grandmother, Delfina Pérez, were included in the 1900 Paris Exposition. Rendón spent his youth in Paris, where his father was the Ecuadorian ambassador, and he was greatly influenced by the modern art movement in France.

Rendón is considered an indigenist artist, but he is equally well known for his cubist-style paintings of men and women in the 1920s and for a series on the *Sagrada Familia* (Holy Family) in the 1940s. He also painted pointillist figurative and abstract works, and did many sketches in pencil and pen and ink. No matter what the medium, he has shown a continuing fascination with line.

LEFT: Oswaldo Guayasamín, Ecuador's most famous painter, in his studio.

Ecuadorian maestro

Oswaldo Guayasamín is the best known of the generation of artists who came of age in the 1930s and 1940s. His father was an *indígena* and Guayasamín has consistently and proudly emphasized his indigenous heritage. Few people are neutral about Guayasamín's work with its message of social protest. His admirers see him as a gifted artistic visionary and social critic, while his detractors see him as a third-rate Picasso imitator whose innumerable paintings of *indígenas* with coarse features and gnarled hands have become parodies of the genre. Make up your own mind by visiting the Museo

reassembled images, notably in his series of monumental paintings *La Edad de la Ira* (The Age of Anger), *Los Torturados* (The Tortured) and *Cabezas* (Heads).

In 1988 Guayasamín continued to make visual political statements with his enormous mural in the meeting hall of the Ecuadorian Congress in Quito, in which 23 panels convey episodes from Ecuador's history. As usual, Guayasamín produced anything but a romanticized picture. Nineteen of the panels are in color, four are in black and white. The latter depict the first Ecuadorian president to enslave the *indígenas*, Ecuador's civilian and military

Guayasamín in Quito (for address see panel on opposite page).

Anyone familiar with the graphic paintings and statues of Christ, agonized and bleeding, in Spanish colonial churches can trace this theme of suffering in Guayasamín's work, although his figures are secular rather than religious. One of his early works, the 1942 painting *Los Trabajadores* (The Workers) is realistic in a manner similar to that of the Mexican muralist José Clemente Orozco. The similarity is more than coincidental as Guayasamín worked with Orozco in Mexico.

Guayasamín went on to develop a style influenced by cubism with its chopped up and oddly

dictators, and a skeletal face wearing a Nazi helmet emblazoned with the letters "CIA."

While Ecuadorians took the mural in their stride, the United States was outraged. The US ambassador called for the letters to be painted out and various US Congressmen discussed cutting off economic aid to Ecuador. Guayasamín regarded this as exactly the kind of bullying that he was protesting against, and the panel has remained unchanged.

An artistic immigrant

Olga Fisch is internationally known for her work as an artist and designer, for her collection of Ecuadorian folk art and textiles and for her promotion of Ecuadorian *artesanías*. She arrived in the country more than half a century ago as a refugee from Hitler, bringing with her a strong background in the visual arts from her studies at the Academy of Art in Düsseldorf, Germany.

Fisch was among the first to recognize the value of Ecuadorian *artesanías* as art and the design potential of traditional motifs. A talented painter, Fisch is best known for her work in textile design, especially rugs and tapestries, based on her interpretations of pottery, embroidery and weaving motifs. She also designs clothing and jewelry, available at her two stores in Quito

three semi-abstract people are delineated by swift, black, brushstrokes. They lean against store fronts in what looks like a seedy downtown neighborhood and the use of yellows and reds contributes to a carnival-like atmosphere. Jácome's 1990 oil *A la Cola* (To the End of the Line) depicts a slashing rainstorm in which three bright-yellow taxis outlined in black divide the canvas diagonally. They are balanced by a mass of frantic people in the upper left, rendered in swirling lines of black and white. The painting effectively conveys the feeling of desperation familiar to anyone who has ever tried to catch a taxi in Quito in the rain.

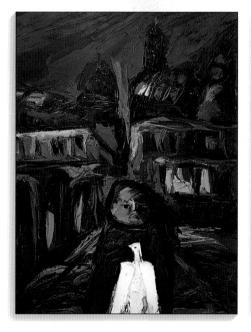

(see the list of stores in the *Travel Tips* section).

The younger generation of painters has moved away from *indígenismo* to more personal, idiosyncratic themes and subject matter. In the 1970s Ramiro Jácome was part of the neo-figurative movement, a return to works with recognizable figures. In the early 1980s he changed his style, painting a series of abstract oils, characterized by deep, rich colors. Later in the 1980s he returned to figurative works.

In *Barrio* (Neighborhood) painted in 1989,

LEFT: an example of the indigenist painting style, by Eduardo Kingman. **ABOVE:** recent canvases by Jaime Romero (left) and Washington Iza (right).

WHERE TO SEE IT

The Casa de la Cultura on Avenidas Patria and 12 de Octubre in Quito has a good collection of modern art, with 20th-century sculptures on the lawn outside. The Museo y Taller Guayasamín, at 543 Calle Bosmediano is devoted solely to Guayasamín's work. Egas' paintings can be seen at the Fundación Cinco, Venezuela y Esmeraldas. If you want to buy as well as look, artists display and sell their work on weekends in the Parque El Ejido. Art Forum on Calle Juan Leon Mera 870, just across from the Libri Mundi Bookstore, has changing shows of major modern artists, and a pleasant café.

OUTDOOR ADVENTURES

Climbing, trekking, rafting or biking – the astonishing variety of terrain is a big attraction for many sports enthusiasts

Outdoor enthusiasts of all types have discovered that the diverse topography of Ecuador provides an ideal environment for so-called "adventure travel." The small size of the country makes getting around a logistical dream: nothing is too far away from anything else, and there are roads to almost everywhere..

Yet, for so small a country, Ecuador has an amazing assortment of terrain, while the climate is favorable for almost year-round excursions. Except for February and March, when it seems to be raining everywhere, good weather conditions can be found in one region or another throughout the year.

BE PREPARED
Buy topographical maps at the Military Geographical Institute (IGM) in Quito before starting your trip.

Trekking in the Sierra

Trekking is one of the most popular adventure activities and there is no lack of out-of-the-way places in the Andes to explore. A number of national parks, some newly established, offer uninhabited areas for days of wandering, while the populated highlands of the Sierra are dotted with small villages whose inhabitants usually offer a welcome to back-packing gringos.

One of the most popular treks in Ecuador is the easy three-day hike to the ruins of Ingapirca, the finest example of Inca stonework in the country. Though the ruins are a poor relation to their spectacular cousin in the Sacred Valley of Peru, a trek to them is a worthwhile endeavor for walking enthusiasts.

The hike begins in the charming village of Achupallus, north of Cuenca, 15km (9 miles) off the Pan-American Highway. A dirt track eventually gives way to a cobbled footpath leading to a pass. You have to squeeze through a small cave to get to the other side. After a brief descent, the trail starts to climb again and traverses a mountain slope above the green valley of the Cadrul River. An excellent site for the first night's camp is beside the sparkling waters

of the high mountain lake, Laguna Las Tres Cruces (Lake of the Three Crosses).

After about a half-day walk on the second day – crossing rocky ridges and skirting boggy valleys – the trail drops below the peak of Quilloloma. The remains of the old Inca road appear in the valley below. There is an excellent place to camp near Laguna Culebrillas and some minor Inca ruins, aptly named Paredones (which means ruined walls) because of the surviving crude stonework. A final three- to four-hour hike on the third day follows the grassy Inca road to the ruins of Ingapirca. (For more on Ingapirca, see pages 267–268 of the *Southern Sierra* chapter.)

Trekking in National Parks

Several national parks within the highland region of Ecuador are especially popular with trekkers because of the ease of accessibility, established trail systems and marvelous scenery. In most cases, day hikes supplant longer treks for those who prefer to see the sights with a lighter load. Facilities within the parks are at a minimum, if they exist at all, but that's part of traveling in a developing country. A small park entrance fee is usually charged, and in some cases, permission from the local INEFAN office must be obtained in advance *(see page 53)*.

Cotopaxi National Park not only attracts climbers who come to scale the Cotopaxi volcano, but its wide open *páramo* is ideal for cross-country treks. The lower slope of Cotopaxi is called the Arenal – a word that comes from the Spanish *arena* meaning sand. Actually the slopes are covered by pumice from recent volcanic eruptions.

A four-day trek across Cotopaxi National Park includes camping one night below the peaks of Carachaloma and Rumiñahui near Laguna Limpiopungo, which is home to an assortment of birds such as the Andean gull, American coot and Andean lapwing. The trek circles the perfectly cone-shaped Cotopaxi vol-

PRECEDING PAGES: scaling Mount Cotapaxi.
LEFT: a climber at the summit of Mount Chimborazo.

cano, and the huge Andean condor can sometimes be spotted gliding high above.

Las Cajas National Recreation Area lies about 32km (20 miles) west of Cuenca. Within its 30,000 hectares (74,000 acres) there is a huge variety of landscapes, ranging from the moonscape appearance of granite rock outcrops to barely penetrable cloud forests where mountain toucans and tropical woodpeckers make their home. With the exception of day-hike trails around the ranger station, most of the area is totally without marked trails, yet a cross-country trek of several days is quite feasible. The region is dotted with some 250 lakes of various

canoes in the world. Climbing in Ecuador is especially good for a number of reasons. It is possible to gain valuable high altitude experience on mountaineering routes that require little preparation. With proper acclimatization, most summits can be conquered in a weekend.

Huts, or *refugios*, have been constructed on many of the higher and more popular climbs. Some of the huts are equipped with bunks (bring a sleeping bag), a communal kitchen with gas stove and dining tables, and the services of a hut guardian who knows the present conditions and route descriptions. During the weekends the huts can get crowded and the

sizes and colors, and fishing for trout is not only permitted, but encouraged.

Podocarpus National Park is located south of Loja and was recently added to the national park system in Ecuador (permits to enter the park can be obtained at the INEFAN office). The area is largely cloudforest and is home to the reticent spectacle bear, the flamboyant Andean cock-of-the-rock and the mountain tanager. A trail system has been established which includes several day hikes from the park headquarters.

Mountaineering

The Andean mountain range in Ecuador comprises one of the largest concentrations of vol-

communal kitchen over-used. Bringing your own stove during peak climbing periods is a good idea. Water is available at the *refugios*, but must be treated with purification tablets or boiled before drinking.

Good climbing weather is possible almost year-round, but normally the best months are June through September and during a short dry spell in December and January. Being a tropical mountain range at the equator, the Ecuadorean Andes generate unusual weather conditions. One part of the *cordillera*, or range, may be inundated with rain, while the next section will have clear skies and perfect conditions. This, at least, makes for plenty of options.

Proper equipment is essential for safe climbing, regardless of how straightforward most routes may appear. Any climbs which involve ice or glacier travel are considered to be technical and require special equipment and knowledge of its use. Crampons, an ice axe and rope are necessary, along with the complement of warm clothing which is demanded by high altitude mountain conditions.

A rucksack with plenty of water, food and extra warm clothing is essential for a summit attempt. Flag markers, or wands, are used during the ascent for route-finding as cloudy conditions will often obscure the descent. In

day hikes to higher elevations. Quito is a good choice and there are several strenuous hikes that can help the climber get in shape. At 4,700 meters (14,000ft), Rucu Pichincha overlooking Quito is an ideal climb to start with, before graduating on to harder and higher peaks.

Easier climbs

For would-be climbers with no experience but plenty of enthusiasm, there are a few Ecuadorian volcanoes. The most popular is Tungurahua, towering over the town of Baños at 5,020 meters (16,500ft). With a small glacier at the top, this straightforward climb can be done

addition, a good headlamp with spare batteries is essential since all climbing begins in the early hours of the morning. All mountaineering gear can be hired in Quito, but, as with the trekking equipment, quality can vary.

High altitude acclimatization is an important factor. Many climbs are so short that the need for proper acclimatization is often underestimated, but with major peaks above 5,700 meters (18,000ft), it should not be overlooked. The best way to accustom the system to altitude is to stay in a relatively high city or town, and take a few

LEFT: a trekker on the Inca Trail.
ABOVE: steaming crater of Guagua Pichincha.

YOU GET WHAT YOU PAY FOR

Mountain guides are available for inexperienced climbers, but caution in selecting the proper guide is strongly recommended. There are people who claim to be guides when they do not have the appropriate experience and the result is potentially dangerous. A decent guide charges a decent price, and it is not something that you should economize on. It is best to go with an adventure outfitter or agency which specializes in mountain excursions, or hire a guide recommended by one of the climbing shops or the South American Explorers' Club in Quito (*see page 125*).

almost year-round, though it's a rare day when the weather is completely clear up here. Because it is on the Oriente side of the *cordillera*, clouds rising from the rainforest normally keep the summit well hidden.

Provided that you have appropriate equipment – sturdy hiking boots, possibly crampons and ice axe – Tungurahua can be climbed in two days. Technically the climb is considered easy, but it is physically demanding. A taxi from Baños is the most convenient way to reach the ranger station, the take-off point for the four-hour climb to the well-placed mountain hut.

The most beautiful part of the entire climb is

the trail to the *refugio* which winds through dense vegetation, with wild orchids blooming in season. After a night spent in the hut, climbers begin the ascent in the very early hours of the morning in order to finish the snow traverse before the sun has softened it to make going heavy.

Several hours of scrambling over pumice scree slope brings you to the snowline. From here, it is only another hour across the snow to the highest point. Views from the summit are some of the best, if the cloud lifts. It is a special day when you can look down from the summit over the cloud forest to the line of volcanoes forming the backbone of the Ecuadorian Andes.

Cotopaxi and Chimborazo

For climbers with greater technical experience, the volcanoes of Cotopaxi at 5,900 meters (19,340ft) and Chimborazo, at 6,310 meters (20,700ft) the highest peak in Ecuador, are the main attractions. At weekends during the peak climbing season, the *refugios* are packed with bustling climbers preparing for the rigors ahead.

Start the climb at around midnight for a round trip of about 10 hours. Often large numbers of climbers set out at the same time, and the flickering light from their headlamps is all that is visible as they ascend through the darkness.

Cotopaxi is the more beautiful of the two mountains, with gentle, curving snow slopes and the massive rock wall of Yanasacha just below the summit. It's a pleasurable ascent as the dawn rays of the sun set the whole glacier sparkling. The summit crater seems perfectly formed against the deep blue Andean sky.

Chimborazo holds the attraction of being Ecuador's highest peak. After several hours of negotiating one steep slope after another, the process becomes something of a slog and one begins to wonder if the summit will ever appear. In the end, the persistent achieve their goal, and the final summit views are well worth the effort.

White-water rafting

The attraction of running untamed rivers draws world-class rafters and kayakers to Ecuador. Those with little or no experience can also safely enjoy the thrill of white-water with the growing number of travel adventure companies operating out of Quito, Tena and Baños.

Many of Ecuador's rivers can be run year round, while some of the more technically difficult ones are possible only during certain seasons. The most accessible and commonly run ones are the Río Toachi and Río Blanco, both two to three hours away from Quito. These rivers transcend the Western Cordillera of the Andes, passing through forested canyons interspersed with small farming villages. The best time to go is from February to May.

A popular Class III rafting trip, suitable for both beginners and experienced rafters, is along the Upper Río Napo. It starts near Tena and is a fun trip through tropical rainforest descending the upper slopes of the Amazon basin and passing several indigenous Quichua communities. The trip is possible all year round, but the best months are between March and October.

For the experienced rafter and kayaker Ecuador has many challenging Class IV and V rivers. One of the most exciting is the Río Misahuallí, but beware of the Casanova Falls. The river can be run safely only from October to March in the low water season when, after a set of Class IV rapids, rafters must be able to stop themselves before the falls.

It is a beautiful trip through virgin rainforest – parrots, oropendulas and other tropical birds abound. The combination of spectacular natural scenery and the strong feel-

THE MISAHUALLÍ

The safest time to embark on the exciting Misahuallí river trip is during the low water season, between October and March.

organized easily from Quito (tel: 523-856). Longer trips can be arranged into the Podocarpus Reserve in the very south of Ecuador from the village of Vilcabamba. Make sure the agency knows what your experience is, particularly if you are a beginner and want a gentle horse.

Mountain biking

The best way to get off the beaten track is on a mountain bike exploring the extensive dirt and cobbled roads that pass through villages rarely visited by tourists. The

ing of isolation makes the adventure all the more exciting. Trips down the Río Misahuallí are organized out of Tena.

Horse riding

Horse back riding across the lush valleys and hills of the Sierra has become a popular leisure activity throughout Ecuador. Several agencies offer organized trips out of Otavalo, Baños and Cuenca. If you are short of time, a one-day trip to Pululahua Crater, by the Equator, can be

LEFT: rafters tackling the white water on one of Ecuador's mountain rivers.
ABOVE: taking a break in the *páramo*.

high elevation, hilly terrain and poor road conditions are challenging, but the views and the colorful local communities make cycling well worth the effort.

If you stay off the main paved roads such as the Pan-American Highway – the Ecuadorians are known for their unsafe driving – the unpaved routes selected from a good topographic map will usually offer solitude and pleasant surprises.

A good place to get acclimatized to the elevation is the market town of Otavalo. Using this as a base for exploration, day trips can be made to the surrounding small villages known for their *artesanías* (arts and crafts). Several outfitters in town will rent bikes for the day and give advice about good routes.

A more ambitious ride takes you 600 meters (2,000ft) up a paved road to the Laguna de Cuicocha, a spectacular collapsed volcanic caldera now filled by a lake. A labyrinth of unpaved roads leads back to Otavalo.

A popular day trip is a mostly downhill ride from Baños, where bikes of dubious quality can be rented, to the jungle town of Puyo. You follow the cliff-hugging road along the gorge of the Pastaza River, passing several inspiring waterfalls. In the town of Río Verde bikes may be left with a local shopkeeper while you visit

los, where a bus can be taken back to Quito.

Although several excellent mountain bike stores have recently opened in Quito, renting high quality bikes is difficult. It's best to bring your own. Most airlines will allow this as long as the bike is boxed. Once here, getting around is made easy by buses with top-racks. Just make sure someone's harvest of potatoes doesn't end up on your bike wheel during the loading.

Paragliding

The topography of Ecuador is well-suited for paragliding. One popular launch site is at the refuge (4,200 meters/13,800ft) on Mount

the falls. Buses pass at half hourly intervals, and you can heave your bike on top of the bus and avoid the long, punishing climb back to Baños.

A popular three- to five-day ride takes you past the volcanic crater lake of Laguna de Quilatoa. A long climb from the Pan American Highway to the indigenous village of Zumbagua (can be avoided by taking a bus) is rewarded by views of a volcanic landscape decorated by wheat fields in different stages of growth, from deep greens and golden yellows to the dark brown earth ready for planting. A dirt track leads to the lake. The next day, after a cold night on the crater rim, you wind along the edge of a deeply eroded pumice plain to the town of Sig-

Cotopaxi, where you can ride thermals to the top of the highest volcano in the world. The best time of year to fly is December. Equally exciting is a flight from La Crucita on the coast, catching winds off the ocean, and following a ridgeline nearly 10km (6 miles) long, staying airborn for three to five hours. Some enthusiasts take off from the slopes of Mount Pichincha and soar over the city of Quito. The best times to fly are during August and September.

If you have sufficient time for lessons, there is a paragliding school with an excellent safety record. For details see *Travel Tips* listings.

ABOVE: evening sun on the north face of Chimborazo.

The South American Explorers' Club

The South American Explorers' Club (which is usually abbreviated to SAEC) based in Quito is a valuable information center for travelers, outdoor enthusiasts and members of scientific expeditions. If your ambition is to climb Cotopaxi, collect orchids, find a reliable boat to the Galápagos Islands, go white water rafting, or simply to meet up with compatible hiking companions, then this is the place to come.

The club was founded by Don Montague and Linda Rojas in Lima, Peru, in 1977. Following its huge success, the Quito Club was opened in 1989 and recently had to move to bigger premises to accommodate the ever growing membership. Montague still runs the US headquarters in Ithaca, New York, and edits a 64-page quarterly journal, *The South American Explorer*, an informative and topical magazine. Articles range from archaelogy, anthropology and geology to mountaineering, indigenous peoples and languages.

The non-profit club is funded by membership dues. A well-invested $40 a year (or $60 for a couple) allows you use of all its facilities in the club houses in both Peru and Ecuador. As a member you have access to an extensive library, equipment storage, book exchange, e-mail, postal mail and phone message services, and bulletin boards. There are also first-hand trip reports written by members which provide personal accounts of hotels, transport, guides and agencies, plus advice and directions for the proposed trip, trek, climb or whatever the activity may be; and there are plenty of useful books and maps for sale.

Besides the general services it offers to its members, the club's mission is to support scientific field exploration and research in the social and natural sciences. Its aim is to awaken greater interest in and appreciation for wilderness conservation and wildlife protection. With this aim in mind it invites guest speakers to give presentations on their specialist subjects and encourages follow-up activities. Talks cover a wide spectrum, from the intellectual property rights in relation to medicinal plants, to climbing the active volcanoes of South America, or giving detailed information about wildlife in the Galápagos.

ABOVE RIGHT: scaling the snowy heights.

If you are interested in staying in Ecuador for a little longer than the average vacation trip and would like to become involved in a community aid project, there are bound to be other club members who will be able to help out with information. The club and its members have built up close ties with orphanages and environmental organizations, and can usually provide general information about volunteer opportunities.

If you join the SAEC before you head to Ecuador you will have the advantage of being able to ask for specialist advice on planning your trip. For a small fee to cover the cost of photocopies and postage the staff at the Ithaca headquarters will recom-

mend, select and mail trip reports to members. The club also has its own catalog, offering books, maps, CDs, language tapes and handicrafts, with discounts for members.

The SAEC headquarters in the United States can be contacted at 126 Indian Creek Road, Ithaca, NY 14850, tel: 607-277-0488, fax: 607-277-6122. The e-mail address is: explorer@samexplo.org, website: http://www.samexplo. org.

The Quito Clubhouse, which is open from Monday to Friday, 9.30am–5pm, is at Jorge Washington 311 y Leonidas Plaza (near the US Embassy) in Quito New Town. The mailing address is Apartado 17-21-431, Eloy Alfaro, Quito; member e-mail: member@saec.org.ec enquiries e-mail: explorer@ saec.org.ec.

FOOD

There's no escaping bananas. But Ecuador's topography has led to the development of some very distinctive dishes in different regions

There is no single Ecuadorian cuisine, but several different ones corresponding to the geographical regions of the country: Costa, Sierra and Oriente. And, as in most countries, there are "high" and "low" cuisines: what you'll find in good restaurants is quite different from what most people eat in the countryside and what you will find in market booths and small cafés throughout the country.

Bananas, however, are ubiquitous. Several varieties are grown on the coast and in the Oriente, from tiny finger bananas *(oritas)* to large, green cooking plantains *(plátanos* or *verdes)*. The yellow bananas of the kind we are accustomed to are called *guineos* in Ecuador. Short, fat red bananas called *magueños* are also good to eat raw. Bananas and plantains are trucked up to every highland town and market so you'll have no trouble finding them.

LAND OF BANANAS
Ecuador was the original banana republic. For many years bananas were its principal export and the country is still the world's largest exporter.

Staple foods
Rice *(arroz)* is not an indigenous food, but it is also ubiquitous, although potatoes *(papas)* will often substitute for it in the highlands. You can count on one or the other to come with every meal. And sometimes, for a complete carbohydrate overload, noodles *(fideos)*, potatoes, rice, *yucca* (a white starchy tuber), and *plátanos* will be served, and that's the meal. This is, needless to say, poor people's food and a partial explanation of why many Ecuadorians are short in stature: besides a genetic component, they don't consume much protein.

Ecuador is overflowing with fruit of all kinds, from enormous *papayas* to more exotic treats like passion fruit *(aya-tacso, maracuyá* and *granadilla* are just a few varieties to try). Then there are sweet custard apples *(chirimoyas)* and tart tamarinds *(tamarindos)*, melons *(melones)* of all kinds, *mangos*, pineapples *(piñas)*, oranges *(naranjas)* and tangerines *(manderi-*

nas*)*, avocados *(paltas)* and lots more. The *naranjilla*, a tiny fruit that looks like a fuzzy, orangey-greenish crab apple, makes a tasty drink that is often served instead of orange juice. Don't be put off by the strange color – the juice is delicious.

Just to confuse you, lemons are called *limas* and limes are called *limones*. If you're uncertain about how to eat a fruit, try it as a juice *(jugo)*. You can ask for juice without water *(sin agua)* and without sugar *(sin azúcar)*.

For a really great eating adventure, go to the market as soon as possible after your arrival in Ecuador. Don't be intimidated by the strange-looking array. Instead, buy every fruit you've never seen before, then go back to your hotel or pension and ask the owner to share them with you and tell you the names of the different varieties. You'll discover some delicious fruits which you can then enjoy for the rest of your trip.

Pacific flavors
Cuisine, however, means a style of cooking, so how do Ecuadorians combine their abundant raw ingredients? Many of the coastal dishes are typical of the entire Pacific coast from Chile to Mexico. They include *ceviche*, which is fish *(pescados)* or seafood *(mariscos)* marinated in lemon or lime juice, onions and chili peppers. There's *ceviche* made of shrimp *(camarones* or *langostinos)*, lobster *(langosta)*, sea bass *(corvina)*, crab *(cangrejos* or *jaibas)*, oysters *(ostiones)* and mixed *(mixto)*.

Ecuador's superb *corvina* is served a number of ways, including fried *(frito)*, breaded and fried *(apanada)* and filleted and grilled *(a la plancha)*. Try any sea fish cooked in *agua de coco* (coconut milk). Besides the varieties already mentioned there are clams *(almejas* or *conchas)*, grouper *(cherna)*, mackerel *(sierra)*, marlin *(picudo)*, snapper *(pargo)*, tuna *(atún)*, and squid *(calamares)*. The *dorado*, or dolphinfish which is not a mammal like the true dolphin, is also popular.

A thoughtful Ecuadorian custom for regulating the spiciness of food is to serve hot sauce (*salsa picant*) made from chili peppers (*ají*) in a little side dish so that you can add as much or as little as you like.

Tastes of the Oriente

Coastal and Oriente foods are similar because of the two regions' low elevation and tropical climate, although there is more game hunting in the jungle (everything from monkeys to tapir and *paca*, a large rodent) and river fish instead of seafood. In both places you'll find lots of *plátanos, yucca,* rice and fried fish. There are several dishes served only in the Oriente, however. One is *piranha* fish, although it surprises many visitors that the notorious carnivorous fish is itself good for eating. The Oriente rivers also have lots of catfish (*challua* or *bagre*), which people make into a stew with plantains, chili peppers and *cilantro* (coriander).

For a jungle salad, try *palmitos* (palm hearts) or chonta palm fruits (*frutas de chonta*), both considered delicacies. *Chucula* is a tasty drink made of boiled and mashed plantains, which resembles a banana milkshake.

Sierra cuisine

And now, as we climb to the highlands, a word about the tuber, that traditional mainstay of indigenous life in the Andes. Believe me, there are a lot of tubers in the Andes, beginning with dozens of varieties of potatoes. The potato was domesticated around Lake Titicaca, the region which still has the most varieties – some of which are so specialized they grow only at altitudes above 2,400 meters (8,000ft). As already mentioned, potatoes (*papas*) are served with almost every meal in the highlands, usually boiled, but sometimes cut up into thick soups. If you don't like potatoes you're in for trouble in Ecuador. They are the food of the common people and, as in Inca times, everyone plants and eats thems. The great Inca terraces used to be reserved for corn, which was usually made into *chicha*.

Besides regular white potatoes in many sizes and varieties, you will come across the sweet potato (*camote*) as well as the *oca*, which looks like a long, skinny, lumpy potato. One Ecuadorian potato specialty is *llapingachos*, potato pancakes made with mashed potatoes, cheese and onions. A better lunch cannot be had.

Soups are the essence of Sierra meals. Before the Spanish conquest *indígenas* did not have ovens for baking, which meant that most food

Yaguar locro contains the heart, liver and other internal organs (which is to say tripe, or *mondongo*) of a cow *(vaca* or *res)*, pig *(chancho)* or sheep *(borrego)*, and is sprinkled on top with blood sausage or the animal's dried blood. *Fanesca* is an incredibly rich soup served only during Holy Week (the week before Easter). You name it and *fanesca* has it: fish, eggs *(huevos)*, cheese *(queso)*, corn and every imaginable grain and vegetable, but no meat. *Mazamorra* is a thick soup made with a ground corn base and cabbage, potatoes (of course), onions and spices. *Sancocho* is a stew made with *plátanos* and corn. Most soups and stews

was boiled, a custom which survives today. Soup is called *caldo, sopa, chupe* or *locra*. Generally, a *sopa* or a *caldo* is a thin soup with potatoes and various unidentified floating objects of the faunal variety. A *locro* or *chupe* is a thick, creamy soup. *Sopa seca* or just plain *seco* (which means dry) is more of a stew than a soup, with meat and vegetables added according to the budget and whim of the cook.

One of the most common *locros* is *yaguar locro* (blood soup), a favorite in the countryside.

LEFT: *anticuchos*, a type of kebab, ready for the grill.
ABOVE: *ceviche*, made from a variety of fresh seafood, is popular on the coast.

are liberally seasoned with *cilantro* and many are given a yellow or orange color by the addition of *achiote* seeds.

Corn *(maíz* or *sara)* is another staple, especially in the Sierra. Unlike in Mexico and Central America, corn in the Andes is not ground and made into tortillas. In northern Ecuador corn is most commonly served on the cob *(choclo)*. Ecuadorian corn has enormous, sweet kernels arranged irregularly, and it's the best corn-on-the-cob imaginable. In the north corn is also eaten as parched kernels *(kamcha)* or a popcorn *(cangil)*. In southern Ecuador it is co monly served as boiled kernels *(muti* or *mo¹ Humitas* are corn tamales: cornmeal seaso and steamed in the leaf. Don't eat the leaf – unwrap it and eat what's inside. *Tostadas de maíz* are corn pancakes; they make a good breakfast or snack.

Miracle grain

Other grains grown locally include *quinua*, wheat *(trigo)* and barley *(cebada)*. *Quinua*, like the potato, is native to the Andes. This tiny, round grain is an amazingly nutritious food, consisting of 15 percent complete protein, 55 percent carbohydrate and only 4 percent fat. The Incas regarded *quinua* as sacred and it was their second most important food crop. *Quinua* is

Andes) are called *habas*. After the *haba* harvest these huge fresh beans are boiled and served hot, dipped in salty *campo* cheese.

In search of meat dishes

After all this fish, fruit and vegetables, you may be wondering about the possibility of getting a good steak. You should ask for *lomo* or *bifstec*, or *chuleta* if you want a chop. *Parrilladas* are steak houses or grills, where the meat is sometimes charcoal-grilled at your table. *A la parrilla* means grilled and *churrasco* or *lomo montado* is meat (usually beef) topped with fried eggs. You can also order veal *(ternera)*,

usually served in soup, but it can also be eaten as a side dish, in the same way as rice.

Most barley is ground up and used in soup, but wheat flour is used to make a variety of good breads and rolls *(pan* and *panecitos)* and *empanadas*, which are baked pastries filled with cheese or meat. Around Latacunga you'll hear women at street stalls calling *allullas, allullas!* ⌐ronounced azhúzhas). These are homemade ⌐. good when hot and fresh, but hard when ⌐t cold.

⌐ s the usual vegetables, Ecuador has ⌐es. What we call lima beans (which ⌐ounced as in Lima, the capital of ⌐ ley were domesticated in the

FROM PET TO POT

If you'll settle for something smaller than a sirloin, try guinea-pig *(cuy)*. Until the arrival of the Europeans, *cuy* was the main source of meat in the Andes. Every family had guinea-pigs running around the kitchen, and some still do. *Cuy* is eaten only on special occasions, when one is scooped up, killed, gutted, cleaned, rubbed with lard and spices, put on a spit and roasted in the fire or baked in the oven. If you can bring yourself to try *cuy*, you'll find that there's not much meat, but what there is is delicious, and, as the Ecuadorians put it, what else are guinea-pigs good for?

lamb *(cordero)* or pork *(puerco* or *chanco; kuchi* in Quichua). *Lechón* is suckling pig. *Salchicha* means sausage, while *chorizo* refers to pork sausage. Bacon is *tocino*, ham is *jamón.*

Asado, which means roasted, always refers to whole roasted pig in Ecuador, unless otherwise modified. Every food market has at least one vendor and sometimes a whole row of them selling *asado. Fritada* (fried pork) is also ubiquitous. *Fritada* is cooked in large copper and brass *pailas* (wok-like pans), visible in the market or in the doorways of small restaurants throughout the country. *Chicharrón* is fried pork skin, crispy and good.

Other sources of dietary protein include chicken *(pollo)* or hen *(gallina),* and eggs served in the usual ways, as well as pasteurized cow's milk *(leche),* which is sold in unwieldy liter-sized plastic bags, and excellent cheese *(queso),* the quality of which has soared in recent years with the arrival of Swiss and Italian immigrants who have introduced European varieties. As for fish, in the Sierra many streams and lakes have been stocked with tasty, if rather bony, trout *(trucha).*

Slaking your thirst

Bebidas is the term for beverages in general, alcoholic or otherwise. Ecuadorian wine *(vino)* is unlikely to win any international awards although occasional bottles can be quite good. Argentinian and Chilean wines are often excellent, but expensive. You're better off sticking to beer *(cerveza),* soft drinks *(gaseosas)* or mineral water *(agua mineral),* among which Güitig – pronounced *wee-tig* – is the most common brand. There is also tea *(te),* herb tea *(agua aromática)* hot chocolate *(chocolate caliente)* and coffee *(café).*

The latter is usually boiled until it becomes a sludge, which is set on the table in a small carafe. Known as *esencia,* it looks just like soy sauce and causes some interesting culinary confusion in Chinese restaurants *(chifas).* The *esencia* is poured in your cup and hot water or milk is added. Sometimes instant coffee substitutes

> **QUICHUA CONTRIBUTION**
> The Quichua language has contributed one word to English: "jerky", which is derived from *charqui,* meaning dried meat.

for *esencia* but the taste, unfortunately, is the same. Black coffee is *tinto,* coffee with milk is *café con leche* and coffee with hot water and milk is *pintado* (which literally means "painted").

Api is a hot drink made from ground corn, and sometimes so thick it might be considered a soup. *Chicha morada* is a sweet, non-alcoholic drink. When it comes to liquor, what you get is the most potent intoxicant with the highest imaginable octane rating: a distilled sugar cane liquor known as *trago,* which burns with a clear

blue flame. Local brands include Cristal and Sinchi Shungu (Strong Heart); there are also several nameless varieties which are produced illegally in the countryside. Tequila is another highly intoxicating drink which is cheap and popular – although not so popular the next morning.

Hervidas are hot drinks served at every fiesta, consisting of *trago* mixed with honey and *naranjilla* or blackberry juice; *guayusas* are *trago* mixed with sugar and hot *guayusa* tea, while *canelazos* are *trago* spiced with cinnamon, sugar and lime. These drinks tend to sneak up on you like Jack the Ripper.

As they say in Ecuador "¡Buen provecho!"

LEFT: whole suckling pig, called simply *asado,* is sold in many markets. **ABOVE RIGHT:** mountains of fresh vegetables in the domestic market at Otavalo.

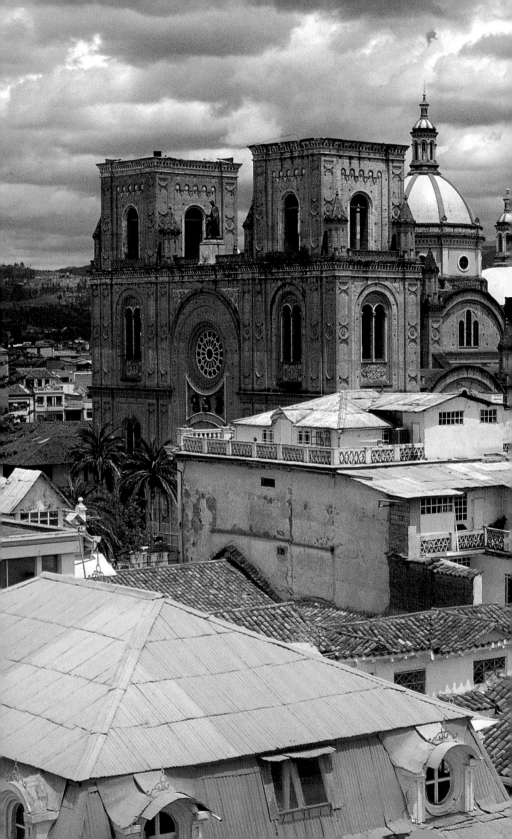

PLACES

*A detailed guide to the entire country, with principal sites
cross-referenced by number to the maps*

Ecuador is the smallest of South America's Andean republics and without doubt the easiest to explore. The capital city, Quito, is the perfect base for travelers – and, for most, their point of arrival. Located only 24km (15 miles) south of the Equator, Quito's Andean setting ensures that it has a pleasant, spring-like climate all year round. Unlike other Latin American capitals, Quito has not been swamped by a population explosion: its elegant colonial heart is preserved in the 18th century, while the modern "new town" offers every comfort from the 20th.

The Andean highlands remain Ecuador's heartland. The classic excursion from Quito, and one of the country's most famous attractions, is a short hop north for the Saturday handicraft market in Otavalo. Then, stretching south of Quito, is the lush mountain valley that the German scientist Alexander von Humboldt dubbed "the Avenue of the Volcanoes." The city of Cuenca, considered Ecuador's most beautiful colonial relic, marks the beginning of the Southern Sierra – a remote and strongly traditional region that boasts some of Ecuador's most unusual *indígena* communities and the country's only Inca ruins.

But Ecuador offers much more than Sierra cultures and the spectacle of ice on the equator. Just 20 minutes west of Quito by air is the Pacific coast. Moving to a more languid rhythm of life than the highlands, the Costa is washed by warm sea currents from the northern Pacific – making the coastline lusher and swimming more pleasant than at the icy beaches of Peru and Chile. Comfortable resorts are dotted along both Ecuador's north and south coasts, which travelers often decide to reach directly rather than passing through the tropical city of Guayaquil, Ecuador's chaotic and rarely attractive commercial heart.

Twenty minutes by air east of Quito is the Oriente region, the most accessible section of the Amazon basin in South America. Jungle lodges, floating hotels and canoe trips explore the farthest reaches of this endangered region which, paradoxically, is fast becoming the continent's greatest travel attraction.

Finally, the Galápagos archipelago is in a class of its own. Easily reached on tours or independently by three-hour flights from Quito, this naturalists' paradise alone can justify the journey to Ecuador. A several-day-long cruise – either in a luxury liner or small chartered boat – is an expensive treat, but remains one of the world's great travel experiences.

PRECEDING PAGES: view from the summit of Mount Cotopaxi; old-style locomotion across the tropical lowlands; a Quito mural; the colonial splendor of Cuenca.
LEFT: Mount Sangay erupting.

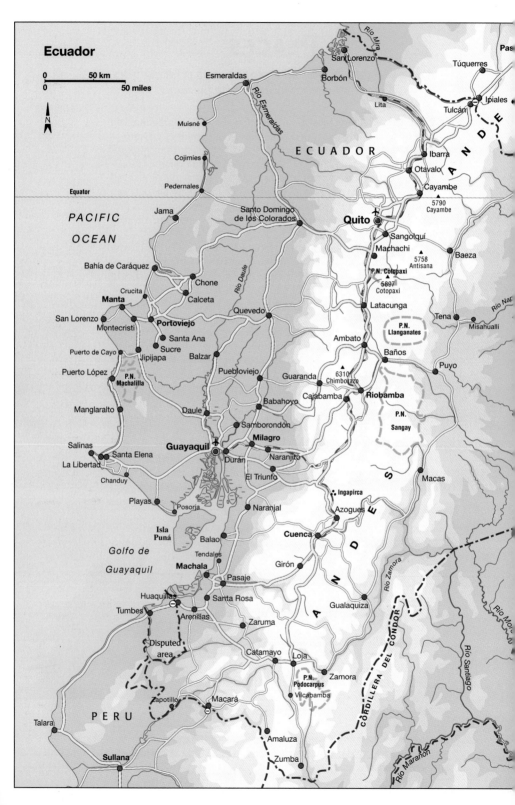

Ecuador

0 50 km
0 50 miles

N

PACIFIC
OCEAN

Equator

ECUADOR

PERU

Pas
Túquerres
San Lorenzo
Borbón
Ipiales
Esmeraldas
Lita
Tulcán
Muisné
Cojimíes
Ibarra
Otavalo
Pedernales
Cayambe
5790
Cayambe
Jama
Santo Domingo
de los Colorados
Quito
Sangolquí
Machachi
Baeza
5758
Antisana
Bahía de Caráquez
P.N. Cotopaxi
5897
Cotopaxi
Crucita
Chone
Calceta
Quevedo
Latacunga
Tena
Río Nap
Manta
P.N.
Llanganates
Misahuallí
San Lorenzo
Portoviejo
Santa Ana
Ambato
Montecristi
Sucre
Baños
Puyo
Puerto de Cayo
Jipijapa
Balzar
Puerto López
Puebloviejo
Guaranda
6310
Chimborazo
Riobamba
P.N.
Machalilla
Babahoyo
Cajabamba
P.N.
Manglaralto
Daule
Sangay
Samborondón
Salinas
Guayaquil
Milagro
Santa Elena
Durán
Naranjito
Macas
La Libertad
Chanduy
El Triunfo
Ingapirca
Playas
Posorja
Naranjal
Azogues
Isla
Puná
Balao
Cuenca
Tendales
Girón
Golfo de
Guayaquil
Machala
Pasaje
A
N
Huaquillas
Santa Rosa
Gualaquiza
D
E
S
Tumbes
Arenillas
Zaruma
Río Zamora
CORDILLERA DEL CONDOR
Río Morona
Disputed
area
Catamayo
Loja
Río Santiago
Zapotillo
Macará
P.N.
Podocarpus
Zamora
Vilcabamba
PERU
Amaluza
Talara
Zumba
Río Marañón
Sullana

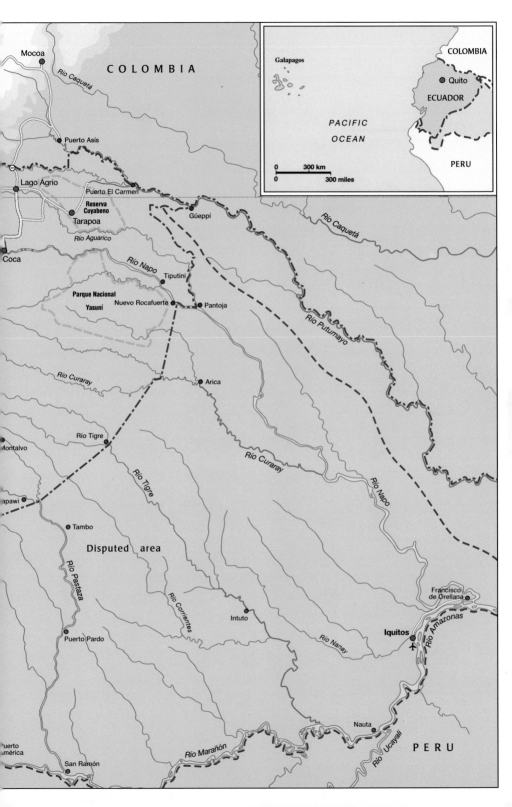

QUITO

Latin America's most beautiful church is here, along with splendid colonial buildings and some bargain shopping. A grid system makes it easy to find your way around

Map, inside back cover

Quito
ECUADOR

Old Town map page 148
New Town map page 160

PRECEDING PAGES: Quito and Cotopaxi seen from Pichincha. **LEFT:** statue of the Virgin of Quito. **BELOW:** Quiteña.

Surrounded by snow-capped volcanoes but only 24km (15 miles) from the Equator, Quito is a strange and beautiful city with a spring-like climate all year round. Although an important Indian city in Inca and pre-Inca times, its indigenous buildings have been erased and today it is divided between the colonial architecture and sculpture of its Spanish conquest days and the clean lines of its modern section. This combination of superb well-preserved colonial churches and convents and shining glass and sleek contemporary architecture makes Quito one of the most beautiful cities in the whole of Latin America.

Nestled at the foot of 4,790-meter (15,710-ft) high Rucu Pichincha, Ecuador's capital owes its name to the Quitua Indians. When the Inca empire spread as far as Ecuador under the leadership of Huayna-Capac, the Indians living in what is now Quito put up impressive resistance to the invaders from Cuzco. But, in the end, Huayna-Capac not only added the area to the empire but he married a beautiful princess from the conquered tribe and set up the Incas' northern capital in Quito. A road was built to link Cuzco with Quito, from which Huayna-Capac preferred to rule.

His decision to divide the Inca kingdom into northern and southern regions – and his fathering of sons in both – were key factors in the downfall of the empire. When Huayna-Capac died, his legitimate heir in Cuzco, Huascar, claimed the throne at the same time as the leader's illegitimate (but some say favorite) son, Atahualpa, declared himself Inca in Quito. The rights to the throne were clouded, too, by the Inca line of succession – which was not based solely on birth order. In many instances, the first son of an Inca was passed over for younger siblings who showed greater leadership skills, wisdom and courage. And, in the case of Huascar and Atahualpa, their subjects at each end of the kingdom supported the local son.

A razed city

A year after Francisco Pizarro had Atahualpa executed on the main plaza of Cajamarca, now in northern Peru, Sebastian de Benalcázar, accompanied by *conquistador* Diego de Almagro, arrived to claim Quito for the Spanish crown. They skirmished with Atahualpa's general, Rumiñahui (Face of Stone), and when it became clear he would be overcome, he angrily set the Inca palace on fire. The flames spread and the city the Spanish finally claimed was razed. (Rumiñahui, meanwhile, was captured and executed.) For that reason Quito has no Inca structures; all that remained of those magnificent buildings perched on the city's beautiful high plain were massive rock foundations. On those bases, the Spanish conquerors built churches, convents and palaces in the exuberant style of the Latin American baroque.

By the end of the 16th century, the new colonial city's population reached 1,500 and it was declared the seat of the royal *audiencia*, a legal subdivision of the New World colony. The proliferation of churches, convents and monasteries won Quito the nickname "The Cloister of America" and, in 1978, the same colonial buildings prompted the United Nations to declare the city a World Cultural Heritage Site.

In early colonial Quito, changes came slowly but steadily as wheat farming was introduced, the Indians were converted to Christianity and colonial rule and laws replaced the Indian culture. In the centuries that followed, Quito became a center for art and sculpture in the New World, with the School of Quito producing an art form characterized by violent Christian themes, such as saints drawing their last breath in horrifying and bloody scenes of martyrdom, painted in rich dark colors and gold brushwork, similiar to the work of the School of Cuzco, Peru.

The growth and development of Quito was not problem-free. There was a bloody rebellion against a royal sales tax in 1592 and another in 1765, when a

Urban transport.

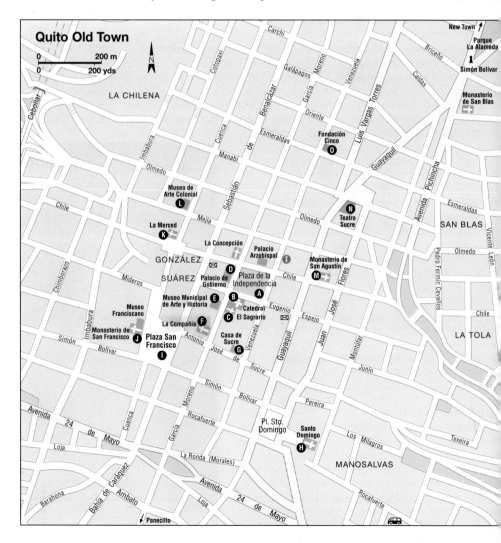

rumor spread that government-dispensed rum had been poisoned to eliminate the poorer classes. But things remained relatively peaceful until full-scale insurrection occurred when the winds of independence spreading across the continent reached this city. In August of 1809 the first sparks of revolution flew in Quito and, on May 24, 1822, the city fell into the hands of the independence troops, led by Marshal Sucre, after a bloody battle in the foothills of Pichincha shadowing the city. (May 24 is now a national holiday.) For eight years Ecuador was part of La Gran Colombia – modern-day Colombia, Venezuela and Ecuador united under a single government – but, in 1830, separated itself, against the wishes of Simón de Bolívar, architect of the scheme, to become independent under the presidency of Juan Flores.

Map, page 148

Colonial buildings, modern problems

Although Quito's old town – called the *casco colonial* – with its churches, convents and whitewashed houses with red tile roofs has not changed much physically since colonial times, social upheavals have been frequent, and it is now exeriencing many of the problems common to urban areas in the late 20th century. In its narrow, cobblestone streets, traffic, with its consequent pollution, is thick and annoying during the day. And behind the doors of the great mansions that once housed the city's richest residents in the oldest part of Quito are now the divided-up homes of the poor.

Quito flies the flag.

Quito today extends far beyond the old town's borders, even spreading up the slopes of Pichincha on the west side. On the eastern side of the city is the **Los Chillos** valley, which has experienced considerable urban development in recent years due to a new highway connecting it with the city. In northern Quito, huge business centers have sprung up complete with banks, shopping arcades, embassies and government buildings. This part of Quito is also where upper-class residential areas are concentrated. The homes of the poor are largely on the city's south side, together with the factories and heavy industry that stretch along the Pan-American Highway, known locally as the Pana.

BELOW: posing for the camera in the Old Town.

The city's rapid recent growth – including a threefold swell in inhabitants from 1950 to 1974 when people from the rural areas moved to the town in search of work and the population reached 600,000 – has brought serious problems, including street crime, marginal housing, pollution and a lack of basic services such as water and electricity. However, Quito is still one of the few Latin American capitals where living conditions, as well as being extremely good for the wealthy, are sustainable, if nothing more, for working-class people – although there has been a disturbing increase in the number of beggars in the plazas in the past few years.

Quito from above

In order to get an idea of the city's layout before you start exploring, it's a good idea to go to a spot that offers a fine panoramic view of Quito and the surrounding volcanoes. **Cerro Panecillo**, a hill dominating the old city and topped by a statue of the Virgin of the Americas with an observation deck, lures those who want to survey the basin in which Quito sits. A series of steps and

In 1534 the layout of the city was designed with 48 blocks, and divided by streets 10 meters (33ft) wide. The checkerboard outline was not completely regular due to slopes and ravines.

paths from García Moreno and Ambato enable you to walk up the hill but assaults are frequent and visitors are strongly advised to ascend El Panecillo only by taxi. The hill stands on what was once an Inca site for sun worship. An even more splendid view is available from the **Cima de la Libertad**. Founded on the site of the 1822 Battle of Pichincha, this spot has a **museum** built by the Ministry of Defense and dedicated to the independence era in Quito. The museum exhibits flags, weapons, a model of this pivotal battle and a sarcophagus containing the remains of its heroes. Dramatically, their tomb is guarded by an eternally-burning flame.

Also overwhelming is the view from **Cruz Loma**, one of the two antenna-topped peaks overlooking Quito on the eastern slope of **Rucu Pichincha**, but muggings have made it a dangerous spot that is best avoided.

Strolling through the past

Walking around the hilly, narrow streets is the best way to see old Quito, the heart of which is the **Plaza de la Independencia** Ⓐ. Also known locally as the Plaza Grande, this attractive palm-shaded square is dominated by **La Catedral** (Metropolitan Cathedral) Ⓑ (open daily, except when masses are in progress; admission free). The other sides of the plaza are flanked by the Palacio de Gobierno, the Archbishop's Palace and the disappointing modern City Administration Building which was erected in 1978 to replace a colonial structure that was beyond rescue. At the center of the plaza is the city's bronze and marble monument to liberty.

The cathedral is easy to find not only because of its size, but because it has written on its façade *Es Gloria de Quito el Descubrimiento del Rio Amazonas*

BELOW LEFT: make your calls here.
BELOW RIGHT: view over Quito.

Quito's Glory is the Discovery of the Amazon River) – although, in fact, Ecuador no longer contains any portion of the Amazon. The cathedral is believed to have existed first as a wood and adobe structure before the official church was built on the site in 1565. Earthquake damage has forced restoration on three occasions, including after the 1987 tremors that damaged many of the city's colonial buildings. The cathedral is filled with paintings and artwork by some of Ecuador's finest early artists from what became known as the School of Quito. Outstanding among these is the famous *Descent from the Cross* by Indian artist Caspicara. Like many churches built in Quito (and Cuenca) during the 16th and 17th centuries, the Cathedral shows definite Moorish influences.

One of the side altars contains the remains of Venezuelan-born Marshal Antonio José de Sucre, leader of the liberation army that annihilated the royalists in the Battle of Pichincha. It is in his honor that Ecuador's currency is called the *sucre*. Left of the main altar is a statue of Ecuador's first president, Juan José Flores, and behind the altar is a plaque showing where President Gabriel García Moreno died on August 6, 1875, from gunshot wounds he received while returning to the Presidential Palace after mass. He was carried back across the street to the church but attempts to save his life were futile. And this was not the only murder committed within the sanctuary of the cathedral. In 1917 a bishop of Quito died during mass when he drank poisoned altar wine.

The **Administration Building** is worth visiting to see the huge brightly-colored *naif* murals of Quito life, but you'll have to get past the plethora of children seeking to shine your shoes in order to do so. Around the corner from the cathedral on Calle García Moreno is **El Sagrario Ⓖ**, built between 1657 and 1706 as the cathedral's main chapel but now used as a separate church. This

Map, page 148

a must see!

BELOW: the Plaza de la Independencia.

building is under restoration but allows visitors to look at the painstaking work needed to save these centuries-old colonial buildings. Among the rescued works are frescoes by Francisco de Alban painted in the church's cupola.

Roller-coaster politics

Detail from a Kingman painting.

On the northwest side of the plaza is the **Palacio de Gobierno** (Government Palace) , also known as the **Palacio Presidencial** (Presidential Palace) (access only to entrance area), with Ecuador's flag atop it and its entrance flanked by guards in red, blue and gold 19th-century uniforms, which seem somewhat anachronistic in contrast with the automatic rifles they carry, and which they used during a 1976 coup attempt. In fact, this building has seen a great deal of activity, especially in the early days of the republic. From 1901 to 1948 alone, Ecuador had 39 governments and four constitutions, and at one point there were four presidents in a span of 26 days. Sightseeing is usually limited to the courtyard with its fountain and columns (the iron balconies were a gift from the French government) and Oswaldo Guayasamín's famous mosaic mural depicting explorer Francisco Orellana's jungle voyage to the Amazon. It was Orellana's journey, which began in Ecuador and culminated in Orellana's naming of the Amazon River near what is now Iquitos, Peru, that led Ecuador to declare itself "The Amazon Nation."

The palace, nearly 400 years old, is an unusual mix of the formal and informal and must be one of the world's few presidential offices where the street-level floor has been converted into small shops that sell souvenirs, including Panama hats, postcards and handicrafts.

Half a block from the plaza, at Eugenio Espejo 1147, is the **Alberto Mena**

BELOW: consulting guide books on the cathedral steps.

Camaño Museo Municipal de Arte y Historia ❺, in an early Jesuit house that later served as barracks for the royal Spanish troops in Quito. The stone column in the patio was the pillory and where prisoners were executed. Underneath it is the dungeon where 36 revolutionaries of the 1890 uprising were imprisoned for nine months before they were executed. Wax figures in the museum graphically illustrate their deaths. The museum contains ecclesiastical art from the 16th and 17th century as well as a handful of works from the 1800s. It is currently undergoing restoration but will reopen in 1999.

The museum was believed to have been built by Jesuit Friar Marcos Guerra, who is also credited with contructing other buildings around the city before he and the other Jesuits were forced out of Quito in 1767 under a decree issued by King Carlos III. What had been the San Luis Seminary was then expropriated for government use.

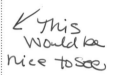

Map, page 148

Latin America's most beautiful church

Almost next door to the museum is the impressive church of **La Compañía ❻** (open early mornings and after 4pm; admission free). This Jesuit church, which has been undergoing restoration, took 163 years to finish and is the most ornate in the country; some say it is the most splendid in Latin America. Richly intricate both inside and out, it is a masterpiece of baroque and Quiteño colonial art. Its altars are covered in gold leaf and the fine paintings on its vaulted ceiling have earned it the nickname "Quito's Sistine Chapel." The pulpit and confessionals are of delicately carved wood and the walls are covered with School of Quito murals, including the painting of the *Last Judgment* at the entrance to La Compañía. The designs on the columns inside the church clearly show a Moorish

✓ This would be nice to see

BELOW: guarding the Palacio Presidencial.

influence and the columns themselves are said to be copies of those by Bernini in the Vatican; they are reproduced in the main altar.

However, the church's most precious treasures, including an emerald and gold-laden painting of the *Virgen Dolorosa*, are kept in the country's Central Bank vaults and taken out only for special religious festivals. Last time it was assessed, the painting was valued at more than $10 million. And the church's original holdings were far, far richer than what exist now. In 1767 when a decree banned the Jesuits from Spanish domains, the treasures in La Compañía were put into 36 boxes and shipped to Spain to pay war debts. What remained – mostly silver – was put up for sale but the devout Quiteños refused to buy it, saying that the items in question belonged to God.

At the foot of the altar in La Compañía are the remains of Quito's saint, Mariana de Jesús. In 1645, a combination of measles and diphtheria epidemics and an earthquake killed 14,000 people in Quito, prompting a frantic attempt to break the city's streak of bad luck. It was then that 26-year-old Mariana de Jesús stepped in. The orphaned daughter of an aristocratic family, she had already given all her wealth to the poor and was said to have miraculously healed the sick. Now she made a bargain with God, offering him her own life if the rest of the city's population could be saved. As the story goes, she fell ill immediately after the public offer of self-sacrifice and, with her death, the plagues on the city ended. Just before she died, doctors bled her – as was the custom – and threw the blood into the garden of her home. It was said that a lily grew where the blood touched the earth and, for that reason, when the Pope canonized Mariana, he called her the "Lily of Quito."

When you come out of La Compañia go left down Avenida de Mariscal Sucre

Quito was severely damaged by an earth-quake in 1987. FONSAL, the Cultural Heritage Protection Fund, has since carried out 300 restoration projects in the colonial quarter.

LEFT: Olga Fisch, businesswoman and artist, in her home.
RIGHT: lavish gold interior, La Compañía church.

and between the streets of García Moreno and Venezuela you will find the **Casa de Sucre Historical Museum**  (open Mon–Sat 8am–4pm; entrance fee) with its collection of weapons, clothing, furniture and documents from the independence era. This was once the home of national hero Marshal Antonio José de Sucre, victor of the Battle of Pichincha, and signatory of the country's subsequent Act of Independence.

A statue of Sucre, pointing in the direction of Pichincha where he led independence troops to victory in 1822, is two blocks away at Bolívar and Guayaquil on the busy little Plaza Santo Domingo. Also in the square is the **Iglesia de Santo Domingo**  (open daily; admission free), a church that is especially attractive in the evening when its domes are illuminated against the dark sky. Unfortunately, the interior of the church has not been as well preserved as others in the city.

Santo Domingo is known for its fine religious sculptures, especially those of the Virgen del Rosario, donated by Spanish King Charles V. The Dominican museum, **Museo Fray Pedro Bedón**, attached to the church, also has an impressive collection of art (the friar himself was a painter). The museum is home to the astonishing silver throne used to carry the Virgen del Rosario during religious processions. A street off the plaza features arches that join the houses together above eye level.

Roaming La Ronda

From the Plaza Santo Domingo, turn down Guayaquil to Calle Juan de Dios Morales, the area known as **La Ronda**, the neighborhood offering the most romantic slice of colonial Quito, with its bright white buildings trimmed with

Map, page 148

← good to see @ Night

sounds nice

BELOW: the house of Marshal Sucre, now a museum.

Riding the bus to school.

blue window frames and doors and touched by pots of red geraniums. Narrow streets of polished cobblestone are bordered on both sides by beautiful old houses with Spanish balconies. This graceful maze of passages and stairways runs from Carrera Venezuela to Calle Maldonado under two bridges. Its name comes from the guitar serenades – or *rondas* – that drew crowds here during colonial days and the musical history of this neighborhood is not forgotten. At intervals along the way are tile portraits of famous Ecuadorian musicians and composers. Sadly, this area is not as safe as it once was. Thefts from tourists are a problem, particularly at night, when a saunter down these streets is a near guarantee of robbery or assault, born of the poverty suffered by some residents.

From here it is only three blocks to the next destination, the Plaza San Francisco, but en route you will pass the two main streets – Carrera Venezuela and García Moreno – which lead from Plaza de la Independencia to the Avenida 24 de Mayo, crested by a new concrete building which has been used as a market hall since street markets were officially abolished in 1981. Despite this ban, lively street trading still goes on at markets from Sucre down to 24 de Mayo and from the San Francisco church west past Calle Cuenca in the most indigenous section of the city. Peek into the buildings on the way by. Many are colonial structures which now house auto supply shops and five-and-dime stores.

Grand tribute to a patron saint

The wide **Plaza San Francisco** ❶ is named for its monastery church, **El Monasterio de San Francisco** ❶ (open Mon–Sat 9am–6pm; Sun 9am–12 noon; entrance fee) honoring Quito's patron saint. The Flemish missionary Fray Jodocko Ricke directed construction of the church and monastery on the site of

the Inca palace only 50 days after the city's 1534 founding – making this the continent's oldest church. Fray Ricke, who was also responsible for introducing wheat to Ecuador by planting the first seeds in this plaza, is honored by a statue in front of the church.

The San Francisco religious complex with its 104 Doric columns is the largest structure in colonial Quito, comparable in size to Spain's El Escorial and with a sumptuous Spanish baroque interior. But the Indian heritage of Quito is represented in this Christian enclave; the church ceiling is decorated with images of the sun, the Inca divinity. Its main altar is spectacularly carved and the side aisles are banked with paintings by School of Quito masters, including the *Virgen Imaculada de Quito* by Bernardo de Legarda. This is reportedly the only winged image of the Virgin Mary to be found in either Europe or the Americas.

The complex's finest artwork, including paintings, sculptures and furniture from the 16th and 17th centuries, is found in the **Museo Franciscano** to the right of the main entrance to the church, in a building which was originally established by Fray Ricke as a school of art and religious instruction for indigenous children. Note the details of the intricately wrought furniture; some pieces have literally thousands of mother-of-pearl mosaics in their construction.

To one side of the San Francisco atrium is the **Cantuña Chapel**, which is believed to have been built by the Indian Cantuña, a Christian convert, and financed by treasures from the Inca empire. (Cantuña's remains lie in the church.) The chapel has a magnificent carved altar – the work of Bernardo de Legarda – and its walls display finely carved wood.

Not far away, at Calles Cuenca and Chile, is another of Quito's churches – there are more than seven dozen in all. This one is **La Merced** at the corner of Calle Cuenca and Chile. Its monastery contains the city's oldest clock, built in 1817 in London. Other non-religious features of this complex include the statue of Neptune on the fountain in the cloister's main patio, which is considered one of the most beautiful patios in Quito. (Visits to the cloister must be arranged in advance at the monastery.)

The castle-like La Merced – constructed from 1700 to 1734 – was one of the last churches built during Quito's colonial period, and it has the old city's tallest tower (47 meters/154ft) and its largest bell. Its walls are pink and white reliefs displaying more than three dozen gilt-framed School of Quito paintings, among them several with unusual scenes of erupting volcanoes and an ash-covered city. Bernardo de Legarda, one of the most important figures in the Quito School, carved the main altarpiece in this serenely beautiful church.

From here, the **Museo de Arte Colonial** (Museum of Colonial Art) **L** (open Tues–Fri 10am–6pm; Sat–Sun 10am–2pm; entrance fee) is just a block away at Cuenca and Mejia, located in a beautiful 17th-century colonial house which provides a splendid and appropriate setting for the works on display. The former home of the Marquis of Vallacis now exhibits selected artwork from the School of Quito. Among its paintings, sculptures and crafts are works by Samaniego, Caspicara, and, once again the Master Bernardo de Legarda.

Map, page 148

LEFT: street in La Ronda. **RIGHT:** enjoying the sunshine in the Plaza de la Independencia.

Quito's gold convent

If you are in the mood for more history and architecture, turn down Calle Mejia when you leave the museum, and at the corner of Mejía and Flores streets you will find the **Monasterio de San Agustín** (open Mon–Fri 9am–12.30pm, 3–6pm; entrance fee) where Ecuador's first (short-lived) Act of Independence was signed in August 1809. Inside its flower-filled patio, robed monks pace, praying against a backdrop of oil paintings by Miguel de Santiago, who spent most of his life in the monastery illustrating the life of St Augustine. The third floor of one wing of the cloister, which is open to the public, houses restoration workshops of the Cultural Heritage Institute. The interior of the San Agustín church is an intriguing mixture of Gothic and arabesque styles and the complex was once dubbed the "Gold Convent" by Quiteños for its rich decor.

Quito's new trolley system is 11km (6 miles) long with 40 stops, and carries 14,000 passengers an hour.

The room where the independence document was signed is called the Sala Capitular and contains a portable altar in 18th-century baroque style attributed to the Indian artist Pampite. In San Agustín's catacombs are the remains of the independence leaders killed by the Spanish loyalists a year after they joined the revolution.

If you walk northeast along Calle Flores (that is, towards the New Town), you find the **Teatro Nacional Sucre** , the city's most beautiful theater, where both concerts and plays are staged. This is the home of the National Symphony Orchestra, which usually performs here regularly, but at present the theater is closed for restoration. Continue for two blocks up Calle Guayaquil and turn left on Esmeraldas to the **Fundación Cinco** (opening hours vary) located in a graceful colonial mansion. Funded by the Banco Central, it stages changing modern art exhibitions.

BELOW: watching the world go by in colonial Quito.

Where old meets new

From here, Calle Guayaquil, with its 19th-century buildings, leads toward the area where the past is left behind. The **Monasterio de San Blas**, in fact, is one of the last colonial complexes before you come to modern Quito lying ahead at the point where old meets new. The landmark is the long, triangular **Parque La Alameda** with an impressive monument of the liberation leader Simón Bolívar. The park contains a number of other busts and statues in honor of famous Latin Americans. Among them is Manuelita Saenz – the Quito-born woman who was Bolívar's companion throughout the revolution. There are also monuments here commemorating the French mission that traveled to Ecuador in 1736 to measure the arc of the equatorial line in order to work out the circumference of the earth. Charles-Marie de la Condamine, the expedition's leader, and Pedro Maldonaldo, an Ecuadorian member of the team, are the best known.

It was in 1598 that Spanish officials in Quito obtained permission to build the Alameda, an area for recreation, brightened by gardens, flowers and shade trees. The consensus was to place this park at the juncture of a natural lagoon – nowadays used by canoeists. At the center of the park is South America's oldest observatory, the **Observatorio Astronómico** ℗ started in 1864 and completed 23 years later. It is used by meteorologists and astronomers and is open to visitors on Saturday mornings.

The small church of **El Belén** ℚ (open daily; admisssion free) on the park's north side is a favorite subject of Quito's artists. It marks the site where the first mass in Quito was said after the city was founded by the Spanish. Simple and graceful, this church's lone nave contains a magnificent Christ believed to be the work of Indian artist Caspicara.

Map, page 160

BELOW: the Casa de la Cultura Ecuatoriana.

Modern reflections.

Two blocks up Avenida 6 de Diciembre and right on Calle Montalvo is the **Palacio Legislativo **, a new government building with the history of Ecuador immortalized in carved stone along its north side. If you take the Avenida Gran Colombia from here to Avenida Paz y Miño, you can see the hilltop home of the **Instituto Geográfico Militar** (Geographical Military Institute) (open Tues–Fri 8am–noon, 2–4pm; entrance fee). There is a museum and a planetarium, distinguishable by its white dome, where shows, lasting about half an hour, take place several times a day.

If you turn right, however, from the Palacio Legislative, and continue up 6 de Diciembre, you will come to the **Parque El Ejido**. This park, the largest in central Quito, is a favorite spot – especially at weekends – for shy Otavalo Indians, picnickers, soccer players, couples out for a stroll, energetic children and street vendors seeking the park's shady trees as respite from the warm sun. Here women carry huge trays of food on their heads, offering for sale *fritada, papas y mote*, portions of grilled meat, potatoes and corn.

Banks, boutiques and bargains

At the north end of El Ejido, from Avenida Patria to Colón, lies Quito's modern tourist and business area with hotels, offices, banks and restaurants. **Avenida Amazonas** is home to travel agencies, art galleries, money exchangers, outdoor cafés and the double-decker airport buses. This is the best spot for strolling and shopping, with stops for cool drinks or snacks at the many restaurants and pastry shops along the route. Shopping bargains range from well-made handicrafts to clothing in boutiques carrying the latest fashions. In the **Colón Internacional Hotel** at the south end of the street is a shopping gallery with a branch of Libri

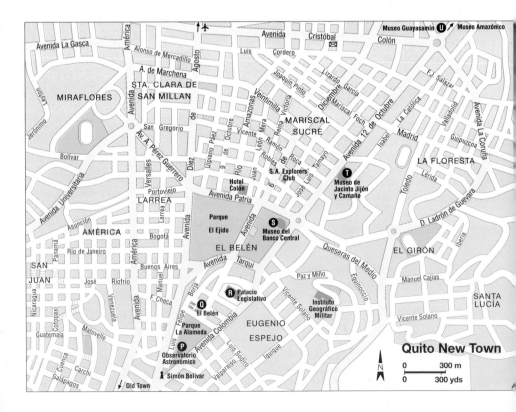

Quito New Town

0   300 m
0   300 yds

Mundi, the city's top bookstore carrying English-language titles and maps. You should also follow the parallel street, Juan León Mera, another good place for cafés and shopping, to the bookstore's main branch, and the popular Art Forum Café. Rather surprisingly for a capital city, most of the shops in Quito close on Saturday afternoons, and it is not unusual to find streets such as Amazonas, which are bustling during the week, almost empty at the weekend.

If you feel in the mood for more culture, instead of shopping and eating, head eastward from the park, along Avenida Patria, to the **Casa de la Cultura Ecuatoriana**, a large circular glass building which houses the **Museo del Banco Central** 🛇 (open Tues–Fri 10am–6pm; Saturday and the second Sunday of the month 10am–noon; entrance fee), which was inaugurated in June, 1995. This stylish presentation of Ecuadorian history, demonstrated through its art works, should not be missed. The spacious museum actually includes five connected salons, devoted respectively to archaeology, gold, colonial art, republican art and modern art.

As you walk through the collections in chronological order you will gain a sense of Ecuador's proud history as seen through the eyes of its artists. Each of the pre-Colombian cultures is represented by artifacts – including pottery, tools, jewelry – and well constructed dioramas. The highlight of the gold room is a ceremonial mask made of gold and silver. The transition to the colonial collection is marked by a gold sun, the god of the Incas, and a silver cross inlaid with precious stones, an early piece fashioned by the conquering Spanish. The museum also contains pieces from the famous Quito School, including one of only two known sculptures of the pregnant Virgin Mary.

The republican art collection has wonderful paintings of mountain and jungle landscapes as well as themes exploring national identity and social change. The indigenous people's struggle for freedom is forcefully presented in the paintings of Eduardo Kingman in the modern collection. The museum also displays many works by Camilo Egas, one of Ecuador's best known contemporary artists, who died in 1961 at the age of 73 (see *A Nation of Painters*, page 113). Another salon is reserved for presentations of work that are rotated every month – it's worth checking what is on while you are in the city.

Written explanations throughout the museum are in Spanish and English and guided tours are available in Spanish, English, German and French.

The **Museo de la Casa de la Cultura Ecuatoriana** (opening hours as for the Museo del Banco Central, above) is housed in the same building, and contains a less comprehensive collection of art from the republican period to modern times. A separate room of the museum displays musical instruments, many of them several centuries old, from all over the world. There is also a display of traditional dress from various indigenous cultures. A movie theater and concert hall are also housed in the Casa de la Cultura.

Just two blocks away, another fine museum with archaeological artifacts is run by the Universidad Catolica on Avenida 12 de Octubre. The **Museo de Jacinto Jijón y Camaño** 🛈 (open Mon–Fri 9am–4pm; entrance fee) contains the private collection donated by

Map, page 160

Shops Closed Sat. P.M.

Av. Río Amazonas

Most tourists gravitate towards Amazonas.

BELOW: skyscrapers over El Ejido park.

the family of the aristocratic archaeologist after his death. It was the work of Jijón y Camaño that provided the basis for the modern-day theories on how pre-Hispanic Indians lived in Ecuador; his books on the subject are valuable rarities. The museum's collection includes *aribalos*, the graceful fluted-mouthed jars with pointed bottoms that are synonymous with pre-Inca cultures throughout the Andes, as well as a wide assortment of religious idols, masks, weapons and shell and bone works. The museum also houses a small collection of the School of Quito colonial art.

Art and artifacts

If you continue for a few minutes along the pleasant tree-lined Avenida 12 de Octubre you will come to the **Museo Amazónico** (12 de Octubre 1430 y Wilson; open Mon–Fri 9am–1pm, 2–6pm; entrance fee), which used to be called the Museo Shuar.

A brand new stadium in the north of Quito, the biggest in Ecuador, opened in 1997 with a capacity for 55,000 people.

This interesting little museum is run by the Salesian Mission, and has a collection of artifacts from Amazon Indian tribes and a number of cultural publications. The Hotel Quito, the Hotel Radisson and the Hotel Oro Verde are all situated nearby.

BELOW:
Guayasamín's sculptures at the museum.

But this is a slight diversion from the route numbered on the map, which takes you to the **Museo Guayasamín** ❶ (open Mon–Fri 9.30am–1pm, 3–6.30pm; Sat 9.30am–1pm; entrance fee) at Calle Bosmediano 543, in one of the city's most beautiful modern houses perched on a hillside overlooking Quito, in the Bellavista district. It is quite a trek uphill and it might be better to take a taxi – drivers always know where to find the museum – or catch a Bellavista bus. This is perhaps the most intriguing colonial art collection in the city. Set up by artist

Oswaldo Guayasamín, the complex is divided into three: a colonial art gallery (Guayasamín's own collection), the artist's gallery where he displays and sells his work, and a studio used by him and his students.

Map, page 160

Provocative and political, Guayasamín's art has made him perhaps the country's best-known artist and the gallery of his works should not be missed. Born of an Indian father and *mestizo* mother, his work delves heavily into themes connected with his mixed culture and this museum complex represents 30 years of planning (see *A Nation of Painters,* page 113). A collection of sculpture is displayed on the flower-splashed tile roof. After your visit to the museum, stroll through the eucalyptus forests in the **Parque Metropolitano**, which has splendid views of Quito and the nearby peaks of Cotopaxi and Cayambe, before going back into town.

If you would like to see what Quiteños do in their spare time, you could wander back down Bosmediano to the large **Parque Carolina** located just off Avenida Eloy Alfaro. The playing fields on weekends are crowded with soccer and volleyball players and runners, and there are usually groups of people picnicking. During the month of August, Sunday outdoor concerts are given by the Banda Sinfónica.

The **Museo de Ciencias Naturales** (Natural History Museum) (open Mon–Fri 8.30am–4.30pm; Sat 9am–1pm; entrance fee) is located on the south side of the park, at the corner of Rumipamba and Los Shyris. It has a good collection of endemic species and is worth a visit before you go to see the flora and fauna in the wild, as it will help you to identify some of the species you may find. Nearby a game of outdoor life-sized chess can be enjoyed at the **Café Ajedrez** (Chess Café), adding to the diversity of things to do and see in Quito.

BELOW: the Banco de Azuay in Quito's New Town.

COLONIAL ARCHITECTURE

Catholic concepts, indigenous motifs and inspiration blend together with Arabic influences to create the Colonial style which has been carefully preserved in Quito and Cuenca

When the Spanish conquered Ecuador they brought with them priests from different monastic orders: Franciscans, Augustinians and Dominicans, and later the Jesuits. Within 50 days of the foundation of Quito in 1534 the Franciscan monks had begun constructing their own church. This was the first classic example of Colonial architecture.

Each religious order was assigned land by the Spanish Crown and each competed against the other in the construction of churches, convents and plazas. Brother Jodocko Ricke, a Flemish Franciscan, set up an informal school for indigenous children to teach them religion and art. It was the first school of fine arts in South America.

The Franciscans discovered the creative skills of the indigenous people and also brought over talented converted Muslims. Sun motifs (the Sun being the principal Inca god) are commonly found along side Madonna and child representations, and ceilings often show Mudejar influence. This blend of European and indigenous ideas created the Quiteño school of art and architecture.

The Jesuits strengthened the arts movement when they arrived in 1586. In the following 250 years ornate churches with richly adorned sacristies, carved choirs and fine paintings flourished. Workshops and guilds were established and by the middle of the 18th century 30 guilds in Quito controlled all artistic production.

ALTAR ▷
As the influence of baroque art became more prevalent the altar pieces grew more and more elaborate. Some were overpowering three-dimensional structures, decorated in gold leaf with rich paintings and statues

△ **STAINED GLASS**
This stained glass window depicting Moses, which brightens Cuenca cathedral, is a fine example of the florid Colonial style

△ **CUENCA: A COLONIAL INHERITANCE**
The center of Cuenca, founded on the site of the Inca city of Tomebamba, has numerous 16th- and 17th-century churches which demonstrate the apogee of Colonial architecture.

THE SCHOOL OF QUITO

The niches of early Colonial altar pieces were first decorated with paintings, but polychrome statues became dominant later additions. When the first Colonial buildings were constructed, statues were shipped over to Ecuador from Andalucia in Spain. However, by the 18th century a distinct style of Quiteño art had emerged.

Baroque, rococo and neo-classical styles from Europe reached Quito and were interpreted in a new way. Artists used different mediums: stone, ivory, tagua, clay, porcelain and metal, but polychrome statues made from wood were the most popular. Pictured above is a typical 17th-century figure from the church of San Francisco.

Native cedar wood and sometimes alder from the hills surrounding Quito were used. Smaller figurines were usually made from balsa wood. Trees were cut only at the full moon so that the sap would have risen to the highest level possible, making the wood stronger for carving. First the artists primed the statues and then painted directly on them with bright primary colors. They developed attention to detail and realism, reddening the cheeks, using false eyelashes and nails and glass eyes. The figures were sometimes dressed from head to toe in sumptuous colors and floral designs.

◁ **DOMES AND BELL TOWERS**
The domes and bell towers of the 17th-century building boom dominate the whitewashed buildings of Quito in Renaissance and baroque styles with many later neo-classical additions.

△ **FLOURISHING FIGURES**
By the 18th century, as artistic individuality flourished, secular figures, including nudes, were incorporated with the religious themes.

△ **PILLARED PORTAL**
This doorway in Cuenca's old cathedral illustrates another intrinsic facet of Colonial architecture: the great variety of columns, spiral, smooth and striated, which were used in portals, facades, altars and towers. The building was begun in 1557, the year the city was founded.

DAY TRIPS FROM QUITO

Mountains, forests, thermal springs, and wildlife sanctuaries all are within easy reach of the capital – and the Virgin of El Quinche is renowned for her miracles

Map, page 168

Quito

ECUADOR

Quito makes a good starting point for many day-long excursions into the lush surrounding Andean Sierra. By hiring a car, taking a tour or using public transport or taxis, there are several popular trips into a region crowded with mountain views, waterfalls, thermal baths, and peaceful villages.

Buses to the Equatorial Line Monument, **La Mitad del Mundo ❶**, leave every half-hour from the market place near La Merced church in Quito's old town, or you can pick them up on Avenida America in the new town. It's about a half-hour trip to the monument (22km (14 miles) to the north of Quito, located right on latitude O°, which provides an irresistible opportunity to straddle both hemispheres. The monument is a rather clumsy looking thing, topped by a huge brass globe, but it's a very popular spot, particularly at the equinoxes (March 21 and September 21) when the sun is directly overhead and neither monument nor visitors cast a shadow. The monument forms the focal point of a park and leisure area with gift shops and restaurants. (including the Equinoccio, which distributes certificates recording your visit), and has a good museum inside (open Tues–Fri 9am–3pm; Sat–Sun 10am–1pm). A lift leads to the top for fine views.

About 4km (2 miles) beyond the monument, toward the village of Calacalí, at Km 4 to the right, is the **Reserva Geobotánica Pululahua ❷**, centered on the biggest volcanic crater in South America. A paved road leads to the rim of the volcano, from where the view of farms on the crater floor is impressive. A rough path leads down from the rim, and the interior of the crater has its own micro-climate, with rich vegetation and diverse bird life.

Also to the north of Quito is the **Reserva Biológic Maquipucuna ❸** (contact the Quito office at Baquerizo 238 y Tamayo, tel: 507-200). Take the new coast road through Calacalí to Nanegalito (61km/35 miles). In the village, take a right turn. It is 19km (12 miles) from Nanegalito, signposted along the way. The reserve consists of steeply-sloped, undisturbed cloudforest, with a great diversity of fauna and flora. The Reserva Bellavista (tel: 09-490891) is on the old road to Mindo at Km 68, also located in lush forest, with great views over the valley. The **Bosque Mindo-Nambillo**, near Mindo, is a protected reserve that is home to a wide range of birds, as well as orchids and bromeliads.

Just below the Hotel Quito lies the tiny village of **Guápulo** with its four-century-old church containing work by some of the country's best known 17th-century artists, for this was the founding spot of the School of Quito. This church and former convent has a pulpit carved by Indian sculptor Juan Menacho which is unquestionably the loveliest in Quito, with Christian and Indian images intertwined in the carving.

Carry on down the mountain, crossing the Machán-

LEFT: Cotopaxi, seen from Quito. **BELOW:** the monument, La Mitad del Mundo.

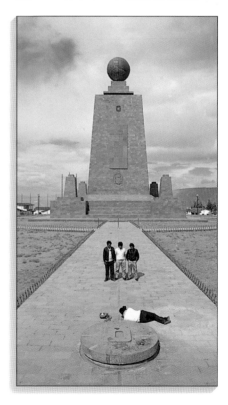

gara river. The next major road on the right (14.3km/11 miles from Quito) leads to the warm-water swimming pools of Cununyacü (open daily, 7am–3.45pm). Back on the main road you reach the village of Cumbayá where a road branches right to Guangopolo, a favorite picnic spot along the river and a fine place for birdwatching. It continues to the valley of Chillos, through unpopulated countryside, winding along the San Pedro river. The road joins up with the new bypass, the Nuevo Oriental, which hooks into the road to **Tumbaco** ❹ which has a good restaurant, El Tambo, and many Quiteño weekend houses.

For horse riding enthusiasts, trips can be arranged from the Reserva Geobotánica Pululahua.

Miracles and hot springs

The road through the Tumbaco valley, passes through the sanctuary of **El Quinche** ❺, a point of attraction for pilgrims from the whole of the northern Sierra. The Virgin of El Quinche is renowned for her miracles, and is a favorite among drivers and transport workers. The walls of the church, covered in gold-leaf, are hung with paintings of miracles performed during the past four centuries, each with its explanatory inscription. Devout Catholics from Quito go to ask the Virgin's blessing whenever they undertake some new venture.

Descend the main road from El Quinche to the south (unpaved but well-maintained). The view is wonderful, and snow and sub-tropical forests lie close together. At Km 59, the small Lago Papallacta 6 is renowned for trout-fishing. (The village of Papallacta is better known for the oil pipline which emerges here.) At Km 60, a narrow road branches off to the springs of Huanonumpa, more commonly known as the thermal springs of Papallacta. Recently renovated and expanded, these are the most attractively developed hot springs in Ecuador. Stay overnight in the comfortable hotel and go for a dip in one of its pri-

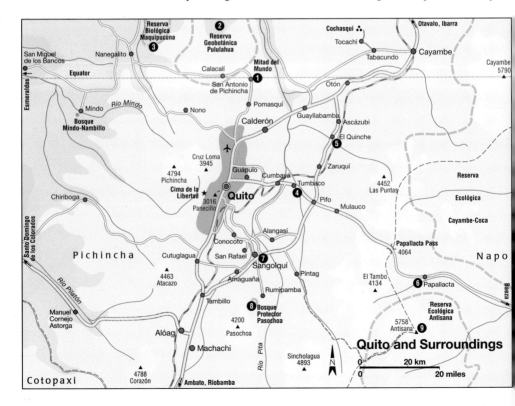

Quito and Surroundings

vate pools. The public pools by the restaurant are crowded on weekends. Reservations can be made in Quito: Foch 635 y Reina Victoria, tel/fax: 548521.

The **Valle de los Chillos**, an area of thermal springs, lies east of Quito. There is a fine descent into the valley on the Via Oriental and the Autopista de Los Chillos. The highway crosses the valley's main road in San Rafael (12km/ 8 miles). Ahead lies the village of **Sangolqui** ❼. Its Sunday market attracts indigenous people in traditional dress, and there are thermal baths nearby.

To the north of here (taking a left at San Rafael) are the thermal springs of Ushimana, El Tingo and La Merced. The Hostería Angamarca has a swimming pool, restaurant and comfortable rooms. The pools of La Merced have picnic and camping areas nearby.

To the south of Sangolqui is the village of **Amaguaña** which can be reached by bus from Quito (about an hour's drive). A few kilometers from Amaguaña, set around an extinct volcano, is the **Bosque Protector Pasochoa** ❽. This small protected area is the only one near Quito that has kept its Andean vegetation intact, and the woods are a sanctuary for tropical birds and native plants (orchids bloom from February to May). For excursions contact Fundación Natura in Quito at Rumipamba 1019 y Yugoslavia, tel: 242758).

The road to the Antisana mountains begins at the main plaza of the village of Alangasí (just north of Sangolqui and 33km/20 miles from Quito) and continues southwards past some unusual lava formations. The road to the foot of the volcano requires a 4-wheel drive vehicle. **Volcán Antisana** ❾ has three peaks, covered by snow and glaciers, which are very difficult to climb. In the surrounding ecological reserve condors, rainbow ducks and other birds may be seen. It is well worth the effort to get to this extraordinary wilderness.

Map, page 168

LEFT: the church at Guápulo. **RIGHT:** miracles recorded at El Quinche.

GOING NORTH

*From Otavalo, Ecuador's greatest market,
to the surrounding lakes and artisans' villages
and up to the Colombian border*

Map,
pages
174/5

he province of **Imbabura**, just a short step north of Quito, is one of
Ecuador's most popular destinations. Its numerous Andean volcanoes,
lakes and valleys combine to make a landscape of extraordinary beauty,
while the variety of local indigenous groups mean that the northern Sierra is one
of the most culturally vibrant regions in the country. Even more beguiling for
many travelers is that Imbabura Province is a rich source of handicrafts: it is
home to the woodcarvers of San Antonio, the leatherworkers of Cotacachi and
– most famously – the weavers of Otavalo.

Beyond the capital

Leaving **Quito ①** behind, most visitors take the shortest route to Imbabura,
some 100km (60 miles) along the paved Pan-American Highway passing
straight through the barren landscape of northern Pichincha. But for those who
have time to explore, there are a number of ways of reaching the province and
several places worth visiting on the way. There are buses from Quito to the towns
numbered on the map on page 174. Getting to some of the villages takes a litle
more ingenuity if you don't have your own transport, but many are walkable
from the nearest town, and round-trip taxi journeys are not expensive.

The main road passes through **Guayllabamba**. Surrounded by dry rocky hills, sparsely covered with tufts
of grass, the Guayllabamba valley is warm and fertile,
famous for its orchards and local fruit, such as the *chi-
rimoya* (custard apple) and the local variety of avocado
pear, which is small, roundish and black-skinned. Visitors are pressed to buy the produce, and the local
women compete by offering a *yapa* (one extra for the
same price). A specialty is the tasty *locro de cueros*
(potato soup with pork rind) with avocados on the side.

Two roads lead out of Guayllabamba towards
Cayambe: the left-hand one, via **Tabacundo**, follows a
deep ravine, with curious rock formations. After crossing the Río Guayllabamba it is possible to make a
detour along the river-side down to the tranquil villages
of **Puellaro** and **Perucho**, where oranges grow, and little seems to have changed for several decades.

Another option is a visit to the archaeological site of
Cochasqui, on the southern slopes of **Mount Mojanda**, a short distance from Tabacundo. Some 15 flat-
topped pyramids and 30 mounds are believed to have
been built by Caranqui Indians around the 13th century,
although some date from AD900. Take a short or an
extended guided tour from the resident guardian, and
learn about religious and funeral practices, living styles
and even the astrological discoveries made in that era.

The small town of **Cayambe**, under the perpetual
vigilance of the extinct volcano of the same name, is

PRECEDING PAGES:
Otavaleña displays
rich tapestries.
LEFT: headgear of
Otavalo women.
BELOW: Saturday
market in Otavalo.

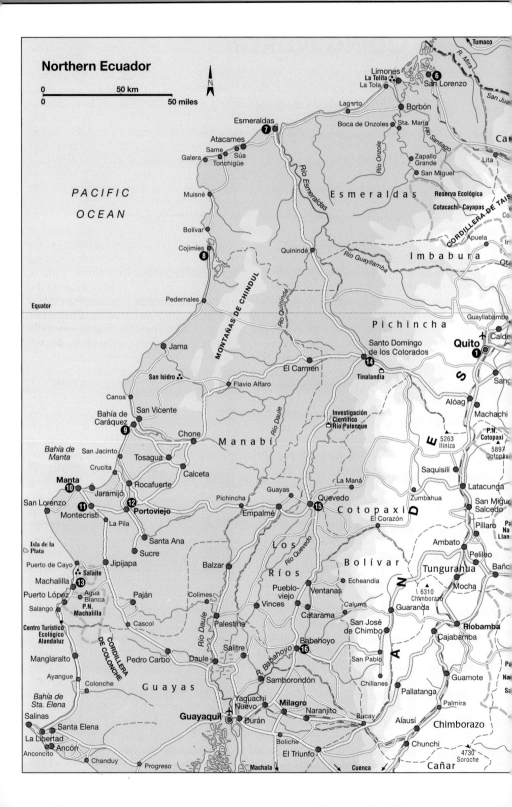

Northern Ecuador

0   50 km

0   50 miles

N

PACIFIC

OCEAN

Equator

Tumaco

R. Mira

Limones
La Tolita
La Tola
San Lorenzo ⑥

Lagarto

Borbón

Esmeraldas ⑦
Boca de Onzoles   Sta. María

Río Santiago

R. San Jua

Ca

Atacames
Same   Súa
Galera   Tonchigüe

Zapallo
Grande
San Miguel

Lita

Río Onzole

Río Esmeraldas

Muisné

Esmeraldas

Reserva Ecológica
Cotacachi-Cayapas

CORDILLERA DE TAI

Bolívar

Apuela

Ir

Cojimíes ⑧

Quinindé

Río Guayllamba

Imbabura

Ot

Pedernales

Río Quininde

MONTAÑAS DE CHINDUL

Guayllabamba

Pichincha

Calde

Jama

Santo Domingo
de los Colorados ⑭

Quito ①

San Isidro

El Carmen

Tinalandia

Sang

Flavio Alfaro

Canoa

Alóag

Bahía de
Caráquez ⑨

San Vicente

Investigación
Científico
Río Palenque

Machachi

Chone

Río Daule

5263
Iliniza

P.N.
Cotopaxi

5897
Cotopax

Bahía de
Manta

San Jacinto

Manabí

Saquisilí

Manta ⑩

Tosagua

Crucita

Calceta

La Maná

Latacunga

Rocafuerte

Pichincha

Guayas

Quevedo ⑮

Zumbahua

San Migue
Salcedo

San Lorenzo ⑪

Jaramijó

Portoviejo ⑫

Empalmé

Cotopaxi

El Corazón

Píllaro

Pa
Na
Llan

Montecristi

La Pila

Santa Ana

Los

Río Quevedo

Bolívar

Ambato

Pelileo

Tungurahua

Baño

Isla de la
Plata

Sucre

Jipijapa

Balzar

Ríos

Echeandía

Mocha

Puerto de Cayo

Salaite

Pueblo-
viejo

Ventanas

6310
Chimborazo

Machalilla ⑬

Puerto López

Agua
Blanca

Paján

Colimes

Vinces

Caluma

Guaranda

Salango

P.N.
Machalilla

Catarama

San José
de Chimbo

Riobamba

Centro Turístico
Ecológico
Alandaluz

Cascol

Palestina

Babahoyo ⑯

Cajabamba

Río Daule

CORDILLERA DE COLONCHE

Salitre

San Pablo

Manglaralto

Pedro Carbo

Daule

Río Babahoyo

Guamote

Na

Ayangue

Colonche

Samborondón

Chillanes

Pallatanga

Sa

Guayas

Bahía de
Sta. Elena

Yaguachi
Nuevo

Milagro

Palmira

Salinas

Guayaquil

Durán

Naranjito

Bucay

Álausí

Chimborazo

Santa Elena

La Libertad

Ancón

Boliche

Chunchi

Anconcito

Chanduy

Progreso

El Triunfo

Machala

Cuenca

4730
Soroche

Cañar

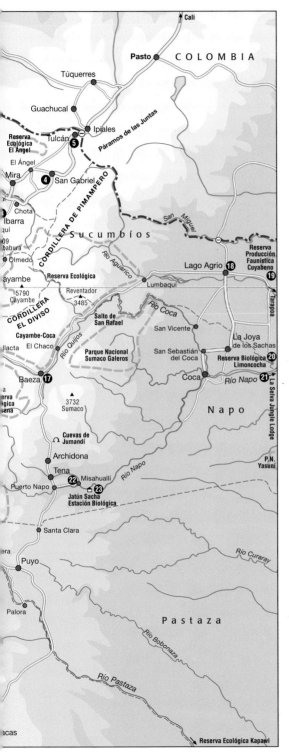

worth a stop-over to try its famous local cheese, especially *queso de hoja*, and the *biscochos*, a savory shortbread.

A few kilometers south of Cayambe is the **Hostería Guachala**, a *hacienda* dating back to 1580, and said to be the oldest in the country. It was renovated and converted into a hotel in 1993. Set in pleasant grounds with a swimming pool and opportunities nearby for horse-back riding, it is an attractive place where it is easy to conjure up the rich history that its owner, Diego Boniface, is more than willing to reveal to you.

Going north from Cayambe, a turn in the main road unexpectedly brings into view Laguna San Pablo and, towering behind it, **Volcán Imbabura**, with its concave slopes covered in tiny fields. Opposite, though often enveloped in clouds, is its sister mountain, **Cotacachi**, and on the flat valley floor between the two, known as "the valley of the dawn," lies the town of Otavalo.

Ecuador's greatest market

At dawn on Saturday mornings, the market square (called the Poncho Plaza) in **Otavalo ❷** gets busy as the stall-holders set up their displays. Handicraft workers from the outlying districts come to negotiate their wares with traders before the tourists arrive. By 9am the square is a feast of colors and textures: rolls of cloth, thick blankets for the cold mountain nights, woollen tapestry wall-hangings with pictures of mountains and llamas, embroidered blouses and dresses, chunky hand-knitted sweaters, long patterned belts or *fajas,* such as the Indian women wind round their waists, and *cintas*, tapes they use to bind their long hair. The square is a maze of stands and narrow alleys with just enough room to pass.

Tourists making day-trips from Quito arrive by bus at around 10am, and the haggling begins. The Otavalo Indians are experienced in business, can size up their customer, and know just how far to lower their price. Several of them even speak English. Despite the crowds, the atmosphere is calm and relaxed – muffled, perhaps, by the walls of cloth. Most of the handicrafts are tailored to foreign tastes, although some of the Otavaleño designs are reworkings of traditional motifs. The style of clothing sold to the public is adjusted each year according to fashion and demand, and many high-quality handicrafts are sold in Quito or abroad, and never appear at all at the Otavalo market. But there is plenty to choose from: the Otavaleño work is always attractive and usually well made (though finishings are sometimes careless), and at prices that seem a dream to most foreigners.

Saturday is also market day for the local population. At the north end of the Poncho Plaza is hot prepared food and a corner market for such animals as *cuys* (guinea-pigs) and rabbits. The market plaza for the larger farm animals is at the western edge of town. Just follow the unmistakable evidence left by these animals along Calle Morales and across the Pan-American Highway.

In parts of the Poncho Plaza and along Calle Jaramillo vendors sell every item of Otavaleño traditional dress, including the intricate hand embroidery of the Indian women's blouses, as well as fleece, yarn, loom parts, aniline dyes and carders. Vendors also sell clothing worn by other indigenous groups in Imbabura Province and by *mestizos* and whites.

The incredible food market

Calle Jaramillo runs south into the permanent food market, which overflows on Saturdays with a mind-boggling array of vendors and food. You'll find every kind of fruit, vegetable, grain and meat imaginable as well as some you'd rather not imagine, much less eat. Don't become so engrossed in your shopping spree in the Poncho Plaza that you miss the food market because if weaving represents one means of subsistence, agriculture represents the other.

A young Otavaleña in typical distinctive dress.

BELOW: the colonial Hostería Cusín near Otavalo, now a hotel.

Map, page 178

Outside the town

While day tours to Otavalo from Quito are popular, many independent travelers arrive on the Friday night before the market and stay for the weekend to explore the lush surrounding countryside. Probably the best base for doing this from is the most unusual hotel in the Otavalo region and a tourist attraction in itself: the **Hostería Cusín**. Located several kilometers out of town, the Hostería was once the main *hacienda* of the area. The new British-born owner has restored the building to its former splendor: the rooms are crowded with antique Spanish religious paintings, wooden armchairs and candelabra, while outside are elegant gardens with ponds and banks of glorious flowers. A night at the hostería is cheap, and the price includes three meals from one of the best kitchens in Ecuador – creating *haute cuisine* versions of the local specialties. You can also drop in for lunch or dinner, or look in as part of a taxi-tour around the area.

The crystal-clear **Laguna San Pablo** Ⓐ is easily accessible from the hostería. On its shores there are several places where you can hire boats and horses. A walk around the lake shore is delightful and there is also a regular bus route. It is a favorite place for water sports, and during September there is an annual race across its width – though it takes courage to plunge into the icy waters.

Also worth visiting are the beautiful **Lagunas de Mojanda**, about 18km (11 miles) south of Otavalo. A dirt road leads to the lakes, divided by hills, the habitat of wild rabbits. There are places to camp, although the nights get very cold.

Artists at work

The villages close to Otavalo provide a chance to see another aspect of the handicraft trade: the craftsmen themselves at work. In nearby **Carabuela**, they make

BELOW: one of the Lagunas de Mojanda, near Tabacunda.

scarves, woollen gloves, ponchos and *fajas*, some still using the pre-Hispanic loom. Other craftsmen in the village specialize in making Andean harps.

The village of **Peguche ᴮ**, too, has its weavers, and is well worth a stop. Peguche is about 3km (2 miles) northeast of Otavalo, and is the home of several Indian musical groups – among them is *Ñanda Mañachi*, an ensemble that has become famous in Europe and North America for its haunting Andean tunes.

About 3km (2 miles) east of Peguche, **Agato ᶜ** is worth a visit if you are interested in textiles. The Tahuantinsuyo Workshop still uses the traditional looms and natural dyes and makes some lovely items, which are often for sale at the Hostería Cusín. You can reach Agato by bus or taxi from Otavalo.

Another nearby village of artisans is **Ilumán ᴰ** (there are occasional trains and buses, or it's an easy walk). The inhabitants make double-sided ponchos, felt hats and tapestries. But Ilumán is also famous for its traditional healers or *curanderos*, who use guinea-pigs, candles and ritual stones, as well as herbs and alcohol, to diagnose sicknesses and chase away evil spirits or negative energy.

The best-known shaman of the region is the legendary "Taita Marcos," who lives in **San Juan de la Calera** near Cotacachi. His house is worth a visit: he uses an altar built with thousands of bottles donated by grateful patients from all over the world, and adorned with pictures of saints.

Master leatherworkers

About 15km (10 miles) north of Otavalo is the village of **Cotacachi ᴱ**, Ecuador's leatherwork center. Mostly made of tough cowhide, the goods have increased in quality recently, and there is an excellent choice of jackets, skirts and boots, as well as briefcases, bags, riding equipment and wallets.

Handicrafts strictly for the tourist market.

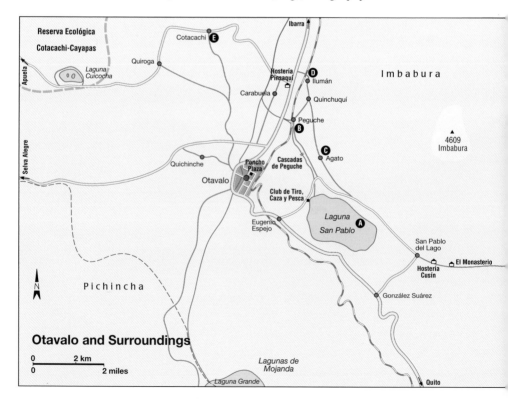

Otavalo and Surroundings

It is worth tasting the typical dish of Cotacachi: *carne colorada*, made of sun-dried and fried pork or beef, colored with *achiote* (a red seed), and served with avocados, jacket potatoes, a cheese, onion and egg sauce, and corn. The chefs at the restaurant El Mesón de la Rosas are said to have invented this dish.

Map,
pages
174/5

Further north
The highway northwards from Otavalo curves around Volcán Imbabura and descends towards Ibarra, passing through **Atuntaqui**, which is reputed to have the best *fritada* (deep fried pork) of the whole region.

Shortly before entering Ibarra, a right-hand turn leads into **San Antonio**, where the specialty is woodcarving. The visitor can watch the craftsmen at work and see the finished articles on sale. Typical examples are the ornamental carved figures of people and animals, in any size from 7cm (3 inches) to 1.2 meters (4ft) tall; they also make furniture, chessmen, lamps and mirror frames.

A shorter, much slower, but very attractive route to Ibarra is along the old Pan-American Highway from Cayambe, heading around the far side of Volcán Imbabura via the villages of **Olmedo** and **Zuleta**. This narrow cobbled road, full of pot-holes, winds through several of the region's oldest *haciendas*: along the way, it presents an image of the traditional rural structure of Ecuador, mixed with modern farming techniques. The *hacienda* at Zuleta, famous for its embroiderers, has several handicraft shops.

The white city
The provincial town of **Ibarra ❸**, about 22km (13 miles) north of Otavalo, is quite large, with a population of 80,000, and enjoys one of the best climates of

BELOW: final touches to a carving at San Antonio.

the Sierra – neither too hot, nor too cold – due to its moderate altitude of 2,225 meters (around 7,000ft). Despite severe damage and destruction in at least two earthquakes, Ibarra has retained a colonial style. Its streets are cobbled, and the town's low red-roofed buildings all have white-painted walls, which has earned Ibarra the nickname of "the white city." The population is an interesting cultural mix of Indians, blacks and *mestizos*.

Typical foods include *arrope de mora* (blackberry syrup) and *nogadas* (a sweet made with walnuts). And the original *helados de paila* (water ices) can be found at the Rosalia Suarez ice-cream parlor. These ices are made by continuously beating fruit juice in a copper *paila* or round-bottomed pan, while it sits on a pile of ice.

You may hear Ibarra's nickname "the white city" translated into Spanish as La Ciudad Blanca.

Close to Ibarra is **Lago Yaguarcocha**. Its name means "blood lake" in Quichua, because in the 15th century the tough inhabitants of this region held out against the Inca invaders for some 16 years, until they were finally defeated and massacred on the shore. Today the lake is sometimes used for sailing, but is mainly known for the motor-racing track that surrounds it. Car races take place on this circuit during the September festival celebrations.

Sugar cane valley

On the other side of the mountain lies the warm **Chota Valley**, the lowest point in the northern Sierra, where sugar-cane, vines and tropical fruits grow. There are several thermal springs in this valley, such as **Chachimbiro**, though the road to them is somewhat arduous.

The Chota Valley is the only zone of the Sierra which has a predominantly black population. Today peaceable farmers, the older members still tell tales of

LEFT: trinkets for sale at Otavalo market.
RIGHT: bargaining for a cow.

their ancestors who fought against slavery on the plantations of Colombia.

In the village of **Chota** (about an hour's drive from Ibarra) a concert hall regularly presents the *bomba negra* music of the local black population, which is a mixture of the Indian music of the Sierra with African-style instruments and rhythms. One of the typical "instruments" is played by blowing tunes on a leaf held between the hands.

On the Colombian border

The highway north from the Chota Valley climbs steeply with twists and turns into the Province of **Carchi**, over the high pass of **El Angel**, and down to the frontier town of Tulcán. This is rich agricultural country, which produces dozens of varieties of potatoes. It also has a thriving trade in contraband goods with Colombia. Carchi, incidentally, is the only province of the Sierra that has practically no indigenous population. The **Reserva Ecológica El Angel** preserves a large expanse of this region, where Andean condors can sometimes be seen.

From El Angel you can do a great hike heading down toward the coast through the **Reserva Cerro Golondrinas**. For more information contact the foundation at Isobela la Católica 1559, Quito, tel: 226602.

About 40km (25 miles) south of Tulcán is Carchi's sanctuary, the **Grotto of La Paz**, near the village of **San Gabriel ❹** where pilgrims go to see the statue of the Virgin sheltered in a natural cave. There are also two splendid waterfalls just outside the village. In **Tulcán ❺**, the border town, the main attraction is the topiary garden in the cemetery, where huge cypress hedges are clipped into the shapes of animals, houses and geometric figures. It is a bizarre and impressive sight, and worth a visit if you are overnighting here on your way to Colombia.

Map, pages 174/5

BELOW: topiary at the Tulcán cemetery.

THE WEAVERS OF OTAVALO

Ecuadorians have kept their traditional dress but can now afford more luxurious fabrics. The weaving families of Otavalo have transformed this demand into an impressive business

Typical Otavalo tapestry work.

BELOW: an Otavaleña takes her baby to market.

For as far back as anyone knows, the people of the high, green Otavalo valley have been spinners, weavers and textile merchants. Because Ecuador lacks the mineral wealth of Peru and Bolivia, the Spanish were quick to exploit the country's human resources, and this included their textile skills. Under the *encomienda* system the colonizers were given the right to use forced Indian labor in return for christening the workers, and by mid-1550s an *obraje* (textile workshop) using forced indigenous labor was established in Otavalo. While the Spanish were busily exploiting the native population, they also introduced the European technology which has formed the basis for the present prosperity: carders, spinning wheels and treadle looms.

Between 1690 and 1720 the *encomiendas* were abolished by the Spanish Crown, but native land fell into white hands and many *indígenas* entered into a system of debt peonage *(wasipungo)* whereby they were virtual serfs on large *haciendas*, many of which continued to operate weaving workshops.

The modern industry got its start in 1917 when *indígenas* on the Hacienda Cusín were encouraged to make imitations of imported British tweeds *(casimires)*. These proved successful in the national market and *casimir* weaving spread to other families and villages in the Otavalo valley. In 1964 the Agrarian Reform Law outlawed debt peonage and granted *wasipungeros* title to their plots of land, leaving *indígenas* free to weave at home or to hire out their labor. Many of the most prosperous contemporary weaving families are descendants of the *wasipungeros*.

The Agrarian Reform coincided with an increase in tourism to the region. In 1966 there was one crafts store in Otavalo. By 1990 there were about 80, most of them *indígena* owned and operated. It's a mistake, however, to think that the textile industry is mainly dependent on tourism. It's a rare Ecuadorian who doesn't own something from Otavalo and most textiles are sold to other South Americans. There is also a substantial export business to North America, Europe and Japan which brings several million dollars a year into the region.

About 85 percent of the estimated 45,000 Otavaleños in the valley are involved in the textile industry either full- or part- time as spinners, weavers, knitters, finishers, wholesalers or retailers, including store owners, market vendors and traveling merchants. Almost all families have at least one spinning wheel or loom in the house. Involvement ranges from widows who spin 2kg (5lb) of wool yarn a week, to families weaving a few ponchos a month on the backstrap loom, to the Tejidos Rumiñahui company in Otavalo, which produces up to 300 ponchos a day on electric looms.

Each weaving and merchant family seeks an economic niche to occupy and the marketing acumen they evince is impressive. One family in Quinchuquí make several hundred acrylic ponchos each month, which are exported to Venezuela. A family in Iluman produce acrylic dresses and shawls which they market in Guayaquil. A family in Peguche weave wool scarves, ponchos and capes which are sold to a North American exporter. Another family in Peguche make high-quality *tapices* (tapestries) which are sold to the major folk-art stores in Quito, to visitors to the family home, and at a kiosk in the Otavalo market.

Increased prosperity has not meant the abandonment of traditional dress, but the use of more luxurious fabrics. The women's skirt wraps *(anakus)* and shoulder wraps *(fachalinas)* were traditionally made of handspun wool or cotton; today wealthy women wear velvet. The women's dress, incidentally, is one of the closest in form to the costume of Inca women worn anywhere in the Andes today. The men's dress is less conservative, being a mixture of colonial and modern elements, although the custom of wearing long hair and the use of *alpargatas* are pre-Hispanic.

Although some older *indígenas* and residents of remote communities are monolingual Quichua speakers, most *indígenas* are bilingual in Quichua and Spanish and a few will surprise you by speaking fluent English, French, German or Portuguese.

The Saturday Otavalo Market *(la féria)* is the high point of the week, not only for the hundreds of travelers who come from around the world (including many Colombians and people from other parts of Ecuador), but also for the thousands of *indígenas* who come to buy, sell and socialize. The market takes place in the three main plazas and the surrounding streets. For more detailed information on this colorful event, see the *Going North* chapter, on page 173.

Map, page 178

BELOW: traditionally dressed Otavaleñas selling fine rugs.

THE PACIFIC COAST

Map,
pages
174/5

*Palm-fringed beaches are the lure. But there's much more to a
coastal trip: marimba rhythms, mangrove swamps, the
bustling port of Manta, and an echo of Africa*

The north coast of Ecuador, extending as far south as Guayaquil, is one of the best places on the continent to take a break from the often demanding rigors of travel. Much of this varied coastline consists of largely empty, palm-fringed beaches, presenting the ideal opportunity to practice one of the foremost customs of ancient Ecuador: sun worship

This area bore the brunt of the devastating *El Niño* floods of 1982–83, when roads, beaches, trees, crops and a significant number of dwellings were washed away. Recovery has in many cases been slow, for in the tropical languor of a sweltering landscape, the tendency to consign things to *mañana* is pervasive. As a string of holiday resorts springs up along the coast, however, the last signs of destruction fade. This development testifies to Ecuador's growing stature as a tourist destination – due partly to its own charms, and partly to its neighbors' ill-fortunes. A holiday in Colombia, with its cocaine-related civil disturbances, is not for the faint-hearted, while the Peruvian coastline is endlessly washed by the Humboldt Current, bringing damp, misty weather and ice-cold waters. Because of this, Ecuador has cornered the market in tropical beaches along South America's west coast.

PRECEDING PAGES:
fishing boats on the
tropical coast.
LEFT: oysters and
limes on the
Atacames beach.
BELOW: enjoying a
day by the Pacific.

Land of two seasons

The wet season on the Ecuadorian coast runs from December to June, the remainder of the year being dry – or perhaps "not-so-wet." During the wet, when flooding is commonplace and high levels of humidity make life uncomfortably sticky, the beaches – despite being below par – are well patronized. All things considered, August to October is the best time to visit this relaxed region.

The coastal topography consists of a thin lowland strip which turns from forbidding mangroves in the north to dry scrubland on the Santa Elena Peninsula, west of Guayaquil. A short distance inland runs a range of low, rounded, crystalline hills. The region is cut by numerous rivers slithering down from the Andes, which regularly flood the alluvial plain which lies to the east of the hills. Huge alluvial fans, often consisting of porous volcanic ash eroded from highland basins, spread out from the major river mouths, providing very fertile soil.

The province of Esmeraldas is one of dense, luxuriant rainforest characterized by two main botanical strata: a high canopy of towering evergreen broadleaf species sprinkled with palms; and at eye-level, clusters of giant ferns, shrubs and vines. Among these are spectacular smaller plants such as orchids and bromeliads which proliferate in the Amazonian forest but are rarely found west of the Andes.

South of Esmeraldas is a zone of deciduous scrub

woodland which drops its leaves during the dry season. A narrow strip of tropical, semi-deciduous forest lies just north of Manta; and from here down to
Guayaquil, this mangrove forest is broken only by the infertile scrubland of
Santa Elena. Among the commercially-used plants of the coastal forests are the
balsa tree, source of the world's lightest lumber; the ivory-nut palm (*tagua*),
used to make buttons; and the *toquilla* reed, from which the renowned Panama
hat is manufactured.

The coastal region, which contains almost half of Ecuador's 11 million people, is populated by a veritable melting pot of ethnic groups. Here, more than
in the Sierra and the jungle, the trails of history incorporate all the colors of the
rainbow. At the time of the Spaniards' arrival, the centers of coastal indigenous
habitation were Esmeraldas, Manta, Huancavilca and Puná; these peoples were
either exterminated outright, or else they interbred to the point where their racial
purity was completely extinguished.

A century or so later, the Spanish–Indian mixture (called *mestizo*) was infused
with Negro blood as slaves were brought from West Africa, creating the *mulatto*
(Spanish–Negro mix) and *montuvio* (Indian–Negro mix) races. Indigenous
Caribs were also shipped to Ecuador to work the plantations, adding a fourth
element to this ethnic conglomeration. *Mestizos* comprise the majority of the
coastal population, but the black influence is one of the region's most interesting features, pervading all aspects of life.

BELOW: tranquil
waterways near
San Lorenzo.

From the Colombian border

A journey that begins in **San Lorenzo** ❻, in Ecuador's northwestern corner,
can only get drier. The sea is the town's *raison d'être*, and fresh, salty breezes fill

the pot-holed streets. The land around San Lorenzo is mostly mangrove swamp, navigated by motorized dugout canoes, while the town itself is frequently sodden with rainwater that has nowhere to run-off. A new road has recently been constructed, linking San Lorenzo to Ibarra and Quito, and there is a bus service. However, many travelers who find themselves here are at one end of the spectacular, day-long train trip between Ibarra and San Lorenzo, or may have come up the coast by boat. It should be noted that San Lorenzo has no immigration office, nor any official currency exchange, so crossing the Colombian border to Tumaco is a somewhat risky proposition.

Despite its isolation – during the wet season, even the railway is sometimes impassable – San Lorenzo can generate a certain amount of bustle. It possesses the best natural harbor of the Ecuadorian coast, and a hinterland still largely untouched due to its inaccessibility. The population has grown from 2,000 in 1960 – when, in the days prior to the discovery of oil in the Oriente, this was Ecuador's El Dorado, the alluring, untapped frontier – to 20,000 today. Lumber traders have made profitable incursions into forests rich in mahogany, balsa and rubber, creating industries and bringing itinerant laborers to this long-neglected outpost.

Map, pages 174/5

African legacy

Despite this, San Lorenzo still has the feel of a town invented by Gabriel García Márquez. The descendants of people from distant continents have been washed up by history on this forbidding shore, and made the most of their displacement. African slaves transported in the 17th and 18th centuries were unloaded in Cartagena (Colombia) and marched southwards to man the coffee, banana and cacao plantations; less than half of this human cargo survived the privations of passage to reach their destinations. Despite multifarious interbreeding, the legacy of Africa lives today in the form of ancestor worship and the voodoo rituals of *macumba*, whereby spirits are summoned to cure and curse. Beneath the latinized veneer of regular Sunday mass lies an ancient belief in macabre spirits or *visiones* such as *La Tunda*, who frightens bad children to death and then steals their bodies, or *El Rivel*, who feasts on corpses.

BELOW: parrot from the coastal rainforest.

African rhythms anchor the up-tempo beat of *marimba* music, which can be heard in San Lorenzo. Esmeraldeña *marimba* retains purer links with its origins than does the Colombian style, which has borrowed heavily from the Caribbean jingles of *salsa* and often resembles Western pop music. Talented musicians and dancers of both *marimba* styles can be seen rehearsing on Wednesday nights, and when they hit the downtown bars, San Lorenzo starts jumping. Men are said to come of age when they begin to *andar y conocer* – literally, "to walk and to know," or "to travel and learn." In black idiom, this commonly-used phrase means "to strut," and is heavily loaded with sexual innuendo.

To get to the coast road you have to go by boat from San Lorenzo to **La Tola**. Services are cheap and regular and take about 2½ hours. En route to La Tola lies the island of **La Tolita**, an important ceremonial center from 500 to 100 BC. Tribal chiefs were buried here, their tombs filled with artifacts of gold, silver, platinum and copper. In recognition of its historical significance, La Tolita has been declared an Archaeological National Park and is undergoing extensive excavation.

Like many such sites in South America, La Tolita has been savagely plundered by thieves, its treasures sold on the international black market. Fortunately, however, the government's attention was attracted in time to salvage a substantial portion of the relics, and another gap in the jigsaw-puzzle of ancient Ecuador is slowly being filled.

Frontier town

Opposite La Tolita at the mouth of the Río Santiago is **Limones** (which must also be reached by boat). It is a small town of some importance as the center of the local lumber industry, but without a lot to offer tourists. Timber is floated downriver to the sawmill here, and processed for further distribution.

The lumber camps, isolated in the dense, upriver jungle, were quite notorious in their early days during the 1960s for a form of outpost exploitation worthy of the author Joseph Conrad. The *mestizo* owners forbade their workers – mostly *morenos* (a generic term for blacks) – to leave camp. Instead, prostitutes and alcohol were shipped in each pay-day – a kind of slavery with over-priced fringe benefits.

This delta region is the home of the Cayapa or Chachi Indians, who – along with the Colorados of Santo Domingo – were the only indigenous coastal tribe to evade extermination by the Spaniards. In both cases, survival was due to the inaccessibility of their homelands. Today, the Cayapas number approximately 4,000. They are sometimes seen selling their finely woven hammocks and

The mask of the sun god, found on La Tolita, is the symbol of the Banco Central.

BELOW: passing the time in the afternoon sun.

Map, pages 174/5

basketwork in the markets of Limones and La Tola – and occasionally Esmeraldas – but they prefer the privacy of Borbón and the inhospitable upper reaches of the Río Cayapa.

A turn-off on the La Tola–Esmeraldas road runs to **Borbón**, but this country is decidedly off the beaten track, and travel can be numbingly difficult, especially in the wet season. A better option is to take a motorized dugout from El Bongo restaurant in Limones upriver to Borbón, whence expeditions continue up to **Boca de Onzoles**, at the confluence of the Cayapa and Onzoles rivers. In this far-flung village, a Hungarian émigré called Stefan Tarjany runs a comfortable lodge – Steve's Lodge – and organizes trips to the mission stations of **Santa Maria** and **Zapallo Grande**. He also arranges boat trips to the **Reserva Ecológica Cotacachi-Cayapa**s, but the usual starting point for this trip is **San Miguel**, the last settlement on the river.

The reserve covers some 204,400 hectares (505,000 acres) and its habitat varies from lowland tropical forest, in this region, to cloudforest, to windswept plain, and accordingly has an enormous range of flora and fauna. It is also the home of the Cayapas Indians who continue to live in their traditional way, trying to avoid the encroachment of Western values and influences. The reserve receives protection from the Ecuadorian government and from international conservation organizations. Guided tours in dug-out canoes can be arranged with the park rangers.

Travel in Ecuador is rarely as adventurous as in these quixotic backwaters, which few visitors make the effort to explore. The Cayapas' counterparts in the Oriente – Stone Age tribes such as the Jivaro and the Huaorani – have received far greater international exposure, which in turn has attracted more tourists. This

LEFT: a couple of coastal icons.
RIGHT: fish doesn't come any fresher than this.

exposure may, however, prove beneficial as the search for oil in the Amazon basin is a much greater threat to indigenous lifestyles than anything the Cayapas are up against.

Difficult highways

Esmeraldas took its name from the emeralds found in the river here.

The road from La Tola to **Esmeraldas**  is rough and never ready: *rancheros*, which are open-sided trucks fitted with far too many wooden benches, take five hours to cover the 100km (60 miles). The northern half of this road may suffer severe flooding during the wet season, but otherwise it is a carefree, breezy ride past cattle farms and swamps teeming with birdlife. A few small towns are strung out along the way, but offer little reason to pause.

It was near Esmeraldas that the *conquistador* Bartolomé Ruíz and company landed, the first Spaniards to set foot on Ecuadorian soil. Esmeraldas is named after the precious stone found in bountiful quantities in the like-named river, at whose mouth the city lies. The Cara Indians, who inhabited this area before migrating to the mountain basins around Otavalo during the 10th century, worshipped a huge emerald known as Umina. Today, the treasures are more industrial than geological: Esmeraldas is the major port of the north coast, whence lumber, bananas and cacao are shipped abroad. The 500-km (300-mile) trans-Andean oil pipeline ends here, and the recent construction of an oil refinery has brought new jobs and money to the city.

BELOW: at a village dance in Esmeraldas.

The treatment of previously fatal tropical diseases has contributed significantly to the growth of Ecuadorian ports, notably Guayaquil, Manta and Esmeraldas. The eradication of yellow fever from these towns early this century was the first step, followed by the discovery and availability of quinine as an antidote for malaria, which as recently as 1942 accounted for one quarter of all deaths in Ecuador. The treatment of tuberculosis, cause of almost one-fifth of fatalities in Ecuador just a generation ago, completed the region's health improvement, providing the basis for growing international maritime trade – and, primarily, improved conditions for the people.

Black capital

Esmeraldas' population of nearly 100,000 consists of mostly *mestizos* and *morenos*, with a surprising minority of mountain Indians looking forlorn and far from home in their bowler hats and thick woollen shawls. Esmeraldas is the center of black culture in Ecuador. It is here that the visitor is most likely to encounter a full *marimba* band, complete with huge *conga* drums, led by the *bomero*, who plays a deep-pitched bass drum suspended from the ceiling. Esmeraldas is, like its music, a vibrant, colorful city that embodies the distinctive elements of coastal urban life. The people are gregarious and no-nonsense, playing with far greater enthusiasm than they work. Nothing is high-brow, all culture is popular, and most would rather watch the opposite sex sway by than observe any religious ritual.

The energy level on the streets soars as the sun slips down into the Pacific, and bars and restaurants – serving dishes of delicious *cocado*, fried fish in a spicy coconut sauce – fill to overflowing.

For the more cerebrally inclined, the **Museo Arqueológico** has exhibits on many of the region's pre-Inca cultures: Bahía, Valdivia, Chorrera and Tuncahuan, as well as some small golden masks from La Tolita. There is also a **Casa de la Cultura Ecuatoriana** with a collection of colonial and contemporary art, but don't be surprised if you are the only visitor. Discotheques far outnumber museums in Esmeraldas, which is a fair reflection of the hedonistic spirit of the ancient peoples whose suggestive figures now rest on silent shelves.

Map,
pages
174/5

Golden sands and palm trees

To the immediate southwest of Esmeraldas begins a stretch of coastline containing the finest and most peaceful beaches in Ecuador. The beach suburb of **Las Palmas** presents a pleasant alternative to staying in the rather unattractive downtown area of Esmeraldas. The road to the other, less-visited beaches passes the Petro Ecuador oil refinery and a luxury hotel, the Hostería La Pradera – complete with swimming pool, tennis courts and a statue of the Virgin of the Swan in a garden grotto – before reaching the coast.

The road from Esmeraldas is reasonable and there is a bus service down the coast to Muisné. The small friendly resort town of **Atacames**, 30km (18 miles) from Esmeraldas, is popular with Ecuadorian and foreign tourists alike. It is relatively undeveloped, with just a string of inexpensive hotels and cabins for rent situated directly on the beach – open the door, and there it is. Predictably, most of the restaurants specialize in fresh seafood, and there is little to be done but sit among the palms and enjoy a plate of fish washed down with a cold beer. Atacames has a cooperative of artisans, presided over by *El Tio Tigre* – Uncle Tiger – which manufactures and sells bracelets and chains of black coral, found

BELOW: fish for lunch by the beach.

just offshore to the south. The purchase of such artifacts cannot be encouraged, however, since in many areas the coral has been pillaged to virtual extinction.

While the beach at Atacames looks harmless enough, there is a powerful undertow. There are no lifeguards, so the current sweeps some swimmers to their deaths each year. Sea snakes washed up on the beach pose another risk: they are venomous and should be avoided. A less avoidable problem is theft, which has been steadily increasing in Atacames in recent years. There have also been several reports of assault on the beach late at night, so a solitary midnight stroll cannot be recommended. Despite these warnings, however, the probability of a visitor encountering any trouble remains slim.

Six km (3 miles) further south lies **Súa**, a small, beautifully situated fishing village that is somewhat livelier than Atacames. The fishermen haul their catch right up on to the small beach, which immediately becomes an impromptu market as locals seek out quick bargains. The sky fills with sea birds such as frigates and pelicans, who do a fine job gobbling up fish heads and guts. As a stay in Atacames is chiefly a matter of relishing the elements, Súa offers glimpses of life in a small seaside town with its eye less on tourists than on the next catch.

Luxury and adventure

A further 8km (5 miles) along the ocean road lies an unpaved side track to the beach of **Same** (pronounced Sah-may), perhaps the finest along this stretch. There is little here other than a collection of mostly expensive and tasteful hotels, including the Hotel Casablanca, constructed comparatively recently in Moroccan design. Same does have the air of a place on the verge of over-development, but it remains the quintessential "away-from-it-all-in-comfort" destination.

TIP

The Hotel Súa has rooms with balconies and sea views. The restaurant is recommended both for fish and a wide variety of other meals.

BELOW: guest apartments at the Hotel Casablanca.

The completely undeveloped villages of **Tonchigüe** and **Galera**, both with lovely beaches nearby, lie a short distance west of Same. At this point, the road leaves the coast and cuts southwards through undulating banana plantations before re-emerging at the shoreline opposite the island of **Muisné**, 83km (51 miles) from Esmeraldas. Motorized dugouts ply the short distance from the mainland to Muisné and, since few visitors bother to come this far from Esmeraldas for just another beach, Muisné exudes the alluring, timeless languor characteristic of any remote tropical island. The beaches here are enormous and empty; there is a handful of cheap, basic hotels and good seafood restaurants, and nothing more. The ghost of Robinson Crusoe may well haunt Muisné's beaches: if you see another set of footprints in the sand, it must be Friday.

Inland from Muisné there is an isolated community of Cayapa Indians, some of whom may be seen around town at the Sunday market.

From Muisné to **Cojimíes ❽**, 50km (31 miles) to the south, there is no road. One or two motorized dugouts make the two-hour journey each day, some continuing as far as Manta; the boats hug the coastline all the way, making it a safe and picturesque trip. An adventurous alternative is to head off under your own steam: the town of **Bolívar**, from where boats depart for Cojimíes, is about 23km (14 miles) from Muisne, making a feasible day's walk. There are several rivers to be forded en route, but locating a ferry is usually easy, and an early start should bring you to Bolívar, where there are no hotels, in time to catch a boat to Cojimíes before dark. The wildlife along this pristine, largely uninhabited coastline is unsurpassed on Ecuador's mainland shore: jellyfish and crabs proliferate, as does the full gamut of pelagic birds, while sea snakes and even the occasional beached whale may be encountered.

Cojimíes lies at the northern end of the road that follows the coast down to Manta. It is a quiet and welcoming town, the site of a pre-Columbian settlement that still awaits comprehensive excavation. Transport connections are delightfully whimsical: the unpaved road is impassable in the wet season, and the daily *rancheros* usually run along the beach in a race against the rising tide. About 20km (12 miles) further south, halfway to Pedernales, is the inexpensive Hotel Cocosolo, situated on a deserted beach amid a breezy coconut palm grove. Just south of Pedernales, a town earmarked for tourist development, the road crosses the Equator – marked by a small monument – and then forks. The left-hand turn runs through more farms and plantations to **Santo Domingo de los Colorados**, while the coastal road continues on to the small market town of **Jama**. Another 50km (31 miles) south lies **Canoa**, center of a fast-developing deep-sea fishing industry.

Scenic roadway

The inland loop through Santo Domingo returns to the coast at Bahía de Caráquez, and is a refreshing change for anyone suffering from an overdose of empty, sundrenched beaches. This route through the heartland of Manabí province is among the most scenic in the entire coastal region, and passes several interesting stop-offs. Just 13km (8 miles) from Santo Domingo, a right-hand turn leads to Hostería La Hacienda, a country inn with

Map, pages 174/5

BELOW: coconut milk makes a refreshing drink.

*Freshly caught crabs
in Bahía.*

lovely surroundings and all creature comforts. Past more banana plantations and cattle farms, the road runs to **El Carmen**, whereafter densely vegetated hills rise from the plain.

Much of Manabí, particularly the southern area, suffers a dearth of rainfall, due primarily to the lifeless winds of the Humboldt Current. Nevertheless, the province is the agricultural core of Ecuador, with coffee, cacao, rice, cotton and tropical fruits cultivated widely. The Poza Honda Dam, built mostly with German finance, is fed by the Río Portoviejo and irrigates large areas of previously uncultivatable lowlands.

Chone (population 40,000) prospers on the strength of these industries, as well as the manufacture of leather saddles and a type of straw hat called *mocora*. The banks of the Río Chone, twisting through the undulating **Bálsamo Hills**, sustain increasing numbers of shrimp farms, an indication of Ecuador's modern industrial diversification, although they have also led to the destruction of mangrove forests. The road climbs to a vantage point offering splendid views of Bahía de Caráquez and the mangrove islands dotting the bay, and then slides down to the coast.

The resort village of **San Vicente** stands at the mouth of the Río Chone, opposite Bahía de Caráquez. The recently constructed church of **Santa Rosa** has an ornate, eye-catching façade, but otherwise there are few diversions from the pleasures of the beach. Seventy km (43 miles) inland along a typically makeshift road is the important archaeological site of **San Isidro**. The prehistoric inhabitants of San Isidro excelled in the art of ceramics: their beautifully crafted figurines are today sold throughout Ecuador, and have spawned a flourishing trade in well-disguised imitations.

BELOW: idyllic coastal vista.

Banana centers

Bahía de Caráquez is named after the Cara Indians who, legend has it, came "by way of the sea" and settled in this bay. Formerly an important export center for bananas and cacao, Bahía entered semi-retirement when the focus of banana exporting – in which Ecuador continues to lead the world – shifted south to Guayaquil and Machala. The cacao industry, in turn, has been steadily declining since it was struck down in its prime by a crippling blight in 1922–23, at which time Ecuador was the world's foremost producer.

A stroll along the palm-fringed riverside Malecón, past rows of stately old mansions – some of them in Victorian "gingerbread" style – reveals remnants of former prosperity. Nevertheless, Bahía's strategic river-mouth location ensures its continued existence as a minor port, and it remains the largest coastal town – with 14,000 inhabitants – between Esmeraldas and Manta.

Much of Bahía's energy today is devoted to tourism: unlike many of Ecuador's north coast towns, it is easily accessible on good roads from Quito, and is one of the most popular resorts in the country. While there are few noteworthy sights in the town, it does offer some simple pleasures. An ascent of **La Cruz hill** is rewarded by sweeping views of the river and coastline, and a sojourn at a riverside café affords surprising glimpses of hard work under a burning sun. There is also a collection of pre-Columbian Manabí pottery in the Casa de Cultura. Ferries across to San Vicente depart frequently, providing a means of transport as well as a scenic way to cool off in the midday sun.

Venturing slightly further afield, launches can be hired to visit **Isla de los Pájaros** and **Isla Corazón** in the bay. These two islands, as the former's name indicates, have raucous sea-bird colonies. Twenty km (13 miles) south of Bahía

Map, pages 174/5

BELOW: a typical house, built on stilts.

de Caráquez are the friendly, peaceful fishing villages of **San Clemente** and **San Jacinto**; driving along the beach at low tide may look tempting, but is inadvisable as many cars have died a watery death here. Instead, follow the Portoviejo road and turn off just before **Rocafuerte**: this route leads to San Jacinto, and on to San Clemente 5km (3 miles) away to the north.

Also along this road, which is notable for the giant ceibo trees lining the way, lies **Crucita**, a beach resort in the past rarely visited by foreigners but recently becoming known as a perfect spot for paragliding.

Shortly thereafter, and just 15km (9 miles) east of Manta, is the fishing village of **Jaramijó**, which has twice reared its historical head. It was, first, the site of an extensive pre-Columbian settlement – hardly surprising given the beauty of the place. Second, Eloy Alfaro, one of Ecuador's best-remembered presidents, lost an important naval battle against conservative forces here in December 1884: the wreck of his ship, the *Alajuela*, can still be seen.

The ancient city of Manta had a population of 20,000 and traded with the coastal people of Mexico and Peru.

Pre-Columbian hedonists

For 1,000 years prior to the arrival of the Spaniards, **Manta** ❿ was the center of one of Ecuador's pre-eminent indigenous cultures. It was known as Jocay – literally, "fish house" – by the local Indians, whose exquisite pottery was decorated with scenes of daily life. And what a life it was! The exuberant hedonism of contemporary coastal Ecuadorians can be traced back directly to the ancient Manteños with their pervasive fertility cult and enjoyment of coca. Their concept of physical beauty was based on the art of *trepining*, whereby children's heads were strapped and bound to increase the backward slope of their chins and foreheads. The desired effect – an exaggeration of the rounded, hooked nose – was quite Neanderthal.

BELOW: the deep blue Pacific.

The Manteños sacrificed their prisoners of war by ripping out their still-beating hearts. Their culture was part-settler, part-wanderer as they cultivated fruit and vegetables while also trading with highland Indians – their source of precious metals – and navigating the ocean in rafts and dugouts as far as Panama and Peru, and possibly the Galápagos Islands. Their skill extended to the arts of stonemasonry, weaving and metalwork – in short, a cultural sophistication of great breadth and depth. (See the *Lost Worlds* chapter, page 27.)

The Spaniard Francisco Pacheco founded the modern settlement of Manta just ten days before Portoviejo in 1535. Nine years earlier, however, Bartolomé Ruíz had encountered a balsa sailing raft with 20 Manteños aboard: 11 of them had leapt into the sea in terror, while the remaining nine served as translators before being set free. Perhaps this rare instance of Spanish tolerance has contributed to the unique character of modern Manta, for it is the most relaxed and habitable city of the entire coastal region.

In its previous incarnation as Jocay, the main thoroughfare of Manta was lined with statues of the chieftains and head priests of the "Manta Confederation." Sadly, the Catholic Church ordered their place to be taken by inoffensive jacaranda and poinciana trees. With a population of approximately 100,000, Manta is a major sea port, with coffee, bananas, cotton textiles

Map, pages 174/5

and fish comprising the bulk of the exports. For all this, the city feels much smaller than similarly sized Esmeraldas, the pace of life being much slower due to the presence of large numbers of Ecuadorian tourists.

Manta is divided by an inlet into a downtown and a resort district, the latter called Tarqui. Along the expansive **Tarqui beach**, local fishermen unload and clean their catch – tuna, shark, dorado, eel and tortoise – whipping the attendant gulls and vultures into aerial frenzy. A towering statue of a Manabí fisherman overlooks the proceedings, noticing few material changes from earlier times.

The **Museo Municipal** houses the finest collection of Manteño artifacts in Ecuador and is well worth a visit. Manta's outdoor theater is the venue for occasional performances, especially during the agriculture and tourism exposition held each October. **Playa Murciélago** is an unprotected surfing beach a few kilometers west of town, site of the comfortable Hotel Manta Imperial. In Tarqui, the Hotel Haddad Manabí, dating from 1931, offers central accommodation with a slight touch of faded grandeur.

Ecuador's "Panama" hat

Straddling the highway between Manta and Portoviejo is the deceptively nondescript town of **Montecristi ⑪**, for more than a century the home of the renowned Panama hat. Until recently the majority of Montecristi's 9,000-odd inhabitants were engaged in the weaving of these remarkable headpieces, made from the straw fronds of the *Carludovica palmata*s. Large numbers of them still are, but Montecristi has had to move with the changing times, and some have switched to making fine wickerwork furniture and decorations.

It is the quintessential cottage industry – many houses in Montecristi contain

BELOW: repairing Panamas is still a thriving trade.

TIP

If you are into ice
cream, try Gelato
Veneziano on Calle
Sucre in Portoviejo.

a rudimentary factory and showroom – and the lack of even the remnants of wealth in Montecristi is sad testimony to the inequitable distribution of the industry's hefty profits.

Like Portoviejo, which we will come to next, Montecristi owes its existence to pillaging pirates: in 1628, a group of Manteños left the coast for a nearby inland refuge. Rows of colonial houses in chronic disrepair line the quiet, dusty streets, and in combination with the non-mechanized weaving, this physical neglect creates the air of a town stuck in another time. Montecristi's religious atmosphere is similarly dated, as the beautiful church contains a famous statue of the Virgin to which several miracles have been attributed. And Montecristi's favorite son is now long dead: Eloy Alfaro, president of Ecuador at the turn of the century and a committed liberal reformist, was born here. His statue overlooks the main plaza, and his house is now a mausoleum, with his library and many personal effects on display. Almost alone among towns in coastal Ecuador, Montecristi survives as a relic – an impression heightened by the anachronism of tourists and Panama hat dealers roaring into town in search of a bargain.

Portoviejo's memories

From Montecristi it is only 24km (15 miles) to **Portoviejo** ⑫, a town with a long history. Things blossom quickly in the tropics, and a conscious effort is often required to keep vestiges of the old from being overgrown by the new. In coastal Ecuador, where the *conquistadores* began their epic trek to victory in the relocated Inca capital of Cajamarca, surprisingly little remains of the colonial past. The monuments, which themselves are few and far between, are generally quite recent erections in honor of heroes of the Liberation – Bolívar, Sucre

BELOW: bringing in a
large marlin.

nd San Martín – or favorite republican presidents. It is as if a wilful forgetful-
ness descended on the pre-republican centuries: those long years of disease and
brutality bequeathed a legacy of military dictatorship and silence.

Descendants of the few hundred *criollo* (pure-bred European) families that
have dominated political and economic life since the origins of the *audencia*
still stalk the corridors of power. Since Ecuador returned to civilian government
in 1978, however, historians have – without fear or intimidation – cast revealing
eyes on the excesses of Spanish colonialism. The people whose transplanted
lives are a direct product of that time – all *morenos*, for example – are thus beginning to understand the original forces that have shaped them, their community
and their country.

Given these historical "black holes," the visitor to Portoviejo may not be surprised to learn that it was one of the earliest Spanish settlements in Ecuador. It
was founded on March 12, 1535, just three months after Benalcázar re-founded
Quito atop abandoned Inca ruins. Guayaquil, founded in January 1535, was the
first Spanish coastal community, but the local Indians, based on the nearby island
of Puná, repeatedly launched marauding raids of such ferocity that alternative
sites were sought.

The original settlement, founded by Francisco Pacheco on the orders of Francisco Pizarro and Diego de Almagro, was, as its name ("Old Port") suggests,
located on the coast. The omens, however, were far from auspicious: in 1541, a
fire destroyed the town, and 50 years later the local Indians staged a fearsome
uprising. Finally, when English pirates ravaged the port in 1628, it was decided
that a spot further inland would be out of harm's way.

Since then, Portoviejo has existed in the shadow of Manta, though as capital
of Manabí Province it remains an important adminis-
trative and educational center. Its population has
recently topped the 100,000 mark, most of which is
engaged in commerce, industry and the rich agricultural
pickings of the hinterland. Portoviejo's bustling streets
are prettily bordered with rows of flora, and a stroll
through the **Parque Eloy Alfaro** is perhaps the most
pleasing pastime. Opposite the park is one of Ecuador's
darkest modern cathedrals. Could the Catholic Church
have been short of cash for once? Beside it stands a
statue of Pacheco, the city's founder.

There are two museums: the **Casa de la Cultura
Ecuatoriana**, with a collection of traditional musical
instruments; and the **Museo Arqueológico,** which is
not as good as its counterpart in Manta. Portoviejo has
few old colonial buildings still standing, but otherwise
little testimony to its long and tumultuous history.

Leaving Portoviejo, go back the way you came for 14
km (8 miles) then turn off on the Guayaquil road to the
village of **La Pila**, which is an interesting stop-off. In
the wake of the discovery of exquisite pre-Columbian
ceramics in the area, the resourceful inhabitants of La
Pila began producing indistinguishable "antique" imitations to cash in on their forebears' artistry. Nowadays,
however, they have embraced originality and appear to
have inherited not only the enterprise but also the considerable artistic skill of their ancestors.

In contrast, **Jipijapa** – a town of 28,000 inhabitants

Map, pages 174/5

BELOW: soaking up the Ecuadorian sun.

**Map,
pages
174/5**

situated another 40km (25 miles) along the highway to Guayaquil – appears to have been swallowed up by Ecuador's flourishing agricultural industries, particularly coffee and cotton.

At Jipijapa, a side road climbs into the damp, luxuriant hills of southern Manabí before descending to the coast near **Puerto de Cayo**, a fishing village with pristine beaches. Fifteen km (9 miles) offshore is **Isla de la Plata**, an ancient Manteño ceremonial center currently undergoing excavation. The island is named after an incident in the late 16th century, when Sir Francis Drake – dispatched by Queen Elizabeth to wreak havoc on the Spanish colonies – captured a silver-laden galleon and made camp on the island to tally his spoils. It is today inhabited only by tortoises and blue-footed boobies, and can be reached by hired motorboat – a trip of two hours. Look out for shells of the spondilus oyster, which in pre-Columbian times served as a unit of currency, and as such was regularly interred in the tombs of tribal chieftains.

The well-worn coast road continues on to **Machalilla** ⓫, the center of the culture of the same name which flourished between 1800 and 1500 BC. It is rich in archaeological remains, especially in the vicinity of **Salaite** and **Agua Blanca**, where there is a small archaeological museum. A pleasant 45-minute walk from Machalilla brings you to the deserted horseshoe beach called **Los Frailes** (The Friars). About 10km (6 miles) further south, fleets of heavily-laden fishing boats dock in the village of **Puerto López** each afternoon at about four o'clock: the skippers will happily sell their catch there and then.

A large tract of the surrounding area was designated the **Parque Nacional Machalilla** in 1979. It protects an expanse of tropical dry forest, which is home to a wide variety of bird and animal life, as well as a stretch of coast and a couple of off-shore islands. You can enter the park from the coast road, or from the main Manta to Guayaquil highway, south of Jipijapa.

BELOW: lone fisherman casts his net. **RIGHT:** statue of a fisherman in Manta.

Digging for the past

About 5km (3 miles) south of Puerto López is **Salango**, a small fishing village close to a site where dozens of scientists, students and local volunteers took part in the largest archaeological dig in the country, providing insights into the fragmentary history of pre-Columbian Ecuador. The relics of a host of successive cultures – Valdivia, Machalilla, Chorrera, Engoroy, Bahía, Guangala and Manteño – which inhabited this fertile stretch of coastline as early as 2000 BC were painstakingly recovered. A museum which was opened here in 1987 has been filled with artifacts found in the area.

Some 6 km (4 miles) south of Salango is an interesting ecological resort, called the **Centro Turístico Ecológico Alandaluz** (Alandaluz Ecological Tourist Center), with buildings constructed of locally grown, easily replenishable bamboo and palm-leaf thatch. The cabins and towers are set out attractively among organic gardens overlooking the sea. The aim of the resort is to become completely self-sustaining: the gardens produce much of the food that is served in the restaurant, water and rubbish are recycled, and innovative organic bathroom facilities, using sawdust, convert human waste into fertilizers for the land.

PANAMA HATS

Prohibition gangsters loved them, but do they have a future?

Montecristi is the capital of Panama hat making: for 150 years the best *superfinos* have been woven in this peaceful, nondescript town. It is here that tourists come to buy the genuine article direct from the weavers' hands, thereby circumventing the demarcated process that the hats undergo before they appear in the shops.

The process extends from the weaver to the comisionista, or middle-man, who buys the untrimmed hat and sells it to the factory, which is often owned by the exporter. There it is trimmed, bleached, and hand-ironed and pounded into its finished shape, before being exported. And why is it called a Panama if it comes from Montecristi? A mistake, apparently, attributed to some 19th-century gold-miners who forgot where they bought their innovative headgear.

The Panama hat production trail begins in the low hills west of Guayaquil, a region cooled by the sea breezes of the Humboldt Current, and where rainfall is plentiful but not excessive. Although found from Bolivia to Panama, it is here, in these conditions, that *Carludovica palmata* – named after King Carlos and his wife Luisa by two Spanish botanists in the late 18th century – thrives.

The plant is not often found growing wild these days. It is more commonly cultivated in fields divided according to the families' seniority in the trade. The stalks of the plant can grow as high as 6 meters (20ft) high and are topped by slender leaves. But it is the material inside the stalks that is needed, the new

BELOW: a dealer displays a *superfino* in his Cuenca store.

shoots containing dozens of very fine fronds each about a meter long and a few millimeters wide. These fronds are boiled in water for an hour, and sun-dried for a day. The procedure is repeated to ensure maximum strength when woven.

The finest weaving is done at night or on dull days, as direct sunlight makes the fronds too brittle, and hot sweaty hands don't produce tight weaves. Women and children make the best hats, because their fingers, being smaller, are more agile. A *superfino* – as the best hats are called, those most tightly woven with the thinnest, lightest straw – takes up to three months to complete. The test of a true *superfino* is that it should, when turned upside down, hold water without any leakage. It should also fold up to fit neatly in a top pocket without creasing.

No one knows exactly how long straw hats have been woven in Ecuador, but the craft certainly preceded the Spanish conquest. The *conquistadores* were impressed by the headgear worn by the indigenous inhabitants of Manabí Province, and adapted it for their own use.

A few of the Panamas were sent to the United States in the late 18th century, and by the middle of the next century exports were growing, although it wasn't until the Spanish-American War of 1898, when the hats were considered ideal headgear for soldiers fighting in the Caribbean and the Philippines, that the export market to the US really took off. The hats first hit Europe in 1855 at the World Exposition in Paris, and, as illustrated by many of Renoir's paintings, they soon became a debonair item of contemporary fashion.

Chicago chic

Why tropical military headgear should have proved so irresistible it is hard to say, but America fell in love with the Panama, and for the next 50 years kept the industry going. The gangsters of the prohibition period took such a shine to it that the Manabí manufacturers still call the wide-brimmed variety the *El Capone*.

Ever a mirror of popular taste, Hollywood embraced the Panama hat: a hero, or a villain, wearing a Panama was a man to be reckoned with, regardless of the fact that in Ecuador the hat identified its wearer as a manual laborer – but then much the same could be said of the 20th-century fashion for suntans, once only seen on those who had to labor in the sun to earn their living.

The industry peaked in 1946 when 5 million hats were exported, constituting 20 percent of Ecuador's annual export earnings, a figure exceeded only by cacao, coffee and bananas. In those days every household in Montecristi produced top quality Panamas but numbers have now dwindled to a handful. The international demand has fallen steadily since the late 1940s. China and Taiwan now produce cheaper imitations that are sufficiently like the genuine item to satisfy all but the most discerning, and many of the weavers of Manabí now earn their living by making mats and wickerwork furniture.

There are some in the business who believe that the manufacture of *superfinos* will not survive for much longer. For the sake of the weavers' livelihoods, and Ecuadorian pride, let's hope that is an over-pessimistic view, but the heyday of the hat is undeniably gone – probably for ever.

Map, pages 174/5

BELOW: Panama hats before they are trimmed.

THE WESTERN LOWLANDS

Agriculture has become vitally important in this region.
As you travel south from Santo Domingo, you'll find rice
on the roads, bananas in bags and houses on stilts

Map,
pages
174/5

Many visitors to Ecuador claim that the most frightening bus journey in the country is the two-and-a-half-hour drive from Quito to **Santo Domingo** in the western lowlands. The road, which is the main link between the capital and the lowlands, drops almost 3,000 meters (10,000 ft) down the western slopes of the Andes and is often shrouded in fog, especially in the afternoons. Truck and bus drivers rely on headlights and horns as they hurtle down the road, paying scant attention to the poor visibility or oncoming traffic. Surprisingly, accidents are rare, but it is not without some sense of relief that the traveler finally arrives.

Home for healers

Santo Domingo's full name is **Santo Domingo de los Colorados ⓮**, after the Colorado Indians who once dominated the area. Their appearance was distinctive: both sexes painted their faces with black stripes and the men plastered down their bowl-shaped haircuts with a brilliant red dye of *achiote*, a local plant (see the picture on the left). Some of the men, notably the Calazacon brothers, built up a nationwide reputation as *curanderos* (medicine men). Until a decade ago, patients from all over Ecuador came to be treated for a variety of ills, but the custom is now dying out.

Travelers still come to Santo Domingo in the hope of seeing the Colorados in their authentic finery or perhaps witnessing a curing ceremony. Some are lucky, for the traditions do still exist, but many are disappointed to find that most of the Colorados now wear Western dress, no longer paint their faces, and have largely lost interest in their traditional appearance and customs.

Santo Domingo has a tropical climate and is the nearest place for Quiteños to come and enjoy the lowland heat. Hence it has developed a couple of small resort hotels, where visitors can relax by a pool in a tropical garden, or try their luck in the casino. It is also the hub of a network of paved roads radiating out into the western lowlands.

Into banana lands

The road south of Santo Domingo leads through vast plantations of bananas and African oil palms. Until the discovery of petroleum in the Oriente in the late 1960s Ecuador was the archetypal banana republic, with bananas being by far the most important export. Even today, Ecuador remains the largest exporter of bananas in the world, with annual exports averaging some US$650 million.

Bananas were not always so important. Friedrich Hassaurek, who served as US minister to Ecuador from 1860 to 1864, reported that the main export was cacao.

PRECEDING PAGES: banana plantations in the western lowlands. **LEFT:** chieftain and his wife, Santo Domingo de los Colorados. **BELOW:** red and green macaws.

This crop was raised along the rivers of the western lowlands, and floated down to Guayaquil for export. In the 1930s, cacao remained the principal export, followed by coffee, which was also grown in the western lowlands. After World War II, banana production became increasingly important and cacao had dropped to second place by the 1970s. Heavy floods during the *El Niño* phenomenon of 1982–83 severely disrupted the cacao industry, and although it has since recovered, bananas and coffee are the two most important export crops.

The banana trees in the plantations are arranged in regular rows for ease of harvesting, and travelers driving past are soon mesmerized by the monotonous repetition of lines of plants. The monotony is broken occasionally by the sight of workers collecting the ripe fruit with long-handled shears. Often bunches of bananas are sleeved in large blue plastic bags before harvesting; the polyethylene in the bags acts a chemical signal which ripens the fruit more quickly.

Market center

An hour and a half's drive south of Santo Domingo lies the largest market town of the western lowlands, **Quevedo**. ⓰ Not only bananas, but cacao, coffee, rice, sugar, African palm oil, citrus and tropical fruits pass through this important center. Quevedo was founded in the mid-1800s and is thus a relatively modern town. You may sometimes hear it referred to as "the Chinatown of Ecuador" because many Chinese immigrants, some of whom came to work on the railway construction around the turn of the century, settled here. Most of the better restaurants along the main streets are *chifas*, as Chinese restaurants are called locally.

In the past, produce from the area was able to reach the coast at Guayaquil

BELOW: *curandero,* or healer, in Santo Domingo.

along the narrow and convoluted Río Quevedo which runs a few blocks north of the city's downtown area.The journey was a difficult and hazardous one, with frequent sand banks, log jams and shallows to obstruct the unwary. Today, with the construction of a good paved road to Guayaquil, the river is used as a playground by the local children seeking relief from the tropical sun. Although the river port is no longer used, the accompanying street market is still found along the banks of the river.

South of Quevedo, a number of rivers form a mosaic across the land, which becomes increasingly subject to flooding during the rainy season which lasts from January to April. It is after these rivers that the province, **Los Ríos**, is named. This kind of terrain is admirably suited to the cultivation of rice, and paddy fields are often seen. The occasional trees between the fields serve as roosts for flocks of wading birds. White American egrets look especially pretty at sunset, when they gather like hundreds of huge white flowers, virtually blanketing the treetops.

During the dry months, rice is set out to dry on huge open-air platforms of concrete in the many commercial *piladoras* found along the road. *Piladora* is a local word meaning a drying and husking factory. Some of the poorer farmers are unable to afford the cost of the *piladora* and so they spread out their modest crops on the nearest available flat and dry surface. In many cases, this proves to be the Tarmac top of the highway, and drivers do their best to avoid running over the crops which are spread out on the road to dry.

Rice and other agricultural products frequently make their way through **Babahoyo** ⓰, the provincial capital of Los Ríos. The city is a modern one, but it has a long history. An Indian settlement existed here before the arrival of the *con-*

Map, pages 174/5

LEFT: brown sugar for sale. **RIGHT:** river valley near Tinalandia.

Map,
pages
174/5

quistadores and Spanish records indicate the presence of a town here as early as 1576. The present city dates from 1867, after a catastrophic fire destroyed the previous town.

Before the building of the road, Babahoyo was an important port known as Bodegas, meaning store houses. There were frequent steamships linking the coast at Guayaquil with the inland river port of Bodega, where goods were stored to await transport to the highlands and Quito by mule.

Houseboats and stilts

The city is a mere 7 meters (23ft) above sea level and flooding always seems to have been part of the way of life. Friedrich Hassaurek, the US minister to Ecuador, noted during his visit in 1860 how most of the houses were built on stilts to raise the sleeping rooms above the annual floodwaters. Today, some of the inhabitants live in a picturesque floating village of houseboats on the Río Babahoyo. Even during the unseasonably high floods of 1983, when the entire population had to wade knee-deep to get anywhere in town, the houseboat village floated safely above the floodwaters.

The western lowlands are an important part of Ecuador's agricultural and tropical life. The exotic crops, equatorial climate, gorgeous birds and interesting people make this a fascinating area to visit. Yet it is very much off the beaten track. Most travelers do no more than take an express bus through Los Ríos, and Babahoyo is the only one of Ecuador's 21 provincial capitals which didn't merit a mention in the index of one of the most renowned of guidebooks to the continent, *The South American Handbook*.

BELOW: children in a western lowlands village.

Ancient forests

This region was not always rich in agriculture. At one time much of the area was covered by dense tropical rainforest. The renowned British mountaineer, Edward Whymper, arrived in Guayaquil in December, 1879, with the aim of climbing Ecuador's major peaks. In his *Travels Amongst the Great Andes of the Equator* he describes his journey through the western lowlands, where he saw "forest-trees rising 150 feet high, mastlike, without a branch, laden with a parasitic growth."

This terrain was very different from the Amazonian forests to the east of the Andean chain. The pronounced rainy and dry seasons produced a distinctive array of plants and animals which contributed to Ecuador's great variety of species. Ecuador holds the record for the highest biological diversity per unit of land of any Latin American country.

Some of this biodiversity can be seen at the **Centro de Investigación Científico Río Palenque**, about half way between Santo Domingo and Quevedo. Surrounded by plantations, the research station is a small island of tropical rainforest with one of the most accessible and varied arrays of plants remaining in the western lowlands. This forest island is too small, however, to have saved much of the animal wildlife that once abounded in the area, although some exotic birds, such as the pale-mandibled aracari (a member of the toucan family), may still be seen.

Birdwatching

E cuador is a birdwatcher's paradise. The wide variety of habitats, from tropical rainforests to windswept highlands, from mangrove swamps to hilly forests, provide a wider range of species than any other country in the Americas. More than 1,500 bird species have been recorded here, twice as many as in the USA and Canada combined.

In the *páramo* (plateau) habitat of Cotopaxi National Park, a place high on the list of many birdwatchers, one of the most surprising sights is a tiny hummingbird, the Andean hillstar, which survives the freezing nights by lowering its body temperature from about 40°C (104°F) in the daytime to about 15°C (59°F) at night – a remarkable feat for a warmblooded creature. At the other end of the size scale is the Andean condor, which, with its 3-meter (10-ft) wing span, is one of the largest flying birds in the world.

Other *páramo* species include the carunculated caracara, Andean lapwing, Andean gull, páramo pipit, great thrush, and barwinged cinclodes. If you camp out, you may hear the loud hoot of the great horned owl as it searches for prey, or the eerie drumming of the Andean snipe's outer wing feathers as it careens by in the dark.

The Andes of Ecuador are split into two ranges between which lies the temperate central valley. The less extreme elevation of 2,800 meters (9,200 ft) ensures a pleasant climate and attracts a variety of fascinating birds. Hummingbirds are great favorites. They begin to increase in number as the elevation drops and the climate becomes milder. More than one-fifth of Ecuador's 120 or so species of hummers are found here.

The Fundación Natura, Ecuador's leading conservation agency, runs Pasochoa Nature Reserve, an hour's drive from the capital. In one of the last original stands of temperate forest in the central valley, 11 hummingbird species, plus a variety of doves, furnarids, tapaculos, tyrant flycatchers, honeycreepers, and tanagers can all be seen.

Spend a couple of days driving to Mindo down the Chiriboga and Nono roads, heading towards the western lowlands, looking for the cock-of-the-rock, plate-billed mountain toucans and mountain tanagers.

On the eastern Andean slopes the road to Coca takes you over the Papallacta Pass through the *páramo*, dropping down through cloudforest, with its barred fruit eaters and gray breasted mountain toucans, into the Amazon Basin. Once there, bird-watching can get a little tricky. Most transport is by dug-out canoe and the lush vegetation hides a huge diversity of birds. You will need considerable patience and experience if you are to see many of them.

Many people find that the best thing to do is to take an organized tour or have a guide to point out some of the 550 bird species found in the area. Parrots, toucans, macaws, vultures, kingfishers, puffbirds, antbirds, herons and hummingbirds are all there, waiting for the patient birdwatcher. Sacha or La Selva Lodge, or the Tiputini Biodiversity Station, are good options if you are looking for experienced guides. (See *Travel Tips* for more details.)

RIGHT: the Andean cock-of-the-rock.

THE ORIENTE

Map, pages 174/5

Reptiles, anacondas, piranhas, toucans, howler monkeys and jumping spiders all await you in the Amazon Basin. Your transport can vary from floating hotel to dugout canoe

You may go to the Oriente only once in your life, so it is worth asking yourself what you want from your trip. How important is comfort? Do you need a specialist guide and are you more interested in wildlife, plants or indigenous culture? Also, what impact is your visit going to have on the rainforest? When you've answered these questions, you can start making plans.

Most people find that a previously organized trip is the best way to see the Oriente: options include a wide range of jungle lodges, the Amazon riverboat *Flotel Orellana,* or the burgeoning number of "adventure tourism" groups. Trips can be organized from Quito or arranged in Misahuallí, Baños, Tena or Coca. If you are looking for an expert guide or a comfortable lodge, you would do best to organize the trip in Quito, although they can be cheaper elsewhere. See the *Travel Tips* section for tour organizations.

River trips

For the adventurous, the best way to experience primary tropical rainforest is a week-long canoe trip down one of the rivers of the Oriente. Several qualified guides organize float trips on the Río Tiputini or in the Reserva Cuyabeno where you can see wildlife close up. During the day you will see woolly and howler monkeys grazing in the trees, toucans or parrots in flight, or if you are lucky an anaconda lazing in the sun. At night you will be serenaded by a symphony of insects and an occasional unidentified animal.

Floating hotel

At the other end of the scale from canoe trips is the *Flotel Orellana,* run by Transturi. The tour can be arranged through the company's offices in Quito or through Metropolitan Touring, and involves a flight to Lago Agrio.

Looking somewhat like a Mississippi riverboat, the three-level flotel takes some 60 passengers on trips down the Río Aguarico. The idea is to allow travelers to dip into the rainforest and return to a certain amount of luxury. Small but comfortable rooms provide the amenities of a modern hotel, while the flotel has a bar, observation deck and dining room where excellent meals are served. Unlike traditional jungle lodges, the slow but sure flotel allows visits to different parts of the Río Aguarico, and permits deeper penetration of the rainforest (the further away from Lago Agrio, naturally, the more chance of seeing wildlife). Passengers are taken ashore in a motorized dug-out canoes, with gumboots, raincoats and insect repellent all provided, for twice-daily forages into the jungle.

Most people who have arranged river tours or visits to jungle lodges in advance will arrive by air, leaping suddenly from one climate to another. Daily flights dive

PRECEDING PAGES: sinuous tributary of the Amazon; vine snake hypnotizes its prey.
LEFT: giant tree in the rainforest.
BELOW: cruising in a motorized canoe.

from Quito to the towns of Lago Agrio and Coca deep in the jungle, covering in only 30 minutes the same distance that can take 12 gruelling hours by land, as well as providing spectacular aerial views of the changing landscape. The dazzling white of the snow-capped Andes gives way to an endless mattress of green stretching into the horizon. Dozens of rivers snake beneath huge gray clouds, ready to drop their loads of moisture onto the rainforest.

The highway from Quito

Travelers who want to observe from the ground the subtle shifts in flora between the Sierra and Oriente gladly sacrifice comfort and speed for a bus window seat along the eastern highway (even though almost all elect to return by air).

An hour east of Quito, the bus labors over the snow-covered Papallacta Pass – at 4,100 meters (13,400ft) one of the highest points in Ecuador that can be reached by public transport. Shivering in the early morning cold, the passengers pull their thin clothes tightly about them and comfort one another with the observation that it will soon be hot. And indeed it is, for as the narrow gravel road plunges down in a series of ear-popping curves from the snowy pass to the Oriente the temperature rises steadily and the landscape alters dramatically.

The Oriente, as Ecuador's Amazonian region is called, lies less than 100km (60 miles) away from the **Papallacta Pass** as the vulture glides. But the eastern slopes of the Andes tumble precipitously, and the road passes lush cloud forests full of giant Andean tree ferns, spiky bromeliads, delicate orchids and brightly colored birds. This is the very rim of the Amazon basin, and the steepness of the terrain combines with the thick vegetation to make it almost impenetrable.

The heavily forested subtropical slopes of this transitional area are also the

Making friends with an anaconda.

BELOW: the *Flotel Orellana.*

haunts of a variety of wildlife, including the spectacled bear, the only bear found in South America. Its name derives from the light markings around the eyes of this otherwise dark animal. It is mainly vegetarian, often climbing trees in search of succulent exotic fruits. The spectacled bear is shy and rarely seen which is perhaps why it has survived so long. Nevertheless, as its habitat is encroached upon by colonists, numbers of the bear continue to fall and it is now protected by Ecuadorian law.

Thirty minutes' drive past the Papallacta Pass is the town of **Papallacta** and its nearby hot springs, a must for anyone in need of a little relaxation. The road drops towards the jungle taking the line of least resistance – a river valley. Amazonian climate patterns ensure heavy rainfall almost year round, and there are hundreds of minor and major rivers flowing down the eastern Andes towards the Oriente. Although at this point they are only 240km (150 miles) away from the Pacific, these rivers will merge with the waters of the world's greatest river system and finally join the sea at the Atlantic 3,200km (2,000 miles) away.

At first the road follows the valley of the Río Papallacta, and finally ends up in the first important Oriente town, **Baeza** ⑰, near the Río Quijos (named after an Indian tribe that lived in the region at the time of the conquest). Baeza is a small, ramshackle, subtropical outpost whose tin-roofed appearance belies its long and interesting history. Since before the Spanish conquest, lowland forest Indians stopped here on their way to the highlands on trading expeditions. Recognizing the area's strategic importance, the Spaniards founded a missionary and trading outpost here in 1548, only 14 years after conquering Ecuador.

Perched on the edge of the Amazon basin at 1,400 meters (4,600ft) above sea level and 80km (50 miles) east of Quito, Baeza remained Ecuador's last outpost

Map, pages 174/5

BELOW: the jumping spider.

in the northern Oriente for more than four centuries. Today, it is its gateway, and can also be reached by a popular road from Baños further south, via the jungle town of **Puyo**. Like most towns of this area, it has little of inherent interest, unless you are a wildlife enthusiast, and most travelers will press on into the newly-opened areas beyond.

Transformed by oil

Until the middle of this century, this Andean rim of the Amazon basin was as far as colonists and travelers went. Wildlife and Indian groups lived relatively undisturbed further on in the Oriente. This suddenly changed in the late 1960s with the discovery of oil in the jungle. Almost overnight, a good all-weather road was pushed from Quito beyond Baeza and deep into the heart of parts of the Oriente which until then could be reached only by difficult river travel or by light aircraft. The new 180-km (110-mile) road stretched from Baeza to **Lago Agrio** ⑱ (literally "Sour Lake"), an oil town built in a trackless region in the middle of the jungle.

For much of its length, the road to Lago Agrio parallels the trans-Ecuadorian pipeline, which pumps oil 495km (310 miles) from the oil fields of the Oriente, up across the Andes and down to the Pacific Coast for processing and export. At irregular intervals along the pipeline, little communities have been created. Some are next to oil pumping stations, whilst others have been founded by colonists near flat pieces of land which they have cleared.

The road is the main communication link in the area and the accompanying pipeline has taken on a new and unusual function. Here, where the frequent tropical downpours turn the edges of the road into quagmires, the people use the

BELOW: crucifix and canoe in a mission chapel.

pipeline as a sidewalk. Groups of boisterous schoolchildren, clad in the gray uniforms worn by pupils of all the local schools, skip and nudge one another as they run precariously along the pipeline, seemingly oblivious to the national wealth flowing beneath their feet. Colonists swinging the ubiquitous machete trudge home from the fields along the pipeline, and even the family dogs trot along behind. The top of the metal tubing has been worn smooth by the many feet treading it every day.

The famous **San Rafael Falls** are on the Río Quijos, about half way between Baeza and Lago Agrio. With a height of about 145 meters (475ft), they are the highest falls in the country. They can be glimpsed from the bus as it travels along the new road, but for an impressive close-up look you should get off at the UNE-CEL electricity station at **Reventador**. From here, it is a 20-minute walk down an overgrown trail through lush forest to a viewpoint where, if the wind is right (or wrong, depending on your point of view) you can be sprayed by the light mist caused by the crashing water. Sometimes the spray can be so thick that it obliterates the view of the cascading river; at other times the mists clear for a magnificent sight of the falls. This is also a great place for birdwatching. The active volcano of Reventador nearby shows its peak above the cloud forest. A three-day hike will bring you to the summit and the fumaroles steaming from the vents.

Lago Agrio itself is one of the fastest growing places in Ecuador, although not much to look at. It's officially called Nueva Loja (New Loja), named by the first Ecuadorian colonists in the area who mainly came from the province of Loja in the south of the country. But homesick North American oilmen working for Texaco nicknamed the town Lago Agrio after the small Texan oil town of Sourlake, and despite what it says on the maps, that's what everyone now calls

Map, pages 174/5

LEFT: the San Rafael waterfall. **RIGHT:** a woolly monkey.

it. Lago Agrio was part of the huge jungle province of Napo, whose capital is **Tena**, an all-day drive away over bad roads. Tena is not an oil town and the citizens of Lago felt that their very different interests were not represented. But Lago's importance became apparent after an earthquake in 1987 isolated the town, cutting the oil flow and bringing the economy to a grinding halt. In 1989, Lago Agrio was made the capital of Sucumbios, Ecuador's twenty-first and newest province.

A hot and humid climate pervades the town. Even the newest buildings begin to look decayed within a few months. The unpaved streets are often filled with mud, and rubber boots are the usual footwear. Yet it is a lively and progressive place; late model jeeps churn the mud in the streets, the bustling market is thronged with shoppers, and the several banks are always busy. There is a palpable air of civic pride.

Meet the capybara – the world's largest rodent.

Into the jungle

It is well worth making the effort to get from Lago Agrio to the **Reserva Biológica Cuyabeno ⓳**, up towards the Colombian border, where some 655,000 hectares (162,000 acres) of incredibly bio-diverse land, consisting of a great deal of flooded and pretty much intact forest, have been turned into a national park. It's a full day's travel by bus and motorized canoe along the Río Aguarico to reach the reserve itself. Most tour companies use *cabañas* (cabins), opensided platforms or tents as accommodation. Visits to the Siona-Secoya communities on the reserve can sometimes be arranged.

Metropolitan Touring *(see Travel Tips* for details) arrange three- to six-day programs staying in their comfortable camps within the reserve. **Imuya Camp**

BELOW: a spectacled caiman enjoying the sun.

s by one of the blackwater lakes, home to the pink river dolphin and Amazon manatee. In the lakes and streams nearby you can also see the paiche, the giant catfish, and four species of caiman. **Iripari Camp** is by Lago Iripari, the largest lake in the Ecuadorian Amazon. This is a perfect spot for birdwatchers to observe oatsins in their lakeside nests or climb the observation tower into the canopy to see tanagers, cotingas and other birds not easily glimpsed from the forest floor.

Map, pages 174/5

Other, longer, trips take you down the Río Napo. One destination is **Lago Panacocha**, a beautiful lagoon on the Río Panayacu, located in a small protected area of 56,000 hectares (138,400 acres) between the Napo and Aguarico rivers. Colonists, deterred by so much flooded forest, have not taken over here. There is some provision for tourists, with several modest *cabanas* and shelters. Walks along remote trails give a good chance of seeing birds, butterflies and fresh jaguar tracks.

Close encounters with piranhas

There may be the opportunity on one of these trips to try some piranha fishing. Small pieces of raw red flesh are used as bait on hand-lines, bringing the infamous creatures out in their hundreds. These small fish are surprisingly easy to catch, although watch your fingers as you bring them aboard: their small, triangular teeth are razor sharp. Piranhas make a fine meal and you can keep their jaws as a souvenir of the jungle.

Contrary to popular belief, it is quite possible – if not exactly relaxing – to swim in piranha-infested waters. The variety of piranha found in Ecuador will only ever turn on large mammals such as humans and horses if there is a huge quantity of blood in the water. Even so, such is the reputation of the fish that

BELOW: the notorious piranha.

TIP

Contact CECIA, the
Ecuadorian Ornithol-
ogy Foundation, for
more information on
birds and their habi-
tats. Nacional 304 y
Telégrafo, Quito,
tel: 433-238.

swimming here is rather unnerving, and many prefer to endure the Amazonian heat rather than test the murky waters.

Red eyes in the darkness

Another unforgettable Oriente experience is night-time caiman-watching. Slip out on a canoe at night and shine a flashlight into the reeds by the lake side: hundreds of red eyes stare back, the reflections from caimans' retinas (rather like the "red eye" effect in flash photography). The more adventurous guides will take the boat right in among these harmless but vicious-looking reptiles – an experience that can feel a little too adventurous if you happen to be in an unstable dug-out canoe. Some guides will even grab a small caiman by the tail, to bring it alongside the canoe and give everyone a closer look.

If you have a few days to spare it is possible to visit **Limoncocha** (Lemon Lake) down river from Coca. Oil exploration nearby seriously threatened this birdwatchers' haven, but protests from the local community and the creation of the **Reserva Biológica Limoncocha** ⑳ put pressure on the oil companies to divert the road. The less edible bird population has more or less recovered. There is accommodation available here in a fairly basic jungle lodge.

About 8km (5 miles) from Limoncocha is the Capuchin mission of **Pompeya**. A bridge was built to the island by the oil company MAXUS, but access is strictly controlled. Among the houses on wooden stilts are an altar with a crucifix above a colored Indian canoe, as well as a curious museum. Here you can handle the various blow pipes used by Amazonian peoples to hunt – many are surprisingly long and heavy, often used to shoot directly upwards into the trees with a dart coated with natural venom that would paralyze the prey.

BELOW: a bar in the Oriente.

Map, pages 174/5

Opposite Pompeya is **Isla de los Monos** (Monkey Island), where you can wander freely and spot howler monkeys high in the trees above. You will need a little patience, but you should be well rewarded. There have been regrettable changes, however: not long ago the island was literally packed with monkeys, but the Ecuadorian army chose it as the site for survival training, and hundreds of these endangered creatures ended up in the soldiers' stews.

Amazon lodges

Not every visitor to the Oriente wants to bathe in a jungle river and sleep on the floor of an Indian hut at the end of a hard day of hiking in the jungle. For those wishing to visit the virgin rainforest, yet return to a comfortable room with a private shower at night, there are several well-known options.

La Selva Jungle Lodge ㉑, owned and operated by an American-Ecuadorian couple, Eric and Magdalena Schwartz, is perhaps the best known of the lodges. Getting to La Selva is half the adventure. As the crow flies it is along the Río Napo, going east from Limoncocha, but most people get there by taking a twin-propeller TAME aircraft trip from Quito to the jungle town of **Coca**, at the confluence of the Río Coca with the Napo. In Coca, passengers are met by lodge staff who drive them to the Napo for a two-and-a-half hour boat ride down to the La Selva dock. At this point, 96km (60 miles) from Coca, the Napo is about a kilometer wide. Visitors disembark and make a short hike along a rough boardwalk through the rainforest to **Laguna Garzacocha** (Heron Lake). Here they are met by simple dug-out canoes and paddled across the lake to the lodge.

The buildings at La Selva, up on stilts and with thatched roofs, have been well constructed to withstand extremes of jungle climate. One thing missing though

BELOW: the air service to Lago Agrio.

ABOVE AND BELOW: scenes on the River Napo. Panning for gold, and travel by local thatched transport.

is electricity. Rooms are lit with kerosene lamps, and the lack of a thumping generator outside the cabins ensures that guests are able to hear the myriad strange and startling sounds of the rainforest. La Selva is a mecca for birdwatchers: parrots, tanagers, toucans and numerous other species can be seen. Expert naturalists, many of them English-speaking, are on hand to guide visitors on walks and canoe rides through the jungle.

Sacha Lodge is another excellent option offering plenty of creature comforts (including electricity and hot water) and as great a variety of trails and trips as anyone could ask for. Just north of the Río Napo, it is reached by a three-hour motorized canoe trip from Coca. The lodge's observation tower enables you to climb 40 metres (130ft) into the canopy for an unobstructed view of miles and miles of intact rainforest, close-up views of plants and birds, and maybe the occasional sloth hanging from a tree-top. (A lodge with an observation tower is essential.) After a long day exploring the magic of the rainforest a dip in the Pilchicocha Lagoon in front of the lodge may be welcome. Details of how to book at these and other jungle lodges can be found in the *Travel Tips* section.

If you are short of time, on a budget and just want a taste of the rainforest there are plenty of trips on offer starting from the small town of **Misahuallí 22**, in the headwaters of the Río Napo. Here guides can be hired for about $30–40 a day. The area has been colonized and the forest here is secondary growth. The large mammals and birds have mainly been hunted out, but a short trip will give you an experience of the jungle and a look at a variety of plants, insects and smaller birds.

Near Misahuallí, on the Río Napo, is **Reserva Biológica Jatún Sacha**, a center dedicated to conservation, education and research, where a number of

Map, pages 174/5

unknown species have been discovered. Next door are the **Cabañas Alinahui** offering comfortable cabins, canoe trips, visits to nearby indigenous communities and walks along a great variety of trails in the area. Tourists can visit the station and see field work in progress. For butterfly lovers this area is paradise: besides hundreds of birds and plants an astonishing 765 butterfly species have been identified at Jatún Sacha.

One aspect of forest life which can be observed around Misahuallí is colonization: small coffee *fincas* (estates), oil palm plantations, cattle ranches, and yucca plots are prevalent. As you journey down the nearby river, you may occasionally notice workers washing and sifting material. They are panning for gold – modern descendants of the long line of settlers obsessed with dreams of El Dorado.

A little further down the Río Napo is **Yachana Lodge**, run by Funedesin, a non-profit organization. Innovative community projects are being developed as role models for sustainable ways of living in the rainforest. Funedesin, which is a foundation for the education and development of indigenous people, can be contacted in Quito at Andrade Marín 188, tel: 541862.

The fragile ecosystem

Any thinking person visiting the Oriente must ask themselves whether they are harming the environment and the lifestyles they are so keen to see and to preserve. This is a particularly pertinent question when it comes to visiting communities of indigenous people. One group which has so far resisted much contact with outsiders is the Huaorani who live in relative isolation in an area around the Río Cononoco.

The political organization ONHAE is working to protect the Huaorani from colonization, following the discovery of oil in the region, but it is difficult to predict whether Ecuador will be able to walk the tightrope between economic development and protecting the Huaorani and the rainforest ecosystem. Most of the Huaorani people, who maintain a hunter-gatherer way of life, do not welcome tourist visits to their communities and it is advisable to respect their wishes.

Living along the Río Aguarico, a small group of Cofan Indians are trying a different survival tactic. Working with the help of US-born Randy Borman, they encourage tourists to visit their village of **Sabelo** on carefully organized tours. Once there, visitors experience the Cofan lifestyle, sleeping on the floors of Cofan-style houses, traveling in dugout canoes, and hiking into the jungle in search of medicinal plants.

The ideal behind the enterprise is to hold on to the jungle and to offer the Cofan group the opportunity to control the rate of change, so that they can retain their language and their sense of themselves as a people. Some people feel that bringing tourism to a region in need of preservation is self-defeating, but Borman and the village leaders disagree. All the money generated goes to the Cofans, who are able to use and display their traditional knowledge of the Oriente, both for personal survival and as their singular contribution to a rapidly changing world (see *The Gringo Chief*, page 99).

BELOW: Oriente settlers.

ORIENTE WILDLIFE

*Everyone wants to see the armadillos and tapirs, the big cats
and the prolific birdlife. But the armies of insects which
most people try to avoid are no less interesting*

Map,
pages
174/5

The Oriente has such a diverse variety of wildlife that for many people the chance to see some of it in its natural habitat is reason enough to travel to Ecuador. Whether your interest is in birds, beasts, reptiles or insects you will find fascinating species in the Amazonian forest.

Fantastic bird life

Some 550 species of birds have been recorded in the Napo region alone, and professional and amateur ornithologists and birdwatchers flock to the area to see species with such exotic names as green and gold tanager, greater yellow-headed vulture, purple-throated fruitcrow, puffbird and toucan.

For many visitors, the parrots and macaws are the favorites. One of the highlights in a trip to La Selva or Sacha Lodge is a boat ride further down river to two large patches of soil laden with mineral salts. These natural salt licks attract hundreds of parrots which require the minerals in their diets. Birdwatchers at dawn can witness a magnificent display of hundreds of squawking, squabbling parrots feeding at the *salados*, as the salt licks are known. Species such as the blue-headed, orange-cheeked, and yellow-crowned parrot as well as the dusky-headed parakeet and scarlet-shouldered parrotlet have been observed here.

LEFT: the great egret. **BELOW:** a golden tanager.

Mammals of the rainforest

The minerals in the salt licks also attract a variety of jungle mammals. Most of these feed at night and leave only footprints for the curious visitor to observe in daylight. An adventurous person could spend the night by a salt lick and perhaps be rewarded with moonlit glimpses of a variety of mammals. These may include the nine-banded armadillo, or a rodent called the paca which has spotted fur, weighs up to 9kg (20lb) and is considered excellent food by local hunters, or perhaps the capybara, the world's largest rodent at 64kg (140lb).

Some salt licks attract a huge, strange mammal, the South American tapir. The largest land mammals in Amazonia, tapirs can weigh in excess of 270kg (600lb). Their closest relatives are the other odd-toed ungulates, the rhinoceros and the horse. Members of the tapir family are among the most primitive large mammals in the world and are well adapted to life in the jungle. Their short sturdy legs, thick, strong necks, and barrel-like bodies covered with incredibly tough skin enable them to shove through the dense forest undergrowth like a living tank. One of their strangest features is a short trunk which gives them an excellent sense of smell and is used to pull leaves off bushes and into their mouths.

Tapirs are much sought-after game animals. Local Indian hunters are able to feed an entire village if they are fortunate enough to shoot one. Apart from the meat,

The toothless armadillo is armed with bands of bony plates.

LEFT: a red howler monkey. **RIGHT:** a young puma.

the tapirs' fatty tissues yield an oil which is much prized for cooking, and the thick skin makes good-quality leather. The South American tapir lives in the Oriente lowlands and the mountain tapir inhabits the upper Amazonian basin and the Andean flanks. Hunting is not as much of a threat to the latter as is habitat destruction, and the mountain tapir is regarded as an endangered species by the Ecuadorian conservation organization, the Fundación Natura.

Apart from man, the tapir's greatest enemy is the big cat of Amazonia – the jaguar. A fully grown male can reach 113kg (250lb) in weight and, when hungry, will attack almost any large animal it comes across. Jaguars will leap onto tapirs' backs and attempt to kill them by breaking their necks in their powerful jaws. The tapirs' defense is twofold: the fact that the thick neck is protected by the tough, leathery skin and a bristly mane; and their habit of charging wildly through the dense undergrowth when threatened, thus making it difficult for a predator to hold on long enough to deliver the fatal bite.

Jaguars do not roar, as do most other big cats. Instead, they emit a low, coughing grunt, especially when hunting.Generally, jaguars are afraid of humans and only the luckiest of visitors catches a glimpse of them in the wild. Most travelers in the Oriente must be content with foot-prints in the soft earth or thrilling stories told by local residents.

You are also unlikely to see another resident, the spectacle bear, because it is a very shy creature, which is perhaps why it has survived for so long. The only bear found in South America, it ranges from 200 meters (650ft) to 4,200 meters (13,800ft) on the heavily forested subtropical slopes. It is mainly vegetarian, often climbing trees in search of succulent fruits. The bear's habitat is being encroached upon by colonists, and it is now protected by Ecuadorian law.

Howling monkeys

The mammals which most visitors do get to see often, however, are the monkeys. The most vocal of these is the very aptly named howler monkey. The males of this species have a specialized, hollow, and much enlarged hyoid bone in the throat. Air is passed through the hyoid cavity producing an ear-splitting call which can easily carry for well over a kilometer in the rainforest. This is an astounding feat when one remembers that the forest vegetation has a damping effect on sound. When heard in the distance, the call has been variously described as sounding like the wind moaning through the trees or like a human baby crying. Close up, the call can be quite terrifying to the uninitiated visitor.

The purpose of the call is to advertize a troop's presence in a particular patch of rainforest. This enables troops to space themselves out in the canopy and thus avoid competing as they forage for succulent young leaves. Occasionally, troops do meet in the tree tops and the result is often chaotic with howling chasing, threatening and even fighting. The energy used in these meetings is better expended in feeding and thus it pays for a troop to make its presence known by frequent howling.

Several other species of monkeys are frequently seen, including woolly, squirrel, spider and tarmarin monkeys. Often, the best way to observe monkeys is from a dug-out canoe floating down a jungle river. A local trained guide will spot a troop of monkeys early enough to stop the boat in a position which offers a clear view of the animals foraging in trees along the banks. From within the rainforest, on the other hand, animals may be difficult to see in the tree tops. In addition, monkeys may display their displeasure at human intrusion by hurling sticks, fruit, and even faeces down on the unfortunate visitor's head!

Map, pages 174/5

BELOW: a stunning blue butterfly.

Map, pages 174/5

Wildlife beneath your feet

Many people come to the Oriente hoping to see exotic birds and mammals, but also trying to avoid the myriad insects. Yet it is the insects which are the most common and, in many ways, most fascinating creatures of the rainforest. Some are simply beautiful, such as the breathtaking blue morpho butterflies whose huge wings flash a dazzling electric blue as they leisurely flap along jungle rivers. Other species have such complex life cycles that they are still not fully understood by tropical ecologists. Among these are hundreds of ant species, particularly the army ants and leaf-cutter ants, both of which species are commonly observed in the forest.

Colonies of leaf-cutter ants numbering hundreds of thousands live in huge nests dug deep into the ground. Foragers search the vegetation for particular types of leaves, cut out small sections and, holding the leaf segments above their heads like small umbrellas, bring them back to the nest. The ants can be quite experimental, bringing back a variety of leaves and even pieces of discarded plastic wrappers. Workers within the nest sort out the kinds of leaves which will mulch down into a type of compost; unsuitable material is ejected from the nest after a few days. The composted leaves form a mulch on which a fungus grows. Ants tend these fungal gardens with care, for they provide the main diet for both the adults ants and for the young which are being raised inside the nest.

The story does not end there. When a particularly good source of leaves has been located, ants lay down a trail of chemical markers, or pheromones, linking the nest with the leaf source, often 100 meters (330ft) or more away in the forest. People frequently come across these trails in the jungle, with hundreds of ants scurrying along carrying leaf sections back to the nest, or returning empty handed for another load.

BELOW: a tree boa, ready to strike.

Other species, for example army ants, may want to prey on this ready and constant supply of foragers. To combat this the leaf cutter ants are morphologically separated by size and jaw structure into different castes. Some specialize in tending the fungal gardens. Others have jaws designed for cutting the leaf segments, and yet others are soldiers, armed with huge mandibles, who accompany the foragers and protect them from attackers. Close observation of the foragers will sometimes reveal yet another caste, a tiny ant so small that it can ride on the leaf segments without disturbing the foragers. Biologists suggest that they act as protection against parasitical wasps which may try to lay their eggs on the foragers.

A colony of leaf cutter ants may last for a decade or more. New colonies are founded by the emergence of a number of potential queens, who mate and then fly off to found another nest, carrying some of the fungus used for food. This is essential to "seed" the new nest. The rest of the new queen's life is spent laying tens of thousands of eggs, destined to become gardeners, foragers, soldiers, riders, or even queens.

Such complicated interactions make the rainforest interesting to biologists and tourists alike. A day with a trained naturalist guide will bring to light many such stories about the habits of the forest's vast population of creatures great and small.

The Vanishing Rainforest

The plight of the world's tropical forests is becoming increasingly well known. Huge areas of forest are being logged or burned every day; so much deforestation is occurring that, at present rates, most of the world's rainforests will have disappeared by early in the next century. Of the almost 2 million known species of plants and animals, about half live only in the rainforest. Scientific estimates of species yet to be discovered are numbered in millions. Most of these unknown species live in the tropical forests, which have by far the greatest biodiversity of any region on the globe. Thus deforestation is causing countless extinctions, many of plants and animals as yet unknown.

Numerous medicines have been extracted from forest plants, ranging from malarial prophylactics to anaesthetics, from antibiotics to contraceptives. Quinine, used as a basis for the prevention and cure of malaria, was first recorded in the 17th century in the forests of southern Ecuador. Many more useful drugs will undoubtedly be discovered in the forests, if they are not destroyed first.

The diversity of species growing in the rainforests also comprises a storehouse of new strains of agriculturally important plants which may be destroyed by disease or drought. For example, if bananas were to be seriously threatened by disease, scientists could search the rainforests for disease-resistant strains to cross into the commercially grown varieties.

The forests are also essential for the survival of indigenous peoples. Hundreds of tribal groups living in the jungles of Latin America, and in Africa and Asia, are threatened by rainforest loss.

On a worldwide scale, the moderating effect of the rainforest on global climate patterns is only recently becoming understood. Deforestation could cause severe global warming, leading to melting ice caps, rising ocean levels, and flooding of coastal regions.

RIGHT: the rainforest is vital for the survival of the planet.

Climates would be altered to the extent that some major crops, such as wheat, would no longer grow.

The main reason the rainforest is being cut down is simple: money. Ecuador and other less-developed countries need to take advantage of the natural resources that the forest has to offer: lumber, cattle pasture, plantations, mineral wealth. This is, however, a short-sighted view. The essential long-term importance of the rainforest must be recognized, both by the host countries and the developed nations.

Debt-for-nature swaps, whereby foreign debts are paid off by the lenders in return for protection of the rainforest, are a move in the right direction, but the developed countries which lend the money must ensure that such incentives reflect the full value of the forests.

Sustainable use, such as rubber-tapping and brazil-nut harvesting, also help to a certain extent. Rainforests such as the Oriente are vital for our survival. Whatever the methods used, it is essential that they are protected.

RAILWAY JOURNEYS

Train journeys in Ecuador can be slow, crowded, and completely idiosyncratic, but they can also be a remarkably exhilarating experience

▷ **BUCAY BELLE**
Ecuador's favorite locomotive steams out of Bucay station.

Ecuador's trains are a colorful, part of the landscape, much-loved by tourists, but they are becoming increasingly uneconomical and, as roads and long-distance bus services improve, increasingly seen as time-consuming and inconvenient. Soon these idiosyncratic steam trains and "iron cars" may become the preserve of dedicated train enthusiasts rather than travelers, so enjoy them while you can.

THE IRON CAR

The Ibarra–San Lorenzo line was opened in 1957 after two French companies spent five years hacking a way through the wilderness. Until the recent construction of a highway, this was the only means of overland access to the coastal port of San Lorenzo in the north-western tip of the country.

This train is actually an antiquated bus, an autoferro ("iron car"), complete with brakes that feed on sand, mounted on a train's chassis and fitted with a diesel engine. It drops from Ibarra at 2,210 meters (6,630 ft) down to San Lorenzo, 190 km (120 miles) away, passing through 20 tunnels, clinging to the edges of vertiginous valleys, and at times almost suffocated by tropical vegetation.

It's not a smooth ride: landslides and derailments are common. All you can do then is wait for normal service to be resumed.

△ **IBARRA-SAN LORENZO**
The "iron car" makes one of its frequent unscheduled stops on the slow and scenic route between the sleepy capital of Ibarra and San Lorenzo on the untamed northern coast. The old bus seats 56 and half as many again huddle in the aisles and on the roof

▽ **MUSEUM PIECE**
Steam locomotives such as this romantic red monster draw many train enthusiasts to Ecuador. It regularly runs through the mountains, but In many countries these engines would be proudly displayed in railway museums.

△ **PIG STOP**
At Huigra station, about halfway between Bucay and Alausí on the Nariz del Diablo route, there's a stop for rather unconventional refreshments – slices from a whole roast pig (*asado*) are popular snacks. The Virgin Mary above the counter bestows a blessing on travelers.

△ **ROOF-TOP VIEW**
Riding on the roofs of trains is an Ecuadorian custom, and a way of escaping the heat of the carriage. Watch out for low-roofed tunnels.

GETTING UP THE DEVIL'S NOSE

Train travel in Ecuador began in 1910, when the Quito–Guayaquil line was opened after more than 30 years and a great deal of money had been spent on its construction. Built with US technical and financial assistance, it was immediately acclaimed as one of the "great railway journeys of the world," and reduced to two days a former nine-day trek along a mule path impassable half the year due to rain.

The most hair-raising train journey in Ecuador, and said to be one of the most spectacular in the world, is the section called El Nariz del Diablo (the Devil's Nose, pictured above) on the Quito–Guayaquil line between Alausí and Bucay. The elderly red steam train switchbacks down the precipitous descent, crossing spindly bridges over heart-stoppingly deep ravines – usually with passengers sitting on the roof, a rather alarming Ecuadorian custom, but one that ensures the best view.

Much of the track was destroyed by landslides during the devastating El Niño floods of 1982–83 but has since been repaired. Although it involves a distance of only about 65 km (40 miles), this part of the journey takes at least three hours – and they are spellbinding hours that no new traveler is likely to forget in a hurry.

▷ **WATER BREAK**
Having completed the most exciting part of its route, the steep descent from Alausí, the steam train stops to take on more water before continuing its journey to Durán on the outskirts of Guayaquil. The adrenaline rush over, many people get off at Bucay and take the bus the rest of the way.

HIGH STREET TRACK
Milagro, near Guayaquil, the train makes stately progress through the main street and no one hurries out of the way.

THE AVENUE OF THE VOLCANOES

The "spine" of Ecuador has hot springs and ethnic markets as well as a long line of breathtaking snowcapped mountains

Map, page 242

Quito

ECUADOR

The Andes are often thought of as the spine of Ecuador, but a ladder is a better analogy. Think of the Eastern and Western cordilleras as the sides of the ladder, with the lower east–west connecting mountains (called *nudos* or knots) as the rungs. Between each rung is an intermontane valley at about 2,300 to 3,000 meters (7,000 to 9,000ft) in elevation, with fertile volcanic soil. The valleys are heavily settled and farmed today and were the territory of different ethnic groups in pre-Inca times. Both the Pan-American Highway and the railroad run north–south between the cordilleras, bobbing up and down over the *nudos* past fields, farms and startled cows beneath a range of dormant and active volcanoes, some of which have permanent snowcaps.

In 1802 the German explorer Alexander von Humboldt named this route the "Avenue of the Volcanoes." Ecuador's position on the equator means that you can travel through the avenue past orchids and palm trees, with tundra vegetation, glaciers and snow visible in the mountains above. By leaving the valley and hiking or climbing up, you can pass through all the earth's ecological zones from sub-tropical to arctic.

A splendid way of traveling down the avenue is by train: not the quickest or most dependable way, but it does allow you to get an intimate look at life along the tracks, traveling through people's back yards, so to speak, rather than down the main road. The route suggested in this chapter, however, takes the Pan-American Highway, with detours and side roads to places of interest on the way.

The road south

Leaving **Quito ❶** by car or bus for the south can seem to take forever, as the streets leading to the Pan American Highway are usually jammed. However, there is now a bypass, the Nuevo Oriental, which connects with the Pan-American Highway on the outskirts of south Quito, and makes driving much less stressful. The road goes through the **Valle de los Chillos** and connects up with the main highway about 8km (5 miles) farther south. The traffic eases up a bit as you wind down off the Quito plateau and into the first intermontane valley. Way off to the east the snowy peak of **Volcán Antisana** (5,750 meters/18,720ft) can be seen.

Looming over the region is **Volcán Cotopaxi** (5,897 meters, 19,347ft), Ecuador's second highest peak and one of the world's highest active volcanoes. On a clear day you can see its perfect, snowcapped cone from north of Quito. In the Western Cordillera, almost directly across from Cotopaxi, is **Volcán Illiniza**

PRECEDING PAGES: Cotopaxi crater. **LEFT:** the basilica at Baños against an Andean hillside. **BELOW:** man from the bleak *páramo*.

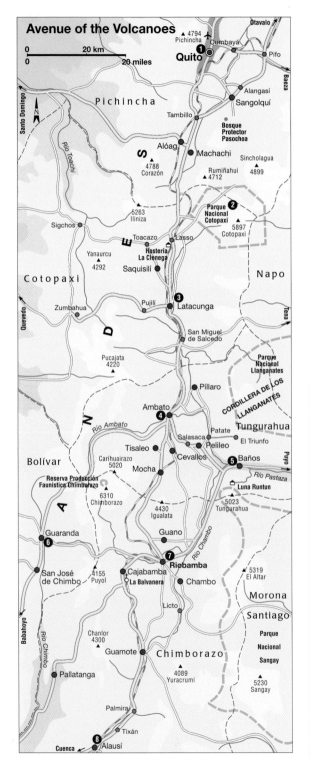

Avenue of the Volcanoes

(5,2635 meters, 17,280ft) – or the Illinizas as they are called, for there are actually two peaks. The lower, northern peak is a satisfying climb for non-technical climbers and hikers, while the southern one, Illiniza Sur, is only for the experienced.

Some 32km (20 miles) beyond Machachi, just over the first pass, is the entrance to the **Parque Nacional Cotopaxi** ❷. Both sides of the highway are covered by a dense forest of Monterrey pines, many of them dying from a fungus disease. The pines are not a native species; they were introduced to Ecuador from California for a forestry project and are a textbook example of the dangers of monoculture, because the pines have crowded out the indigenous vegetation and the fungus has spread rapidly from tree to tree.

The national park centers on Cotopaxi, of course, but there are several other peaks which attract climbers, including **Rumiñahui** (4,710 meters/

FIESTA DE LA MAMÁ NEGRA

Latacunga's festival of the Virgen de las Mercedes, commonly known as the Fiesta de la Mamá Negra (the Festival of the Black Mother) takes place on September 23 and 24. It's a lively event with obvious Indian influences despite its Christian name and outward trappings, which of course include paying homage to the figure of the black-faced Virgin Mary.

There are huge street parades with allegorical figures, often making satirical social or political points, masquerades, local bands, noisy firework displays and dancing in the streets until all hours of the night. There is also a solemn midnight mass (misa de gallo) although some of the celebrants are a little less than solemn. It is one of the best-known such fiestas in the country and well worth seeing, if your visit happens to coincide with these dates.

5,430ft), and there is also a great variety of wildlife, ranging from falcons and highland hummingbirds to tiny deer and the endangered, and rarely seen, Andean puma.

Map, page 242

Haciendas and markets

As elsewhere in Latin America the prime agricultural land in the valley was taken from the indigenous population soon after the Spanish conquest and turned into large Spanish-owned estates (*haciendas*), many of which still exist and include vast landholdings, despite the Agrarian Reform of 1964. Back on the highway, at Km 68 from Quito, you come to the entrance to **Tambo Mulaló**, a *hacienda* which has been converted to tourist use, offering excellent typical food (*comida criolla*). A *tambo* in Inca times was a way station or inn for travelers. During the colonial era, Tambo Mulaló was a retreat for Jesuits, then an inn for travelers on the road to Quito. It is now a dairy farm with a small bullring and horse-back riding.

A hop down the road is the tiny town of **Lasso** and the turn off to the west for the **Hostería La Ciénega**. Now a hotel and restaurant, its main house – a stone mansion with huge windows, stone-cobbled patios and Moorish-style fountains – was built in the mid-1600s for the Marquis de Maenza and was occupied by his family for more than 300 years. The stone chapel has a bell, still rung on Sunday mornings, which was installed in 1768 in thanksgiving when Cotopaxi ended 20 years of devastating eruptions. Von Humboldt stayed here in 1802 when he surveyed Cotopaxi, and the de Maenza-Lasso family plotted Ecuador's independence from Spain on this site in the 1800s. The comfortable rooms are well furnished. Besides opportunities for excellent birdwatching in the gardens you

BELOW: horseman on the windswept Sierra.

The Hostería La Ciénega.

BELOW: chicken transport, economy class.

can ride horseback from here and make day trips to Cotopaxi National Park.

The little towns in the valley, and the larger city of **Latacunga** ❸ (pop. 40,000), are interesting primarily for their fiestas and market days. Some 90 km/54 miles from Quito, Latacunga is somnolent and pleasant, with a number of buildings constructed from local gray volcanic rock. It was founded in 1534 on the site of an Inca urban center and fortress. There are busy Saturday and Tuesday markets, where crafts are sold, especially *shigras,* baskets and ponchos.

Latacunga's town hall *(municipio)* and cathedral are on the main plaza, the Parque Vicente León, which has topiary and a well-maintained garden. Behind the cathedral is a converted colonial building housing an arcade with shops, offices and an art gallery. Five blocks west down Calle Maldonado at Calle Vela there is a small ethnographic museum in the **Molinos (Mills) de Montserrat** (open Tues–Sat 10am–5pm) which is operated by the Casa de la Cultura Ecuatoriana. After that, it's easy to get the small town blues, but Latacunga makes a good base for side trips to other parts of Cotopaxi Province.

Some 10km (6 miles) west of Latacunga is Pujilí, which has a lively market on Sunday, but otherwise very little going for it except the Corpus Christi festivities in June, the most colorful celebration of the fiesta you will find.

A wild and scenic loop west of Latacunga takes you through the market towns of Zumbagua, Chugchilan, Sigchos and Saquisilí, then back to Latacunga. Zumbagua's market is on Saturday, when stalls are stocked with colorful fresh produce. Half an hour's drive further on is Lake Quilotoa, an azure colored volcanic crater, still considered active. Indigenous people from the Tigua valley nearby sell naive, brightly-colored enamel paintings on sheepskin at the crater rim. Going north from here to the village of Chugchilan is the Black Sheep Inn, an

Map,
page 242

ecological farm with delicious home cooking and great views over the sierra. The whole loop back takes several hours along mainly dirt roads, so a stop here is a welcome break.

Saquisilí only comes out of its torpor on Thursday market day. The market is an economic hub for the surrounding region, with *indígenas* buying and selling everything from cattle to cotton. The market is decidedly a local, rather than tourist, affair and a favorite with many travelers for that reason.

Back in Latacunga, the Pan-American Highway continues south, deep into the central Sierra. About 11km (7 miles) from Latacunga on the outskirts of San Miguel de Salcedo, is the **Hostería Rumipamba de las Rosas**, yet another converted *hacienda*. Rumipamba has the best food in the region. It has an especially good Sunday buffet, with folk musicians playing traditional music. It's also a good place to stay, with comfortable rooms, a swimming pool, a playground for children, and a rather sad-looking zoo.

Some 10km (6 miles) further south you cross the provincial boundary and enter Tungurahua Province named, like most of the highland provinces, after the area's dominant volcano. The region is known for its relatively mild climate and production of vegetables, grain and fruit, including peaches, apricots, apples, pears, and strawberries, and you will encounter roadside vendors along the highway on both sides of Ambato.

Provincial center

At 128km (80 miles) from Quito, **Ambato ❹** is the capital of Tungurahua Province. Arriving in the city brings you abruptly face to face with the 20th century. Ambato was almost totally destroyed by an earthquake in 1949 and then

BELOW: a colorful Tigua painting on sheepskin

rebuilt, so virtually nothing of the colonial town remains. With a population of about 120,000, the city is the fourth largest in Ecuador, after Guayaquil, Quito and Cuenca.

Industries include some textiles (especially rug weaving), leather goods, food processing and distilling, but the most interesting aspect of the city is its enormous Monday market, the largest in Ecuador. Thousands of *indígenas* and country people come into town for the different activities, which take place in various parts of the city. Several plazas contain nothing but produce vendors, while the streets are lined with kiosks selling goods of all kinds. To reach the textiles, dyes, and crafts (ponchos, ikat blankets and shawls, *shigras,* belts, beads, hats, embroidered blouses) follow Calle Bolívar or Cevallos about 10 blocks north from the center of town to the area around Calle Abdón Calderón.

Guinea-pig for sale: for a pet or the pot?

After the market is a good time to visit Ambato's two central plazas. The main one, the **Parque Montalvo**, is named after the writer Juan Montalvo (1833–99), and has an imposing statue of him. Montalvo's nearby house, at Calles Bolívar and Montalvo, is open to the public. On the north side of the Parque Montalvo is Ambato's modern **cathedral**, with some fine stained-glass windows. Opposite it is the the post office. The **Parque Cevallos**, a few blocks to the northwest, is green and tree-lined, and is the site of the **Museo de Ciencias Naturales** (open Mon–Fri 8am–noon, 2–6pm; entrance fee), packed with stuffed animals and birds of the region.

BELOW: cooking up a storm at Ambato market.

The Río Ambato flows through a gorge to the west of the town center. A walk south along the river leads to the suburb of Miraflores, where there are several fine old *quintas* (country homes) which have gardens open to the public. A paved road leads out of Ambato to the east, past Volcán Tungurahua and down into the

Oriente, forming one of the main east–west links between jungle and Sierra.

From Ambato, catch a bus or truck 20km (12 miles) northeast to the small town of **Píllaro**. This is the way to get to the **Parque Nacional Llanganates**, perpetually wrapped in fog and covered with virtually impenetrable cloudforest vegetation. These remote mountains appeal to the Indiana Jones in all of us because of various accounts of General Rumiñahui hiding Quito's gold here, before Benalcázar and the *conquistadores* could get to it.

Map, page 242

Defiant and distinctive

About 14km (8 miles) east of Ambato on the road to Baños is **Salasaca**, the home of a small, beleaguered indigenous group, which is struggling to hold on to its land and maintain its customs in the face of enormous pressure from whites in the surrounding communities. The Salasaca are said to have been *mitmakuna*, part of the Incas' divide and rule policy, under which groups of people were moved from one part of the empire to another. They are said to have originated in Bolivia and been sent to Ecuador by the Incas as punishment for a revolt, although there seems to be no documentary evidence for this.

Salasaca men wear black and white ponchos and handmade white felt hats with broad, upturned brims at the front and back. Unique to Salasaca are the men's purple or deep-red scarves dyed with cochineal, a natural dye that comes from the female insects that live on the Opuntia (prickly pear) cactus. Salasaca women wear the same hats as the men, brown or black *anakus,* cochineal-dyed shoulder wraps, handwoven belts with intricate motifs, and necklaces of red and Venetian glass beads.

A few kilometers past Salasaca is **Pelileo**, a little town in which you wouldn't

BELOW: Salasaca *indígenas* returning from market.

want to invest in property: it has been leveled by earthquakes four times in the past 300 years. As the last quake was in 1949, the present Pelileo is an entirely modern town. There is a small Saturday market, which is attended by many *indígenas* from Salasaca. It is also Ecuador's major production center for blue jeans.

Sub-tropical climate

Beyond Pelileo the highway drops 850 meters (2,780ft) to Baños in only 24km (15 miles), following various tributaries and then the Río Pastaza itself in its headlong rush to the Amazon basin. The region produces sugar cane for distilled alcohol, and many kinds of fruits and vegetables.

Baños ❺, with a population of only about 15,000, probably has more hotels per acre than any other community in Ecuador. The main attraction is the thermal hot springs bubbling out of the side of the wild and unruly **Volcán Tungurahua** (5,020 meters/16,465ft) which broods above the town. There are also several private hot baths connected with the various hotels. The Piscina El Salado baths, with pools of varying temperatures, half a kilometer back up the road to Ambato, are often less crowded than are the baths in town.

Baños has its own Hard Rock Café – but it's a quaint little place, completely unrelated to the rest of the chain.

The gentle, sub-tropical climate and vegetation around Baños (altitude 1,800 meters/5,886ft) is another draw, especially after the chill of the highlands. The region is a hiker's paradise: you can walk up the slopes of Tungurahua along many different trails leading out of town, or head for the Pastaza river gorge where there are dozens of waterfalls, some on the Pastaza, others cascading off Tungurahua into the Pastaza's tributaries. Jungle trips and white-water rafting can be arranged in Baños, and you can also rent horses by the hour or day.

BELOW: thermal baths beneath a waterfall in Baños.

Follow the main highway east toward Puyo and the Oriente you come to the spectacular Río Verde falls, about 20km (12 miles) from Baños. Many varieties of orchids grow along the road, and the area is excellent for birdwatching.

If travelers come for the hot springs and hiking, thousands of Ecuadorians come to pay homage to the Virgin of Baños, known as **Nuestra Señora del Agua Santo** (Our Lady of the Holy Water), whose statue is housed in the basilica in the center of town. The Virgin is credited with many miracles including delivering people from certain death in a fire in Guayaquil, and saving the lives of travelers when a bridge over the Pastaza River collapsed. The walls of the basilica are hung with paintings depicting these events. The basilica grounds have a small museum with moldering stuffed tropical birds and the Virgin's changes of clothing. The tiny zoo with dejected tropical birds, tapirs and a few snakes and tortoises has now moved to near the San Ignes Falls, 3km (2 miles) west of Baños.

A mountain detour

From Baños, return to Ambato (buses are frequent and the journey takes about an hour) and make a trip to the west. A paved road circles around **Volcán Carihuairazo** (5,020 meters/5,886ft) and **Volcán Chimborazo** (6,310 meters/20,571ft) and heads for Guaranda and the coast. Chimborazo, of course, is the highest peak in Ecuador and it looms over the provinces of Chimborazo, Bolívar and southern Tungurahua like a

giant ice cube, dominating the landscape (see page 119 for climbing information). The **Reserva Producción Faunística Chimborazo** (Chimborazo Fauna
Reserve) is also worth a visit.

Map,
page 242

The Western Cordillera outside Ambato is the land of emerald mountains.
Every inch of the vertical hillsides is farmed by the Chibuleo *indígenas,* turning the land into a patchwork quilt composed of every imaginable shade of
green. Every so often, either Carihairazo or Chimborazo pokes its snowy head
out above the clouds. The road climbs to the *páramo* above 4,000 meters (13,000
ft), with some superb views of Chimborazo, then drops again to Guaranda,
which is 85km (53 miles) from Ambato. Midway through the journey you enter
Bolívar Province.

Art and fireworks

About 90km (55 miles) from Ambato, the capital of Bolívar Province,
Guaranda ❻ (2,670 meters/8,725ft) is a small, sleepy town of 14,000 people,
that comes alive on Saturday with the weekly market. It is set among seven hills,
one of which, Cruz Loma (Cross Hill), has a giant statue of an indigenous chief,
El Indio de Guarango, a *mirador* (lookout) and a small, circular museum with
pre-Hispanic and colonial artifacts. There are three other small museums in the
town with mixed collections including colonial art and ethnographic material:
the **Museo Municipal**, the **Museo de la Casa de la Cultura Ecuatoriana**, and
the **Museo del Colegio Pedro Carbo**. Opening hours are variable: check on
arrival. The **Parque Central** has a monument to the liberator, Simón Bolívar,
which was a gift from the government of Venezuela.

BELOW: hotels, bars
and Coca Cola
on the main
street of Baños.

Guaranda is the market center for the **Chimbo Valley**, a rich agricultural

A pregnant Virgin Mary in the Riobamba museum.

region that produces wheat and corn (*maiz*). A 16-km (10-mile) ride through the valley south from Guaranda takes you to **San José de Chimbo**, an ancient town with colonial architecture and two thriving craft centers. The *barrio* (neighborhood) of Ayurco specializes in fine guitars, handmade from high-quality wood that is grown in the province, while the *barrio* of Tambán produces hunting guns and fireworks.

But these aren't just any old fireworks. Bamboo frames (*castillos,* or castles) are fabricated in the shape of giant birds, huge towers or enormous animals, with fireworks attached. They are set off to striking effect at fiestas throughout the country. It's not uncommon for the *castillo* to fall over, shooting sky rockets directly into the crowd. Cowardly gringos generally jump for cover behind the plaza fountain, but the Ecuadorians love it.

Ancient center

There is a rough dirt track from from Guaranda to **Riobamba** ❼, capital of Chimborazo Province, but most people return to Ambato and travel the 65km (40 miles) on the Pan-American Highway. The Pana climbs up to the *páramo* past the small town of Mocha, skirts the eastern slopes of Carihuairazo and Chimborazo, crosses the pass and then drops down into the Riobamba Valley. However, a new road is being constructed from Guaranda to Riobamba.

BELOW: mules cautiously cross a mountain bridge.

In 1541 the Spanish chronicler, Pedro de Cieza de León, began an epic 17-year horseback journey in Pasto, Colombia, riding south along the Royal Inca Highway through Ecuador, Peru and Bolivia. By 1545 Cieza was in central Ecuador heading for Riobamba. "Leaving Mocha," he wrote, "one comes to the lodgings of Riobamba, which are no less impressive than those of Mocha. They

are situated in the province of the Puruhás in beautiful fair fields, whose climate, vegetation, flowers, and other features resemble those of Spain." Chimborazo is still primarily an agricultural province, growing crops such as wheat, barley, potatoes and carrots, with some grazing land for small herds of sheep, llama and cattle.

It's only an hour from Ambato to Riobamba, but for each half hour of travel you feel as if you were going back a century. Two more completely unlike provincial capitals located so close to each other would be hard to imagine.

Although Riobamba, at 2,750 meters (8,993ft) is only 180 meters (589ft) higher than Ambato, it feels much colder, perhaps because of the wind sweeping down off the glaciers of Chimborazo.

The original Riobamba, the city the Spanish founded on the site of a major Inca settlement, was located 21km (13 miles) away where the modern town of Cajabamba stands, but the old town was flattened by an earthquake in 1797 and a new location was chosen. The new Riobamba (pop. 70,000) has the architecture and ambience of an 18th-century town; stately, quiet and slow – except, of course, on Saturday, which is market day.

Map, page 242

Indigenous peoples

Chimborazo Province was the pre-Inca territory of the Puruhá tribe. Such modern towns as Guano, Chambo, Pungalá, Licto, Punin, Yaruquies, Alausí, Chunchi and Chimbo were Puruhá settlements. But the Incas moved people around, as they did throughout the empire. For example, they settled *indígenas* from Cajamarca and Huamachuco, Peru, in the Chimbo region and moved many Puruhá people to the south.

BELOW: the town of Riobamba, beneath Mount Chimborazo.

Today Chimborazo has an amazing mixture of people who wear different kinds of traditional dress, although there aren't necessarily special names for all these groups. Chimborazo was the site of many *obrajes* (textile sweatshops) in colonial times and the more recent locale of *haciendas* with enormous land-holdings, so that the indigenous population became increasingly impoverished and marginalized through succeeding centuries as they were pushed by new settlers into the mountains or became attached to the country *haciendas* as *wasipungeros* (serfs).

The Chimborazo *indígenas* did not take mistreatment and injustice lying down. There have been many revolts over the centuries including an uprising of 8,000 *indígenas* around Riobamba in 1764, a revolt in Guano in 1778, and a rebellion in Columbe and Guamote in 1803. Land shortages are still a problem and men from many communities frequently migrate temporarily to the larger cities in search of work. Chimborazo has also seen intensive Protestant Evangelical missionizing, which has often exacerbated ethnic tensions.

Dark fedoras are taking over from the traditional white.

The most obvious ethnic marker in Chimborazo is hats. While *indígenas* are increasingly using dark, commercially made fedoras, a large number still wear the handmade white felt hats, especially for fiestas and other special occasions. In the Guamote market you can spot as many as 15 different kinds of white handmade hats being worn. Such variations as the size and shape of the brim and crown and the color and length of the streamers, tassels or other decorations all indicate the wearer's community or ethnic group.

BELOW: the main plaza of Riobamba.

Two areas of the Riobamba market are of special interest to travelers. Traditional indigenous garments, including such items as hats, belts, ponchos, *ikat* shawls, fabric, *shigras,* hats and old jewelry (beautiful beads, earrings and *tupus*)

are sold in the **Plaza de la Concepción** on Orozco and 5 de Junio, along with baskets and *ikat* blankets. In one corner of this plaza people set up their treadle sewing machines and mend clothes or sew the collars on ponchos, while other vendors sell aniline dyes. Just south of this plaza on Calle Orozco is a small cooperative store selling crafts made by the *indígenas* of Cacha.

Map, page 242

Another important craft of the Riobamba region is *tagua* nut carving. The egg-sized seeds of the lowland tagua palm are soft when first exposed to air but then harden to an ivory-like consistency. *Tagua* is carved into jewelry, chess sets, buttons, rings, busts and tiny kitchen utensils. Stores opposite the railroad station located on Avenida Primera Constituyente sell *tagua* crafts. (The Avenue of the First Constitution acquired its name because, after winning its war of independence from Spain, Ecuador's first constitution was written and signed in Riobamba on August 14, 1830.)

About eight blocks northeast of the *artesanías* plaza is the **Plaza Dávalos**, where *cabuya* fiber (made from Agave americana cactus, the century plant) and products are sold. *Cabuya* crafts have been an important local industry in the region since colonial times. *Indígena* women spin the fiber into cordage, which is used for such items as the soles of *alpargatas,* rope, *shigras,* saddle bags and vegetable sacks.

After the market the town empties rapidly and lapses into somnolence for another week. This is your opportunity to visit the **Museo de Arte Religioso** (open Tues–Sat 9am–12.30pm, 3–6.30pm; Sun 9am–12.30pm) housed in the Covento de la Concepción on Calle Orozco at España. Among the items on display are statues, vestments and a fabulous gold monstrance encrusted with diamonds and pearls.

Riobamba is home to three other small museums. The museum in the **Colegio Nacional Pedro Vicente Maldonado** on Avenida Primera Constituyente 2412 has natural history exhibits. The **Museo de la Escuela Politécnica Superior de Chimborazo** displays archaeology and contemporary art, while the **Museo del Banco Central**, in the new bank building downtown, has ethnographic and modern art exhibitions. Opening times for all these museums are erratic, so it is worth checking at the tourist information office on Calle 10 de Agosto, near the main plaza. Riobamba also has some majestic old churches, including the **cathedral** on 5 de Junio and Veloz and the completely round **Basilica** (the only one in Ecuador) on Veloz and Alvarado in the Parque La Libertad.

At sunset climb to the top of the **Parque 21 de Abril** (located on Calle Argentinos north of the center of town). With luck you can catch the last light on mountains Chimborazo, Carihuairaso, Tungurahua and **Altar** (5,319 meters/17,457ft). The latter, which is the brooding hulk south of the city in the Eastern Cordillera, is also known in Quichua as *Capac Urcu* (meaning Great or Powerful Mountain).

BELOW: elegant park and statue, Riobamba.

Exploring the region

Riobamba is a good base for excursions to the rest of Chimborazo Province. For a day trip to buy rugs and visit the artisans at work, catch a bus or cab 12km (7 miles) north on a subsidiary road, not the Pan-American Highway, to **Guano**. The town is known for its cottage-industry production of fine rugs, handknotted on huge vertical frame looms. Most shops have a workshop attached where you can watch the weavers at work.

Cabuya fiber comes from the agave plant and is similar in texture to cotton.

Just a kilometer or two beyond Guano (there is a bus service) is the small town of **Santa Teresita**, which specializes in the production of carrot or potato sacks woven from *cabuya* fiber. Many of the weavers have enormous warping frames in their yards, with hundreds of meters of *cabuya* on them, and you may also see the woven yardage stretched out along the road. At the edge of town is the **Balneario Las Elenas**, with two cold-water swimming pools, one warmer pool, all fed by natural springs, and a cafeteria.

Most of Chimborazo Province lies to the south of Riobamba, and it's a part of Ecuador worth exploring. The road to Licto climbs above Riobamba and offers good views of the city and the volcanoes.

Another quiet, but extremely traditional Sunday market, drawing *indígenas* from the Laguna Colta area and the usual assortment of vendors, is held in **Cajabamba**, 13km (8 miles) south of Riobamba on the Pan-American Highway. This was the site of the old Riobamba, which was originally a Puruhá community and then the Inca settlement of Liripamba when it had fine, mortarless stonework, including a temple of the sun, a house of the chosen women and a royal *tambo*. The stones from the Inca buildings were incorporated into the Spanish town, which was destroyed in the 1797 earthquake and subsequent landslide. The only building surviving from the 18th century is the chapel.

BELOW: Indians farming near Alausí.

About 2km (just over a mile) beyond Cajabamba is the tiny town of **Balvanera** (also spelled Balbanera), on the shores of **Laguna Colta**. Colta *indígenas*

graze their cattle and sheep along the marshy shores of the lake, and use the totora reeds in the lake to make mats *(esteras)* and baskets *(canastas)*.

The story is that the little church, with its image of the Virgin of Balvanera, is the oldest church in Ecuador, constructed by the *conquistador* Sebastián de Benalcázar and his troops after a victory over the Inca forces, but there is no documentary evidence to support this.

If the journey from Ambato to Riobamba takes you back two centuries, the trip to **Guamote** (51km/32 miles south of Riobamba) is yet another time warp. The Thursday market is the major weekly fair for the southern part of the province. *Indígenas* on horseback or leading llamas laden with produce arrive from communities where no road reaches. At the animal market much of the bargaining takes place in Quichua, but at the food and clothing markets more vendors speak Spanish. You will see more *indígenas* in different kinds of traditional dress here than at any other market in Ecuador.

Map, page 242

Switchback railway

From here, the highway drops down past Tixan and into **Alausí** (2,356 meters, 7,704ft). Alausí was once used as a resort to escape from the heat of Guayaquil, and now it has the feel of a place past its prime. But it has charm, and an interesting Sunday market. Alausí's is still famous, however, for the **Nariz del Diablo** (Devil's Nose) railway which switchbacks back and forth between here and Sibambe, dropping precipitously, on its way between Quito and Guayaquil. The switchbacks were washed away in the *El Niño* storms of 1982–83, but the railroad has been repaired and trains are once again making the hair-raising trip between Guayaquil and the highlands. (*For more details, see pages 236–37.*)

BELOW: llamas transport produce to market.

THE SOUTHERN SIERRA

*Beautiful colonial Cuenca, the Inca ruins of Ingapirca
and the valley of Vilcabamba are just three of many reasons
for visiting Cañar, Azuay and Loja Provinces*

Map,
page 265

T he southern Sierra, consisting of Cañar, Azuay and Loja Provinces, is the least visited part of the highlands, mainly for reasons of accessibility rather than for lack of attractions. The Andes broaden and flatten out somewhat here, with none of the dramatic snowcaps of the central and northern highlands, but with plenty of stunning green vistas and mountain roads guaranteed to give you an adrenaline rush.

Hub of the south

The jumping off point for most trips in the south is **Cuenca ❶**, capital of Azuay Province, with a population of 153,000, making it Ecuador's third largest city. Until about 35 years ago, Cuenca was isolated from the rest of Ecuador by the lack of good roads, but now it is connected to both Guayaquil and the northern Sierra by paved highways, as well by daily flights to Quito and Guayaquil, and (when the railway is working) *autoferro* connections with the Guayaquil-Riobamba-Quito line at Sibambe.

The Cuenca basin is a major *artesanías* center, producing ceramics, *paja toquilla* (Panama) hats, baskets and Christmas ornaments, gold and silver jewelry, and *ikat* shawls, ponchos and blankets. Other industries include textiles, furniture and automobile tires. The city is the economic and intellectual center of the southern Sierra, with a state university and a long history as the birthplace of artists, writers, poets and philosophers.

Most Ecuadorians consider Cuenca to be their country's most beautiful city and it's hard to find anyone who would argue. Cuenca means river basin or bowl in Spanish, and the city is situated at 2,549 meters (8,335 ft) on the banks of the **Río Tomebamba**. It has retained its colonial architecture and feel, with new construction in a neo-colonial style that is compatible with existing structures. The blue domes of the new cathedral dominate the skyline.

Because of its cobblestone streets, interior patios and public plazas overflowing with flowers and greenery, and whitewashed buildings with huge wooden doors and ironwork balconies, Cuenca is a walker's delight. In fact, you really need to wander at a slow and gentle pace to appreciate and absorb the details of the city.

Originally, Cuenca was a major Cañari settlement. After the Inca conquest, it became an important city called *Tumipampa*, the Plain of the Knife (Hispanicized as Tomebamba), intended to be the Cuzco of the north.

Very little of that Inca city remains. If you follow Calle Larga southeast as it goes downhill along the Tomebamba River (near the junction of Calle Tomás Ordoñez with Calle Larga) you will come to the ruins of **Todos Santos**. This small site includes four perfect

PRECEDING PAGES:
patchwork fields of
the southern Sierra.
LEFT: colonial
streets of Cuenca.
RIGHT: after a storm
on the *páramo*.

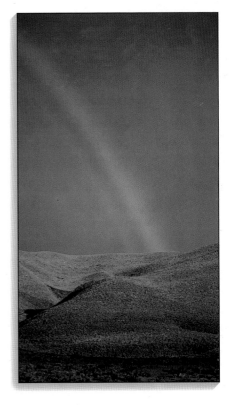

Inca trapezoidal mortarless stonework niches, and the remains of the colonial mill of Todos Santos, which was constructed with stones taken from Inca buildings. There are remains of Inca walls on the hillside above the mill, where ceramics and other evidence of Inca occupation were excavated.

Colonial culture

In 1532 the Inca armies retreated north before the advancing forces of Sebastian de Benalcázar. The Spanish city of Cuenca was founded on this site in 1557, and named Santa Ana de los Cuatro Ríos de Cuenca.

The bells for Cuenca's cathedral, donated by Germany, have remained at the entrance to the nave ever since construction of the tower ended.

As soon as the Spanish arrived in an area they built a church, and Cuenca was no exception. The **Catedral Vieja** (Old Cathedral) **A**, on the east side of the main plaza, the Parque Calderón, was started in 1557, the year the city was founded. But the city outgrew this simple old church and construction on the **Catedral Nueva B** began in 1880. The new church, dedicated to the Immaculate Conception of the Virgin Mary, was built to hold 10,000 celebrants during religious events and is opposite the old cathedral on the Parque Calderón.

The neo-Gothic New Cathedral was intended to be 42.5 meters (141ft) wide and 105 meters (351ft) tall, which would have made it the largest church in South America. It is constructed from alabaster and local marble with floors of pink marble imported from Carrara, Italy. But the architect miscalculated and designed bell towers too heavy for the structure to support, so work on the towers was halted in 1967.

The **Parque Abdón Calderón** is Cuenca's main square, with the Municipio (town hall) on the south side. Just off the southwest corner of the square, on Calle Sucre, is the **Casa de la Cultura Ecuatoriana. C** This small colonial-

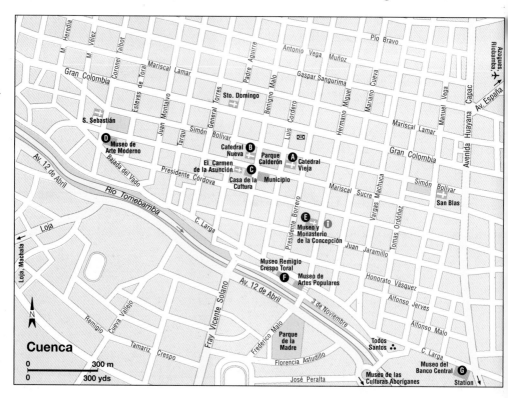

Cuenca

0 — 300 m
0 — 300 yds

Map,
page 260

style building frequently has good exhibitions of local art. On the same block is the **Monasterio del Carmen de la Asunción**, founded in 1682. The church has a fine old carved stone façade and the pulpit is gilded and embellished with mirrors. However, the building is often closed, so you may have to be content with the exterior architecture. A daily flower market is held in the tiny plaza in front of the church and for as little as a few sucres you can brighten your hotel room considerably.

Is modern art more to your taste? The **Museo de Arte Moderno** (Modern Art Museum) **Ⓓ** (open Mon–Fri 9am–1pm, 3–6pm; admission free) is also on Calle Sucre, at Coronel Talbot. This museum has rotating exhibitions of contemporary art as well as art workshops for children.

If you're not tired of churches (Cuenca has 27), go back along Calle Sucre and turn right at Calle Hermano Miguel to the **Museo y Monasterio de la Concepción** (Church and Museum of the Conception) **Ⓔ** (museum open Tues–Fri 9am–4pm, Sat 9am–noon; entrance fee).The entrance to the church contains 17th-century tombstones. The cloister, built between 1682 and 1729, was recently restored by the Banco Central. The cloister's museum contains an unusual collection of religious art including toys presented to the convent by novices entering the order, a silver nativity scene, and an altarpiece of carved wood and gold by the sculptor Manuel Machina.

As for other museums in Cuenca, the **Museo Municipal Remigio Crespo Toral** **Ⓕ** (open Mon–Fri 9am–1pm) on Calle Larga 707 at the intersection with Borrero, gives new meaning to the word decrepit. The building is ancient, with creaking stairways and crumbling plaster, but somehow it's the perfect setting for all kinds of old artifacts, from pre-Hispanic ceramics and goldwork from the

BELOW: cupolas in Cuenca.

Detail of a mural in El Turi, Cuenca.

Cañari and Chordeleg cultures to colonial paintings, furniture and religious sculptures.

The new **Museo del Banco Central** ❻ (open Mon–Fri 8.30am–5.30pm; Sat 9am–1pm; entrance fee) is located on Avenida Huayna-Capac across Calle Larga, above excavations of some Inca walls. The museum has permanent archaeological, ethnographic, colonial and republican art collections, as well as old photographs of Cuenca.

The Museo del Banco Central inherited the collection of the late Father Crespi, a Salesian priest who died in the late 1980s. Father Crespi's artifacts consist of an amazing variety of pieces from pure junk to fine pre-Inca ceramics, which the museum is in the process of sorting and dating. Crespi firmly believed that Ecuador was settled by the Phoenicians who sailed up the Amazon.

Also try the **Museo de las Culturas Aborígenes** (open Mon–Sat 9am–noon, 3–6pm; entrance fee; tel: 811 706 for guided tour) at Avenida 10 de Agosto 4-70, on the south side of the Río Tomebamba. It holds a fascinating private collection of pre-Colombian archaeology from various cultures throughout Ecuador.

Indigenous groups

Many of the Cuenca valley people occupy an intermediate position between *indígenas* and whites. They are generally artisans and country people and are called *Cholos Cuencanos*, and represent a mixture of Inca, Cañari, and Spanish blood. The rich *cholo* culture is slowly disappearing as young people adopt modern-style clothing and move to the cities or to work in the United States.

In rural areas and especially at the markets in Sigsig, Gualaceo, Chordeleg, and sometimes in Cuenca you will still see people in traditional *cholo* dress,

Art in Cuenca, past and present: **LEFT:** cathedral door, **RIGHT:** mural in El Turi.

Map,
page 265

which includes Panama hats for both men and women and colored ponchos, especially burgundy and red, for men. For fiestas many *cholo* men wear beautiful handwoven *ikat* ponchos (see chapter on *Artesanías,* page 107, for details).

If you're in Cuenca mid-week for the Thursday weekly fair or for the smaller Saturday market, check out the plaza between Calle Mariscal Lamar and Sangurima off Calle Hermano Miguel, where *artesanías* are sold, including baskets, wool and *ikat* shawls (*paños*). (The permanent food market is on the other side of town, on Calle Cordova off Padre Aguirre.)

Southern Ecuador is well-known for its crafts. The Organization of American States has a permanent center in Cuenca for the preservation and promotion of traditional *artesanías:* the Centro Interamerico de Artesanías y Artes Populars (CIDAP), whose offices and museum located on the stairs where Calle Hermano Miguel intersects Calle Larga and descends to the Río Tomebamba.

Excursions into the countryside

Gualaceo is about 36km (22 miles) from Cuenca on paved roads. Buses run regularly between the two places, heading north of Cuenca on the Pana, turning east at El Descanso and following the Río Paute. It is a pretty town situated on the banks of the Río Gualaceo and is the site of *quintas,* summer homes for people from Cuenca and Guayaquil. The slightly lower elevation makes it ideal for growing peaches, apricots, apples, cherries, guayabas and chirimoyas. There are several good restaurants along the river, and an inn, the **Parador Turistico Gualaceo**, which has comfortable rooms, a restaurant and a swimming pool.

Chordeleg, a pre-Inca Cañari town, has artisans of all kinds: ikat poncho weavers, *paja toquilla* hat and basket weavers, potters, embroiderers and jew-

BELOW: laundry drying on the outskirts of Cuenca.

elers. The town is just a few kilometers up the mountain south of Gualaceo, a 10-minute trip in the local bus. The road leading into Chordeleg from Gualaceo is lined with jewelry stores selling silver and gold jewelry at very reasonable prices in styles ranging from colonial filigree to modern. Other local *artesanías* (and textiles from Otavalo) are sold in gift shops around the main plaza. CIDAP has a small but excellent ethnographic museum on the plaza, with displays of local crafts and a gift shop. The exhibit showing the process used in making *ikat* textiles is especially informative.

There are pre-Inca ruins in the Chordeleg area, including an enormous snake-shaped stone walkway near the entrance to the town, and sites on nearby hilltops which have been archaeologically excavated. Chordeleg has a small Sunday market, but most people from the town attend the larger market in Gualaceo. From the plaza in Chordeleg you can catch a bus to **Sigsig**, 20km (12 miles) farther south. Sigsig is a tiny colonial town with an equally tiny Sunday market, but the trip along the river is gorgeous. Two archaeological sites, Chobshi and Shabalula, are close by; ask residents for directions.

If you are more interested in wilderness adventures consider visiting the **Area Nacional de Recreación Cajas** 30km (19 miles) northwest of Cuenca. The park contains hundreds of clear, cold lakes, streams and rivers at altitudes from 3,500 to 4,200 meters (9,000 to 13,000ft) on the *páramo* beneath jagged mountain cliffs. You can go swimming (if you're brave), but the fishing for rainbow trout is even better and there are miles of hiking trails, camp grounds and a small refuge. Recently herds of llamas and alpacas have been brought in as part of a breeding program to re-introduce these animals to the southern highlands. It is also a wonderful spot for birdwatching, especially around the lakes, where numerous exotic species can be found. Buses to Las Cajas (as the park is known) leave in the early morning from the Church of San Sebastián, at calles Bolívar and Talbot in Cuenca and return late in the afternoon).

Independent traditions

Cañar Province, north of Cuenca, home of the Cañari *indígenas*, has the largest and the most complete accessible Inca ruins in Ecuador. While Cañar is considered a highland province, about one-third of its territory is in the western lowlands, where sugar cane, cocoa, bananas and other tropical fruits are grown. In both the lowlands and Sierra, extensive territory is given over to cattle grazing on large tracts of land owned by *haciendéros*, despite the Agrarian Reform of 1964.

The Cañaris have never had an easy time of it, at least not since the arrival of the Incas in the 15th century. They were once the principal indigenous group in all southern Ecuador. At first they resisted the Incas fiercely, at one time defeating them and throwing them back to Saraguro.

When civil war broke out in 1527 between two claimants to the throne, Atahualpa in Quito and Huascar in Cuzco, the Cañaris sided with Huascar. Atahualpa routed Huascar's army in battle at Ambato and in revenge killed most of the men and boys of the Cañari tribe, despite their surrender and pleas for mercy.

A year after the Spanish captured and killed

TIP

It is worth noting that entrance to the Cajas National Park costs $6, but a taxi to the information center in the heart of the park will set you back about $15–20.

BELOW: pots for sale.

Atahualpa in Cajamarca, a Spanish force under Sebastián de Benalcázar marched north to plunder Quito. When Benalcázar reached Tumipampa he was joined by three thousand Cañari warriors, eager for revenge against the Quito Inca forces. The Cañaris fought with the Spanish throughout the conquest of Ecuador, but received scant recognition from the Spanish for their help. By 1544 many thousand Cañari men were working in the gold and silver mines of southern Ecuador and the tribe was so reduced that in 1547 the Spanish chronicler Pedro de Cieza de León noted that the ratio of women to men was 15 to 1.

Currently there are about 40,000 Quichua-speaking Cañari *indígenas* scattered throughout Cañar, the highest province in Ecuador. Most are farmers, but some are sheep and cattle herders. They are, on the whole, averse to outsiders and have a reputation among whites and other *indígenas* for being bellicose.

Cañari men's dress includes the *kushma,* a fine *ikat* poncho for fiesta use, black wool pants, a white cotton shirt with embroidery on the sleeves and collar and an extremely fine double-faced belt with motifs from local life including animals, Inca pots and skeletons, buses and trains, and designs taken from chil-

Map, page 265

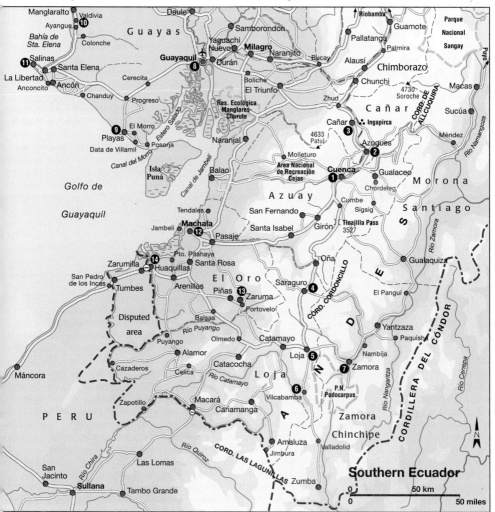

Southern Ecuador

0   50 km

0   50 miles

Temporary housing for dispossessed Cañari people.

BELOW: hoof-cutting in the Sierra near Cuenca.

dren's school books. Like the men of Saraguro and Otavalo, Cañari men wear their hair in a long braid. The sheep herders also wear sheepskin chaps and carry a small whip with a wooden handle, which is worn over their shoulder. The typical Cañari hat, worn by both men and women, is handmade of white felt with a small round crown and narrow brim, turned up in front. Cañari women wear an embroidered blouse, a shoulder wrap held shut with a *tupu,* and a wool *pollera* skirt in various colors.

Exploring Cañar

The Pan-American Highway climbs out of Cuenca to **Azogues ➋**, the capital of Cañar Province with 30,000 inhabitants. Azogues has a quiet colonial air, with wooden balconies and shutters aslant on ancient whitewashed houses. *Azogue* means mercury, and the town was named after the nearby mercury mines.

The **Convento de San Francisco** towers above Azogues on a hill to the southeast. The Spanish practice of building churches on pre-Hispanic Inca holy places (*wakas),* many of which were located on mountain-tops, accounts for the large number of churches that are perched at ridiculous heights. If you need the exercise and want the view, it's a half-hour climb to the top.

As befits a provincial capital, Azogues has two museums. The **Museo Ignacio Neira** in the Colegio Julio Maria Matavalle has zoology, archaeology and minerology displays, but is open only on request. The **Museo del Colegio de los Padres Franciscanos** houses religious art and archaeological artifacts. The opening times vary – check when you arrive.

The Pan-American Highway winds past Azogues and into **Cañar ➌**, which is 65km (40 miles) from Cuenca and 36km (22 miles) from Azogues. Cañar is

Map,
page 265

high and chilly at 3,104 meters (10,150ft); this is barley, potato, quinua (a highly nutritious grain) and cattle country. The town has a fascinating market on Sundays, when *indígenas*, including mounted Cañaris with ikat ponchos, whips (*chicotes*) and sheepskin chaps (*zamarro*), come down off the *páramo* to buy, sell and trade.

The Cañari men's belts are extremely fine, made in a complex intermesh double-faced technique with all kinds of motifs representing local life and folklore. The best place in town to buy belts is the jail (*la carcel*), where *indígenas* doing time don't waste time, but spend it weaving. The jailer will unlock the door and let you into the main patio where you will be besieged by friendly prisoners with belts and sometimes ponchos to sell.

Ecuador's greatest ruins

Many people visit Cañar for the market and then go on to **Ingapirca** (open daily). The ruins are not easy to reach as there are no buses, and trucks run infrequently. You can chance it and wait by the side of the road for a truck to come along or you can rent a taxi for the day in Cuenca, rent your own vehicle, or go on an organized tour. Ingapirca can be reached by roads on either side of Cañar. About 2km (1 mile) south of Cañar a sign on the east side of the Pana announces the ruins, which are 15km (9 miles) down an unpaved road. A kilometer north of Cañar a better, shorter, road (8km/5 miles) goes east through El Tambo .

Ingapirca means Inca Stone Wall; the name was given to the site by the Cañaris. We know that the Inca Huayna-Capac built Ingapirca in the 15th century on the royal highway that ran from Quito to Cuzco and stationed soldiers there to keep the Cañaris under control. Throughout the Inca empire outlying Inca settlements had multiple functions and were intended to be models of Cuzco on a much smaller scale. From what remains of Ingapirca, the site probably had storehouses, baths, a royal *tambo* or inn for the Inca, dwellings for soldiers and others, and a sun temple, the remains of which can be seen in the beautiful elipse, made of green diorite and modeled after the Koricancha, the main temple in Cuzco. The high-quality stonework indicates that Ingapirca was a very important site.

Not surprisingly, the Incas often chose hilltops for their settlements, both for defensive reasons and to free flat valley land for cultivation. Much of Ingapirca was dismantled over the centuries by local people who used the stones for building.

Various other remains surround the main buildings. The Ingachungana, or Inca's playground, is a large rock with carved channels; similar rocks exist in Peru. The Ingachungana may have been used for offerings or for divination, with water, chicha or the blood of sacrificed llamas or guinea-pigs poured in the channels. Near the Ingachungana is a chair or throne cut in the rock and called, logically, the **Sillón del Inca** (the Inca's Chair). Below in the gorge are several zoomorphic rock carvings which appear to be a monkey and a turtle, and the **Cara del Inca** (the Inca's Face), a large stone outcropping that is probably natural, rather than carved. The site also houses a small museum (open Mon–Sat) with

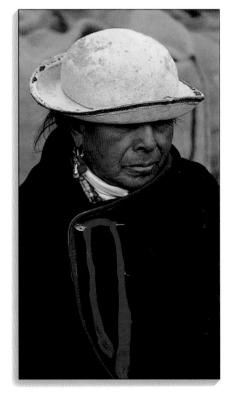

BELOW: woman from Cañar.

ethnographic and archaeological exhibits. The archaeology displays include such artifacts from the Cañari and Inca cultures as ceramics, jewelry and textile fragments. Less than a mile away is the village of **Ingapirca,** which has a crafts cooperative store next to the church and a basic restaurant where the food looks better and better as the day goes on.

The far south

Tucked away deep in southern Ecuador between Azuay Province and the border with Peru, **Loja Province** is the least visited of the highland provinces, mainly because of its isolation. There are flights to the capital city, Loja, from Quito and Guayaquil, but not from Cuenca, so travelers heading directly south from Cuenca must go overland along the paved Pan-American Highway. Loja is primarily rural and agricultural and there are only a few small towns along the road.

The Pana south of Cuenca passes through rich, green valley land until **Cumbe** (14km/9 miles), where it begins to climb to **Tinajilla Pass** at 3,500 meters (11,445ft). The Pana traverses the *páramo* of **Gañadel,** which is usually misty and fogged in. In the middle of this wilderness, figures bundled in shawls and ponchos will appear out of the fog to flag down the bus. The clouds sometimes part to surprise you with extensive views of the Western Cordillera and sunlight streaming through in the distance, a sight that looks like the dawn of creation.

From here the road twists a few miles to **Saraguro ❹**, a high, chilly town of about 3,000 inhabitants, mainly *mestizos* and whites. It is the social and commercial center for the Saraguro *indígenas,* relatively prosperous farmers and cattle traders who live in a number of smaller communities (called *barrios)* surrounding the town.

Saragueños are said to be descendants of the Incas, who replaced the indigenous Palta people sent to Bolivia by Tupac-Yupanqui.

BELOW: ruins of Ingapirca, Ecuador's major Inca site.

The Saragureños are said to be descendants of the Inca conquerors of Ecuador, who were brought to the region after the Inca Tupac-Yupanqui's conquest of the region around 1455. Under Inca rule, each ethnic group was required to retain its traditional costume, especially its headdress and hairstyle. The Spanish outlawed certain kinds of Inca headgear and introduced brimmed hats, but in typically conservative fashion each ethnic group insisted on wearing a distinctive style, which accounts for the plethora of hat styles seen in the Andes today.

Map, page 265

The *indígenas* of Saraguro were never serfs on the *haciendas* or laborers in textile sweatshops. They have survived as farmers and cattle traders, supplying much of the beef for southern Ecuador. Because of a shortage of pasture in the Saraguro region the Saragureños drive their cattle over the continental divide and down unto the jungle around Yacuambi. The cattle are fattened and driven back up over the Andes to be sold at the Sunday Saraguro market. The Saragureños value education and are among the best educated *indígenas* in Ecuador, with their own high school in Saraguro, and Saragureños attending the universities in Cuenca and Quito. The community now has its own indigenous doctor and nurse.

Remembering the Inca

Saraguro dress is black or dark indigo-blue wool, which many *indígenas* say they wear in mourning for the death of the Inca Atahualpa. Most of the dress is handspun and handwoven and everywhere you travel in the Saraguro region you will see women and girls with distaffs and spindles, spinning wool for their family clothing.

Most striking, though, is the women's jewelry. Several white jewelers in

BELOW: fine Inca masonry at Ingapirca ruins.

Saraguro specialize in making the large nickel or silver shawl pins *(tupus)* which females use to close their shoulder wraps. Fine silver *tupus* are heirlooms, passed down from mother to daughter, as are filigree earrings. Females also wear beaded necklaces. One style has rows of tiny, seed beads strung in zig-zags, and the colors of the beads and number of rows indicates her community.

Saraguro has two very basic *pensiones* and a couple of bad restaurants, but is worth visiting for the Sunday market which draws *indígenas* and white farmers from the region. Some crafts, especially the traditional jewelry, are sold in small shops in the main market building and surrounding streets.

Saraguro was also an Inca settlement and there are extensive ruins, which are impossible to find without a guide, outside the town in the forests on the slopes of Mount Acacana. The ruins, called **Inga Iglesia** (Inca Church), are large, but overgrown, and contain fine mortarless stonework walls and channels carved in the rock for the water system.

The Cuenca–Loja bus continues on to Loja after a stop in Saraguro to pick up passengers. If you decide to stay in Saraguro a local Saraguro–Loja bus also makes the roundtrip between the two places several times a day. Loja is another 61km (38 miles) from Saraguro, a 2-hour ride along a dizzying corkscrew road.

Woman with a distaff, a common sight in the Saraguro area.

Colonial center

Loja ❺ is the provincial capital of the province, and provincial it is: provincial and old. Because the Spanish invasion of Ecuador began in Piura on the north coast of Peru, Ecuador was conquered and settled from south to north. Loja was founded in 1548, which makes it one of the oldest cities in the country. Cieza de León commented on the prosperity of the region and on the vast herds

BELOW: skipping Mass in Saraguro.

of llamas, vicuñas and guanacos when he rode through Loja on the Royal Inca Highway, but the Spanish conquerors soon hunted them to extinction.

Loja has about 95,000 inhabitants and is nestled among the mountains at a pleasant 2,225 meters (7,275ft). Because it is so close to the Oriente it is a major entry point to the southern jungle and the province of Zamora-Chinchipe. The city has two universities, one of which has a law school and a music conservatory. It has the inevitable colonial art collection housed in the **Convento de las Conceptas** near the main plaza. A permit from the bishop of Loja is necessary in order to see this collection, a piece of bureaucracy which may lead you to decide that you have already seen enough colonial art. A local branch of the **Museo del Banco Central** (open Mon–Fri 9am–3.30pm) recently opened in a colonial mansion at 10 de Agosto and contains archaeological, ethnographic and colonial art collections.

As for churches, the **Cathedral** and the churches of **San Martín** and **Santo Domingo** have nicely painted interiors, but are otherwise nothing to write home about. The statue of the Virgin of Cisne is kept in the Cathedral from August to November. The fiesta of the Virgin takes place on September 8. The religious observances and the accompanying agricultural fair attract pilgrims from throughout northern Peru and the southern part of Ecuador.

Valley of the ancients

For a change of pace a popular excursion using Loja as a base is to **Vilcabamba** ❻, 62km (38 miles) due south. Vilcabamba gained a certain reputation in the 1970s as the valley of the ancients, where an unusual percentage of old people were said to live to be 100 to 120 years old. Disappointingly for those looking for

Map, page 265

BELOW: Saraguro women at a bus stop.

Map, page 265

TIP

Charley's Cabañas provide an inexpensive and totally relaxing place to stay in Vilcabamba, and horse riding can be arranged in the valley.

BELOW: old man from Vilcabamba.
RIGHT: young cousins in Saraguro.

the fountain of youth, these tales turned out to be exaggerated. One book on Vilcabamba, for example, contained a document purporting to be a birth certificate proving that one man was 128 years old. The document, on closer scrutiny, turned out to be a land title in his grandfather's name, which his descendant shared. There is no documentary evidence to support the stories of a large population of centenarians.

Still, there are a number of very healthy, active people in their seventies, eighties and nineties, bounding around the hilly countryside like wizened mountain goats, and there is good reason for their vitality. Vilcabamba is located at a comfortable, mild 1,500 meters (4,905ft) and the people lead active lives, farming on the mountainous slopes and eating a balanced, primarily vegetarian, diet. In other words, they follow all the prescriptions Europeans and Americans are given for living to a jolly old age: physical exercise, a strong family life, worthwhile activities that give life meaning, a balanced diet that is low on animal fats, and a relative lack of stress.

The Vilcabamba region is also a visual delight, green, gentle and pretty. PREDESUR, the Ecuadorian government agency responsible for development in the south, has established a recreation area, **Yamburara**, on the river bank about a mile outside Vilcabamba. Here is a small zoo, whose animals gaze wistfully at the hills where they would obviously prefer to be, gardens with many sorts of flowers, including orchids, a swimming pool and fish ponds.

Gold rush outposts

Although strictly speaking part of the Southern Oriente, **Zamora** ❼ is only 60km (40 miles) from Loja, but admittedly they are slow and bumpy miles. A

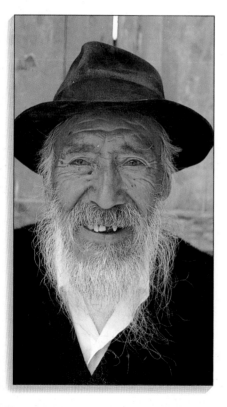

colony was founded here by the Spanish in 1549 at about 970 meters (3,180ft) above sea level in the headwaters of the Río Zamora. This colony was soon wiped out by Indian attacks but, undaunted, the Spaniards reestablished it and pursued their feverish quest for gold. Around 1560 they refounded the colony, giving it the fanciful title of the Royal Mining Village of the Rich Hill of San Antonio of Zaruma. Gold was then successfully extracted for some 70 years before the colony died out once more.

Several attempts were subsequently made to re-establish Zamora, the most recent in 1869. It has held on to its existence somewhat precariously since then. In the 1930s there were fewer than a dozen buildings, but by 1953 Zamora had become the capital of the isolated province of Zamora-Chinchipe, even though the only access was still by mule. The first vehicle made it to Zamora in 1962.

In the 1980s, a new lode of gold was discovered some 15km (10 miles) northeast of Zamora, in the **Nambija** area, traditional mining grounds of the Incas. Zamora's population has since risen to more than 6,000, a new road is under construction on the south side of the river, and the area has experienced a small gold boom. Ecuadorian prospectors, hoping to strike it rich, make their way to the Zamora area with their hopes as high as those of their predecessors. The urge to find gold is not something that goes out of fashion.

GUAYAQUIL AND THE SOUTH COAST

The vibrant port city of Guayaquil and the beach resorts of the Santa Elena peninsula show a different side of Ecuadorian life

Many visitors to Ecuador are surprised to learn that the seaport of **Guayaquil ❽** is the country's largest city, with a population of some 1.7 million inhabitants, nearly half as large again as Quito. But size is not the only surprise in this bustling commercial city which offers the nation's finest hotels, restaurants and shopping along with one of its most thriving red-light districts and plenty of mosquitoes. Guayaquil is not for the meek.

Situated on the west bank of the busy Río Guayas, navigable for the biggest of ocean vessels heading in from the Pacific via the Golfo de Guayaquil, this city handles 90 percent of Ecuador's imports and 50 percent of its exports. It has a reputation for being hot and humid with too many inhabitants and few tourist attractions. This may be true, but it overlooks the rough-and-ready hospitality and gutsiness of Guayaquil and its inhabitants.

During the rainy season, January to April, the heat and humidity are, indeed, oppressive, but from May to December the climate is pleasant with little or no rain and cool nights. And Guayaquil, prosperous despite its rundown façades, is dotted with wide concrete boulevards, spacious parks and colorful gardens, as well as beautiful monuments, attractive residential neighborhoods, museums with rich archaeological and art collections and excellent restaurants.

Its most obvious attraction is the **Guayas** itself. The chocolate-colored river teems with ships, small boats, dugout canoes and rafts loaded with produce from the inland villages and plantations. Considered one of the cleanest deepwater ports in this part of the world, it is also a controversial spot. Although Ecuador is not considered a major drug-trafficking country, Guayaquil figured prominently in a drug scandal a couple of years ago when three tons of cocaine in boxes labeled 'Ecuadorian cocoa" were shipped from that city to the United States.

But the so-called Great Chocolate Cocaine Caper was an exception to the mostly legitimate traffic that moves on the Río Guayas. In Guayaquil, a number of travel agencies offer river tours, taking visitors past small settlements, farms and cattle ranches along this lush, tropical river and through locks into the Salado estuary where the city's new seaport area is located.

A name inspired by tragedy

Although Spanish explorer Francisco de Orellana – credited with discovering the Amazon River – claimed to have founded Guayaquil, it was actually inhabited long before the Spanish arrived. The Valdivia Indians flourished in the area around 2000 BC, followed by the Huancavilcas. Legend has it that the Huancavilcas'

PRECEDING PAGES: gathering shrimp larvae in the Guayas. **LEFT:** art for sale in Guayaquil. **BELOW:** the city's bustling center.

Cemitterio General

Julian Coronel

Julian Coronel

Julian Coronel

Vicente Piedrahita

Galecio

Quito

Lorenzo de Garaicoa

Riobamba

Jimena

Avenida Boyacá

Baquerizo Moreno

García Moreno

Avenida Machala

Avenida

Pedro Moncayo

Galecio

Chimborazo

Antepara

TARQUI

Alejo Lascano

Mendiburo

General Córdova

José de

Luis Urdaneta

Rumichaca

Padre Solano

Escobedo

Avenida Rocafuerte

ROCA

Riobamba

Junín

Luis Urdaneta

Roca

★ Las Peñas /
Durán Ferry

Avenida 9 de Octubre

Victor Manuel Rendón

D
Museo del
Banco Central

C
Casa de
Cultura

Parque
del
Centenario

La Merced

Plaza
La Merced

Avenida Machala

E
Piscina Olímpica
Hotel Oro Verde

Vélez

Avilés

Avenida 9 de Octubre

Panamá

Malecón Simón Bolívar

ROCAFUERTE

Aguirre

Lugue

Avenida Boyacá

San Francisco

B

Vélez

La Rotonda
H

Quito

Parque
Victoria

Juan Pío Montúfar

Clemente Ballén

Francis

Aguirre

Chile

Pedro Carbo

Museo
Nahim
Isaías B.

★

i

Unicentro

Palacio de
Gobierno

Pedro Moncayo

10 de Agosto

Catedral
A

Parque
Bolívar

✉

Avenida

Colón

6 de Marzo

Rumichaca

Sucre

Avenida Boyacá

Museo
Municipal
F

Pichincha

Pedro Carbo

Palacio
Municipal

Torre
Morisca
G

Alcedo

Colón

Pedro Pablo Gómez

Fco. Campos

Chimborazo

Chile

Mercado
La Bahía

BOLÍVAR

Ayacucho

Benalcazar

Lavayen

Luzarraga

Villamil

Simón Bolívar

Franco Dávila

Lorenzo de Garaicoa

Avenida Olmedo

Huaynapac

R í o   G u a y a s

Guayaquil

Noguche

OLMEDO

Chimborazo

Avenida Olmedo

Malecón

i

Manabí

0   300 m
0   300 yds

Huancavilca

chieftain, Guayas, killed his beautiful wife Quil then drowned himself so that he Spaniards would not capture them. The tragedy of this doomed couple is supposed to be what inspired the city's name.

While fairly calm and conventional Quito was worrying only about infrequent earthquakes, Guayaquil spent its first 400 years fending fires. The last major blaze, in 1896, destroyed a large number of Guayaquil's charming wooden houses (some of which had long survived their main enemy – termites).

The different natures of Quito and Guayaquil – one a sophisticated center for art and culture, the other a rapidly growing center of commerce occupied by tattooed sailors and hard-working, hard-drinking laborers – bred a rivalry between the cities. It is common for competing presidential candidates to be from one or the other, and while Quiteños think the Guayaquil residents rough and unrefined, Guayaquil dwellers think the residents of the capital are dull and backward, not to mention foolish for living in a city with no nightlife and no beaches. Guayaquileños claim that they make the country's money and the Quiteños spend it.

Map,
page 278

Brassy wealth

Despite its development problems Guayaquil is a growth area, a center of industry with oil and sugar refineries, cement mills, breweries and all types of manufacturing. It is an attractive destination for visitors seeking luxurious hotels, fine restaurants, clubs for tennis, golf, yachting and swimming, exciting discotheques and upscale shopping – including a bevy of duty-free stores. The main blotches on its record are a high crime rate and an unstable water supply, characterized by sporadic shortages in some of the downtown neighborhoods.

BELOW: Guayaquil's urban sprawl.

A model ship in the Museo del Banco Central.

There is no straightforward way to see the sights of Guayaquil, but a suggested route is to visit the scattered downtown places of interest first, then follow the Malecón along the water's edge, past the docks to the Las Peñas district. Start with a visit to the neo-Gothic **cathedral ⓐ** on the west side of Parque Bolívar, on Calle Chile between 10 de Agosto and Clemente Ballen. The cathedral was built in 1948, with lovely stained-glass windows and Cuenca marble altar. Its side altars are overwhelmed by innumerable votive candles lit by the devout; some people even hold candles in their hands while walking around the church praying. The original wooden cathedral built in 1547 burned in one of the city's many fires.

Parque Bolívar (also known as Parque Seminario) is perhaps the most interesting park in the city, The old, well-maintained botanical garden earned its nickname from its equestrian statue of Bolívar; around the statue's base are bas-relief depictions of that mysterious Guayaquil meeting between Bolívar and San Martín (see page 282). Turtles paddle in the park's pond and iguanas roam freely, delighting children who gather to watch them. The pavilion and gates in this nearly century-old park came originally from France.

On the other side of the park is the ultra-modern **Unicentro Shopping Center**. The **Unihotel**, at this sparkling indoor gallery of shops and services, has gained a reputation for its cocktails, including its *jipijapa*, a blend of orange aguardiente, grenadine and lemon served with a slice of pineapple.

From here, walk two blocks along Calle Chile to the plaza and church of **San Francisco ⓑ**. The church was built in 1603 and beautifully restored in 1968. You'll also see that many streets in the central district preserve porticos protecting pedestrians from the sun or rain. Going west along Avenida 9 de Octubre

BELOW: the church of San Francisco, Guayaquil.

you will come to the **Parque del Centenario**, the city's largest plaza, covering four city blocks. It is filled with monuments, the most important being the patriotic Liberty monument with the likenesses of Ecuador's heroes and smaller statues representing history, justice, patriotism and heroism.

Map, page 278

Pre-Columbian artifacts

Just outside the park on 9 de Octubre and Moncayo is the **Casa de Cultura Ecuatoriana C** (open Tues–Fri) with a display of pre-Columbian artifacts found in archaeological digs on the country's coast. Reopened following a 1987 fire, this museum once had an impressive collection of gold items in its Carlos Zevallos Menendez Hall – reported to be Ecuador's most valuable pre-colonial gold collection – but many of them mysteriously disappeared; those that remain at the museum are not publicly displayed. Current exhibits now range from clay whistles known as *ocarines* to molds for casting gold masks and colonial art. Other artifacts and archaeological displays – including ceramics, textiles, gold and ceremonial masks – are located at the **Museo del Banco Central D**, three blocks to the west on the same street, beside the US Embassy and opposite the **Hotel Oro Verde**, the best spot in town for a *gringo* breakfast, if you got up early enough to be needing a second breakfast by now.

Go south from here down Calle García Moreno, and you will find the **Piscina Olímpica** (Olympic Swimming Pool) **E**.

To reach the most intriguing museum in town you need to walk four block south then turn left on Calle Sucre and head back towards the Malecón to the **Museo Municipal F**, which has a macabre collection of the Jivaro *tzantzas* – or shrunken heads – prepared by jungle Indians using secret processes scientists

BELOW: monument to the meeting between Simón Bolívar and José de San Martín.

are still unable to unravel. There are, of course, theories on how the human heads were reduced to fist size without losing their original features, but there is no consensus. A 1988 auction at Christie's in London brought in bids of several thousand dollars apiece for such shrunken heads and tourists in Ecuador are occasionally offered *tzantzas* for sale, although authorities say those bargains are not only illegal but are almost certainly monkey – not human – heads. This museum also has displays of Inca and pre-Inca ceramics from the Huancavilca and Valdivia Indians, colonial art, modern art and local handicrafts.

If you like a party, come to Guayaquil on July 24/25, when riotous celebrations mark Bolívar's birthday and the founding of the city. Hotels are booked in advance.

On the waterfront

From the museum, go back to 10 de Agosto where a right turn will take you to the **Malecón Simón Bolívar**. This seawall area along the waterfront offers a microcosmic view of the city's light and dark sides. Children selling slices of fresh pineapple and vendors with soft drinks as armor against the hot sun share the same benches as idle sailors. This area is always filled with people, from beer-bellied shirtless men exchanging stories and couples embracing under trees, to pickpockets. A right turn and down a handful of blocks will lead to the beginning of the chaotic informal outdoor market where anything from cameras with phony trademarks to misspelled T-shirts are sold. Contraband fuels much of the commerce at this jostling, noisy gathering place. Prostitutes line up along the walls of cut-rate hotels here and theft is common, but there is little physical danger during the day.

Directly ahead of you is the **Torre Morisca** (the Moorish Clock Tower) **G** dating from 1770. Visitors can climb the steep, narrow winding stairway inside its base (which is used as a city office) and go up to the room with the clock

BELOW: the Moorish-style clock tower.

workings, even stepping outside onto a ledge to get a good look at the city. The gardens around the clock are a favorite meeting spot for young couples and in the early evening this area is full of strollers looking for relief from the last blast of daytime heat.

Across the street is the splendid **Palacio Municipal**, separated from the severe **Palacio de Gobierno** by a plaza with a statue dedicated to General Sucre, hero of Ecuador's war of independence.

A little further along, at Aguirre 104 and Malecón, is the national **Tourist Office**, CETUR (Oficina de Turismo). You may prise a city map out of the staff there but, like much in Guayaquil, the mood is laid back.

Meeting place of the liberators

Continuing along the Malecón to the foot of Avenida 9 de Octubre you will see the semicircle of **La Rotonda** **H**, with its statue commemorating the historical but mysterious meeting between the continent's two great liberators, Venezuelan Simón Bolívar and Argentine General José de San Martín. Bolívar had freed the countries to the north and San Martín was responsible for the independence of Argentina and Chile but their final plans differed – Bolívar wanted the countries united under a democracy with an elected president and San Martín envisioned a monarchy.

The meeting resulted in the Acuerdo de Guayaquil (Guayaquil Accord), which established the short-lived

Gran Colombia, uniting Venezuela, Colombia and Ecuador. There was no witness to the exchange between the two men and the only thing that is known for sure is that when the meeting ended, Bolívar remained and San Martín went into exile in France.

La Rotonda is built so that people can stand on either side of the statue, whisper, and hear one another. From here you can enjoy an impressive view of the hill known as Cerro del Carmen and, far beyond, the Guayaquil–Durán bridge – the country's largest at 4km (2½ miles) long and the link to the Durán rail terminal.

At the upper end of the Malecón, past restaurant boats, working docks and the Durán ferry exit, Calle Numa Pompilio Lloma mounts the side of Cerro Santa Ana and enters the picturesque bohemian district of **Las Peñas.** Here, the wooden architecture shows the influence of the Pacific naval yards during the period of Spanish colonization. On the small **Plaza Colón**, where the narrow winding street with its original cobblestone paving begins, two cannons commemorate the defense of the city against pirate invasions. The romantic 19th-century houses bordered by jasmine bushes are today mostly inhabited by artists; peek into open doors on the way by. There are a few art galleries here and No. 186 is the residence of the well-known painter Hugo Luis Lara.

From the top of the **Santa Ana** hill there is a spectacular view of the city, salt estuaries, new port and river, although it is not advisable to climb the hill alone. This area also has an open-air theatre – Teatro Bogotá – and, just behind, the oldest church in Guayaquil, **Santo Domingo**, founded in 1548 and restored in 1938. A patio at the left-hand side of the church's nave contains a spring credited with miraculous healing powers. Stairs to the right of the church and the steep Buitron Street lead to **Cerro del Carmen**, topped by the Cristo del Consuelo

Map, page 278

BELOW: the historical Las Peñas district.

monument. (Because of the isolation of this spot and crime problems, this is best visited on an organized tour.) At the foot of the hill is the dazzling white cemetery, the **Cemeterio General** with its avenue of royal palms leading to the grave of 19th-century President Vicente Rocafuerte, elaborate marble sculptures and imposing Greco-Roman mausoleums.

Beaches of the south

Guayaquil is an important meeting city for business executives but rarely the sole destination of tourists. Rather, it is the jumping-off point for the beaches of Ecuador's southern coast. Except for Salinas, these are generally undeveloped stretches of sand lapped by warm salt water and toasted by the tropical sun. (People with fair skin should take precautions under these burning rays; sometimes less than half an hour of unprotected sun can cause severe sunburn.) Although weekends and the December to April vacation season see much beach activity, the area is all but deserted during the week. There are a few hotels and official camping sites, although camping is allowed everywhere.

The road south from Guayaquil passes through dry scrubland, with the scenery undergoing an astonishing change from wet fields of rice and bananas to an arid – but attractive – landscape with strange bottle-shaped kapok trees and scattered bright flowers. Traffic on the coastal road, which passes the busy villages of **Cerecita** and **Progreso** about 70km (42 miles) outside of Guayaquil, is heavy from January to April during local vacation months and at weekends. In Progreso (officially called Gomez Rendón), the road forks right to Salinas and Santa Elena. A left-hand fork leads to the popular beach resort of Playas, Guayaquil's closest beach at 100km (60 miles) from the city.

Selling salsa by the sea.

BELOW: a bus will take you to the beach.

Playas ❾, which is officially General Villamil, is an important fishing village. Old balsa rafts, similar to craft used in pre-Inca times, line the beaches, and are found only in this area. They are still used by some of the fishermen who bring in a catch every afternoon.

Map, page 278

However, the main focus of this little town is tourism, and the sandy beaches are the lure for weekend crowds. An alternative to the main beach with its hotels, including the popular Playas, Rey David and Cattan, and the holiday villas used as escape destinations for Guayaquil residents, is the beautiful beach to the north, called the Pelado, a long and lonely stretch set against the backdrop of a cliff. For overnight stays in Playas, the best lodgings are to be found in the more expensive *hosterías* Bellavista and Los Patios on the main road to Data just outside the village.

About 14km (8 miles) south along the coast from Playas is **Data de Villamil**, interesting for its traditional wooden shipbuilding industry. An inland road from here passes the old village of El Morro with its huge wooden church, and farther along is the fishing village of Posorja with commercial boats and hundreds of seabirds wheeling around the **Canal de Morro**, used by overseas vessels bound for Guayaquil. Shrimp farming produced an economic boom in the village, which has grown rapidly over the past few years. This is a pleasant stop on a day trip even though the beaches are not really good for swimming.

Opposite Posorja is the large island of **Puná**, which was already inhabited in pre-Inca times as evidenced by the traces of two settlements from the Valdivia culture which archaeologists have found there. The island is difficult to reach, although boats can be hired in Guayaquil: contact the Capitanía del Puerto or the Yacht Club for details.

BELOW: welcome refreshments on a hot afternoon.

Cactus and tuna

To reach the Santa Elena Peninsula you must go back to Progreso, and take the right-hand road to Salinas through an increasingly dry, cactus-covered landscape. At Km 35.6 outside Progreso is the road to the fishing village of **Chanduy**, a mecca for archaeologists who have made important discoveries while excavating the remains of Valdivia, Machalilla and Chorrera Indian settlements. This is considered to be the oldest agricultural settlement on the continent where ceramics were made, and may have been a ceremonial center. Nowadays, like all the fishing villages along this route, the biggest catches are brought close to the shore with the cold Antarctic-born Humboldt Current. The tuna and marlin feed here on smaller, warm-current fish.

Just before reaching Chanduy is the recently inaugurated **Museo Real Alto**, which takes the form of two giant huts covered with straw roofs. Poorly marked, it is to the left of a directional sign reading *Fabrica Portuguesa*. Among the exhibits at this museum is one demonstrating how the local inhabitants of the area now live.

Back to the main roadway, at Km 49.5, a right-hand deviation in the road leads to the **Baños de San Vicente**, a large complex in which water is channeled into swimming pools and mud baths are said to have curative powers. The Hotel Florida is pleasant; reservations can be made in advance in Guayaquil.

Farther down the main road is **Santa Elena**, interesting only for its church and usually bypassed in favor of La Libertad and Salinas. However, on the outskirts of the town near a Mormon temple with a small tower is **Los Amantes de Zumba** (The Lovers of Zumba) archaeological site. Two human skeletons estimated to be 3,500 years old are caught in an after-life embrace in the grave, which falls under the auspices of the Archaeological Department of the Banco Central in Guayaquil. Roberto Lindao is the warden at the site and special permission must be obtained for the grave to be opened to visitors.

La Libertad, the largest town on the peninsula with 45,000 inhabitants, is a busy port with a bustling market and serves as the hub for bus services further north. The waterfront Samarina Hotel, about a kilometer outside town, offers guests a bar, pool, restaurants, tennis court and bungalows for families. Take the right-hand fork in the road going north towards Manglaralto. There are several fishing villages along this piece of coast, where Guayaquileños have vacation homes, but there are no restaurants or hotels. However, these are marvelous spots for a day of swimming. **Punta Blanca** has an exquisite, isolated beach that attracts shell collectors. **Ayangue**, 45km (28 miles) further north, has white beaches, a gentle slope and no big waves, making it ideal for children.

Valdivia ⑩, 5km (3 miles) up the coast, is the center of Ecuador's oldest culture, established around 3,000 BC, and has an interesting museum full of local finds (although its best pieces are on display in museums in Quito and Guayaquil).

At Manglaralto, at the end of this scenic road, there are basic restaurants and bed-and-breakfast establishments at some of the local homes. Travelers with four-wheel-drive vehicles can continue along the coast

Fragments of multi-colored female figures have been unearthed during archeological digs on Valdivian sites.

BELOW: children enjoy Santa Elena beach.

through lush and dense vegetation to Puerto López, in Manabí province (see the *Pacific Coast* chapter, page 187).

Map, page 278

Summer beach mecca

Retrace your steps down the coast to reach Ecuador's most fashionable resort town, **Salinas** , lying in a half-moon bay on the tip of the **Santa Elena Peninsula**, a total of 150km (90 miles) from Guayaquil. It has a pleasant beaches, tall buildings, excellent hotels, good restaurants, a casino and a yacht club which lure throngs of swimmers and sun baskers. It is also the site of a naval base. The best place to stay is the Hotel Miramar, which has air-conditioning, a pool and casino. Other hotels are the first-class El Refugio, the modern and reasonable Salinas and the inexpensive but noisy Yulee. Salinas is famous for sport fishing and annually hosts international deep-sea fishing competitions. "Pesca-Tours" organizes fishing trips and provides all the equipment for those looking for king-size dorados and black marlin (*picudos*) weighing in at up to 580kg (1,300lb).

About 9km (5 miles) from Salinas is **Punta Carnero** with a beach several kilometers long. From the Carnero Inn situated on a cliff, you have a marvelous view of the ocean and the hotel has a good restaurant, pool and bar. Fishing charters can be arranged from here, and it's also a good spot to see wading birds. For the best seafood in town, try the Mar y Tierra; for vigorous nightlife there is the Barba Negra discotheque.

The deep south

To get to the next destination you must return to Guayaquil and take the road toward Azogues, turning off after about 20km (12 miles) towards Machala in

BELOW: the sandy beach at Salinas.

Map,
page 278

TIP

Machala has a wide
range of inexpensive
Chinese restaurants,
known in Ecuador
as chifas.

El Oro, the southernmost of Ecuador's provinces, which owes its name to the rich gold deposits mined here during the 16th century. It is now Ecuador's leading banana and shrimp-producing region. The fields here are blanketed by massive banana plantations, the ripening fruit protected by light-blue plastic bags. **Machala ⑫**, the main city, is known as the "World Banana Capital." The International Banana and Agricultural Festival is held here every year in late September and draws large crowds. In fact, with 144,000 inhabitants, Machala is Ecuador's fourth largest city. Although not particularly attractive, it is a thriving town with some comfortable hotels and an international port, **Puerto Bolívar**, near the popular **El Coco** beach.

Some 1 million tons of banana and shrimp exports pass through Puerto Bolívar annually, and from its boat pier motorized dugouts can be taken to the archipelago of **Jambelí**, an extraordinarily beautiful area that is little explored.

Other side trips are available from Machala, including a journey to the pleasant farming center of **Santa Rosa**, on the Loja road, and then on to the beautiful old coffee-growing town of **Piñas** (take a left-hand turn about 20km/12 miles from Santa Rosa) before reaching the mining town of Zaruma. The road is flanked by banana, coffee and cacao plantations.

Town among the ruins

The road from Piñas continues to **Portovelo** from where you can see the town of **Zaruma ⑬** stuck to the mountainside like a swallow's nest. This mining town of 5,000 inhabitants was founded during the colonial-era gold boom and recently attracted renewed interest with the discovery of pre-Columbian ruins at Chepel, Trencillas, Payama and Pocto. Although the ruins have not yet been fully excavated, they have led archaeologists to conclude that the area was densely populated in pre-Inca times.

The town conserves much of its colonial past: its wooden houses with elaborately decorated balconies and the church are well worth seeing. From the main plaza and the no-frills Hotel Municipal, there is a fantastic view of the surrounding valley. Visits to an abandoned gold mine can be arranged through the city council – **Consejo Municipal** – and a stop at the **Museo Municipal** (opening hours vary)with displays of archaeological artifacts, colonial art and Zaruma's history is recommended. As well as the Municipal, the Hotel Pedregal, 3km (2 miles) outside Zaruma, is recommended

To the far south of Machala, the route ends at **Huaquillas ⑭** and the (still disputed) border with Peru. Although the border at these two cities is clear, the area to the east is not and appears as Peruvian territory on maps produced in that country and as Ecuadorian territory on Ecuador-printed maps. This border not only marks the beginning of the Peruvian coastal desert but is one of the continent's main cross-border commercial centers – although much of what is bought and sold is contraband.

Huaquillas is a busy, dusty and unattractive town with stagnant water lying on its rutted roads and a reputation for pickpockets – who generally seek out tourists, sometimes returning stolen passports if a reward is proffered and no charges are pressed. The only decent hotel is the government-run Parador Turistico, north of town, with a restaurant and swimming pool, the latter being a welcome relief from the insufferable heat and dust.

ABOVE: Machala is the banana capital of Ecuador. **RIGHT:** a parade in Guayas province.

The main street of Huaquillas leads to the **International Bridge** into Peru and is lined with street vendors, aggressive money changers, police and border officers, and children and adults alike offering to carry luggage pretty much like many other border crossing. Travelers must cross the bridge on foot unless they are driving their own car.

THE GALÁPAGOS ISLANDS

"Seeing every height crowned with its crater, and the boundaries of most of the lava streams still distinct, we are led to believe that within a period geologically recent, the unbroken ocean was here spread out. Hence, both in space and time, we seem to be brought somewhat near to that great fact, that mystery of mysteries – the first appearance of new beings on this earth."
— CHARLES DARWIN, *The Voyage of the Beagle*

The Galápagos Islands had their fame guaranteed in 1835 when the 26-year-old naturalist Charles Darwin landed on one of their black volcanic coasts. Although an indifferent student, Darwin had begun revealing his extraordinary powers of observation during a voyage around the globe on HMS *Beagle*. No other place would prove to be quite as fertile for his work as the Galápagos. Some 20 years later (in 1859), Darwin published *The Origin of Species*, making the creatures of the Galápagos a cornerstone of his theory of evolution by natural selection, in one stroke overturning the whole train of western scientific thought.

Wildlife is still the main reason why tens of thousands of visitors fly the 960km (570 miles) from mainland Ecuador to the Galápagos archipelago every year. Even those who have no particular fascination with animals find themselves reduced to a childlike glee by the experience: the islands are the ultimate natural zoo, where bizarre fauna exist totally free and fearless of man.

Giant lumbering tortoises, blue-footed boobies and equatorial penguins carry on their daily routine, indifferent to their audience of human visitors only feet away. Baby sea lions play with swimmers in the water, grabbing their flippers and performing somersaults. Approach as close as you like, but the dozens of marine iguanas sunning themselves on black rocks will just sit and stare blankly back.

Although these animals have been able to thrive on the Galápagos, the islands' landscapes are mostly bleak and sunburnt. Until recently, permanent human settlement had been kept to a minimum. In 1959, the Ecuadorian government declared the islands a national park and restricted human settlement to the small outposts already established. Today the Charles Darwin Research Station on Santa Cruz, created in 1964, and the Marine Research Reserve, founded in 1986 have their hands full trying to restore the Galápagos to the days before humans began to upset the delicate ecological balance.

But the sad fact is that however hard they work, it is possible that the only way the islands and their inhabitants will be preserved unharmed is by ending tourist visits altogether.

PRECEDING PAGES: volcanic eruption on Isla Isabela; marine iguana colony, Punta Espinosa; giant tortoises near Volcán Alcedo.
LEFT: marine iguanas sunbathe on the cliffs at Plaza Sur.

THE GALÁPAGOS: DARWIN'S ZOO

Map, page 318

The volcanic archipelago teems with rare bird and marine life which can be seen nowhere else in the world

The "living laboratory" of the Galápagos archipelago is set in the Pacific Ocean some 960km (570 miles) west of the Ecuadorian coast. It consists of 13 major islands, six small ones and 42 islets that are barely more than large rocks. All are of volcanic origin and spread over roughly 80,000 sq. km (30,000 sq. miles) of ocean. Their highest point is Volcán Wolf, at 1,707 meters (5,600ft) on Isabela, which, at 4,600 sq. km (1,800 sq. miles), is by far the largest island.

Visited at different times by explorers from around the world, most of the islands have two or even three different names. British pirates gave them solid, Anglo-Saxon names like Jervis and Chatham; the Spanish dubbed them from their standard stock of place names, such as Santa Cruz and Santa Fe; while the Ecuadorian government in 1892 tried to clear up the confusion by giving the islands official titles: the effort was unsuccessful and each usually has at least two names still in use. Even the name Galápagos has been changed several times before being officially restored in 1973: taken from a Spanish word for tortoise, it refers to the giant creatures that most astonished the first explorers.

An eccentric climate

The Galápagos year can be divided into a two "seasons:" the "hot" or "wet" season lasts from January to early May with an average temperature of 28°C (82°F); while the "cool" or "dry" season from May to December has an average of 18°C (64°F). The cooler period is also referred to as the *garua* season, named after the bank of clouds that generally settle over the islands at this time. Altitude also has an effect on the climate: it can be hot and dry in the low-lying parts of the islands, and almost cold and humid in the highlands (above 22 meters/72ft). The winds, the marine currents and finally the geological formation of the soil can alter the climatic conditions considerably: generally, the beaches with white sands are cooler on the feet, while stretches of black lava can reach temperatures of up to 50°C (120°F).

Two marine currents pass along the archipelago. The cold Humboldt Stream originates in the south of Chile and brings the *garua* with it in May – it has a moderating effect on the whole climate of the Galápagos, which, since they sit directly on the equator, should be more punishing than it actually is. The other current is the warm northern stream called *El Niño*, "the boy child," because it arrives around Christmas time, although its effects are rarely welcome: it brings heavy rains and – on occasion – floods and tidal waves to the Ecuadorian mainland.

LEFT: king of the islands. **BELOW:** the naturalist Charles Darwin, who visited the islands in the early 1830s.

Geology of the islands

What we see of the Galápagos islands is actually the tips of various gigantic "shield volcanoes" poking up some 10,000 meters (30,000ft) from the ocean floor and composed entirely of basalt. Some scientists once believed that the islands were the remains of a sunken continental platform that was linked to the South American continent during the Miocene era. But today it is widely accepted that the archipelago was formed mainly by the accumulation of lava from successive underwater volcanic eruptions.

It appears that the earliest of the islands were formed roughly 4 to 5 million years ago, and that some of the western islands, such as Fernandina and Isabela, are only 1 million years old. The process of island formation is in fact still going on. The Galápagos lie on the northern edge of the Nazca tectonic plate – one of the several huge land masses that, over millions of years, slowly move around the earth's surface. Over time, this gradual continental drift takes them towards the southeast – precisely over one of the world's so-called "hotspots." These volatile, unmoving points beneath the tectonic plates build up heat over time to create a volcanic eruption that will rise above the ocean's surface. The southeastern islands of the Galápagos were the first formed in this way, and the more recent, western islands still have active volcanoes. The scientist Morrel witnessed an eruption on Fernandina in 1825 that sent the surrounding sea to a temperature of 65°C (149°F). More recently, Volcán Cerro Azul on Isabela erupted in 1979 and again in 1982.

Relatively fresh basalt lava flows can still be seen around the island of Isabela, often making fascinating patterns. They include "pahoehoe" or "ropy" lava – where the skin of the lava flow has been wrinkled by the heat of the still-flow-

Preserving the surface.

BELOW: cactus thrives on lava flows.

ng lava beneath. Another type is "aa" – pronounced "aah aah" – and looks like twisted black caramel.

Map, page 318

Colonization

Obviously, the volcanic lumps that first burst forth from the Pacific 4 million years ago were utterly devoid of life. Yet now the islands are teeming with plants and animals. Somehow they must have made their way from South America – and, since the islands were never connected to the continent, this fauna and flora must have crossed the 1,000-km (620-mile) stretch of water.

Only certain types of creatures could survive the journey: this explains the present-day predominance of sea birds (which could fly), sea mammals (which could swim) and reptiles (which apparently floated across from the American coast on accidentally formed vegetation rafts and, unlike amphibians and land mammals, could survive for long periods without food or water). Meanwhile, plant seeds and insects could have come across stuck to birds' wings or in animals' stomach contents.

Thor Heyerdahl is among those who believed that the Inca Tupac-Yupanqui organized an expedition to the islands in the 15th century, but there is no evidence to support this theory.

Once they had landed on the bleak islands, only certain animals could survive. Those that did found that their traditional predators had been left behind on the South American coast. The animals' lack of timidity probably stems from this general absence of predators – a fact that also explains why recently introduced domestic goats and pigs are able to wreak havoc so easily.

Charles Darwin was the first to observe how each arriving species had adapted over time in order to thrive. The most famous case may be "Darwin's finches" – the 13 similar species of finches that probably descended from one original species. Each modern species has certain differences that suits its particular

BELOW: Sullivan Bay and Pinnacle Rock, Bartolomé Island.

environment on different Galápagos islands: some have short, thick beaks so that they can split seeds; others have long, thin bills to catch insects.

Many years after his visit to the Galápagos, Darwin attributed the process to natural selection. After their arrival on the Galápagos, each finch produced offspring that were imperceptibly different from the parent. In this strange new environment, some chicks were better able to survive. They were the ones that reached maturity and produced young, passing on new genetic traits to their offspring. Over thousands of generations, some traits were thus "selected" as fitting the finches' new home – until the differences between the new creature and the original qualified it to be re-named as a new species.

Darwin propounded this theory in his classic work *The Origin of Species*. It became particularly controversial when applied to man, not only suggesting that the animal kingdom did not spring ready-made from the hand of God, but that man is in many respects no different from other forms of animal life.

The human history

There is a possibility that the Inca Tupac-Yupanqui organized an expedition to the Galápagos during his rule in the 1400s, but most historians accept that the islands were first discovered by accident in 1535 by the Spanish cleric Fray Tomás de Berlanga, bishop of Panama. On the way to Peru, his boat was becalmed and drifted to the Galápagos. The cleric landed in search of water but "found nothing but seals and tortoises, and such big tortoises that each could carry a man on top of itself" and birds "so silly that they do not know to flee." He dubbed the islands "Las Encantadas," the Bewitched Ones, because they tricked his navigator's eyes and seemed to appear and disappear in clouds of mist.

BELOW: National Park wardens measure a giant tortoise.

For the next two centuries, the islands, far from the Spanish trade routes, were a hideaway for Dutch and English buccaneers. They began the practice of killing large numbers of giant tortoises for their meat – having found that the creatures could be stacked upside-down in their ships' holds without food and water for over a year and still be turned into fine soup. This practice was taken up most devastatingly by the 19th-century whalers. Between 1811 and 1844 there were said to be more than 700 whaling ships in the Pacific, and many of them called into the Galápagos Islands to stock up on tortoise meat.

The first permanent colonist on the Galápagos was an Irishman named Patrick Watkins, who arrived at Floreana in 1812. His story is included in a series of sketches called *The Encantadas* by Herman Melville. Melville's portrait of the islands was not a flattering one: "Take five and twenty heaps of cinders dumped here and there in an outside lot; imagine some of them magnified into mountains, and the vacant lot the sea; and you will have a fit idea of the general aspect of the Encantadas."

When the Ecuadorian government claimed the islands in 1832, Floreana was given as a reward for bravery to a local Creole officer. He brought 80 people from the mainland and kept them enslaved using giant dogs. But the so-called "Dog King of Charles Island" was forced to flee when his slaves rebelled. A brutal penal colony was set up on San Cristóbal in the 1880s, with the prisoners worked to death, flogged mercilessly and marooned on desert islands to die slowly of thirst as punishment for misdemeanors.

When the United States entered World War II, it chose the Galápagos as a defense base against attacks on the Panama Canal. An airstrip was built on Baltra Island that is still in use today. In 1958 the last convict colony was closed,

Map, page 318

BELOW: a graceful diving penguin.

and in the 1960s regular passenger flights began to operate. Tourists discovered that the islands were within reach, and began to make the long journey.

Since then, tourism has been ever-increasing. In September 1995, the islands were brought to a halt when locals led by the Deputy of the Galápagos, Eduardo Veliz, seized San Cristóbal airport, the National Park office and the Charles Darwin Center, demanding more control of and benefits from tourism. Some kind of peace was secured, but only after two weeks of fierce protesting, complete suspension of all visits, and intense negotiations in Quito.

Taking an iguana to the beach.

Concern for conservation

Scientists have been observing the Galápagos periodically ever since Darwin's work in the mid-19th century. In this century, it became obvious that many of the animals introduced by man had gone feral and were devastating the natural ecology of the islands. Everything from goats to pigs, rats, dogs and cats were breeding furiously. They were taking other animals' food, devouring turtle eggs and baby land iguanas, eroding the soil and destroying the plants.

In 1930 an expedition led by Gifford Pinchot from the United States suggested the possibility of creating a wildlife sanctuary in the archipelago. Five years later, laws were passed to protect the fauna of the islands, but it was not until 1959 that the Galápagos were declared a National Park, with the aim of protecting the islands and encouraging scientific research.

BELOW: great frigate male with fully inflated pouch.

Also created in 1959 was the Charles Darwin Foundation for the Galápagos Islands, an international organization under the auspices of UNESCO and the International Union for the Conservation of Nature. In 1964 the foundation established the Charles Darwin Research Center, with scientific, educational and protective objectives. The scientific program provides assistance for experts, and biology students who visit the islands. The educational program is aimed at improving environmental awareness, particularly among students. And the protective program attempts to overcome the negative effects of introduced animals, and prevent other man-made disasters.

Various protective programs have been undertaken in cooperation with the National Park administration. So far, they have been successful in eliminating all black rats on Bartolomé, while all wild goats were hunted on Santa Fe, Española (Hood) and Rábida. A campaign against dogs, which attack young tortoises and land iguanas, started recently.

Tourism takes off

Before the 1960s, a visit to the Galápagos involved a long and uncomfortable sea-voyage on the old ship *Cristóbal Carrier*, which ran once a month from Guayaquil to the archipelago. Travel between the islands was spartan and often nearly impossible: travelers sometimes had to wait weeks to find a boat heading where they wanted to go. Not surprisingly, most visitors were from the ranks of the wealthy who could afford their own yachts and cruise the islands at leisure.

All this changed overnight when regularly scheduled air transportation was made available to the public, and passenger ships were run by Ecuadorian tourist agenes. In 1970, an estimated 4,500 tourists arrived; in 1978 the figure was 12,000; ɔw more than 45,000 make the trip every year. This figure is worryingly high. ʼildlife and vegetation are in danger of being severely affected if tourism con- ɴues at this rate. The government claims that it wants to control the number of ᵢsitors to the islands, but is not enforcing its restrictions.

Tourism on the islands themselves is strictly controlled. The national park ᵉrvice has made a selection of about 54 visitor sites and 62 marine sites where ᵢurists are allowed outside of towns – and then only in the company of trained ɟides. Trails are marked with small stakes painted in white. They stop you ʼushing plants and animals underfoot, and also keep crowds away from crater ɔrders, where serious erosion can occur.

Map, page 318

range of plant life

ᵥery island on the Galápagos is unique, although only a committed naturalist ɔuld plan to visit them all. Many are virtual deserts. Others, more mountainous, ᵉ relatively lush. Thanks to the icy Humboldt Current, the islands are not as hot ᵢ you would expect them to be on the equator, but the sun can still be punishing, ɪd few can stand more than a few hours' hiking steep trails.

There are six different vegetation zones on the Galápagos, beginning with the ᵢoreline and ending with the highlands. The low islands are the driest, as clouds ᵢss by here without discharging. Meanwhile, the mountainous islands often ᵢock clouds, which turn into fog, drizzle or rain showers and help flora to thrive.

The area of the shoreline or littoral zone is populated by plants that can toler- ᵉ high levels of salt – mangroves, saltbush, myrtles and other minor aquatic ᵢnts. Next comes the arid zone, characterized by thorny plants with small flow-

BELOW: opuntia cactus grows in the arid zone.

The scalesia zone.

ers: different types of cactus (particularly *opuntia* and *cereus*), inextricabl
brushwood (*matorrales*), the ghostly-looking *palos santos*, carob trees (*algar
robos*) and lichens (*liquenes*). In the transition zone, perennial herbs and smalle
shrubs are dominant, among them the *matasanos*, and the pega pega (*Pisoni
floribunda*).

The high humid area – called scalesia after the zone's dominant tree, typicall
covered with bromeliads, ferns and orchids – extends between 200 and 50
meters (650 and 1,650ft) above sea level. Several typical plants are found in thi
zone: locust and guava trees, *passiflora* and fungus. Above 500 meters (1,650ft
is the miconia zone, which is also the main area used for cultivation and pas
ture on the inhabited islands, where coffee, vegetables, oranges and pineapple
are planted. In the highest zone, called fern-sedge, grow mainly ferns an
grasses, including the giant Galápagos fern tree which can sometimes reach
meters (10 ft) in height.

Of the 875 plant species so far recorded on the island, 228 are endemic. But al
the plants did come originally from the South American continent, and hav
since adapted to the harsh new environment.

Fascinating wildlife

Fifty-eight resident bird species have been recorded here, of which 28 ar
endemic. The others are either found in other parts of the world or are migra
tory, spending some part of the year living or breeding away from the islands
They can be classified into sea birds and land birds: among the latter are the
famous Darwin finches, mocking birds (distinguished by their gray and brow
streaks), the Galápagos dove and the endemic Galápagos hawk.

BELOW: waved
albatrosses perform
their courtship
dance.

Sea birds tend to be more impressive for non-naturalist visitors. The world's entire population of 12,000 yellow-billed, waved albatross lives on the single island of Española (Hood). These magnificent creatures are famous for their extraordinary courtship displays, dancing about and "fencing" with their beaks – literally, standing face to face and clicking their beaks together at a great rate.

Map, page 318

One of the most common birds is the blue-footed booby, which is not endemic. They are an unforgettable sight, as their feet really are a bold, striking blue. They were named "boobies" after the Spanish word "bobo" (dunce) by early sailors, who were amazed that the birds would not fly away when men approached to kill them. The boobies also have a somewhat comical courtship ritual: they "dance" towards one another, plodding about with blue feet working up and down, "skypoint" (pushing their wings up to the heavens) and give one another twigs as presents. They are often seen diving into the water from heights of 20 meters (65ft) to catch fish.

Another common sea bird is the frigate bird. They can look quite sinister when hovering overhead, and are not above preying on other birds' young. The males' puffed scarlet chest sack makes an impressive sight when they are mating. With only 400 pairs still alive, the Galápagos lava gull is said to be the rarest bird species on earth. The Galápagos also have the world's only two flightless sea birds: the Galápagos penguin and the flightless cormorant. The penguin is a big favorite, clumsily waddling about on land but speeding like a bullet under the waves. They are the most northerly penguin species, probably first coming up from the south with the icy Humboldt Current. They are mostly found on Isabela and Fernandina, although they can also easily be seen on Bartolomé.

Like the penguin, the endemic flightless cormorant makes an entertaining

BELOW: flightless cormorant drying its wings, Isla Fernandina.

sight – if you are lucky enough to spot one, since there are only some 700 pairs in existence, found on the remote, far coasts of Isabela and Fernandina. The flightless cormorant has no enemies to fear, so does not suffer from its inability to fly – it scampers along flapping what look like the shreds of lost wings. It is, however, a good diver and can easily catch the fish it needs for its food.

The flightless cormorant cannot fly because it lost the keel of its breastbone long ago. Its aquatic mating dance routine can last for 40 days.

Prehistoric creatures

It was Darwin who called the Galápagos "a paradise for reptiles." Most common are the endemic black marine iguanas, often found sunning themselves on cliffs and shorelines. Darwin himself found their dragon-like appearance rather horrifying: he called them "imps of darkness… of a dirty black color, stupid and sluggish in [their] movements."

They are probably relatives of a land-going reptile species that died out 100 million years ago. But these creatures have adapted themselves to the ocean to feed on seaweed, often diving to 12-meter (40-ft) depths. They have developed unusual glands connected to their breathing systems that accumulate the excess of salt in their bodies. Every so often the salt is snorted out through the nose – not an attractive sight. While they are usually black (a suitable color for "imps of darkness"), the males change skin color during mating to some surprising tones of orange, red and blue.

The rarer-to-spot land iguanas are yellow in color and often larger than their sea-going relatives. They are one of the species that was hardest-hit by the animals introduced by man. Tiny lava lizards can be found on all the Galápagos islands, frequently seen doing somewhat absurd "push-ups" on pathways, which is a sign that they are marking out their territory against intruders.

BELOW: marine iguana with young.

Slow-moving giants

No doubt the most famous of the Galápagos reptiles is the giant tortoise. Countless thousands were killed for their flesh by whalers during the 18th and 19th centuries, and now only an estimated 15,000 remain. There were 14 subspecies of giant tortoise here – distinguished most easily by the different shell shapes – but three are now extinct (the last example of one species was found at the turn of the century by an expedition from the San Francisco museum: the scientists promptly despatched the creature to take its shell back for study).

The giant tortoise is one of the most ancient of reptiles, but also among the rarest – it exists only here and on the island of Aldabra in the Indian Ocean. Weighing up to 250kg (550lb), it has two types of shell: the dome-shaped is found in humid environments such as Santa Cruz, where vegetation is low and abundant. This type of tortoise has short legs and neck. The second type has a shell that resembles a horse's harness and lives on islands with uneven soil and no low grass, such as Española (Hood). These tortoises are more agile (relatively speaking!) and have long legs and necks in order to feed themselves. The shell indentation allows them to protrude their necks further.

Legend has it that these tortoises can live for centuries. One, given to the Queen of Tonga by Captain Cook in the 1770s, is said to have survived until 1966, but there is no certain evidence for them living for more than 100 years.

Saving these magnificent creatures has been a major task of the Darwin Research Station: a program of breeding and reintroducing the animals to their natural habitat seems to be successful. On Española (Hood), only 10 males and two females of a subspecies were still alive until, after years of breeding in captivity, some 100 healthy specimens were returned to the island. But the tortoise

Map, page 318

BELOW: a giant tortoise munches leaves.

population is still at risk: on Santa Cruz a mysterious disease killed several of them in 1996 and for a while visitors were banned from the National Park.

There is only one survivor, however, of one subspecies from the island of Pinta, and he goes by the name of Lonesome George. Despite a US$10,000 reward for a female of the species, no mate has been found for him to carry on the line. But hope has not been surrendered and scientists at the Charles Darwin Research Center are still searching for a female counterpart.

Easier to spot in the wild seems to be the Pacific green sea turtle, which snorkelers can often observe underwater.

There is a serpent in paradise: the Galápagos snake. There are three endemic species, they grow up to 1 meter (3ft) long, but are not poisonous and very rarely seen.

Playful sea lions and dolphins

There are fewer land mammals than there are birds or reptiles because they were much less likely to survive the journey across from coastal South America. Storms may have blown the hoary bat to the Galápagos, while the rice rat may have made it across on a vegetation raft. Sea mammals, however, simply followed the currents to the islands, and these days they make up some of the Galápagos' creatures most popular with the visitors.

Topping the list is the sea lion, related to the Californian species. The young are incredibly cute and playful – they will swim about snorkelers and tease them, even staring into your goggles and pretending to charge you before turning away. The *machos*, or older males, do, however, stake out their territory very jealously. They can turn aggressive and have been known to bite swimmers, so a degree of caution should be used in their presence (guides will know which areas are the preserve of the bull lions).

BELOW: swimming with sea lions.

Fur seals have more hair than sea lions, they are smaller and very shy: they

prefer to live in colonies, on distant cliffs. Bottle-nosed dolphins are often seen surfing the bow spray of boats, while no less than seven whale species have been sighted at or near the Galápagos archipelago, but getting a close look at them is fairly unlikely.

Map, page 318

An underwater world

Under the waves, snorkelers will be constantly surrounded by many of the 307 species of fish recorded in the Galápagos – and more are being discovered every year. Schools of brightly colored tropical fish pass over the sea floor and around rocks, making a spellbinding sight. There is also a variety of sharks that can be seen in the water, but they are not dangerous. They are much too well fed to bother about attacking humans, and apparently have never attacked a swimmer in the Galápagos – if that's any consolation when you see one! Although the thought is somewhat unnerving, the grace of these creatures is said to be particularly impressive.

Keep an eye out for the different types of rays that glide majestically along the ocean floor. The giant manta ray can sometimes be spotted leaping out of the sea and landing with a loud slap on the waves. None of the rays are dangerous except for the stingray – on some beaches they lie in shallow water beneath a layer of sand, and can give quite a sting if trodden on. It's worth giving the sand a shuffle with your feet to scare off any basking rays.

Animals that do not have backbones are called invertebrates – creatures such as jellyfish, sponges, molluscs and crabs. The most commonly seen of these is the bright yellow and orange Sally Lightfoot crab, which can be found on almost every rock in the Galápagos.

LEFT: a Sally Lightfoot crab. **RIGHT:** a blue-footed booby.

BIRDS OF THE GALÁPAGOS

From the marbled godwit to the black-necked stilt, the birdlife on the Galápagos Islands, which taught us about evolution, is still rich, rare and rewarding

Where else will birds practically come out to greet you? Life without predators has made the birds of the Galápagos fearless, which means that many of them are easy to spot. There are 58 resident species, of which 28 are endemic, as well as about 30 migratory birds. The seabirds are the most frequently seen: in the dry coastal areas you are likely to spot three species of the booby family, the waved albatross – found nowhere in the world except on the island of Española – and the world's only flightless seabirds, the Galápagos penguin and the flightless cormorant. The best time to come is in winter (October to February) when most migrants are visiting, and birds are reproducing. Then, a serious ornithologist might see 50 species in a week, and even a dilettante should be able to spot two dozen.

There are dangers in paradise, however: the introduction of domestic animals has been bad news. Some prey on the birds, others destroy or compete for their habitats. Farming on the inhabited islands also destroys habitats, and a natural phenomenon, the *El Niño* current, brings mosquito-carried disease and disrupts the food chain.

△ **PEREGRINE FALCON**
The peregrine falcon (*Falco peregrinus*) is a migrant frequently seen on the islands of Española, Isabela, Baltra and Santa Cruz. From November to March, the falcon can reach very high speeds when it is swooping to attack prey

◁ **GALAPAGOS HAWK**
The female Galápagos hawk (*Buteo galapagoensis*) mates with up to four males in order to ensure that breeding will be successful

◁ **BLUE-FOOTED BOOBY**
The blue-footed booby (*Sula nebouxii excisa*) has a wonderful courtship ritual, in which the male ostentatiously displays his brightly-colored feet in order to attract a mate. Two or three eggs are laid and both of the parents share the task of incubating them. Once they have become independent, the young birds leave the islands and do not return to breed until some three years later.

THE SECRET OF DARWIN'S FINCHES

The finches of the Galápagos were vitally important in the development of Charles Darwin's ideas about evolution and the formation of species. When he set off on his voyage around the world on HMS *Beagle* (1831–36), he believed, like most people of his time, in the fixity of species. But on the Galápagos he observed that 13 different species of the finch had evolved from a single ancestral group, and it was this (together with his observations of the islands' tortoises) which led to his contention that species could evolve over time, with those most suited to their natural environment surviving and passing on their characteristics to the next generation.

The main differences he noted between the finches was the size and shape of their beaks, leading him to conclude that the birds which survived were those whose beaks enabled them to eat the available food.

The 13 species of finch are divided into two groups: ground finches (pictured above is the large ground finch, *geospiza magnirostris*) and tree finches, of which the mangrove finch, found only in the swamps of Isabela Island, is the most rare. You are unlikely to see all of them on a short visit, but it's a challenge to see how many you can spot.

◁ **VERMILLION FLYCATCHER**
The vermillion flycatcher (*Pyrocephalus rubinus*) is an attractive little bird and quite unlike any other bird to be seen on the Galápagos Islands. It has a high-pitched, musical song and builds a distinctive cup-shaped nest, on which the female incubates the eggs.

△ **FRIGATE BIRDS**
 The magnificent frigatebird (*Fregata magnificens magnificens*) and its close relation, the great frigatebird, can be seen near the coasts of many islands. Both males and females have long forked tails and the male is remarkable for the red gular pouch which puffs in the mating season.

◁ **LAVA GULL**
The lava gull (*Larus fuliginosus*) is believed to be the rarest species in the world It roosts on the shores of saltwater lagoons and builds solitary nests along the coast.

△ **BROWN PELICAN**
The brown pelican (*Pelecanus occidentalis urinator*) is a huge, cumbersome bird which can often be seen following fishing boats in search of food.

VISITING THE ISLANDS

*Uncontrolled, tourism could destroy this Pacific paradise.
The thousands of visitors who follow in Darwin's
footsteps need to follow strict guidelines*

Map,
page 318

Most travelers to the Galápagos arrive by air, except for a few who have pre-arranged trips on one of the larger cruisers, which occasionally depart from Guayaquil. Flights leave from both Quito and Guayaquil. TAME flies daily to the island of Baltra, from where a bus and ferry will take you across to Puerto Ayora on Santa Cruz. SAN-Saeta has flights four days a week to Puerto Baquerizo Moreno on the island of San Cristóbal, where a second airport has recently been built. On arrival, you must have your passport ready and US$80 entrance tax payable to the National Park – without these two essentials, you will not be able to enter the islands.

Many travelers will have pre-arranged their cruise around the islands on one of the larger luxury ships. The best two are the *Galápagos Explorer*, a liner owned by the airline SAN-Saeta, and which leaves from San Cristóbal in conjunction with their new air service; and the *Santa Cruz*, run by the Ecuadorian agency Metropolitan Touring, which leaves from Baltra airport with the TAME flights. Both offer all the comforts of a five-star hotel, with excellent food, swimming pools, evening slide shows and the like. They also have English-speaking guides who are qualified naturalists. Although the capacity of these ships is 90 people, they operate with groups of no more than 20 – landing them by small dinghies called *pangas* for twice-daily excursions. The large boats have the advantage of covering a lot of territory by night, easily reaching the more remote islands without unduly rough passages.

PRECEDING PAGES:
the lunar landscape
of Isla Bartolomé.
LEFT: siesta hour at
the Hotel Sol y Mar,
Puerto Ayora.
BELOW: transport to
the islands.

Independent (and less pecunious) travelers often choose to organize their own cruise on one of the dozens of smaller boats on the islands. This can be arranged in Quito or Guayaquil, but is cheapest when done in Puerto Ayora (some small boats operate from San Cristóbal, but relatively few). The idea is to take your time, meet up with other like-minded travelers, find a captain and agree a price. All this usually takes two or three days, but if you have the time but not much money it's worth doing

The main advantage of organizing your own trip is flexibility: you can pick and choose which islands you want to visit, for how long, and when. However, the guides often don't speak English, and rough weather conditions can make night journeys on these boats difficult for those with delicate stomachs. Still, for younger, independent travelers, this is definitely an experience not to miss.

A guide to the visitor sites

The only places that boats may land on the islands are at the 54 designated visitor sites, and even then visitors must be accompanied by a guide. Some of the more fragile sites are further restricted so that only small

groups are allowed to visit, or limits are imposed on the numbers each month. The landing by *panga* is either wet or dry – your guide will tell you which. Wet landings simply mean that you leap into the water up to your ankles (sometimes up to your knees), so keep your shoes aside; dry landings are at natural or man-made jetties, where you should keep your shoes on.

The most densely populated island in the Galápagos (in human terms), as well as its second largest (at 986 sq. km/380 sq. miles), is **Santa Cruz**. Most tours start here at the township of **Puerto Ayora**, and even those that begin at San Cristóbal call here to visit the **Charles Darwin Research Station ❷**.

With 3,400 people, Puerto Ayora has the air of a relaxed and easygoing fishing village. The wide turquoise **Academy Bay** is full of small boats and makes a picturesque sight, while the town docks are usually crowded with small children running, swimming and playing with sea lions. Ayora has plenty of small hotels and restaurants, the most eccentric being the **Sol y Mar**. It sits right on the waterline and its porch is always crowded with marine iguanas (the little beasties will even walk over your feet while you're having breakfast, which can be something of a surprise until you get used to it).

The main attraction remains the Research Station. This is the classic place to have your photo taken with one of the giant tortoises: mature specimens of several subspecies are kept in pens here, fascinating, ancient-looking creatures. While you often see pictures of tourists riding tortoises, this can actually damage their shells and is prohibited. The station also has a tortoise breeding-house, where the young can be seen, and a small museum and information center. Paths run from the station into littoral vegetation: fine examples of various varieties of cacti can be found, as well as thick expanses of mangrove.

Dried lava patterns.

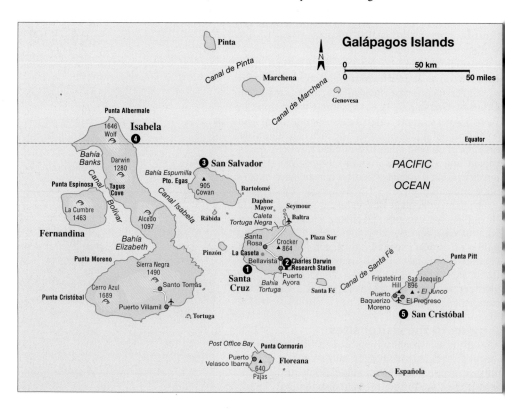

There are several trails from Puerto Ayaro that are worth exploring if you have the time. Seven km (4 miles) towards the west is **Tortuga Bay** (Turtle Bay), with fine white sands and waters rich in lobsters. You can go here for swimming and relaxing without a guide, although the fish and animals are still protected.

The highland interior of Santa Cruz, in the National Park, offers several attractions: the **Lava Tubes** are long underground tunnels made when lava solidified on the surface of a flow but kept going underneath. Climbing **Cerro Crocker,** an 860-meter (2,800-ft) high hill, shows the range of vegetation zones on the island. And a day excursion can be made to the **Tortoise Reserve** which is one of the few places to see giant tortoises in the wild. Organize your trip beforehand with a tour guide in the town or visit independently: you need to take a jeep and then a two-hour walk to find these creatures wallowing in the mud.

The central islands

The islands close to Santa Cruz are the most often visited, although not necessarily the most interesting for naturalists. Day trips are run by various agencies from Puerto Ayora: this means a lot of traveling time on the water if you want to visit more than one. It is more fun and – if properly organized – only slightly more expensive to visit several on your own cruise.

Only 24km (15 miles) from Puerto Ayora is **Isla Santa Fe** (also known as Barrington). A wet landing is the start of a short trail into a dry landscape crowded with *opuntia* cactuses. Santa Fe is one of the best places to see the shy land iguana, but the steep path is one of the more difficult on the Galápagos, so a swim from the beach near the landing site comes as a welcome relief.

On the northeastern coast of Santa Cruz is the tiny island of **Plaza Sur**. Only

Map, page 318

BELOW: the harbor at Puerto Ayora.

13 hectares (32 acres) in area, its coast is so crowded with sea lions that everyone on the *panga* needs to clap and shout to clear a landing space. Swimming is not encouraged here, since the *macho* or bull sea lions are particularly aggressive. Plaza Sur is unusually crowded with animal life: there are plenty of land iguanas and its impressive black cliffs are populated with sea birds. Nearby is a convalescent home for bachelor *macho* sea lions: after losing a brawl over territory, they come here to recuperate before returning to the fray.

Isla Seymour is separated from the larger island of **Baltra** by a channel. But whereas Baltra has little to interest a visitor, Seymour is considered one of the Galápagos' best breeding grounds for sea birds. Blue-footed boobies are so common on this island that visitors have to be careful not to step on any of the nests that may have been built on the trails.

The strange, block-shaped island of **Daphne** is 10km (6 miles) away. Access is restricted to only a few boats a month. Landing here is also difficult, with a leap onto nearly-sheer rocks that becomes somewhat hair-raising in rough weather. But it is worth the effort: at the end of a trail, a large crater is dotted with hundreds of blue-footed booby nests, making a decidedly surreal sight.*

Volcanic rock and iguanas

One of the larger islands, relatively close to Santa Cruz, is commonly known as either **Santiago** or **James**, although its official title is **San Salvador ❸**. It has a number of landing sites, although by far the most popular is **Puerto Egas** on the west coast. This is one of the best places to see hundreds of marine iguanas sunning themselves on black volcanic rocks, while fur seals can be spotted swimming nearby. The **Sugarloaf Volcano** dominates the horizon here. Swimming is good at Espumilla Beach and Buccaneer Cove. If you are in a small group, try snorkeling at the **fur seals' grotto**. You can swim with these characters for hours through the crystal pools that have been formed under natural-stone archways.

BELOW: preparing lunch on a charter boat.

Sitting off the west coast of San Salvador, the small (120 hectares/300 acres) island of **Bartolomé** is one of the most photographed in the Galápagos. The centerpiece of a visit is the steep climb up **Cerro Bartolomé**: the view is spectacular, looking over lunar fields of dried lava, craters and out over the jutting, honeycombed **Pinnacle Rock**. The heat is also quite intense, so after working up a sweat most people transfer to the second landing site, one of the most pleasant beaches on the islands. The snorkeling is excellent, especially around Pinnacle Rock itself: apart from the tropical fish moving in formation, you have a chance of spotting teams of penguins hunting underwater. A path leads over to the other side of the island, where dozens of reef sharks patrol only meters from the edge of the water.

South of Santiago is the island of **Rábida** (Jervis), which is famous for its beach with dark red sand (due to its high iron oxide content) along which lounge hundreds of bloated sea lions. Indolent and clumsy on land, they are surprisingly energetic in the water: this is a great place to play with the baby sea lions. A path into the interior of the island passes a marshy lake full of bright pink flamingos (the pinker the flamingo, the healthier it is – the color comes from the shrimps they sieve through their beaks). In the trees by the beach are also a large number of brown pelicans.

Another unusual point on Rábida that is well worth visiting is **Caleta Tortuga Negra** – "Black Turtle Cove." This tidal lagoon leads into a maze of mangroves: it can be visited only by *panga*, cutting the motor and paddling quietly through the natural tunnels made by trees. The brackish waters of the area are full of white-tipped sharks and mustard rays. But it is most famous as a mating spot for the green Pacific turtles. With luck, you can spot the two heads coming up for air during copulation, which lasts for many hours.

When cruising the south coast of Jervis/Santiago, keep an eye out for **Sombrero Chino** – literally "Chinese Hat," named for the island's sweeping conical shape. One of the more recent islands, it has a 400-meter (1,300-ft) path around its circumference, along which sea lions relax in abandonment.

The western islands

At 4,588 sq. km (1,770 sq. miles), and 120 km (75 miles) in length, **Isabela ❹**, the largest of the Galápagos islands, is still recovering from fires which blazed across the island in 1994. The fires were eventually extinguished, but not without a severe impact on vegetation. One of the island's main attractions, the giant tortoises, were thankfully rescued by helicopter and taken to the other side of the island to a breeding center. Isabela is also one of the islands that still has volcanic activity, and there are five cones still visible: **Wolf** at 1,645 meters (5,395 ft); **Alcedo** at 1,097 (3,600); **Santo Tomás** (also called Sierra Negra) at 1,490 (4,885); **Cerro Azul** at 1,690 (5,540) and **Darwin** at 1,280 (4,200).

Some 950 people live on Isabela, mostly in and around **Puerto Villamil** on

**Map,
page 318**

BELOW: Galápagos penguin surveys the scene.

Iguanas don't object to posing for photographs.

the south coast. Cruise ships rarely visit the outpost since it is difficult to enter the bay, especially when the sea is rough. It does, however, have a fine sandy beach, an old cemetery and several basic hotels and restaurants. Eighteen km (11 miles) away is the village of **Santo Tomás** and the "Wall of Tears" – built in the convict colony that was closed in 1959.

The crater Santo Tomás has a diameter of 10km (6 miles), making it the second largest in the world, while Alcedo has a still-steaming fumarole and scores of giant tortoises living at its rim. It can be reached by climbing a difficult 10-km (6-mile) trail from Shipton Cove. It is an overnight project: there is a camping site here but you must bring your own food and water (a special National Park permit is also needed to camp here). For those who want an easier hike, the rim of Santo Tomás is easier to reach (9km/5 miles from Santo Tomás).

Most of the visitor sites on Isabela are situated on the west side of the island. Probably the most popular is **Tagus Cove**. Here you can climb up a path to see lava fields stretching for miles. A *panga* ride along the cliffs will reveal colonies of penguins, as well as the usual range of sea birds. It is probably also the best place to see the unique flightless cormorant.

Other landings can be made at **Urbina Bay**, **Elizabeth Bay** and **Punta Moreno**. The flightless cormorant was common at **Punta García** but it has become more difficult to sight in recent years.

On the other side of Isabela is **Isla Fernandina**. One of the least-visited islands because of it is so remote, it is also the most westerly in the Galápagos. It has one visitor site at **Punta Espinosa**, with some impressive lava flows (this was probably the most recently formed major island, and still has some volcanic activity). Along its shores are more penguins and hordes of marine iguanas.

A whalers' post box

Of historical interest on **Isla Floreana**, to the south of the archipelago, is the post box at **Post Office Bay**, where whalers used to leave mail way back in the late 18th century. Since replaced several times, the box is still in use. It is the custom to look through the mail and take anything addressed to your destination, putting a local stamp on it when you arrive and sending it on its way.

Of the visitor sites on Floreana, **Punta Cormorant** is a beach with a greenish tinge from the tiny crystals of olivine in the sand. From here a trail leads to a lagoon, where occasionally some magnificent pink flamingos nest and circle around. Nearby is a second beach with glistening white sands. The **Devil's Crown** is a sunken crater that forms a semi-circle of rocks: this is perhaps the best site for diving in the whole archipelago. Apart from the schools of brilliant tropical fish, you will probably be joined by some baby sea lions who will race snorkelers through a natural underwater archway.

The outlying islands

The most southerly island in the Galápagos is **Española** (Hood). Like the northern island of Tower, Hood is famous for its sea birds – particularly the waved albatross. Twelve thousand pairs nest here, almost the world's entire population. During the mating season,

BELOW: a tuna catch.

they begin "fencing" by knocking their beaks together and waddling about "like drunken sailors," as one observer put it. The whole astonishing range of sea birds can be seen on this island, as well as the beautiful beach of Gardner's Bay. Keep an eye out for the "blowhole," which spouts water 50 meters (165ft) into the air whenever waves hit.

Map,
page 318

At the eastern point of the archipelago lies **San Cristóbal** (Chatham) ❺, the second human population center after Santa Cruz: some 2,800 people live in the sleepy town of **Puerto Baquerizo Moreno**, the provincial capital. The recent introduction of SAN's flights here has meant a development boom, and now several hotels and restaurants service the town. There is a small **museum** run by the Franciscan fathers, a monument to Darwin and, at the entrance to the port, a rock called **Leon Dormido** which can be climbed for a good view of the island.

A road leads from the capital to the village of **El Progreso** and the 895-meter (2,935-ft) high **Volcán San Joaquín**. The **El Junco Lagoon** is a freshwater lake within a crater, surrounded by ferns. **Frigatebird Hill** is, as the name suggests, a good place to see frigate birds and is only a short walk from the town. **La Loberia** is a beach crowded with sea lions and **Puerto Grande** a small cove particularly popular for swimming.

Other far-flung islands include **Marchena**, **Pinta** and **Genovesa** (Tower). Genovesa is home to the main colony of red-footed boobies, three types of Darwin finch, and everything from red-billed tropic-birds to storm petrels.

Preserving the islands

Tourism to the Galápagos has been described as a two-edged sword: it can be a force to preserve the islands; or, uncontrolled, it can destroy them. The follow-

BELOW: messages at Post Office Bay, Isla Floreana.

Map, page 318

ing are guidelines to ensure that the Galápagos are left unaltered by your visit.

No natural object – plant, animal, shell, bone, or scrap of wood – should be removed or disturbed. It is illegal and alters the islands' ecological conditions.

Be careful not to transport any live material to the islands, or from island to island. Before leaving the boat, check your shoe soles for dried mud, as it may contain plant seeds and animal spores. Inadvertent transport of these materials represents a special danger to the Galápagos: each island has its own unique fauna and flora, and introduced plants and animals can quickly destroy them. Obviously no other animals or plants should be brought to the islands. One of the most destructive forces in the Galápagos are domesticated species gone wild.

For the same reasons, do not take any food to the uninhabited islands. Together with the food may come insects or other organisms which might threaten the fragile island ecosystems. Fresh fruits and vegetables are especially dangerous. A dropped orange seed, for example, may become a tree.

Animals may not be touched or handled. They will cease to be tame if fondled by humans. Young animals that have been handled may be rejected by their mothers because of their smell. They soon die as a result.

Animals may not be fed. Not only can it be dangerous but in the long run it can destroy the animals' social structure and affect their reproduction.

Do not startle or chase any animal from its resting or nesting spot. Exercise extreme caution among the breeding colonies of sea birds such as boobies, cormorants, gulls, or frigate birds. These birds will fly from their nests if they are startled, often knocking the egg or chick to the ground or leaving it exposed to the sun. (A recently hatched booby chick will die in 20 to 30 minutes if it is exposed to the sun; frigate birds will also eat any unguarded chick.)

Do not leave the designated visiting sites. Where trails to points of interest are marked with wooden stakes, you should remain within the stakes.

Litter of all types must be kept off the islands. Disposal at sea must be limited to certain types of garbage which can be thrown overboard in selected areas. Keep all rubbish in a bag or pocket, to be disposed of on your boat. The crew of your vessel is responsible to the National Park for proper trash disposal. You should never throw anything overboard.

Do not buy souvenirs or objects made from plants or animals. Black coral is now endangered by islanders' carvings. If anyone offers you any of these souvenirs, please advise the National Park.

Camping anywhere within the Galápagos without a permit is against the law. Camping is permitted only in certain sites designated by the National Park. Contact the National Park office in Santa Cruz for information.

All groups visiting the National Park must be accompanied by an approved, qualified guide. The visitor must follow the guide's instructions, while the guide must ensure compliance with the National Park regulations relating to the conservation of the flora and fauna.

Notify the National Park service if you see any serious damage being done. You may be a decisive factor in the preservation of the islands. The office is a 10-minute walk east of the main town of Puerto Ayora, open Mon–Fri, 8am–noon and 2–6pm; Sat 8–10am.

BELOW: a dip in the waters off Isla Bartolomé.
RIGHT: dolphins ride a boat's spray.

INSIGHT GUIDES

Travel Tips

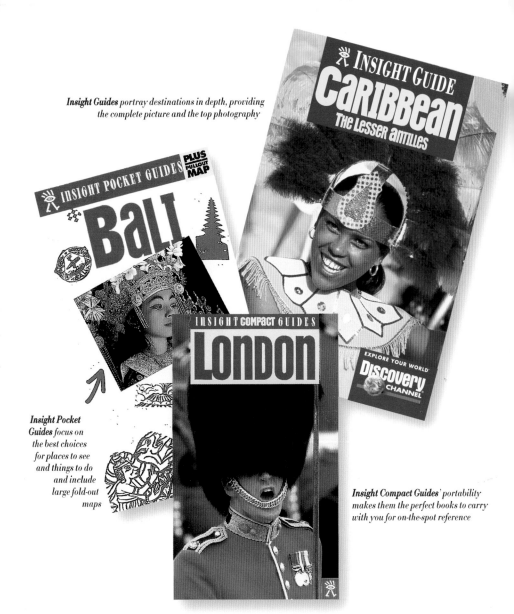

Insight Guides portray destinations in depth, providing the complete picture and the top photography

Insight Pocket Guides focus on the best choices for places to see and things to do and include large fold-out maps

Insight Compact Guides' portability makes them the perfect books to carry with you for on-the-spot reference

Three types of guide for all types of travel

INSIGHT GUIDES Different people need different kinds of information. Some want *background information* to help them prepare for the trip. Others seek *personal recommendations* from someone who knows the destination well. And others look for *compactly presented data* for on-the-spot reference. With three carefully designed series, Insight Guides offer readers the perfect choice. Insight Guides will turn your visit into an experience.

The world's largest collection of visual travel guides

CONTENTS

Getting Acquainted

The Place

Ecuador is located on the northwestern coast of South America, between a latitude of 1° 27' North and 5° South. It owes its name to the equatorial line that runs through the mainland just north of Quito, as well as through the Galápagos Islands. The country is bordered by Colombia to the north, Peru to the east and south, and the Pacific Ocean to the west.

Mainland Ecuador is divided by the Andes into three distinct areas: the Sierra (highlands), the Costa or coast, and the Oriente (Amazon basin).

The Sierra is shaped by two Andean mountain chains, the Eastern Cordillera and Western Cordillera, which create 10 mountain valleys, in which Sierra *indígenas* (Indians) live at altitudes of 2,200 to 2,800 meters (6,600 to 7,400 ft).

The inhabitable highland area is often referred to as the *páramo*. Scattered along the Eastern and Western Cordilleras are several active volcanoes. The highest peak is Chimborazo at 6,310 meters, or 20,702 ft.

The Andes drop steeply down to the tropical coastal lowlands on one side and the Oriente on the other. The coast manages to escape the icy Humboldt Current that washes the beaches of Peru and Chile, so the landscape is lush and swimming a pleasure. Meanwhile, the Oriente (some 30 percent of Ecuador's territory) is mostly flat plain-land.

The Galápagos archipelago

Fact Pack

Total area 270,670 sq. km (108,268 sq. miles)
Capital Quito
Population about 11 million
Language Spanish, Quichua and other Indian languages
Religion 90% Roman Catholic
Time zones mainland 5 hours behind GMT, the Galápagos 6 hours behind
Currency sucre (ECS)
Weights and measures metric
Electricity 110 volts, 60 cycles, AC
Dialling code 593

consists of 17 larger islands and 100 or so smaller ones. Located 1,120 km (672 miles) west of the mainland, they are renowned for their unusual wildlife.

Climate

Because it is on the Equator, Ecuador has only two seasons: wet and dry. Weather patterns vary greatly between the different geographical regions.

In the inhabited inter-mountain basin of the Sierra, the temperature changes little between seasons. However, each day the mornings are generally sunny and fresh, becoming warmer towards midday; in the afternoon it often rains, and towards the evenings it gets chilly, and the nights are cold. Thus, in Quito the daily range of temperature is generally 8° to 21° C (46° to 70° F). There is one rainy season in the Sierra, from November to May, when there is frequent rainfall during the afternoon and evening. However, it rains quite often during the dry season too, and the sun shines in the rainy season for at least a couple of hours every day.

Above 3,800 meters (11,400 ft) no plants grow and temperatures reach freezing during the night. Occasional snow storms also occur.

The coastal lowlands and Amazon basin are very hot all year round, with temperatures ranging from 22° C (73° F) at night to 33° C (100° F) during the day. Humidity is extremely high. The rainy season in both areas is from May to December, although tropical downpours are regular in the dry season also. In the Galápagos Islands, there are also two seasons, produced by the ocean currents: the rainy (warm) and dry (cool) season.

During the rainy season, from January through June, the weather is warm and sunny, while the water temperature is a comfortable 23° C (75° F); heavy, tropical showers occur occasionally. This is the best time to visit. For the rest of the year, a mist called the *garua* settles over the islands and makes the day cloudy, and the water begins to cool. It rarely rains, but it can be windy.

Government

The Republic of Ecuador has been under democratic rule since 1979. The new constitution approved by referendum in 1978 allowed the extension of the vote to include all literate citizens aged over 18.

The president and vice-president are elected directly for five-year terms and cannot stand for office again. The 69-person Chamber of Representatives meets for two months of the year. There is a Supreme Court of Justice whose members are chosen by the Congress, and High Courts in every province.

Each of the country's 21 provinces has a governor, appointed by the president, and a prefect, elected by the inhabitants. The provinces are subdivided into 103 *cantones* (municipalities), headed by elected *alcaldes* (mayors).

Planning the Trip

What to Wear

Ecuador has three very different climactic zones, so what you wear depends completely on where you are headed.

The Sierra is where most travelers begin. Quito is called the "City of Eternal Spring," although eternal autumn (fall) might be more accurate. When the sun is shining, Sierra days are warm and pleasant, but when the clouds roll in and winds begin to blow, you need a warm sweater. Nights can be quite cold, so a warm coat or parka is recommended.

Note that Quito tends to be more conservative in its dress standards than the rest of the country. Ecuadorians, like most Latin Americans, like to dress up when they go out to restaurants and night spots – men will often wear a jacket and tie even in relatively casual surroundings, while women can seem to spend hours grooming themselves.

Of course, this doesn't apply to many backpacker hangouts, and even in the ritzier establishments, traveling gringos are forgiven for a more casual appearance than Ecuadorians. But remember that a night out in a restaurant is more of a big deal for an Ecuadorian, and dressing too unkemptly can seem like an insult to the other clients. If in doubt, err on the side of formality and you can't go wrong.

The coast and Galápagos Islands are tropical regions, so dress for the heat. Take a swimsuit, because swimming and snorkeling on the islands are a joy (most boats have snorkeling gear, so you don't need to bring your own unless you want to). Guayaquil and the coast are very casual, so shorts for men are widely accepted for many social situations (not so widely for women – a light dress is more appropriate). Remember to use protection against the sun.

Dress in the Oriente is even more functional. All clothes should be light, because of the stifling heat, but long trousers and shirts are recommended against insects. Bring some sandshoes for walking.

Rain can strike in any part of Ecuador whether it's the rainy season or not, so bring a decent rain coat.

Entry Regulations

VISAS & PASSPORTS

To visit Ecuador as a tourist, all you need is a valid passport (unless you happen to be from China, Cuba, North or South Korea, Taiwan or Vietnam, in which case you do need a visa). Ecuadorian Immigration Police will give you a free T-3 Tourist Card, which you should keep since it is needed when you leave the country (stapling it into your passport is not a bad idea). It is usually given for 30 days (unless you ask for more), although you can easily extend it for up to 90 days in the Department of Immigration in Quito (Av. Amazonas 2639). Note that tourists can only stay in the country for a maximum of 90 days in any calendar year – but sometimes a one-month extension can be obtained for a few dollars at the end of the 90-day period.

In theory, Immigration Police can ask for an onward ticket or proof of sufficient funds (US$20 a day) before allowing entry, although they rarely do.

Customs

Each traveler may bring a liter of spirits, several bottles (a "reasonable amount") of perfume and 300 cigarettes into Ecuador duty free.

You should carry your passport, or a photocopy of it, at all times, since the police are empowered to arrest those without ID should a check be made. Foreigners are unlikely to be bothered in this way in the streets of Quito, but it is very important to have your passport handy on bus trips in the countryside, where checks are common.

Health

It is a good idea to consult a tropical medicine clinic before traveling. Vaccinations against diptheria, polio, tetanus, typhoid, yellow fever and hepatitis A are strongly recommended. If traveling into the Amazon or the tropical lowlands, anti-malaria pills should be taken. Remember that the course usually starts one or two weeks before your visit and should be continued for at least four weeks after you leave. Remember, too, to cover exposed areas of skin after dusk and use an insect repellent.

If you are hiking or cycling in rural areas a rabies vaccination will mean fewer post-bite shots if you get bitten by a rabid dog.

The most common illness for tourists is, of course, mild diarrhoea – something that hits most visitors at some stage. Sufferers should have plenty of liquids (hot tea without milk is ideal – definitely no coffee), avoid eggs and dairy products and rest as much as they can. Two products, Dioralyte and Rehidrat, taken regularly, help prevent dehydration. Boiled water with a little sugar and salt added has a similar effect.

The symptoms of diarrhoea can be stopped with medication like Imodium. This does not cure the ailment, and is really only useful if you have to hop on a long bus or flight and don't want a sudden attack. If the complaint continues for several days, consult a doctor. Also, if you suffer severe abdominal cramps, fever, or nausea, or if blood or puss is evident in your stool, you need a test to see if you've caught amoebic dysentery. But in almost all cases, diarrhoea is simply a matter of becoming accustomed to strange foods, and the stomach returns to normal after a couple of days.

To avoid diarrhoea, don't drink the tap water in Ecuador. Ask instead for mineral water (*Güitig* is the best brand – pronounced Wee-tig). Stay clear of uncooked vegetables, salads that haven't been properly treated, and unpeeled fruits.

Most food in the large cities of Ecuador, or in the restaurants where most travelers will eat, is perfectly safe. Hepatitis is a danger if you eat food prepared in dirty conditions, and, as mentioned above, it is advisable to have a gamma globulin shot to protect against this. There is also a newer drug, Havirix, which gives 10-year protection, although you need a booster afer the first year.

A more everyday health risk is the fierce equatorial sun, a danger even in the cold Sierra. Newcomers to Ecuador should not expose their skin to the sun for long periods, especially during the middle of the day. Bring strong sunscreen lotion. Wearing a hat is a good idea.

Altitude sickness *(soroche)* can sometimes affect travelers arriving in Quito by air. Most people will need a couple of days to get used to the thin Andean air, so take it easy at first: eat light meals, steer clear of excessive alcohol and don't go

Maps

The best selection of maps of Ecuador is produced by the Instituto Geográfico Militar on top of the hill on Avenida T Paz y Mino, off Avenida Colombia in Quito. Large-scale maps of the whole country, ranging from a 1:1,000,000 one-sheet map to 1:50,000 topographical map are available here. The Sierra has been covered in detail, but the Oriente and parts of the Western Lowlands are not well-served. For a road map, pick up the *Guia Vial del Ecuador*, with 26 partial maps,by Nelson Gomez, Editorial Camino.

on strenuous walks; a chocolate bar can sometimes help. Drink tea, relax and let your body become accustomed to the height.

Mountain sickness is a more serious problem for climbers, who may be exerting themselves at altitudes over 5,000 meters (15,000 ft). Symptoms can include vomiting, rapid pulse and failing blood pressure. The only real cure is to descend to a lower level. Before starting out, most climbers drink *mate de coca* (coca leaf tea) which is the local preventative remedy.

There are several good private hospitals in Quito and Guayaquil, but they are expensive. Visitors are advised to take out travel insurance.

Money

Ecuador's currency is the *sucre*, which devalues fairly rapidly by Western standards. It is traded in bills of 100, 1,000, 5,000, 10,000, 20,000 and 50,000 and coins of 50, 100, 500 and 1000 sucres. Some old bills of 5, 10, 20, and 50 do still exist. A new 100,000 bill is planned. In late 1997 there were just over 4000 sucres to the US dollar.

Foreign currencies can be exchanged in banks and casas

de cambio (exchange houses) in the business districts of Quito (Av. Amazonas), Guayaquil and Cuenca. The easiest currency to exchange is US dollars (which is the unofficial parallel exchange for all Latin America), although in Quito and Guayaquil almost any currency can be exchanged. Outside the major cities, however, it becomes difficult to exchange anything but US dollars, usually only in cash form, and at a dismal rate. Change your money before leaving Quito.

On Sundays and holidays, when banks and casas de cambio are shut, you can always exchange money in the major hotels such as the Colón in Quito. Most smaller hotels, some shops and even many restaurants will change dollars at a rate slightly lower than the official one.

It is worth bringing most of your money in travelers' checks for safety, as these can be changed almost as easily as cash. Most people also bring a certain amount of cash dollars in manageable denominations (say $20 bills).

It is easy to have money transferred to Ecuador, through organizations such as Western Union. You can pick up the sum in US dollars, travelers' checks or local currency.

Major credit cards (particularly Visa and Mastercard) are accepted in the larger hotels, restaurants, and tourist-oriented shops.

In Quito and Guayaquil ATMS from which you can withdraw sucres using Visa or MasterCard are becoming more common.

Public Holidays

JANUARY

1st – National holiday: New Year's festivities; dances, fancy dressers, masquerades, etc.
6th – National holiday: Festival of the Three Kings (Epiphany).
Ambato (Tungurahua): Children's Mass (*misa de niños*), processions, Christmas carols.
Cuenca (Azuay): Children's Mass, processions, Christmas carols.
Gatazo Grande (Chimborazo): Fireworks, hymns, invitations to share food and drink, election of the "prioste" (Steward of the Festival), kings and ambassadors.
Lican (Chimborazo): Hymns, processions, election of the "prioste" and kings.
Montecristi (Manabí): Bands, dances.
Tisalleo (Tungurahua): High Mass, everybody pays homage to the Christ Child in the crib, folkloric presentation in national costume with dances.
Calpi (Chimborazo): Marimbas, processions with "La Mamá Negra."`
15th *Quito-Chillogallo* (Pinchincha): Dances of the Innocent, masquerades, typical bands.

FEBRUARY

1st – *Mira* (Carchi): Festival of the Virgin of Charity (*Virgen de la Caridad*); Fireworks, dances, glove ball games (*pelota nacional*), vaca loca (crazy cow) rodeos.
12th – (*All Ecuador*): Anniversary of the discovery of the Amazon River (*Día del Oriente*) – Fairs in Puyo, Tena, Macas and Zamora; day of the province of Galápagos – civic events.
27th – (*All Ecuador*): Patriotism and National Unity day to commemorate the battle of Tarqui in 1829; oath to the flag by students, civic events.

Changeable date – (*All Ecuador*): Carnival (this precedes Lent, so depends on the date of Easter).

MARCH

2nd to 5th – *Atuntaqui* (Imbabura): Sugarcane and Craftsmanship Festival – dances and *verbenas*.
4th to 10th – *Gualaceo* (Azuay): Peach Festival. Fruits, flowers and craftsmanship exhibition, dances and masquerades.

Holiday Tactics

• When an official public holiday falls at a weekend, offices may be closed on the Friday or Monday.
• When a public holiday falls midweek it may be moved to the nearest Friday or Monday to create a long weekend.
• Major holidays are often celebrated for several days around the actual date.
• Banks and businesses are closed on official public holidays.
• If you plan to travel on a major holiday, book ahead if possible as transportation can be very crowded.

APRIL

19th to 21st – *Riobamba* (Chimborazo): Farming, cattle, handicraft and industrial fair; folkloric dances, parades, allegorical floats, etc.
Changeable date – (*All Ecuador*): Holy Week. Celebrations and processions on Good Friday and Easter Sunday.

MAY

1st – (*All Ecuador*): Labor day – workers' parades.
2nd – *Quito*: Festival of Las Cruzes at La Cruz Verde quarter (corner of Bolívar and Imbabura Street). Typical band, fireworks, dancing in the streets at night.
3rd – *Quito*: Festival of La Cruz at Champicruz (Avenidas Prensa

and Sumaco). Dances, hymns, fireworks, and masquerades.
Checa (Pinchincha): Patron saint's day of the Lord of Good Hope (*Señor de la Buena Esperanza*). Typical band, bonfires, fireworks, serpents, greasy pole climbing and many more attractions.
11th to 14th – *Puyo* (Pastaza): Farming, cattle and industrial exhibition and fair in the Amazon region.
24th– (*All Ecuador*): National civic festivity to commemorate the Battle of Pichincha in 1822. Parades, cultural events.

JUNE

23rd/24th – *Otavalo* (Imbabura), *Tabacundo* (Pichincha), *Guamote* (Chimborazo): Festival of Saint John (San Juan). Dancing, masked parades and other celebrations. In Otavalo it is an all-male festival and may last all week, culminating in rock throwing at San Juan church.
24th and following days – *Sangolqui* (Pichincha). Corn and tourism festivities. Parades, masquerades, craftsmanship exhibition and country bullfights (everybody participates).
24th – *Calpi* (Chimborazo). *Gallo Compadre* and *vaca loca* rodeos.
28th to 29th – *Santo Domingo de los Colorados* (Pichincha). Canonization anniversary. Parades, dances, farming exposition.
29th – *Cotacahi and Cayambe* (Imbabura), and other communities: Festival of Saints Peter and Paul (San Pedro y San Pablo). Dancing, parades, bonfires, and a ceremony of *entrega de gallos* (delivering of roosters).

JULY

16th – *Ibarra* (Imbabura): Celebration of Virgen del Carmen. Fireworks, typical music, masquerades.
22nd – *Pelileo* (Tungurahua): Canonization anniversary.

Country bullfights (everybody participates) and many folkloric attractions.

23rd to 25th – *Guayaquil*: Guayaquil's foundation anniversary. Parades, dancing in the streets, international beauty contest ("Pearl of the Pacific"), art expositions and cultural events.

24th – National Holiday: Simón Bolívar's birthday.

29th – *Pillaro* (Tungurahua): Celebration day of the apostle Santiago the Elder; country bullfights (everyone participates) and other attractions.

AUGUST

3rd to 5th – *Esmeraldas*: Independence Day. Farming, craftsmanship and industrial fair, processions, dances, marimbas, Afro-American folklore, etc.

5th to 7th – *Sicalpa* (Chimborazo): Festival of the Virgin of the Snow (*Virgen de las Nieves*). Religious observance, fireworks, clowns, folkloric presentation in national costume with dances.

10th – National Holiday: National civic festival to commemorate independence in 1809. Military and school parades.

Pillaro (Tungurahua): San Lorenzo festivities. Popular bullfights, masquerades.

Yaguachi (Guayas): San Jacinto festival, with popular pilgrimages.

25th – *Santa Rosa* (El Oro): Agricultural fair. Various shows.

SEPTEMBER

2nd to 15th – *Otavalo* (Imbabura): Yamor festivities. Many attractions, typical music, cockfights, parades, folk-singers, beauty contests, dances in national costumes.

5th to 12th – *Loja*: Festival of Virgen del Cisne, the patron saint. Religious observance, fair, dances, masquerades, horse races, cockfights, folksongs.

6th to 14th – *Cotacachi* (Imbabura): Jora festival. Folkloric dances, typical food.

11th to 16th – *Milagro* (Guayas): Agricultural fair. Car races, shows.

8th to 9th – *Macara* (Loja): Agricultural fair. Folkloric presentations.

8th to 9th – *Sangolqui* (Pichincha): Bullfights, dances and processions.

20th to 26th – *Machala* (El Oro): International Banana Festival.

23rd to 24th – *Latacunga* (Cotopaxi): Festival of Virgen de las Mercedes, the patron saint. Vespers, masquerades, typical bands, fireworks, Midnight Mass (*misa del gallo*) and folkloric festival *La Mamá Negra* (shepherds, musicians, native songs, clowns and other typical attractions).

***Quito*:** Festival of Virgen de las Mercedes. Vespers, typical bands, fireworks, Midnight Mass, religious procession around the church.

24th – *Piñas* (El Oro): Product fair.

24th to 28th – *Ibarra* (Imbabura): Festivals of the Lakes. Parades, folkloric dances, car races in Yaguarcocha, beauty contests, international agricultural and industrial exhibition.

27th – *Espejo* (Imbabura): Indian handicrafts fair.

29th – *Gonzanama* (Loja): Agricultural and industrial exhibition. Several events.

OCTOBER

9th to 12th – *Guayaquil*: National civic festival to commemorate the independence of Guayaquil. International industrial fair, concerts, regattas, dances, parades, shows and general razzmatazz.

12th – National Holiday: Columbus Day (Día de la raza). To celebrate the arrival of the Europeans in America.

14th to 18th – *Portoviejo* (Manabí): Agricultural and

industrial exhibition. Many attractions.

NOVEMBER

1st – National Holiday: All Saints' Day.

2nd – (*All Ecuador*): All Souls' Day (*Día de los Difuntos*). Flower-laying ceremonies in the cemeteries; especially colorful in rural areas, where entire Indian families show up to eat, drink and leave offerings in memory of their departed relatives; typical food is *guaguas de pan* (bread rolls) and *colada morada* (fermented corn syrup).

3rd – *Cuenca* (Azuay): Civic festivity to commemorate Cuenca's independence. Processions, expositions, dances and other cultural events.

4th – *Manta* (Manabí): Manta Day. Parades and celebrations.

11th – *Latacunga* (Cotopaxi): Independence of Latacunga. Parades, several cultural events and popular bullfights.

21st – *El Quinche* (Pichincha): Day of the Virgen of El Quinche, the patron saint. Religious observances, pilgrimages, commercial fair.

DECEMBER

1st to 6th – *Quito* (Pichincha): Anniversary of the Foundation of San Francisco de Quito. Festivities include a series of special bullfights, parades, street dances, greasy pole climbing, and election of the Queen of Quito.

25th – National Holiday: Christmas Day. Nativity scenes in churches and homes, illuminations, Christmas carols, Midnight Mass, folkloric festival *Pasa del Niño* in El Tingo, a village near Quito, and other towns, and especially in Cuenca.

28th: All Fools' Day. Masquerades, dancing clowns, and other attractions.

31st – (*All Ecuador*): New Year's Eve celebrations. Parades and dances culminate in burning of life-size dolls representing politicians, artists, etc., and *el año viejo* (the old year), particularly in Quito, Guayaquil and Esmeraldas.

Getting there

By Air

Travelers heading to Ecuador from the United States can fly directly to Quito or Guayaquil in Ecuador on daily flights from New York, Miami and Los Angeles with the national airline, SAETA Internacional. Its main competitor, American Airlines, has a regular service to Ecuador, from Miami. In Quito, SAETA is based in the España building on the corner of Avenida Colón and Avenida Amazonas. Reservations with SAETA can be made at the following offices:
Bolivia: *La Paz*, Av. 16 de Julio No. 1800, Edif. Commos, 1er Piso. Tel: (591-2) 322-903, 352-079, 376-001. Fax: (591-2) 362-697.
Colombia: *Bogotá*, Calle 82 No. 11-83 Ofic 402. Tel: (571) 218-7144, 218-2644, 218-9233, 218-5033. Fax: (571) 218-3633.
Medellin: Carrera 34 A No. 19 A 87, Local 035, Centro Commercial Automotria. Tel: (574) 262-6400, 262-5906, 262-5868, 262-5786. Fax: (574) 262-3816.
Ecuador: *Quito*, SAETA Av. Colón y Av. Amazonas, Edificio España. Tel: (593-2) 564-969; flight information Tel: (593-2) 502-706.
Quito Airport: Av. 10 de Augosto y Buenos Aires. Tel: (593-2) 441-506. Fax: (593-2) 255-918.
Guayaquil, Av. Carlos Juilio Arosemena Km 2.5. Tel: (593-4) 205-115, 200-277. Fax: (593-4) 293-081. Vélez 206 y Chile. Tel: (593-4) 32-6912, 32-9855, 32-6466. 9 de Octubre 2002 y Los Rios. Tel: 29-6111. Fax: 29-6397.
Guayaquil Airport: Av. las Américas. Tel: (593-4) 28-6909,

29-2737. Fax: (593-4) 397-081. *Ambato*, Bolívar y Montalvo. Tel: (593-3) 826-147. Fax: (593-3) 825-052.
Cuenca, Sucre 770 y Luis Cordero. Tel: (503-7) 831-548. Fax: (593-7) 835-113.
Ibarra, Pedro Moncayo y Olmedo. Tel: (593-6) 957-667.
Peru: *Lima*, Andalucía 174, Mirallores, Lima 18. Tel: (51-1) 422-0889. Fax: (51-1) 422-6919.
Venezuela: *Caracas*, Av. Libertador, Centro Comercial Libertador, PH.NE. Tel: (582) 761-6530, 761-6630, 762-9905. Fax: (582) 71-9322.
United States: *Chicago*, 6N Michigan Avenue, Suite 1313, Chicago, IL 60602. Tel: (312) 701-0200, 701-0402. Fax: (312) 701-0103.
Los Angeles, Skyview Centre, 6033 West Century Blvd, Suite 375, Los Angeles, CA 90045. Tel: (810) 670-0307, 670-0809. Fax: (810) 670-2058. Toll Free: 1-800-86 SAETA.
Miami, Corporate Center Drive, Suite 402, Miami, FL 33126. Tel: (305) 477-2104. Fax: (305) 477-3945. Toll free: 1-8000-82 SAETA.
Miami Airport: Tel: (305) 526-3310, 526-6613. Fax: (305) 871-4345.
New York, Fifth Avenue, Suite 2030, New York NY 10110. Tel: (212) 302-0004. Fax: (212) 302-4008.
New York Airport: Tel: (718) 558-5622. Fax: (718) 917-5623.

From Europe: Air France flies from Paris to Quito several times a week (via French Guiana or Bogotá), Iberia flies from Madrid (via Puerto Rico), KLM from Amsterdam (via Curaçao) and Lufthansa from Frankfurt.
Several Latin American airlines (such as Aerolineas Argentinas, Ladeco, Varig, Viasa and Avianca) offer connecting flights to Ecuador from Europe and the US via their home countries. SEATA operates regular

Agents and Packages

Several operators offer flight combinations and packages, and it is best to shop around. Some companies also offer tailor-made holidays which can include yacht charters, jungle trips, excursions to the Galápagos Islands, and perhaps a stop on the way, for example in Peru.
In the USA:
Eco Travel Services, 5699 Miles Ave., Oakland CA 94618. Tel: (510) 655-4054. Fax: (510) 655-4566, 1800-655-4054.
In Ecuador:
Inti Travel, Quito, Tel/fax: (593-2) 237-549, e-mail: sun@ecnet.ec. Specializes in off-the-beaten-track hiking trips, climbing expeditions and Galápagos tours.
In the UK:
Animal Watch Wildlife Adventures, Granville House, London Road, Sevenoaks, Kent TN13 1DL. Tel: (01732) 741-612. Fax: (01732) 455-441.
Crusader Travel, 57 Church Street, Twickenham, TW1 3NR. Tel: (0181) 892-7606. Fax: (0181) 744-0574.
Ecuador Travel, Palladium House, Argyll Street London W1. Tel: (0171) 439-7794.
Flightbookers, 177/8 Tottenham Court Road, London W1P 0LX. Tel: (0171) 757-2444. Fax: (0171) 757-2277.
Imaginative Traveller, 14 Barley Mow Passage, London W4. Tel: (0181) 741-3113. Fax: (0181) 742-3045.
South American Experience, 47 Causton Street, London SW1P 4AT. Tel: (0171) 976-5511. Fax: (0171) 976-5908.
Worldwide Journeys and Expeditions, 8 Coneragh Road, London W14 9HP. Tel: (0171) 381-8638. Fax: (0171) 381-0836.

flights from Ecuador to the rest of South America.

From Australia, New Zealand, Asia: Travelers have only three options: take the Aerolineas Argentinas transpolar flight from Sydney via Auckland to Buenos Aires, then a connecting flight to Guayaquil; take the Lan Chile flight from Australia to Santiago, then connect with Ecuador; or fly to Los Angeles and take one of the several connecting flights from there.

Ecuador's airports
Ecuador has two international airports, at Quito (Mariscal Sucre) and Guayaquil (Simón Bolívar). While business travelers may want to visit Guayaquil, most tourists will be heading for Quito. However, the largest airplanes cannot land at Quito airport, and some airlines will take you only as far as Guayaquil: you then take the connection to the capital. The flight time is approximately 30 minutes, and the views, if you get a window seat, can be stunning.

Unfortunately, buying a ticket at Guayaquil airport is an experience best avoided. You should therefore make sure that your carrier flies direct to Quito, or does the connecting leg itself, or will at least look after you at the airport.

Chile's excellent Ladeco Airlines, for example, does not fly to Quito but has a special

Air Travel Taxes

• There is a 10 percent tax imposed on all air tickets bought within Ecuador.
• A US$25 departure tax is levied on international flights from Ecuador. It is payable at the airport in sucres or cash US dollars.
• There are no departure taxes for domestic flights.

official at Guayaquil airport to help you find your luggage (no mean task) and ensure that you have a seat to Quito, so you can relax at the bar until the flight leaves. AeroPeru, on the other hand, simply drops travelers in Guayaquil – leaving them to fight their way onto a waiting list.

Always confirm your return flight. In Ecuador this is not just a formality.

By Land
It is common for backpacking travelers to travel overland into Ecuador, crossing at either Huaquillas or Macará on the Peruvian border or Tulcán/Rumichaca on the Colombian side. At both borders, minibuses and trucks run between bus centers on both sides for a small fee. The borderś are usually open from around 8am to 6pm. Make sure you get an entry stamp and tourist card when you come in. REYTUR bus company runs an international service from Quito and Guayaquil to Lima. It is more expensive than buying a ticket to the border, walking across and buying another ticket straight away. And they make you change buses anyway so there is no real advantage in doing this, although it may sound more convenient.

By Sea
It is unlikely that anyone would plan a visit to Ecuador by sea. The only passenger services from Europe are Continental Shipping and Travel, run from 179 Piccadilly, London W1V 9DB. Tel: (0171) 491-4968; and NAVIS, Billhorner Kanalstr, 69, 2000 Hamburg 28, Germany. The US Grace Line is also said to take passengers to South America.

Telephoning Ecuador

The country code for Ecuador is 593. To call a number in Ecuador from abroad, dial the international access code (011 from the US, 00 from Britain) the country code (593) the area code without the 0 (2, 3, 4, 5, 6 or 7 depending on the area) and the six-digit local phone number

Area codes are divided by province. Examples of codes for popular destinations are:
Quito 02
Cuenca 07
Ambato 03
Guayaquil 04
Galápagos Island 05
Esmeraldas 06

Practical Tips

Business Hours

Government offices in Quito are open to the public 8am–4.30pm, Monday–Friday. In Guayaquil, hours are 9am–noon and 3.30–6pm, Monday–Friday.

Banks in Ecuador work from 9am–1.30pm (although some private banks offer a limited service, called *servicio diferido*, in the afternoon). Banks are closed at weekends and public holidays. Private companies generally work 8am–5pm with an hour for lunch.

Stores are generally open 9am–1pm and 3–7pm, Monday–Friday, then Saturday 9am–1.30pm. Shopping centers and small grocery stores stay open until 8pm. Drug stores (*farmacias*) are open continuously 9am–8pm and some are listed "on duty" 24 hours a day (see the daily newspapers for the roster).

Tipping

A 10 percent service charge is added to bills in restaurants, but it is customary to add on another 10 percent for the waiter. Airport porters can be tipped about 50 cents US. Taxi drivers do not expect a tip.

Media

In Quito, there are several good newspapers : *El Comercio, Hoy, Tiempo* and *Ultimas Noticias* are the most established. In Guayaquil, you can choose from *Expreso, El Telegrafo, El Universo* and *La Prensa*.

Postal Services

Letters are often slow to be delivered and are sometimes lost. It is worth having your letters certified *(con certificado)* for about 10 cents – you get a receipt which won't do much practical good, but means that your letter's existence is recorded somewhere and given safer treatment.

The main post office in Quito is in the old town at Espejo 935 and Guayaquil. This is where the *Poste Restante (Lista de Correos)* is located. Users of American Express travelers' checks may have their mail sent to the Amex office in the new town operated by Ecuadorian Tours at Amazonas 399. Mail can be sent most safely to Apartado 2605, Quito, Ecuador.

Photography

Bring sufficient film with you: buying camera gear within Ecuador is expensive and the choice of film is limited. If you are stuck, try one of the photo stores on Quito's Avenida Amazonas and make sure the film date hasn't expired. Processing is unreliable.

Equatorial shadows are very strong and come out almost black on photographs, so the best results are often achieved on overcast days.

Not surprisingly, Ecuadorian *indígenas* resent having a camera thrust in their faces and often turn their backs on pushy photographers. Unless you are taking a shot from a long distance, ask permission beforehand. Many will ask for a small fee or "tip" and it is often more pleasant to comply rather than trying to shoot people without being noticed.

Telecommunications

Every town has a long-distance telephone and telex office (EMETEL), but expect to wait for an hour. Many people will find it more convenient to call from their hotel – a surcharge is added, but the time and effort saved is generally worth it. Calls are expensive (about US$7 a minute to Europe and the US). Rates are discounted after 7pm.

If you make the call yourself, the main EMETEL office in Quito is on Avenida 10 de Agosto near Avenida Colón.

Organized Tours

Tours may be arranged through travel agents in Europe or the US, but it is simple to organize an itinerary on arrival in Ecuador.

There are dozens of travel agents along Avenida Amazonas in Quito, many of which offer similar programs. Popular day trips are to Otavalo and the Mitad del Mundo monument. There are also longer trips to the coastal beaches, the Oriente, Cuenca or the Galápagos.

The largest and oldest travel agency in Ecuador, and one that can be recommended without reservation, is Metropolitan Touring. Its main office is in Quito near the Hotel Colón:

Metropolitan Touring: Av. Amazonas 239, PO Box 17-17-1649, Quito, Ecuador. Tel: (593-2) 506-650. Fax: (593-2) 560-807.

In Guayaquil: Metropolitan Touring is at Antepara 915, Guayaquil. Tel: (593-4)320-300. Fax: (593-4)323-050.

Bookings can be made in the US through: **Adventure Associates**: Suite 110, 13150 Colt Road, Dallas, Texas 75240. Tel: (214) 907-0414, (800) 527-2500. Fax: (214) 783-1286.

Bookings in Europe: **South American Tours**: Adalberstr. 44–48D, 6000 Frankfurt M. 90, Germany. Tel: (069) 770-371-

75. Fax: (069) 707-1107.
Metropolitan Touring will fix anything from tours around Quito to week-long trips to the Galápagos. It also owns the facilities for some of Ecuador's more unusual trips, including:
• The *Flotel Orellana*: journeys on a floating hotel into the Amazon for 3–6 days. Also on offer are excursions into remote jungle lodges. Metropolitan Touring also runs Ecotourism trips into the Oriente. They include staying at the Imuya, Iripari and Aguarico Camps in the Cuyabeño Reserve, with guided treks into the surrounding rainforest.
• Rail adventures through the Avenue of the Volcanoes in the company's own carriages: the trips include stays in Riobamba and/or Cuenca and connections to Guayaquil.
• The *Santa Cruz* : package tours on a luxury liner around the Galápagos Islands. The company also arranges trips on smaller luxury yachts.

Oriente
To visit Randy Borman's Cofan village in the Oriente (see The Gringo Chief, page 99), tours must be organized through Wilderness Travel in Berkeley, California, which offers 17-day trips visiting both the Sierra and Oriente for around US$2,000 plus air fare.The company also offers adventure-oriented group trips to the Galápagos and combines Ecuador with trips to the Andes of Peru. Contact **Wilderness Travel**, 801 Allston Way, Berkeley, CA 94710-9984. Tel: 1 (415) 548-0420, or toll-free within the US to 1 (800).

Adventure Tourism

TREKKING EQUIPMENT
Alta Montaña, Washington 425 y 6 de Diciembre, Quito. Tel: (593-2)
Andisimo, 9 de Octubre 427 y Robles, Quito. Tel: (593-2) 223-030.
Campo Abierto (Next door to

Campo Base), Baquedano 355 y Juan León Mera, Quito.
The Explorer, Reina Victoria y Pinto, Quito. Tel: (593-2) 550-911.
Pamir Adventure Travels, Juan León Mera 721 y Ventimilla, PO Box 17-16-190 CEQ, Quito. Tel: (593-2) 542-605. Fax: (593-2) 547-576.

MOUNTAIN GUIDING-TREKKING
Capac Urcu Mountain Climbing School, Roca 650, Quito. Tel: (593-2) 230-485/569-775. e-mail: jayarza@pi.pro.ec.
Companía de Guias, Washington y 6 de Diciembre, Quito. Tel: (593-2) 504-773.
Inti Travel. Tel/fax: (593-2) 237-549. e-mail: sun@ecnet.ec.
Pamir Adventure Travels, Juan León Mera 721 y Ventimilla, PO Box 17-16-190 CEQ, Quito. Tel: (593-2) 542-605. Fax: (593-2) 547-576.
Safari, Calama 380 y Juan León Mera, Quito. Tel: (593-2) 552-505. Fax: (593-2) 220-426.
Sierra Nevada, Pinto 637 y Amazonas, Quito. Tel: (593-2) 553-658. Fax: (593-2) 554-936.
Surtrek, Amazonas 877 y Wilson, Quito. Tel: (593-2) 561-129.

PARAGLIDING
Parapente Condor, Sanquez y Cifuentes 3-59 y Mejia, Ibarra. Tel: (593-6) 957-332.

Useful Addresses

The Ecuadorian National Parks Service is at: **INEFAN**, 8th floor, Ministry of Agriculture Building, Av. Amazonas y Eloy Alfaro, Quito. Tel: (593-2) 548-924. The main conservation organization is Fundación Natura, América 5663 y Voz Andes, Quito. Tel: (593-2) 447-342.

WHITE WATER RAFTING
Ríos Ecuador, Italia 714 y Mariana de Jesús, Quito. Tel: (593-2) 553-727. Tel: (in Tena) (06) 887-438.
Row, Salazar Gómez 144 y Martinez, Quito. Tel: (593-2) 458-539.
Yacu Amu Rafting, Amazonas 993 y Wilson, Quito. Tel: (593-2) 236-844.

BIRDWATCHING
CECIA (Ecuadorian Ornithology Foundation), Nacional 304 y Telégrafo, Quito. Tel: (593-2) 433-239. e-mail: cecia@uio.satnet.net.

Tourist Information

The government tourist office **CETUR** (Corporación Ecuatoriana de Turismo) has its central office at Eloy Alfaro 1214 y Carlos Tobar by Parque Carolina, Quito. Tel: (593-2) 507-564/224-970. It has smaller offices in most Ecuadorian towns.
A unique resource for backpacking travelers in Ecuador is the South American Explorers' Club (SAEC), Jorge Washington 311 y Leonidas Plaza, in the new town area of Quito. Tel: (593-2) 225-228. This travelers' meeting place keeps up-to-date information on every aspect of Ecuador and is the perfect place to go for advice. Non-members may use the place for one visit and are then asked to sign up: membership (around US$40 a year) also entitles you to a quarterly magazine ($7 charge for postage outside the US). It is well worth the price. They can also help you out if you are robbed or have an accident.
Written enquiries about travel in Ecuador can be sent to the Club at Apartado 21-431, Eloy Alfaro, Quito, or the US office at 126 Indian Creek Rd Ithaca, NY 14850. Tel: (607) 277-0488/247-6700.

Getting Around

Domestic Travel

Until the 20th century, transport and communications in Ecuador were poorly developed. When the Guayaquil–Quito line was completed in 1908, it provided for the first time an effective inter-regional link and cut the travel time between the two cities from 12 days to 12 hours.

Today the railway system is more of a tourist attraction than a commercial link. The total track length is 1,043 km (646 miles); at present the Quito–Riobamba, Riobamba–Alausí–Guayaquil and Ibarra-San Lorenzo stretches are in operation for passengers. The Azogues–Cuenca stretch is out of service.

The road network, on the other hand, has expanded considerably since World War II, and the main roads are generally very good. Of the 38,000 km (23,560 miles) of highways, about 18,000 km (11,160 miles) are open all year round and about 7,000 km (4,340 miles) are paved.

By Air
Air transport is fairly well developed. The Oriente is the one area where airlines have virtually no competition from other forms of transport. There are many villages whose only contact with the rest of the country is by air; besides numerous small strips, 34 airports can handle bigger planes, some of them modern jet aircraft. The only two airports

suitable for international traffic are Mariscal Sucre in Quito and Simón Bolívar in Guayaquil.

There are local domestic flights to all the main cities. Airlines SAN, SAETA and TAME connect the principal urban centers of the country – Quito, Guayaquil and Cuenca – by jet service, with several flights daily each way. Flying time Guayaquil–Quito is about 30 minutes. TAME offers daily service to the Galápagos Islands, landing at Baltra, and SAN flies to the archipelago four times a week, landing at San Cristóbal. TAME flies from Quito to Esmeraldas, Manta, Portoviejo, Tulcan and Loja (via Guayaquil) and from Guayaquil to Machala. In the Amazon jungle Lago Agrio, Coca and Macas are served.

Car Rental

Car rental is as expensive as in Europe or in the United States. Charges are about US$35 a day, with mileage increments.

A valid driver's license from your home country is normally accepted, but some rental companies require an international license. It is worth applying for one in your home country before you leave if you plan to hire a car.

Extra insurance costs may be charged. It is often more economical to hire a taxi for several hours, which will take you to remote areas or to another town: be sure to bargain the costs beforehand.

There are military flights in the more remote Amazon areas. TAO flies small aircraft between Puyo (Shell-Mera) and Macas and ICARO operates charter flights. Two missionary organizations, Servicio Aereo de la Misión Salesiana and Alas de Socorro (Tel: 593-2 441 593), operate

flights to remote jungle communities from Macas and Shell respectively. Air taxis (Cessnas or Bonanzas) can be rented. Small airlines' offices are found at the Guayaquil and Quito airports.

With the exception of flying to the Galápagos Islands, domestic flights are fairly inexpensive (a return flight Quito–Guayaquil is about US$80). Passengers have to show up one hour before the departure of domestic flights, for baggage handling and check-in procedures. Many flights give marvelous views of the snow-capped Andes, so it is worth getting a window seat. Seats are given on a first come, first served basis.

There are no departure taxes for domestic flights.

By Rail
The few trains still operating are rarely comfortable or reliable. Nevertheless the adventurous tourist may try to board the *autoferro* (like a bus mounted on a railway chassis) that runs from Ibarra in the Northern highlands to San Lorenzo on the coast (carry your own food and watch your luggage!). For more details, see the feature on Railway Journeys.

Many hundred kilometers of Ecuador's train system were totally destroyed during the 1982–83 floods. One of the most spectacular train rides in the world, the Quito–Guayaquil railway line, is now working again. It is possible to go with a *tren mixto* (passengers/freight) from Guayaquil (Durán) to Alausí, a stretch which has been made famous in the British TV series *Great Railway Journeys of the World*. The train departs from Durán at 6am every morning, arriving at Alausí 12 hours later. The return trip from Alausí departs at 9am and arrives at Durán at 5pm.

A more comfortable option is offered by Metropolitan Touring in Quito: a railway car refitted with pullman seats, en route meals and a viewing platform, operates on the railway between Riobamba and Chan Chan.

Metropolitan Touring offers a 2-day package: by bus from Quito to Riobamba, down the Devil's Nose to Chan Chan by train, and back to Quito by bus (US$260 per person, twin share occupancy). Alternatively a stay in a *hacienda* can be included on the return to Quito. For more details, contact Metropolitan Touring at Amazonas 239 in Quito, tel: (593-2) 506-650.

Passport Checks

On buses, always carry your passport with you. There are police checks on all the roads leading out of main towns and you can get into serious trouble if you are unable to present your documents.

By Car

Traveling by private car is generally more convenient in Ecuador than in other Andean countries; first, because the main roads are in a good state; second, because the running costs are economical; and third, because the countryside is safer than in the neighboring republics. Nevertheless, when touring by car, beware the bus drivers, who often go very fast, and make sure that your car has good ground clearance.

By Bus

Bus travel is not too comfortable, but numerous companies connect all the main towns at frequent intervals (smaller localities are also served) and the fares are incredibly low.

In general buses leave from central bus terminals; exact schedules exist only in theory, although one can usually buy tickets one or two days in

advance and choose the seat number (the front seats tend to have slightly more leg room than the back seats).

During long holiday weekends or special fiestas, buses are generally booked up for several days in advance, so early booking is recommended.

Four types of buses are used:
• small buses (*busetas*) for 22 passengers which are fast (sometimes too fast) and efficient;
• larger coaches *(buses)* which have more space;
• new luxury buses which have recently been introduced on routes between major cities;
• trucks with roofs, open sides and wooden plank seats, called *rancheros,* which are found mainly on the coast.

All the main towns and cities are served by urban bus lines. The buses are mostly small and usually extremely overcrowded, especially at peak hours.

There is a smart new trolley system operating between the north and south of Quito but this, too, gets very crowded at peak hours. The new large *Selectivo* buses running in Quito's new town area are a pleasant exception.

If you want to get off a local bus, shout *baja!* ("down") or *esquina!* ("corner") – the driver will stop at the next corner.

Taxis

Taxis in Ecuador are very cheap for domestic consumption, but meters are only used by taxi-drivers in Quito. In Guayaquil, meters are installed by law but drivers do not use them: be sure to ascertain the fare before-hand, or you could be overcharged. In smaller towns, meters do not exist; at weekends and at night fares are 25 to 50 percent higher.

Where to Stay

Hotels

There is no shortage of hotels in Ecuador. Every little town, no matter how remote, has somewhere to lay one's head. However, if you want hotels of an international standard, the options are more limited. Five-star luxury accommodation can be found in Quito, Guayaquil, Cuenca, the resort areas of Esmeraldas and Santa Elena, or the jungle lodges and *Flotel Orellana* of the Oriente. Most other areas rely on basic but clean country inns (*hosterías*), *pensiones* or *residenciales*.

During the high tourist season (June to September in the Sierra, December and January on the coast) and during fiestas or the night before market days (in Otavalo particularly), finding accommodation can be tight, so it is worth making a reservation; in other places just turn up. Luxury hotels charge international rates for their rooms. A room in a first class hotel might cost US$80, while a double with private bath in a perfectly comfortable *residencial* can be had for US$20. Decent backpacker hotels with shared bathrooms can generally be found for US$3-6 per person in even the remotest area. In most places apart from budget hotels/ hostals, service and tax charges of roughly 10 percent each will be added to the bill. *For specific recommended hotels in Quito, Guayaquil, Esmeraldas, Cuenca and the Galápagos, see their respective sections.*

Eating Out

What to Eat

Ecuador has a rich, plentiful and varied gastronomic culture, different from that of other Latin American countries. Ingredients and seasonings from other parts of South America and from Europe have blended to create some exciting tastes.

Well worth trying are the following local dishes:

Cuy: whole roasted guinea pig is a traditional food dating back to Inca times. Certainly not served in fancy restaurants, but rather at markets and street stands.
Tamales: a pastry dough made from toasted corn flour or wheat flour and filled with chicken, pork or beef, wrapped in a leaf and steamed.
Humitas: a pastry (sweet or salty) made from corn *(choclo)*, crumbled cheese, egg and butter and wrapped in a corn husk.
Tortillas de maíz: tasty fried corn pancakes filled with mashed potatoes and cheese.
Empanadas de morocho: a delicious small pie stuffed with pork meat and fried, served with hot sauce.
Empanadas de verde: a pie of green plantain, filled with cheese or meat.
Ceviche: raw seafood marinated in lemon, orange and tomato juice and served with popcorn and sliced onions. Can be made from fish, shrimp, mussels, oysters, lobster or octopus. Very popular on the coast.
Locro: a yellow soup prepared from milk, stewed potatoes and cheese, topped with an avocado. It may also contain watercress,

meat, lentils, pork skin etc.
Lechón hornado: roasted suckling pig; a specialty of Sangolqui, near Quito.
Asado (literally, "roasted") generally means whole roasted pig. It is found in many parts of the country.
Llapingachos: mashed potato-and-cheese pancakes usually served with *fritada* – scraps of roast pork and salad.
Seco (stew): It can be based on chicken *(gallina)* goat *(chivo)* or lamb *(cordero)* and is usually served with plenty of rice.
Fanesca: a kind of fish soup with beans, lentils and corn. Eaten mainly during the Easter week, *fanesca* is filling and rich.

On the coast, there is also an amazing richness of gastronomic combinations. Seafood is very good. The most common fish are: white sea bass, called *corvina*, shrimp *(camarones)* and lobster *(langostas)*. Look out for *encocada* (coconut) dishes, and the *sal prieta* of Manabí, a sauce with peanut butter and corn flour.

A surprisingly tasty dessert *(postre)* is *helados de paila*, ice cream made with fruit juice and beaten in a large brass pot *(paila)* which is rotated in another pot filled with ice.

International cooking, can be found in Quito, and all sizeable towns.

Where to Eat

Quito has a very good selection of restaurants serving every-thing from local dishes to international cuisine. Surprisingly, there are few good restaurants in Guayaquil, apart from in the bigger hotels, where excellent food is served. In the provinces it is possible to eat well at reasonable prices. A restaurant need not be fancy to serve delicious and healthy food, but avoid shabby places.

In Quito and Guayaquil there are some very expensive

restaurants, but in a good restaurant you can have a full meal for approximately US$5-10 plus 20 percent service charge and tax. If you order a bottle of wine, however, the bill will be much higher, because wine is imported. It is customary to leave an additional tip of 10 percent for the waiter.

Restaurants are open for lunch from noon until about 3pm. They often offer inexpensive "executive lunches." Dinner is from 7pm until midnight. In the evening, ordering is à la carte. Most restaurants are closed on Sunday or Monday, but hotel restaurants are open every day.

Drinking Notes

There is an amazing choice of juices *(jugos)* such as *mora* (blackberry), *naranja* (orange), *maracuya* (passion fruit), *naranjilla* (a local fruit tasting like bitter orange) or papaya. Beers such as Pilsener, Club and Loewenbrau are quite drinkable. All other beers are imported and rather expensive. The usual soft drinks are known as colas and the local brands are very sweet. The excellent mineral water is called Güitig (pronounced wee-tig) after the best known brand. Coffee is often served after meals. A favorite Ecuadorian way of preparing coffee is to boil it for hours until only a thick syrup remains. This is then diluted with milk and water. Instant coffee is common. Espresso-machines are found only in the better hotels and in a very few restaurants and cafeterias.

Finally a word about alcoholic beverages: rum is cheap and good (commonly drunk with Coca-Cola in a *cuba libre*); tequila is also cheap; whisky is fairly expensive, and imported wines (from Chile and Argentina) cost much more than they do in their country of origin. Local wines cannot be recommended.

Quito
A – Z

Airlines

INTERNATIONAL
(phone code 593-2)
Aeroflot, 18 de Septiembre y Av.
Amazonas. Tel: 545-454.
Aerolineas Argentinas, Av.
Amazonas 1188 y Calama. Tel:
543-257.
Aero Peru, George Washington
718. Tel: 561-699. Fax: 564-
871.
Air France, 18 de Septiembre y
Av. Amazonas. Tel: 524-201.
Fax: 566-415.
Alitalia, Ernesto Noboa 474 y 6
de Diciembre. Tel: 545-652. Fax:
569-143.
American Airlines, Av.
Amazonas 353 y Robles. Tel:
561-144. Fax: 561-425.
Avianca, 6 de Diciembre 511 y
18 de Septiembre.Tel: 508-843.
Fax: 502-746.
British Airways, Colón y Av.
Amazonas, Edif. España. Tel:
540-000. Fax: 228-933.
Continental, 461-486 Av.
Nacionas Unidas y Amazonas,
Edificio La Previsora, 8th floor.
Tel: 261-487. Fax: 462-119.
Copa, Ventimilla 888 y JL Mera.
Tel: 565-969. Fax: 563-358.
Iberia, Av. Amazonas 239. Tel:
560547. Fax: 566-852.
KLM, Amazonas 3617 y Sanz,
Edif. Xerox. Tel: 455-233. Fax:
435-176.
Lacsa, 12 de Octubre 394. Tel:
505-213. Fax: 223-744.
Lan Chile, 18 de Septiembre
238 y R. Victoria. Tel: 508-396.
Fax: 566-682.
Lufthansa, 18 de Septiembre
238 y R. Victoria. Tel: 541-300.
Fax: 566-682.

Saeta, Colón y Av. Amazonas,
Edif. España. Tel: 564-969.
Airport: Av. 10 de Agosto y
Buenos Aires. Tel: 502-706.
Varig, Portugal 794 y República
de El Salvador. Tel: 250-126.
Fax: 436-845.
Viasa, Av. Amazonas 1188 y
Calama. Tel: 568-262.

DOMESTIC
Aeroturismo, 18 de Septiembre
332, Edif. Pichincha. Tel: 563-
996. Fax: 567-940.
Aerogal, Amazonas 7797 y Jorge
Hoguin. Tel/fax: 257-202.
Ecuatoriana, Reina Victoria y
Colón. Tel: 563-003.
Helicopteros Nacionales, Av.
Gonzalez Suarez 1050. Tel: 525-
280.
Icaro, Instituto Civil Aeronáutico.
Tel: 448-626; fax: 439-867.
Saeta, Colón y Amazonas, Edif.
España. Tel: 564-969.
Tame, Colón 1001 y Rabida.
Tel: 554-905.
Transportes Aereos Orientales,
Av. Amazonas y Palora. Tel/fax:
446-779.

Car Rental Agencies

Avis Rent a Car, Airport. Tel:
440-270. A variety of models
is available (including four-
wheeled drive vehicles).
Budget Rent a Car, Av.
Amazonas y Colón. Tel: 237-
026.
Ecuacar, Colón 1280 y
Amazonas. Tel: 529-781.
The company also has a
branch at the airport.
Hertz, Oro Verde Hotel. Tel:
569-130.
Most rental agencies prefer
credit cards.

Airport

Quito's international airport
Mariscal Sucre is 8km (5 miles)
from the city. Taxis to the tourist
area downtown should cost no
more than US$5. Inexpensive
buses run all the way along Av.

Amazonas to the airport. There
is a US$25 (1997 rate)
departure tax on international
flights. There are no luggage
deposit boxes at the airport.
The Icaro flying school offers
flights in small propeller aircraft
along the Avenue of the
Volcanoes. A 7-seater plane
costs around $650 per hour.

Art Galleries

Artists display their works in the
Parque El Ejido, near the big
arch on Av. Patria, at weekends.
Art Forum, J.L. Mera 870. Tel:
504-209.
**Centro de Promoción de
Artistas**, Casa Blanca, Parque
del Ejido. Tel: 522-410.
Fundación Exedra, Carrion 243
y Plaza. Tel: 224-001.
La Galeria, Juan Rodriguez 168.
Tel: 232-807. Modern art only.

Automobile Club

ANETA is located at Eloy Alfaro
218 y 10 de Agosto. Tel: 229-
021. Office hours: 9am–1pm
and 3–7pm.

Books and Periodicals

Librería Científica, Juan León
Mera y Av. Colón. Tel: 552-854.
Libri Mundi, Juan León Mera
851 y Veintimilla. Tel: 234-971.
Branch at Hotel Colón. Tel: 550-
455. Books in English, German,
French and Spanish; large
selection of maps, international
magazines, records.

Banks

American Express, Av.
Amazonas 339 y Jorge
Washington, 5th floor. Tel: 560-
488.
Banco de Guayaquil, Colón y
Reina Victoria. Tel: 566-800 for
cash advance on Visa.
Banco del Pacifico, Av.
Amazonas y Roca. Tel: 507-348
for cash advance on
MasterCard.

Banco de Pichincha, Av. Amazonas y Colón. Tel: 547-006 for cash advance on Diners Card.
Citibank, Juan León Mera 130 y Patria. Tel: 563-300.
Filanbanco, Av. Amazonas 530. Tel: 444-591 for cash advance on Visa.
Thomas Cook, Representative is Ecuacambio, Av. de la República 192 y Almagro. Tel: 540-129.
Lloyds, Av. Amazonas y Carrion. Tel: 564-134.
Western Union, Av. Republica 396 y Almagro. Tel: 502-194. Fax: 563-026. Money transfers and DHL courier.
Casas de Cambios (exchange houses), **Producambio** in old town: Sucre y Venezuela, Galeria Sucre. Tel: 511-364. In new town: Amazonas 370 y Robles. Tel: 564-500.

Apart from changing foreign currencies into *sucres*, they will cash travelers' checks into US dollars (up to US$200 for a small commission).

The airport **cambio** and the exchange desk at the Hotel Colón are the only places in town that will change money on Sunday (mornings only).

Buses

Local buses run frequently and are inexpensive. Destinations are shown on the front of the vehicle. Beware of pickpockets. Long-distance buses leave mainly from the Terminal Terrestre in the southern Villa Flora district, at Maldonado and Cumandá. There are about two dozen bus companies with offices at the terminal. It is worthwhile booking in advance.

There are many buses a day to major destinations including Ambato (3 hours), Bahía de Caraquez (8 hours), Baños (3½ hours), Coca (12 hours), Cuenca (9–14 hours), Guaranda (5 hours), Guayaquil (8 hours), Lago Agrio (10 hours), Latacunga (2 hours), Loja (14–18 hours), Machala (11 hours), Manta (8 hours), Portoviejo (8 hours), Puyo (7 hours), Riobamba (4 hours), Santo Domingo (2½ hours), Tena (9 hours), Esmeraldas (6 hours), Otavalo (2½ hours), Ibarra (2½ hours) and Tulcán (5½ hours). There are no direct buses to Peru or Colombia. Reytur (E. Gangotena 158 y Orellana, Tel: 546-674) run an "international" bus to Lima, but this involves a change at the border. It is cheaper to take a bus to Huaquillas, cross the border and take a **taxi colectivo** to Tumbes, where regular buses connect with Lima. Panamericana (Av. Colón y Reina Victoria) operate a deluxe service from Quito to Huaquillas. Both Panamericana and Reytur offer services to Colombia, but this again involves changing buses at the border.

Consulates and Embassies

Austria, Veintimilla 878 y Amazonas. Tel: 524-811.
Bolivia, C. B. Lavayen y Juan Pablo Sanz. Tel: 458-863.
Brazil, Av. Amazonas 1429 y Colón, Edif. España, 10th floor. Tel: 563-086.
Canada, Av. 6 de Diciembre 2816 y J. Orton. Tel: 543-214.
Chile, Juan Pablo Sanz 3617 y Amazonas. Tel: 249-403.
Colombia, Av. Atahualpa 955 y República, 3rd floor. Tel: 458-012.
Germany, Av. Patria y 9 de Octubre, Edif Consolidado, 6th floor. Tel: 225-660.
Peru, Av. Amazonas 1429 y Colón, Edif. España, 2nd floor. Tel: 527-678.
Sweden, A. Jerves 134 y Orellana. Tel: 509-514.
Switzerland, Av. Amazonas 3617 y Panz, Edif. Xerox. Tel: 464-948.
United Kingdom, González Suárez 111. Tel: 560-670.
United States, Av. 12 de Octubre y Patria. Tel: 562-890.

Drugstores

Regular medicine can be bought without a prescription in most pharmacies (*farmacias*). The newspapers list *farmacias de turno* which are open on Sunday or at night. Most drugstores will give injections as well as the disposable serum needles (beware of non-disposable needles!).

Police and emergency

Fire Tel: 102.
Police Tel: 101.
Radio Patrol Tel: 101.
Ambulance/Red Cross Tel: 131.
General Emergency Tel: 111.

Hospitals and Doctors

Air Ambulance. Tel: 432-368. Most embassies have telephone numbers of recommended dentists, but **Clínica de Especialidades Odontológicas,** Av. Orellana 1782 y 10 de Agosto. Tel: 521-383, can be called in cases of dental emergency 24 hours a day.
Red Cross (Cruz Roja). Tel: 582-479.
Ambulance. Tel: 131 for emergencies or 580-598.
Laboratory Analysis, Clínica Pichincha, Veintimilla 1259 y Paez. Tel: 5540854.
Laboratorio Clínica Patológico, Cordero 410 y 6 de Diciembre, Edificio San Francisco. Tel: 226-990.
Clínica de la Mujer, Av. Amazonas 4826 y Gaspar Villaroel. Tel: 458-000.
Hospital Metropolitano, Av. Marlana de Jesús y Occidental. Tel: 431-520. Best and most expensive in Quito. English speaking doctors available.
Hospital Voz Andes, Villalengua 263. Tel: 241-540. American-run, with an emergency room. Most doctors speak some English.

Hepatitis vaccinations (Havirix): Medcenter, Foch 476 y Almagro. Tel: 521-104.

Hotels

LUXURY

Hilton Colón, Av. Amazonas y Patria. Tel: 560-666. Fax: 563-903. All rooms have cable TV (US programs); shopping mall; several restaurants and bars; coffee shop; disco; sports facilities (swimming-pool, sauna, gymnasium); hairdresser.
Hotel Quito, Av. González Suárez 2500. Tel: 544-600. Fax: 503-556. All rooms with cable TV (US programs) several restaurants and bars; coffee shop; night club; sports facilities (heated pool); quiet, with splendid view and very pleasant gardens.
Oro Verde, Av. 6 de Diciembre. Tel: 566-497. Fax: 569-189. Quito's newest luxury hotel. Numerous suites and executive suites; several restaurants; disco; sports facilities (heated pool, fitness center).
Radisson, World Trade Center, Luis Cordero y 12 de Octubre. Tel: 233-333. Fax: 235-777.

FIRST CLASS

Alameda Real, Roca 655 y Av. Amazonas. Tel: 564-185. Fax: 565-759. Numerous suites; gallery of stores; several restaurants and coffee shop, bar etc. Recently renovated.
Chalet Suisse, Reina Victoria 312 y Calama. Tel: 562-700. Fax: 563-966. Excellent food, night club, casino etc.
Hotel Sebastian, Almagro 822 y Cordero. Tel: 222-400. Fax: 222-500. Comfortable.
Tambo Real, 12 de Octubre y Patria. Tel: 563-822. Fax: 554-961. Opposite the US embassy.

GOOD

Ambassador, 9 de Octubre 1052 y Colón. Tel: 561-777. Fax: 503-712. Newly opened, excellent food, clean, spacious, good service.

Café Cultura, Reina Victoria y Robles. Tel: 224-271. Fax: 224-271. Converted mansion. Great Danish breakfasts.
Hostal Los Alpes, Tamayo 233 y Washington, behind US embassy. Tel: 561-110. Fax: 561-128. Very comfortable.
Real Audencia, Bolívar 220 y Guayaquil. Tel: 512-711. Fax: 580-213. Well-furnished, spacious rooms, restaurant has fine view of Old Quito.
Sierra Nevada, Joaquin Pinto 687 y Amazonas. Tel: 553-658. Fax: 554-936.

Price categories

- **Luxury:** $170–$290
- **First Class** $55–$125
- **Good** $30–$55
- **Inexpensive/hostels** (some with shared rooms) $7–$20

All rates are for double rooms

APARTMENT-HOTELS

Amaranta, Leonidas Plaza 194. Tel: 527-191. Luxurious apartments with kitchenette.
Apart Hotel, Rodriguez 175 y Almagro. Tel: 506-834. Well furnished attractive apartments.
Mariscal, Robles 958. Tel: 528-833. Well furnished, but noisy.

INEXPENSIVE: FOR STUDENTS AND GLOBETROTTRS

Campo Base, Veintimilla 858 y Juan León Mera. Tel: 224-504.
Cafecito, Cordero 1124 y Reina Victoria. Tel: 234-862. Shared rooms. Cafe downstairs.
Magic Bean, Foch 681 y J.L. Mera. Tel: 566-181. Mostly shared rooms, good restaurant, central location in new town.
Marsella, Los Rios y Castro. Tel: 515-884.The pick of the budget hotels, US$6 a double, hot water, friendly atmosphere, rooftop terrace.
Posada del Maple, Rodriguez 148 y 6 de Diciembre. Tel: 544-507. Friendly atmosphere with kitchen and cable TV-room.

AROUND QUITO
SOUTH OF QUITO

Hostería La Cienega, Pan-Americana Sur Km 72, Lasso. Tel: 719-182. Fax: (593-3) 719-182.
Hostería Guachala, on the road to Cangahua, just south of Cayambe. Make reservations in Quito, Reina Victoria 1138. Tel: 563-748. Fax: (593-2) 563 748. One unusual option is to stay at converted colonial *hacienda*:
NORTH OF QUITO
Hostería Chorla VI, Km 4 Pan-Americana Sur, Ibarra. Tel: 932-222. Fax: (593-6) 932-222.
Hostería Cusín, Lago San Pablo, Otavalo. Tel: 918-013. Fax: (593-6) 918-003.
Hostería La Mirage, Cotocahi (Imbabura Province). (P.O. Box 11365 CCNU, Quito). Tel: 915-237. Fax: (593-6) 915-065.
Hostería San Agustín, Pan-Americana Sur Km 1Y2, Ibarra. Tel: 955-888.
  Travelers flock to Otavalo for the Saturday market. Hotels are thus likely to be booked up early on Friday night and empty for the rest of the week. The best hotel is the Hostería Cusín (above).
  If you prefer to stay in town, try the comfortable Hotel El Indio, Bolívar 904. Tel: 920-325.

Language Classes

Quito is considered one of the best places in Latin America to learn Spanish. There are dozens of cheap places offering classes: they advertise in the hotels, bars and restaurants frequented by young gringos. Classes can be taken by the hour, by the day or by the week. Also, many organizations offer intensive courses where you board with an Ecuadorian family and are usually taught on a one-to-one basis.
  Recommended are:
La Lengua: Av. Colón 1001 y J.L. Mera, Edif. Av. Maria. Tel/fax: 501-271. e-mail: lalengua@uio.telconet.net

Simón Bolívar: Leonidas Plaza 690 y Wilson. Tel: 226-635. e-mail: khaugan*aol.com

Nightlife

There is an elegant nightclub and discotheque at the Hotel Colón Internacional. Another is the **Techo del Mundo** at the Hotel Quito. For great salsa dancing go to **Seseribo** at Edificio El Giron, Veintimilla y 12 de Octubre. **Ramón Antigua**, Veintimilla y Isabel la Católica, **Zoo**, La Niña y Reina Victoria and **NoBar**, Calama 442 y Amazonas are popular with young people.

Taberna Quiteña (Amazonas 1259 y Colón, and in the Old Town Calle Manabí y Luis Vargas), has a cellar bar atmosphere and musicians who wander from table to table.

The *peñas* are popular and good for local folk music. Try Nucanchi Peña, Av. Universitaria 496; tel: 540-967. There are casinos at the hotels **Chalet Suisse**, **Colón Internacional**, **Quito** and **Oro Verde**.

Post Office and Communications

The main post office for *Poste Restante* (in Spanish *La Lista de Correos*) service is at Espejo 935 y Guayaquil. The post office in the new town is at Reina Victoria y Colón in the Ecuatoriana building. Packages need to be sent from the branch at Ulloa 273 y Davalos, also in the new town. Letters may be dropped at the reception desk of the hotels Colón and Quito. Stamps may be bought in the hotel bookshops during store hours. Faxes can be sent from both the above hotels or the EMETEL office at Av. 10 de Agosto y Colón. Open daily 8am–10pm Long-distance calls can be made from the same office. English-speaking operators are on duty at all times. Calls are less

expensive from 7pm–5am and all day Sunday (with a three-minute minimum charge).

Railways

Quito's train station is 2 km (1 mile) south of the center, on Av. P. Vicente Maldonado near Llanganates. There is a Saturday service to Riobamba. Tickets need to be bought on the Friday morning from the train station itself. For the Sunday train to Cotopaxi tickets are on sale all week at the administration office in the old town, Calle Bolívar 443 y Benalcazar. **Quito train station** Tel: 266-144. **Ibarra train station** Tel: (06) 950-390.

Religious Services

Roman Catholic services are held regularly in Quito's churches. Services other than Catholic are held at:
Carolina Adventist Church, Av. 10 de Agosto 3929. Tel: 239-995. Meetings on Saturdays at 9am.
Central Baptist Church, Ríos 1803. Tel: 513-074. Sunday services 9am and 6pm.
Church of Jesus Christ of the Latter Day Saints, Almagro y Colón. Tel: 529-602. Sunday service 9.30am.
Lutheran Church, Isabel la Católica 1431. Tel: 234-391. Sunday services: 9am in English; 10.15am in German; 11.30am in Spanish.
Synagogue, Versalles y 18 de Septiembre. Services Friday 7pm.

Restaurants

Most of the best restaurants are in the New Town, around Amazonas, Colón and 6 de Diciembre. There are several outdoor cafés along Amazonas where you can take in the sun and street life during the day.

INTERNATIONAL
El Dorado, In the Hotel Colón. Tel: 521-300. Excellent; good breakfast and pastries in the hotel's cafeteria.
Excalibur, Calama 380 y Juan León Mera. Tel: 541-272. Very elegant and pricey.
Grain de Café, Baquedano 330 y Juan León Mera. Tel: 234-430. Inexpensive tasty food, relaxed atmosphere.
Magic Bean, Foch 681 y Juan León Mera. Tel: 566-181. A well known place for younger people, although it is not cheap. Great coffee and cakes.
Hotel Oro Verde, Av. 6 de Diciembre. Tel: 566-497. Good food, good service. Also excellent Japanese restaurant.

FRENCH
La Belle Epoque, Eduardo Whymper 925 (between 6 de Diciembre and Diego de Almagro). Tel: 222-506.

For Local Dishes

Campo Base, Baquedano 355 y Juan León Mera. Tel: 224-504. Good Ecuadorian food, meeting place for climbers.
La Choza, 12 de Octubre 1821 y Cordero. Tel: 230-839. Typical food, well prepared, nice surroundings.
Las Redes, Amazonas 845 y Veintimilla. Tel: 525-691. Known for its *ceviches* and other seafood specialties in informal surroundings.
Rincón La Ronda, Belo Horizonte 400 y Almagro. Tel: 540-549. Good, typical food, live music at weekends.
La Terraza del Tartaro, Veintimilla 926 y Amazonas. Tel: 527-987. Penthouse elevator in rear of entry, fine view, good food.
Taberna Quiteña, Amazonas 1259 y Cordero. Tel: 230-009. Good Ecuadorian food with live entertainment.

Expensive but excellent. Reservation necessary. **Rincón de Francia**, General Roca 779 y 9 de Octubre. Tel: 554-668. Very good reputation. Reservation necessary.

GERMAN
El Ciervo zum Hirsch, Ramirez Dávalos y Paez (near Amazonas). Tel: 543-116. Excellent German and international food.
Taberna Bavaria, Cordero 1313. Tel: 563-380. Good German food, pleasant atmosphere.

SPANISH
El Mesón de la Pradera, Orellana y 6 de Diciembre. Tel: 504-815. Good food and service in elegant converted mansion.
La Paella Valenciana, La República y Diego de Almagro. Tel: 239-681. Deliciously prepared Spanish dishes.

STEAK HOUSES
La Casa de Mi Abuela, Juan León Mera 1649. Tel: 565-667. Excellent Argentinian beef.
Shorton Grill, Calama 216 y Almagro. Tel: 523-645.

ITALIAN
Pizza Hut – Espejo, downhill from Plaza Independencia.
– Juan León Mera 566 y Carrion.
– Naciones Unidas y Amazonas.
Il Risotto, Pinto 209 y Almagro. Tel: 220-400. Authentic Italian cooking. Home-made pasta and good *tiramisu*.
Romo y Remulo, Juan Léon Mera 1012 y Foch. Tel: 543-900. Delicious, inexpensive pasta dishes.

CHINESE
Casa China, Cordero 613 y Tamayo. Tel: 522-115. Good Chinese food.
Hong Kong, Wilson 246 y Tamayo. Tel: 225-515. Excellent.

ARABIAN
El Arabe, Reina Victoria y Carrion. Tel: 549-414.

CUBAN
La Bodega de Cuba, Reina Victoria 1721 y La Pinta. Tel: 542-476. Good food, pleasant setting and atmosphere.

VEGETARIAN
El Holandes, Carrion y Reina Victoria. Tel: 522-167. Indonesian, Greek, Italian and Dutch dishes.
El Marquez, Calama 443 y Amazonas. Inexpensive, very popular at lunchtime.

Shopping

There are dozens of *artesanías* stores and kiosks in Quito, especially in the Avenida Amazonas area. Several have outstanding selections of high quality folk art and clothing. They include:
Almacén Folklore Olga Fisch, Av. Colón 260. There is also a branch in the Hotel Colón.
Centro Artesanal, Calle Juan León Mera 804.
Exedra, Carrion 243 y Plaza. *Artesania* center.
Galería Latina, Calle Juan León Mera 833.
La Bodega Artesanías Calle Juan León Mera 614.

Sports

There is a public swimming pool at Av. Universitaria y Nicaragua and also one at Cochapata, near Villarroel y 6 de Diciembre. The El Condado Country Club has an 18-hole golf course, a heated swimming pool and riding facilities (temporary membership is available). Fuente de Juventud, Republica 855 y Eloy Alfaro, open Tues–Sun, 9am–9pm, has an indoor pool, whirlpool sauna, steam room, weight lifting and other gym equipment. Tel: 247-722/ 529-152. You can join some of the top hotel gym clubs if staying a while. Membership is about US$100 a month. The Municipal Tennis Club,

Amazonas y Atahualpa (tel: 242-918) has a swimming pool and sauna.

Theaters and Cinemas

Teatro Prometeo, Adjoining the Casa de la Cultura Ecuatoriana.
Teatro Sucre, Calle Flores y Guayaquil. Tel: 216-668. The most fancy and most traditional of the theaters (plays, concerts, shows). Closed for restoration.
Humanizarte Av. Amazonas 1667 y La Niña. Tel: 550-729 has contemporary dance shows. The best cinema is at **Multicine** in the CCNI shopping mall at the north end of Parque Carolina. It has four screens, good sound quality and the latest movies. The **Casa de la Cultura Cinemateca** also shows good films. Tel: 230-505. **The British Council**, Amazonas y La Niña, shows films on Tuesday evenings. Tel: 508-282.

Travel Agencies

There are travel agencies all along Av. Amazonas and in the major hotels. Options include:
Angermeyers, Foch 726 y Amazonas. Tel: 569-960. Fax: 569-956.
Ecuadorian Tours, Amazonas 339. Tel: 560-488. Fax: 501-067.
Ecuagal, Amazonas y Pinto. Tel: 229-580. Fax: 550-988.
Ecuaviajes, Eloy Alfaro 1500 y Severino (by Parque Carolina). Tel: 501-913. Fax: 563-510. Good rates for airline tickets.
Etnotur, Juan León Mera 1238. Tel: 564-565.
Explorer Tours, García y Reina Victoria. Tel: 522-220.
Metropolitan Touring on Amazonas 239. Tel: 506-650. Fax: 560-807.

Cuenca A – Z

Airlines

SAETA, Benigno Malo 727. Tel: 839-090. Fax: 835-5113.
TAME, Gran Colombia y Hno Miguel. Tel: 846-733. (Daily connections with Quito and Guayaquil.)

Buses

The **Terminal Terrestre** is in Av. España, northwest of the City center. All long-distance buses leave from here. (To Riobamba 5½ hours; Ambato 7½ hours; Quito 10½ hours; Loja 4 hours; Guayaquil 5 hours; Macas 11 hours; Gualaquiza 7 hours.)

Hotels

The **Asociación Hotelera, Cordova y Padre Aguirre**. Tel: 821-659. Has information about hotels in and around Cuenca.
LUXURY
El Dorado, Gran Colombia 787 y Luis Cordero. Tel/Fax: 831-390. The best hotel downtown, excellent restaurant, discotheque, sauna, pastry-shop and cafeteria.
Oro Verde, Av. Ordoñez Lasso. Tel: 831-200. Brand-new, out of town, beautifully situated on lake with rowing-boats; belongs to a Swiss hotel chain; excellent restaurant, La Cabaña Suiza, heated open-air swimming-pool, gymnasium, discotheque.

FIRST-CLASS
Crespo, Calle Larga 793. Tel: 842-571. Fax: 839-473. Great variety of rooms, all very clean and cozy, with private bath, color TV, central heating. Some overlook the Tomebamba river. Swimming pool, Turkish bath and French restaurant.
Parador Turístico Gualaceo, Gualaceo. Tel: 828-661. About 36 km (22 miles) outside Cuenca, but a delightful place to stay, with swimming pool.

GOOD
Conquistador, Gran Colombia 665. Tel: 831-788. Fax: 831-291. Good value; discotheque "Fernando's", cheap for International Youth Hostel Federation members.
Posada Sol, Bolívar 503 y Mariano Cueva. Tel: 838-695. Fax: 838-995. Attractive colonial-style building in heart of Cuenca. Owner also runs outdoor trips.
Presidente, Gran Colombia 659 y Hermano Miguel. Tel/Fax: 824-704. New, with restaurant.

BUDGET
Cafecito, Hermano Vasquez 736 y Luis Cordero. Tel: 827-341. Popular with younger travelers. Attractive colonial house.
Hostal Macondo, Calle Tarqui 1164. Tel: 831-198. Colonial house with kitchen and laundry facilities.

Money Exchange

Banco del Pacifico, Vaz Tout, Luz Cordero y Gran Columbia.

Other Addresses

Airport: Tel: 862-203.
Clínica Santa Ana: Av. Manuel J. Calle 1-104. Tel: 814-068. Good medical center. 24 hour emergency service.
EMETEL: Benigno Malo y Sucre.
Red Cross (Cruz Roja): Antonio Borrero 563. Tel: 882-320.
Regional Hospital: Av. del Paraiso. Tel: 811-099.

Restaurants

El Tunel, General Torres 860. Tel: 823-109. Good local food.
Govinda, Honorato Velasquez 756 y Cordero. Vegetarian, excellent juices, clean.
Jardin, P. Cordova 727. Tel: 821-120. One of Ecuador's best restaurants , international food – nouvelle cuisine.
La Napoletana Pizzeria, Solanos 3-4. Tel: 823-172. Great, inexpensive pizzas.
Los Capulis, Presidente Cordova y Borrero. Tel: 832-339. Lively atmosphere, good food and live music.
Rancho Chileno, Av. España 1317. Tel: 800-657. Chilean dishes, pleasant ambience.
Villa Rosa, Gran Colombia y Tarqui. Tel: 837-942. Attractive setting, excellent international and local food.

Shopping

The handicraft shops along Gran Colombia, near El Dorado Hotel, include **Ocepa**, **Productos Andinos**, **Artesanías Atahualpa**, **Arte Artesanías**, **Arte del Pacífico** and **Artesanías Paucartambo**. High quality Panama hats are made by **Romero Ortega**, Vega Muñoz 9-53, Tel: 823-429, who exports hats worldwide.

Tourist Offices

CETUR, Hermano Miguel 686 y Cordova. Tel: 882-058.

Travel Agencies

Eco Trek, Calle Larga 7108 y Cordero. Tel: 842-531. Fax: 835-387.
Expediciones Río Arriba, Hno Miguel y Cordova Esquina. Tel/Fax: 840-031.
Metropolitan Touring, Mariscal Sucre 662. Tel: 831-185.
Rootours, Calle Larga 890 y Benigno Malo. Tel: 835-888.

Esmeraldas A – Z

Airlines

TAME has flights to Quito daily. A bridge over the river at San Mateo (upstream from Esmeraldas) connects with the General Rivadeneira airport, 25 km (15½ miles) away. The TAME office – corner of main plaza, tel: (593-6) 726-863 – will organize a shared taxi to the airport.

Boats

Enquire at the Capitania del Puerto about boat departures (occasionally to Guayaquil and Manta, more often to Limones).

Buses

There is no central bus terminal. Aerotaxi, the fastest line, leaves for Quito from the main plaza (journey time 5 hours, frequent departures); Panamericana has a luxury service to Quito once a day, leaving from Hotel Casino; Transportes Occidentales or Trans-Esmeraldas, Av. Piedrahita 200, have large, slower buses (to Quito 7 hours, Santo Domingo 3½ hours, Guayaquil 9 hours, Machala 12 hours); Cooperativa Sudamericana have buses for Ambato (8 hours); Reina del Camino to Portoviejo (9 hours) and Bahía de Caráquez (8 hours).

Provincial buses leave from the *La Costenita,* or waterfront area. Times: Atacames and Sua (1 hour), Muisné (3½ hours). Frequent departures. Buses run also to La Tola (5 hours). The road is good until Río Verde;

there is a combined bus/boat service to San Lorenzo.

Hotels

FIRST CLASS

Apart Hotel Esmeraldas, Av. Libertad 407 y Tello. Tel: 728-700. All rooms with private bath, air conditioning and color TV; good restaurant.
Costa Verde, Luis Tello 809. Tel: 728-714. Near the beach. Air conditioning and pool. Pleasant restaurant.

GOOD

Cayapas, Av. Kennedy y Valdez. Tel: 711-022. Transformed mansion in colonial style, nice rooms, restaurant.
Colonial, Plata y L. Tello, Las Palmas. Nicely situated, close to the Las Palmas beach, under French management, excellent food.
Del Mar, Av. Kennedy, Las Palmas. Tel: 713-910. New, close to the Las Palmas beach.
El Galeón, Olmedo y Piedrahita. Tel: 713-116. Low prices. Restaurant is adequate but uninteresting.
Estuario, Av. Libertad y Gran Colombia. Tel: 713-930. Modern and spotlessly clean, air conditioning, good restaurant.

Money Exchange

Casa de Cambio Produbanco, Bolívar 516. Tel: 710-460. The Banco de Pichincha and Filanbanco also have branches in Esmeraldas.

Other Addresses

CETUR (Tourist Office), Bolívar 299 y Mejia. Tel: 714-528.
Hospital, Av. Libertad y Parada 8. Tel: 710-012.
Immigration office (Migración y Extranjeria), Av. Olmedo y Rocafuerte. Tel: 720-256.
Police, Sucre 1111. Tel: 711-484.
EMETEL (Post Office /

Telecommunications) J. Montalvo y Malecón. Tel: 728-827.

Tourist Information

The CETUR office is located at Aguirre 104 y Malecón. Tel: 328-312. Open: Mon–Fri, 9am–4pm CETUR organizes individually guided tours of Guayaquil on request.

Restaurants

Atenas Tiffany, Av. Kennedy 707. Recommended.
Budapest, Manuela Cañizarez 216. Hungarian owner.
Chifa Asiatico, Manuela Cañizarez 227. The best of the Chífas, or Chinese restaurants.
Tía Carmen, Sucre y 9 de Octubre. Good but inexpensive. A typical local dish is *encocado* – fish, crabs or shrimp cooked in coconut cream served with rice and plantains.

Guayaquil A – Z

Airlines

INTERNATIONAL

Aerolineas Argentinas, Pedro Moncayo 707 y V.M. Rendón. Tel: 302-141.

AeroPeru, Chile 329 y Aguirre. Tel: 513-691. Fax: 513-671.

Air France, Aguirre 106. Tel: 320-313. Fax: 320-313.

American Airlines, Cordova 1021 y 9 de Octubre. Tel: 566-902.

AVIANCA, Rendon 416 y Cordova. Tel: 314-091. Fax: 310-713.

British Airways, Vélez 206. Tel: 323-834. Fax: 326-419.

Copa, Urdesa, Circunvalación Sur 631-A y Ficus. Tel: 883-751. Fax: 881-528.

Iberia, Av. 9 de Octubre 101. Tel: 329-558. Fax: 327-886.

KLM, Aguirre 411. Tel: 328-028. Fax: 324-130.

Lacsa, Cordova 1040 y 9 de Octubre. Tel: 562-950. Fax: 562-958.

Lan Chile, Malecón 1400. Tel: 324-360. Fax: 534-575.

Lufthansa, Malecón 1400. Tel: 324-360. Fax: 325-477.

SAETA, Vélez 206 y Chile. Tel: 329-855. Arosemena Km 2.5. Tel: 205-115. Fax: 296-397.

Varig, Pedro Carbo 7 Av. 9 de Octubre. Tel: 560-876. Fax: 561-479.

VIASA, Pedro Moncayo 707 y Rendon. Tel: 562-141. Fax: 302-602.

DOMESTIC

SAETA, Vélez 206 y Chile. Tel: 329-855.

TAME, Av. 9 de Octubre 424. Tel: 300-714.

Airport

Guayaquil's international airport Simón Bolívar is 5km (3 miles) from the city center. The taxi fare from the airport to town should not cost more than US$6. There is a *casa de cambio* (exchange house) at the airport as well as a CETUR information office (though the latter is rarely open).

Bookstores

Librería Cervantes, Aguirre 606.

Librería Científica, Luque 225 y Chile.

Librería Universitaria, Chile 410.

Nuevos Horizontíes, 6 de Marzo 924. Book exchange.

Car Hire

Budget Rent-a-car, García Moreno (in front of Oro Verde Hotel). Tel: 328-571.

Hertz, Avis and International have offices at the airport and in the main hotels.

Hertz. Tel: 511-316.

Avis. Tel: 285-498.

Consulates and Embassies

Argentina, Aguirre 104. Tel: 530-767.

Austria, Av. 9 de Octubre 1312. Tel: 282-303.

Bolivia, Cedros 100 y VE Estrada, Banco de Credito building. Tel: 885-790.

Brasil, KM 7,5 Via a Duale, Textiles San Antonio. Tel: 252-899.

Canada, Cordova y Rendón. Tel: 563-580.

Chile, 9 di Octubre 100 y Malecón, Banco La Previsor building. Tel: 562-995.

Colombia, Cordova 812 y Rendon. Tel: 563-308.

Denmark, Cordova 604. Tel: 308-020.

France, Aguirre 503 y Chimborazo. Tel: 328-159.

Germany, Av. Arosemena Km 2.5, Edif. Berlin. Tel: 200-500.

Great Britain, Cordova 623. Tel: 560-400.

Italy, Baquerizo Moreno 1120. Tel: 563-136.

Netherlands, Ycaza 454 y Moreno. Tel: 562-777.

Norway, Av. 9 de Octubre 109. Tel: 329-661.

Peru, Av. 9 de Octubre 411, 6th floor. Tel: 322-738.

Spain, Circunvalación Sur 118 y Calle Unica. Tel: 380-265.

Sweden, Via a Daule Km 6.5. Tel: 254-111.

Switzerland, Av. 9 de Octubre 2105. Tel: 453-607.

United States of America, Av. 9 de Octubre y García Moreno. Tel: 323-570.

Venezuela, Chile 329. Tel: 326-566.

Exchange

Banco del Pacifico, Fco.P. Ycaza 200. Tel: 311-744.

Banco Popular, Pedro Carbo 555 y Av. 9 de Octubre. Tel: 328-980 (changes travelers' checks into cash dollars without commission).

Citibank, Av. 9 de Octubre y Lorenzo de Garaicoa. Tel: 564-650 (changes cash and personal checks only).

Filanbanco, 9 de Octubre y Cabo. Tel: 322-780.

LLoyds Bank, Calle Pichincha 108-110. Tel: 563-360. There are several c*asas de cambio* on Av. 9 de Octubre and on Av. Pichincha. Most of them accept travelers' checks; on weekends, change money in the larger hotels or at *Wander Cambios* in the airport.

Entertainment

There are many cinemas in Guayaquil which show English-language movies with Spanish subtitles. Enquire in the local newspapers or at the reception desks of the better hotels about what is going on. *Peñas* (folk music evenings) normally take place at weekends: recommended is **Rincón Folklórico**, Malecón 208 y Montalvo.

There are endless discotheques. A popular one is Guayacil, in La Garzota neighborhood, playing salsa and merengue, with a restaurant. La Tequila is also popular. In the Alborada Commercial Center there are numerous small discos. The first-class hotels also have discos. La Chiva city tour is a lively open bus with music on Friday nights. Contact Guayatour, Aguire 108 y Malecón. Tel: 322-441.

Casinos are found at the hotels Oro Verde, Unihotel, Continental and Ramada.

Local holidays include Bolívar's birthday July 24, followed by Guayaquil Foundation Day (July 25), when the city celebrates with parties and fiestas and it is difficult to get a hotel room. New Year's Eve is a lot of fun: along the Malecón, life-size dolls representing *el año viejo* (the old year) are carried around. At midnight they are set on fire.

Hotels

LUXURY
Continental, Chile y 10 de Agosto. Tel: 329-270. Fax: 325-454.
Gran Guayaquil, Boyaca y Ballén. Tel: 329-690/329-698. Fax: 327-251. Shares a city block with the cathedral; very comfortable and spacious rooms with air-conditioning and color TV, good restaurant, swimming-pool, sauna, gymnasium.
Oro Verde, Garcia Moreno y Av. 9 de Octubre. Tel: 327-999. Fax: 329-350. Probably the best hotel in town; very comfortable rooms with air-conditioning and color TV; several restaurants serving international cuisine and Swiss dishes; swimming-pool and fitness center.
UNI Hotel, Ballén 400 y Chile.

Tel: 327-100. Fax: 328-352. 46 very comfortable table suites, several restaurants, swimming pool, casino etc.

FIRST-CLASS
Ramada, Malecón y Orellana. Tel: 565-555. Fax: 563-036. Very nice rooms with view of the Guayas river, excellent restaurant, indoor-swimming pool, discotheque, casino.

VERY GOOD
Palace, Chile 214. Tel: 321-080. Fax: 322-887.
Plaza, Chile 414. Tel: 327-140. Fax: 324-195. Comfortable rooms with air conditioning and TV; good restaurant.
Rizzo, Clemente Ballen y Chile. Tel: 325-210. Fax: 326-209.
Sol de Oriente, Aguirre 603 y Escobed. Good Chinese restaurant. Tel: 325-500.Fax: 329-352.

Immigration

Av. Pichincha y Aguirre (Gobernación). Tel: 321-538.

Local Buses

Since taxis are very cheap in Guayaquil, buses and *colectivos* are mostly avoided by foreign visitors. But the *busetas* or minibuses are safe to ride. *Servicio especial* buses, marked with blue and white diagonal stripes are slightly more expensive but relatively efficient.

Long Distance Buses

The **Terminal Terrestre** (Central Bus Terminal) is near the airport and the bridge over the Guayas river, and all long-distance buses leave from here. Journey times are: to Quito (8½ hours), Cuenca (7 hours), Riobamba (5 hours), Santo Domingo de los Colorados (5 hours), Manta (3 hours), Esmeraldas (7 hours), Portoviejo (3½ hours), Bahía de Caráquez (5½ hours), Machala (3½ hours),

Huaquillas (5 hours), Ambato (6½ hours), Alausí (4 hours). There are also frequent buses to Salinas (2½ hours) and Playas/General Villamil (2 hours). There is a shared taxi-service to Machala (2½ hours), leaving from next door to the Hotel Rizzo, downtown.

Medical Services

Clínica Kennedy, Av. El Periodista. Tel: 286-963. Best hospital in the city. English-speaking doctors, consulting rooms for external patients.
Clínica Santa Marianita, Boyaca 1915 y Colón. Tel: 322-500.
Hospital Luís Vernaza, Julian Coronel 404. Tel: 300-300.
Emergency:
Aero Ambulance Aguire, 442 y Cordova. Tel: 308-584. Dental treatment is available at the **Clínica de Odontología Integral**. Tel: 398-371.

Post Office

EMETAL and Correo Central (the main post office) are side by side on Aguirre y Pedro Carbo. Tel: 560-200/531-713.

Restaurants

INTERNATIONAL
El Parque, Top floor of Unicentro. Very good buffet lunch, overlooks Parque Bolívar.
Gran Hotel Guayaquil, Boyaca y 10 de Agosto. Tel: 327-251. Has an excellent restaurant open to non-residents.
La Posada de las Garzas, Circunvalación Norte 536. Tel: 383-256. Exclusive atmosphere, very good international food.
Yacht Club, Malecón Simón Bolívar (at the foot of Av. 9 de Octubre). Tel: 325-225. Request admission from the manager, excellent food in pleasant surroundings.

LOCAL FOOD
Barandua Inn, Circunvalación

Norte 528 B, at the shore of the Salado estuary. Tel: 389-407. Excellent seafood.
Galeria El Taller, Quisquis 1313, between Esmeraldas and Los Ríos. Tel: 393-904. Very typical Guayaquileño food and ambience, recommended.
Hotel Continental, Chile y 10 de Agosto. Tel: 329-270. Good local food in the restaurant.
El Manantial del Marisco, Av. Principal, opposite the gas station, La Garzota neighborhood. Tel: 271-703.

FRENCH
Anderson, Tulcán 810 y Hurtado. Tel: 369-138.

ITALIAN
La Carbonara, Bálsamos 108 y V.E. Estrada, Urdesa. Tel: 382-714. Delicious pasta and pizzas.
Pizza Hut, Av. 9 de Octubre. Good and inexpensive.
Trattoria da Enrico, Bálsamos Sur 206 y la Unica, Urdesa. Tel: 387-079. Very pleasant Italian ambience, rustic-elegant, excellent food.

SPANISH
Juan Salvador Gaviota, Francisco Boloña 603, Ciudadela Vieja Kennedy. Tel: 395-621. Good paellas Valencianas.

CHILEAN
El Caracol Azul, 9 de Octubre y Los Rios. Tel: 280-461. Considered to be one of the best seafood restaurants in Guayaquil.

CHINESE
El Cantones, Av. Guillermo Pareja y Calle 43, La Garzota neighborhood. Tel: 233-644.
Gran Chifa, Pedro Carbo 1018. Tel: 512-488. Fine ambience, not too expensive.

JAPANESE
Tsuji, V.E. Estrada 813 y Guayacanes, Urdesa. Tel: 881-183. Exquisite Japanese food.

ARGENTINE
La Parillada del Nato, VE Estrada 1219 in Urdesa neighborhood. Tel: 387-098. Good grilled meat.

Shopping

Guayaquil has several smart shopping centers: Policentro, Unicentro, Plaza Triangulo, CC La Alborada, Plaza Quil, Entre Rios (biggest, with cinemas) and a new mega one Mall de Sol. To buy handicrafts of good quality **Lo Nuestro** and **Galería Guayasamín** (both at Policentro) are recommended. **Artesanías de Ecuador**, 9 de Octubre 104 y Malecón, is good and reliable. The **Mercado Artesanal** between Av. Loja y Montalia is also good. Be wary of pickpockets.

English books can be bought at the **Librería Científica, Luque y Chile**. Tel: 328-569.

Shopping at the Bahía (black market), located along Calles Pinchincha and Olmedo, is very popular with Guayaquileños.

Sports

There are many sports clubs in Guayaquil. Guests of the **Hotel Oro Verde** can use the facilities of the Tennis Club Guayaquil on request. Nearby there is an Olympic swimming pool, open to the public. There is also a swimming pool at Malecón Simón Bolívar 116. Guests of the **Gran Hotel Guayaquil** can use the facilities of the Terraza Racquet Club (with two squash courts, gymnasium and sauna).

Telecommunications

EMETEL: Offices are located at Pedro Carbo y Aguirre and L. Urdaneta 426. Public telex booths exist, but it's easiest to do everything through your hotel.

Travel Agencies

The travel agencies vie with each other to offer attractive tours to the Galápagos, but other tours and services are also available.
Albatros, 9 de Octubre y Lizardo Garcia. Tel: 453-770. Fax: 287-328.
Ecuadorian Tours, Av. 9 de Octubre 1900 y Esmeraldas. Tel: 287-111. Fax: 280-851. American Express Agent.
Guyatur, Aguirre 108 y Malecón. Tel: 322-441.
Macchiavello Tours, Antepara 802 y 9 de Octubre. Tel: 286-079.
Metropolitan Touring, Antepara 915 y 9 de Octubre. Tel: 320-300, Fax: 323-050. The oldest and largest travel agency network in Ecuador is also probably its most efficient. Tours and ticketing of all kinds can be done here.

Galápagos A – Z

Airlines

Flights are heavily booked so you should confirm and reconfirm your seat and check in early at the airport.

TAME has daily flights at 8.30am to Baltra, with connecting buses making the short trip to Puerto Ayora. Many cruises pick up their passengers directly at the airport and return them there. Note that if you are organizing your own cruise around the islands, Puerto Ayora is currently the best place to do it from.

SAETA flies to San Cristóbal Island every morning at 8am except Sundays. These flights coincide with departures of the company's luxury liner the *Galápagos Explorer* and several other tours. Note that if you want to be on Puerto Ayora, it can be quite difficult to travel between the islands.

All non-Ecuadorian travelers to the islands must pay a US$80 entrance fee to the national park and a $12 tax at Puerto Ayora (which is likely to go up). Both must be paid on arrival at the airport. Payment can be made in sucres or dollars but not by credit card. Keep the receipt: you may have to show it again.

Arranging a Cruise

The Galápagos archipelago is almost entirely a national park, and no visitor is allowed to enter it without a qualified guide on an organized tour. There are various ways that this can be done.

Some travelers choose to take a series of different day trips from Puerto Ayora to the islands nearest Santa Cruz, but, while this is cheap, it is not very satisfying (tour operators on the island will offer these for about US$50 a day). The great majority of visitors go on cruises around the islands, taking at least three nights – the more, the better. If you are going to spend the cash to come all this way, it is a pity to miss out on one of the world's great travel experiences.

Large cruisers: For many, a trip on one of the largest cruisers is the most comfortable and convenient way to visit the islands. The two best are the **Galápagos Explorer** run by SAN/Saeta from San Cristóbal island, and the **Santa Cruz** run by Metropolitan Touring. Both ships have all the comforts of a luxury liner, including excellent food in their dining rooms. By traveling overnight, these cruisers can easily reach outer islands that smaller yachts sometimes struggle to get to. The going is much smoother on a large ship, too. Both boats make occasional trips from Guayaquil to the islands.

Both take around 80 passengers on three- or four- day cruises – one covering the northern islands, another the southern. You can combine both trips to make a seven-day cruise. Passengers visit the islands in groups of 10 on motorboats (*pangas*) accompanied by English-speaking naturalist guides who all have university degrees in their fields.

The cost works out to between US$200 and US$300 per person per night on a twin-share basis (all inclusive, except for bar and airfare), depending on cabin and length of cruise (1997 prices).

Bookings for the *Santa Cruz* can be made at Metropolitan Touring in Quito or Guayaquil, or

their US agents Adventure Associates (see Travel Packages section of *Practical Tips* for contact numbers).

Tours with the *Galápagos Explorer* can be booked in Ecuador at any travel agent or SAETA office. In the US and Europe bookings can be made through **Galápagos Inc**, 7800 Red Rd, S Miami, Fl. Tel: 1 (305) 665-0841. Fax: 1 (305) 661-1457. Toll-free in the US: 1 (800) 327-9854.

Diving

Galápago Sub-Aqua, Av. Charles Darwin, Puerto Ayora, Isla Santa Cruz. Tel/fax: 593-4-314510. Offers scuba and diving tours and diving instruction.

Smaller yachts: Dozens of yachts operate cruises around the islands. Most of work out of Puerto Ayora, although a growing number are now based in Puerto Baquerizo Morena to deal with the influx of tourists from SAN/Saeta flights. They can take from 6 to 20 people, with the bigger boats being most stable in rough weather.

Tours on these boats can be booked on mainland Quito from a number of agencies. Metropolitan Touring, for example, runs five yachts at a luxury standard – check at their office for rates and availability. These trips are somewhat more costly than on the larger cruisers, but are also more intimate and still very luxurious. The agency can even arrange special scuba-diving trips.

Cheaper tours on small boats can be arranged at places such as Galasam on Calle Pinto 523 y Av. Amazonas, tel: 561-470. Check with the South American Explorers' Club in Quito for the latest reports on such smaller operators to make sure you aren't being ripped off. When booking in Quito or Guayaquil, expect to pay around US$90-$120 a day including food.

Situr and Ecoventura operate 20-berth boats with cruises from three to seven nights, and can be booked in the US through Galápagos Network, 7200 Corporate Center Drive, Suite 404, Miami, FL 33126. Tel: (305) 592 2294, toll-free 1-800-633-7972. Fax: (305) 592-6394.

Organizing your own tour: This is the cheapest, most flexible way of visiting the islands, and for many independent travelers the most satisfying. Dozens of backpackers simply turn up at Puerto Ayora and begin getting a few people together to charter a boat – if you look like a candidate, travelers are likely to stop you in the street and ask about your plans. The only drawback is that you need a few days to get the required number of people together and arrange a boat, so it's not a good idea to try to set it up in a hurry.

Boats take 8 or 12 people, and cost about US$50 a day with all meals inclusive. The South American Explorers' Club (Jorge Washington 311 y Plaza) offers the following hints for travelers doing this:

• Boat owners like to fill their boats to capacity. The group is usually expected to share the cost of any unsold passenger space.

• When dealing directly with the boat owner, bargaining is expected.

• Bottled drinks are not included in the cost of the cruise. Bring as much mineral water as you think you will need; it is sold at the Puerto Ayora supermarket (at the docks).

• Boat travel to outer islands such as Española and Genovesa can be quite rough, especially from September to November.

• Make sure the boats have enough sets of snorkeling gear.

The SAEC in Quito keeps lists of reports from travelers indicating which of the many boats are the best.

Camping

There are three official sites on the island of Santa Cruz: near the Darwin Research Station, at the Tortuga Bay and near the *caseta* in the tortoise reserve. For more information about camping sites and special permits contact INEFAN (see page 336 for address).

Exchange

If you are taking a tour on one of the large cruise ships, there is no problem about paying your bill in dollars or Ecuadorian sucres, and exchange facilities are available. Independent travelers can change foreign currency in Puerto Ayora, but at a poor rate, so bring whatever you need in sucres from the mainland.

Hospital

There is a basic hospital in Puerto Ayora. Consultations cost US$10.

Hotels

At Puerto Ayora (Santa Cruz)
FIRST CLASS
Angermeyer, Academy Bay. Tel: 526-186. Fax: 526-571. Reservations best made in Quito at Calama 182 y Almagro. Tel: 222-198. **Delfin.** Tel: 526-297. Situated at the opposite side of Academy Bay, accessible only by boat. First-class, with private beach. Recommended.
Galápagos. Tel: 526-330. Fax: 526-296. First class; comfortable bungalows with private baths, ocean view, good restaurant.

INEXPENSIVE
Fernandina. Tel: 526-122. Reasonable prices, friendly management.

Salinas. Tel: 526-107. Cheap and clean.
Sol y Mar. Tel: 526-281. The best-known hotel in Puerto Ayora, where you share the terrace with iguanas.

Information

CETUR (Tourist office) in Puerto Ayora, near the pier, is open Mon–Fri, 8am–noon and 3–6pm.

Restaurants

At Puerto Ayora
Las Cuatro Linternas, facing Pelican Bay. Good Italian food.
La Garrapata. Popular meeting place for travelers.
Sol y Mar. Tel: 526-281. Good place for breakfast on terrace with iguanas.

Shopping

Food and drink are available in several stores on the main islands of Santa Cruz, San Cristóbal and Isabela, but medicines, sun lotions and film are either not available or extremely expensive.

Avoid buying souvenirs made from black coral, turtle and tortoise shell, as these animals are protected.

Traveling between the Islands

INGALA (Instituto Nacional de Galápagos) has official inter-island passenger services on Tuesdays and Saturdays from Santa Cruz to San Cristóbal, returning on Mondays and Wednesdays. On Thursday the INGALA boat leaves Santa Cruz for Isabela, on Friday Isabela for Floreana, returning at 12.

The INGALA office in Puerto Ayora is next to the hospital, in Puerto Baquerizo Moreno on the road leading inland at the edge of the town.

Language

Anyone with a working knowledge of Spanish will have no trouble making themselves understood in Ecuador, but there are a few interesting local variations. In order to emphasize an adjective, the ending -aso is added: for example, something that is very good would be *buenaso*. An expression you will hear everywhere, and which is difficult to translate, is *no mas*. *Siga no mas* for example, means "Hurry up (and get on the bus/move down the line etc.)." *Come no mas* means "Just eat it (It'll get cold/it's nicer than it looks, etc.)." You will soon get the hang of it.

Indígenas all speak Spanish but you will hear Quichua words which have crept into the language: *wambras* translates as "guys," and *cheveré* means "cool."

VOWELS
a as in father
e as in bed
i as in police
o as in hole
u as in rude

CONSONANTS are approximately like those in English, the main exceptions being:
c is hard before **a**, **o**, or **u** (as in English), and is soft before **e** or **i**, when it sounds like **s** (as opposed to the Castilian pronunciation of **th** as in think). Thus, *censo* (census) sounds like senso.
g is hard before **a**, **o**, or **u** (as in English), but where English **g** sounds like **j** – before **e** or **i** – Spanish **g**

sounds like a guttural **h**. **G** before **ua** is often soft or silent, so that agua sounds more like awa, and Guadalajara like Wadalajara.
h is silent.
j sounds like the English h.
ll sounds like y.
ñ sounds like ny, as in the familiar Spanish word *señor*.
q is followed by **u** as in English, but the combination sounds like **k** instead of like **kw**. *¿Qué quiere Usted?* is pronounced: Keh kee-ehr-eh oostehd?
r is often rolled.
x between vowels sounds like a guttural **h**, e.g. in México or Oaxaca.
y alone, as the word meaning and, is pronounced **ee**.
Note that **ch** and **ll** are a separate letter of the Spanish alphabet; if looking in a phone book or dictionary for a word beginning with **ch**, you will find it after the final **c** entry. A name or word beginning with **ll** will be listed after the **l** entry.
If you have no Spanish, here are some basic words to help you get around:

My name is Mary	*Me llamo María*
Hello, how are you?	*¿Hola, que tal?*
I'm very well, and you?	*Yo, muy bien. ¿Y usted ?*
Very well, thank you	*Muy bien, gracias*
Good morning	*Buenos días*
Good afternoon	*Buenas tardes*
Goodnight	*Buenas noches*
Welcome	*Bienvenido*
Hello	*¡Hola!*
Bye	*Adios*
See you later	*Hasta luego*
How are you?	*¿Qué tal?*
Very well	*Muy bien*
Thank you	*Gracias*
Don't mention it	*De nada*
Please	*Por favor*
Excuse me	*Perdon*
Yes	*Si*
No	*No*
What is this?	*¿Que es esto?*
How much is	

this?	*¿Cuánto es?*
Good morning, where is the Tourist office?	*Buenos días, dónde esta el oficina de turismo*
Straight	*derecho*
To the left	*a la izquierda*
To the right	*a la derecha*
Town Hall	*Ayuntamiento*
Bank	*Banco*
Library	*Librería*
Art Gallery	*Sala de Exposiciones*
Pharmacy	*Farmacia*
Bus stop	*Parada de Autobús*
Train station	*Estación de tren*
Post office	*Correos*
Hospital	*Hospital*
Church	*Iglesia*
Hotel	*Hotel*
Youth hostel	*Albergue*
Camping	*Camping*
Parking	*Aparcamiento*
Sports ground	*Polideportivo*
Square	*Plaza*
Discotheque	*Discoteca*
Beach	*Playa*

1	*uno*
2	*dos*
3	*tres*
4	*cuatro*
5	*cinco*
6	*seis*
7	*siete*
8	*ocho*
9	*nueve*
10	*diez*
11	*once*
12	*doce*
13	*trece*
14	*catorce*
15	*quince*
16	*dieciséis*
17	*diecisiete*
18	*dieciocho*
19	*diecinueve*
20	*veinte*
21	*veintiuno*
25	*veinticinco*
30	*treinta*
40	*cuarenta*
50	*cincuenta*
60	*sesenta*
70	*setenta*
80	*ochenta*

90	*noventa*
100	*cien*
101	*ciento uno*
200	*doscientos*
300	*trescientos*
400	*cuatrocientos*
500	*quinientos*
600	*seiscientos*
700	*setecientos*
800	*ochocientos*
900	*novecientos*
1,000	*mil*
2,000	*dos mil*
10,000	*diez mil*
100,000	*cien mil*
1,000,000	*un millón*
1,000,000,000	*mil*

Days of the Week

Monday	*lunes*
Tuesday	*martes*
Wednesday	*miercoles*
Thursday	*jueves*
Friday	*viernes*
Saturday	*sábado*
Sunday	*domingo*

Months of the Year

January	*enero*
February	*febrero*
March	*marzo*
April	*abril*
May	*mayo*
June	*junio*
July	*julio*
August	*agosto*
September	*septiembre*
October	*octubre*
November	*noviembre*
December	*diciembre*

Further Reading

☞ ☞ ☞

General

HISTORY AND SOCIETY

Bork, A.W. and Mayer G., *Historical Dictionary of Ecuador*, New York, 1973.
Bushnell, G.M.S., *The Archaeology of Santa Elena Peninsular*, Cambridge, 1951.
Cavalho-Neto, P., *Diccionario del Folklore Ecuatoriano*, Casa de la Cultura, Quito, 1964.
Cueva Tamariz, A., *La Literatura Ecuatoriana*, Buenos Aires, 1968.
Drekonja, Gerhard, et al, *Ecuador Hoy*, Bogotá, 1978.
Hagen, Victor Wolfgang von, (ed), *The Incas of Pedro de Cieza de León*, Oklahoma Press, 1959.
Hemming, John, *The Conquest of the Incas*, Penguin, 1987 (the classic account of the Spanish conquest).
Pike, F.P., *The United States and the Andean Republics*, Cambridge (Mass.), 1979.

BIRDWATCHING

Castro, Isabel, and Phillips, Antonia,*The Birds of the Galápagos Islands*, Christopher Helm Publishers, 1995.
Hilty and Brown, *A Field Guide to the Birds of Ecuador*, Princeton, 1986.

OTAVALO

Meisch, Lynn, *Otavalo: Weaving, Costume and the Market*, Ediciones Libri Mundi, 1987.

TRAVEL

Humbolt, Alexander von, *Personal Narrative of a Journey*, abridged and translated by Jason Wilson, Penguin, 1995.
Miller, Tom, *The Panama Hat Trail*, out of print but worth reading if you can get a copy.
Whymper, Edward, *Travels Amongst the Great Andes of the Equator*, Peregrine Books, 1987 (amusing memoirs of the famous British mountaineer).

THE GALÁPAGOS

Castro, Isabel, and Phillips, Antonia, *The Birds of the Galápagos Islands*, Christopher Helm Publishers, 1995.
Darwin, Charles, *The Voyage of the Beagle*, Penguin.
Jackson, M.H., *Galápagos: A Natural History*, University of Calgary Press, 1985 (without doubt the best guide to the islands).
Merlen, A, *Field Guide to the Fishes of the Galápagos*, Ediciones Libri Mundi, 1988.
Treherne, John, *The Galápagos Affair*, London, 1983 (an entertaining account of the scandals and murder occurring on Floreana in the 1930s).

Other Insight Guides

The *Insight Guides* series now has almost 190 titles, spanning every continent. Apa Publications has also created two companion series of guidebooks. *Insight Pocket Guides* provide short-stay visitors with a range of carefully selected timed itineraries and include full-size pull-out maps. *Insight Compact Guides* are handy mini-encyclopedias, ideal for on-the-spot use.

In the *Insight Guide* series, South America and Latin America are covered by books on *Argentina, Buenos Aires, Belize, Brazil, Rio de Janeiro, Amazon Wildlife, Chile, Costa Rica, Ecuador, Mexico, Mexico City, Peru,* and *Venezuela*.
Insight Guide: South America provides a country-by-country overview of the continent in more than 400 pages of incisive text and stunning photography.

ART & PHOTO CREDITS

Abbot, Bill /Wilderness Travel 98
AISA 24
AKG London 32
Archivo Fotográfico Madrid 38, 40, 46
Bärtschi, Andre and Cornelia 20/21, 209, 213, 214/215, 216/217, 221, 224, 225, 230, 232L, 232R, 233, 234
Coleman Ltd , Bruce 53, 224T, 231, 232T
Corbis 169R
County of New York Library /de Nanxe, Vautier 45
Courtesy of El Comercio, Quito 93
Dixon, Katie 169L
Elmendorf, Donna 50, 56/57, 60, 61, 63R, 65, 69, 78, 82, 90, 100/101, 152, 187, 188, 192, 194, 195, 223R, 226, 249, 252, 261
Franco, Bolo 190, 191R, 196, 198, 274/275, 281, 282, 284, 289
Franco, Cesar 197
Gil, Eduardo 22/23, 26, 27, 29, 34, 58/59, 62L, 62R, 63L, 74, 91, 92, 95, 106, 107, 108, 109R, 110, 112, 114, 115L, 115R, 122, 126, 128, 129L, 129R, 134/135, 136/137, 138/139, 146, 147, 149, 154L, 154R, 155, 156, 157L, 157R, 159, 161, 167, 173, 177, 180R, 186, 193, 201, 206/207, 208, 210, 211R, 212, 220T, 228, 246, 246T, 248, 250, 251, 253, 258, 262T, 262L, 262R, 263, 267, 268, 269, 272, 276, 279, 283, 284T, 285, 309, 311L, 322T, 325
Gross, Andreas M. 41, 68, 109L, 150L, 150R, 151, 153, 158, 162, 305, 317, 319

Hooper, Joseph 99, 219,
Hurley, Peter /Wilderness Travel 97
Hutchison Library 79, 83, 163
Kessler, Shari 30, 52, 94, 184/185, 200, 202
Krist, Oliver 25, 141, 152T, 160T, 168T, 228T, 288T
Lawrie, Eric 6/7, 8/9, 10/11, 72/73, 75, 76, 77, 81, 118, 120, 121, 124, 132/133, 140, 144/145, 181, 223L, 241, 243, 244, 245, 247, ,250T, 256/257, 259, 266, 270, 270T, 271
Maier, John 1, 14, 54/55, 84/85, 102/103, 172, 179, 182, 235
Meisch, Lynn 16, 42/43, 67, 80, 86, 104/105, 176T, 273
Perrottet, Tony 18/19, 48, 66, 111, 170/171, 176, 180L, 182T, 183, 191L, 218, 220, 222, 296, 301, 314/315, 316, 318T, 320, 322, 323, 324
Rachowiecki, Rob 96, 116/117, 203, 227, 304T, 321
Rex 49
Roy, Tui de 12/13, 290/291, 292/293, 294/295, 302, 303, 304, 306, 307, 308, 310, 311R, 326
Trimble, Stephen 4/5, 87, 88, 130, 131, 156T, 166, 189, 199, 211L, 244T, 252T, 254, 255, 266T, 286, 300, 306T, 308T
Villon, Selio 125
Walker, Harry 148T, 149T, 298
Wessel, Günther 64, 196T, 277, 280, 280T, 287
Williams, Joby 161T

Picture Spreads

Pages 70/71: Clockwise from top: Andreas M. Gross; Andreas M. Gross; Stephen Trimble; Andreas M. Gross; Stephen Trimble; Andreas M. Gross; Andreas M. Gross; Andreas M. Gross; Andreas M. Gross;
Pages 164/165: Clockwise from top: Andreas M. Gross; Archivo Iconográfico, Barcelona; Stephen Trimble; Tony Perrottet; Stephen Trimble; Stephen Trimble; Stephen Trimble.
Pages 238/239: Clockwise from top: Menaux Photo, Image Bank; Michael Whitehouse/Millbrook House; P. B. Whitehouse/Millbrook House; P. B. Whitehouse/Millbrook House; P. B. Whitehouse/Millbrook House; P. B. Whitehouse/Millbrook House; Michael Whitehouse/Millbrook House; Donna Elmendorf.
Pages 312/313: Clockwise from top: Andreas M. Gross; Natural History Museum, London; Andreas M. Gross; Andreas M. Gross; Andreas M. Gross; Stephen Trimble; Andreas M. Gross; center: Andreas M. Gross.

INSIGHT GUIDE
ECUADOR

Cover photograph **Stephen Trimble**
Maps **Polyglott Kartographie**
Berndtson & Berndtson Publications
Cartographic Editor **Zoë Goodwin**
Production **Mohammed Dar**
Design Consultants
Klaus Geisler, Graham Mitchener
Picture Research **Hilary Genin**

Index

dusky-headed parakeet 231
falcon 243, 312
finch 301–2, 306, 313, 323
flamingo 320–21, 322
flightless cormorant 307, 308, 312, 322
frigate 304, 307, 313, 323
furnarid 213
Galápagos dove 306
Galápagos hawk 306, 312
Galápagos lava gull 307
Galápagos penguin 297, 303, 307, 312, 320, 321, 322
golden tanager 231
gray breasted mountain toucan 213
great egret 230
great horned owl 213
great thrush 213
greater yellow-headed vulture 231
hawk 306
heron 213
hoatsin 225
honeycreeper 213
hummingbird 213, 243
kingfisher 213
lava gull 312–13
macaw 209, 213, 231
mocking bird 306
mountain tanager 213
orapendula 123
pale-mandibled aracari 212
páramo pipit 213
parrotlet, parrots 123, 189, 213, 219, 231
pelican, brown 313, 320–21
penguin, Galápagos 297, 303, 307, 312, 32–2
peregrine falcon 312
plate-billed mountain toucan 213
protection 96, 167, 169
puffbird 213, 231
purple-throated fruitcrow 231
rainbow duck 169
red-billed tropic 323
red-footed booby 323
storm petrel 323
tanager 213, 225, 231
tapaculo 213
toucan 213, 219, 231
tyrant flycatcher 213
vermillion flycatcher 313
vulture 213
watching 168, 213, 226, 231, 243
waved albatross 306, 307

blancos 64
boat trips
Galápagos 304–5, 317, 320
Oriente 36, 219–20, 219
Boca de Onzoles 191
Bolívar 195
Bolívar Province 108, 249–50
Bolívar, Simón 41, *45*
Acuerdo de Guayaquil 45, 282–3
death46
festivals 282
Gran Colombia 45, 149, 282–3
memorials 249, 280, 281
Boniface, Diego 175
Bonpland, Aimé *32*, 41
Borbón 191
Borja Cevallos, Rodrigo 48
Borman, Randy *99*, 229
Bosque Protector Pasochoa 169, 213
Bosque Mindo-Nambillo 167, 213
Bouguer, Pierre 15
Brazil, disputes with 47
bread figures 82, 110
Bucaram, Abdala 15, 49, *49*, 52, 68
Bucay *236*, 237
bullfights *56–7*, 82, 243
butterflies 229, *233*, 234

C

cacao 48, 192, 209–10, 288
Cacha Obraje 108
cactus *300, 305*, 318
caimans 225, 226
spectacled 224
Cajabamba 254
Calacalí 167
Calderon 110
Canal de Morro 285
Cañar 33, 108, 266–7
Cañar Province 264–8
Cañaris 33, 35, *62, 72*, 263–4
clothes 265–6, 267
Incas and 33–4, 38, 264–5
Spanish and 38, 265
Canelos Quichua 110
Canoa 195
canoeing *219*
capybaras *224*, 231
car rental 337
Carabuela 177–8
Carachaloma 119
Caranqui/Caras 33, 34, 173

Carchi *22–3, 27*, 181
Carihuairazo, Mount 248
Casa de la Cultura Ecuatoriana (Quito) 115, *159*, 161
Casanova Falls 123
Caspicara 151, 157, 159
catfish, giant 225
Cayambe *80*, 81, 173–5
Cayambe-Coca Ecological Reserve 53
Cayapas 190–92, 195
Cayapas-Mataje Reserve 53
CECIA (Ecuadorian Ornithology Foundation) 226
Centro de Investigación Científico Río Palenque 212
Centro Interamericano de Artesanías y Artes Populars (CIDAP) (Cuenca) 263, 264
Centro Turístico Ecológico Alandaluz 202
ceramics see pottery
Cerecita 284
Cerro Narrio 29
Chachimbiro 180
Chachis 190–91
Chambo 81, 251
Chanduy 286
Chibuleos 249
Chimbo 251
Chimbo Valley 249–50
Chimborazo, Mount *16*, 17, 41, *124*, 248
climbing *118*, 122
Reserva Producción Faunística 248–9
worship 76
Chimborazo Province 250–5
agriculture 10–11, 250–1
clothes 251–2
crafts 104–5, 108, 252–3, 254
hats 252
fiestas 79, 81, 82
markets 253, 254, 255
peoples 251–2
railway 255
shigras 109
weaving 104–5, 108, 252–3, 254
"Chinatown" 210
Chone 196
Chordeleg 33, 108, 110, 262, 263–4
Chorrera culture 193, 202, 286
Chota, Chota Valley 66, 180–81
Chugchilan 244
Cieza de León, Pedro de 38, 250

The World of Insight Guides

400 books in three complementary series cover every major destination in every continent.